A TIME TO RISE

COLLECTIVE MEMOIRS *of the*
UNION OF DEMOCRATIC FILIPINOS (KDP)

EDITED BY

Rene Ciria Cruz

Cindy Domingo

Bruce Occena

Foreword by Augusto F. Espiritu

UNIVERSITY OF WASHINGTON PRESS

Seattle and London

A Time to Rise was made possible in part by a generous grant from the Hugh and Jane Ferguson Foundation.

4 CULTURE   This publication was also supported by a grant from the 4Culture Heritage Special Projects program.

UNIVERSITY OF WASHINGTON PRESS
www.washington.edu/uwpress

LIBRARY OF CONGRESS CATALOGING-IN-PUBLICATION DATA
Names: Ciria Cruz, Rene P., editor of compilation. | Domingo, Cindy,
    editor of compilation. | Occena, Bruce, editor of compilation.
Title: A time to rise : collective memoirs of the Union of Democratic Filipinos
    (KDP) / editors, Rene Ciria Cruz, Cindy Domingo, Bruce Occena ;
    foreword by Augusto F. Espiritu.
Other titles: Collective memoirs of the Union of Democratic Filipinos (KDP)
Description: 1st edition. | Seattle : University of Washington Press, [2017] |
    Includes bibliographical references and index. |
Identifiers: LCCN 2017015274 (print) | LCCN 2017051641 (ebook) |
    ISBN 9780295742038 (ebook) | ISBN 9780295742014 (hardcover : alk. paper) |
    ISBN 9780295742021 (pbk. : alk. paper)
Subjects: LCSH: Katipunan ng mga Demokratikong Pilipino. | Katipunan ng mga
    Demokratikong Pilipino—Biography. | Filipino Americans—Political activity. |
    Filipino Americans—Politics and government—20th century. | Philippines—
    Politics and government—1946- | Filipino Americans—Biography.
Classification: LCC E184.F4 (ebook) | LCC E184.F4 T548 2017 (print) |
    DDC 959.904—dc23
LC record available at https://lccn.loc.gov/2017015274

Cover photographs: (top) *Tears for Freedom*. Union Square, San Francisco, CA. February 26, 1986. (bottom) *Symbol of Anger against the Dictatorship*. Consulate General of the Philippines, San Francisco, CA. February 27, 1986. Both © Rick Rocamora

To the victims of the Marcos dictatorship and those
who continue to fight for peace and democracy in the Philippines

CONTENTS

FOREWORD

Augusto F. Espiritu

Augusto F. Espiritu is associate professor of history and Asian American studies at the University of Illinois, Urbana-Champaign. He is coeditor of Filipino Studies: Palimpsests of Nation and Diaspora *(2016) and author of* Five Faces of Exile: The Nation and Filipino Americans *(2005). His current research focuses on the politics of race, gender, and national identity in the US insular empire, especially on the legacies of Spanish civilization in Cuba, Puerto Rico, and the Philippines.*

S IMILAR to other Asian Americans, Filipinos in America are often stereotyped as a model minority. As authors Janelle Wong and colleagues explain, "The most insidious assumption [of the myth] as it relates to Asian American politics is not just that Asian Americans are successful in the labor force and other minority groups are not, but that *their success has depended on avoiding explicitly political strategies to advance their group interests.*"[1] The Filipino community in the United States is, however, more diverse than this prevailing stereotype of docility. Indeed, the stereotype belies a rich history of resistance and advocacy for the expansion of democracy, including by those of the anti–Ferdinand Marcos movement and in the Filipino American Left in the United States from the 1960s to the end of the twentieth century.[2] *A Time to Rise: Collective Memoirs of the Union of Democratic Filipinos (KDP)* adds to shattering that model minority stereotype of political passivity, not only because of this book's overt political commitment, but also because of its deeply personal approach.

The early 1970s were an especially important moment for Filipinos in America. Struggles against racism, poverty, and war were moving to a new level of militancy in the wake of the assassinations of Martin Luther King Jr. and Robert Kennedy. The New Left, which under the Students for a Democratic Society had galvanized opposition against the war and mobilized millions of youth, especially white, Jewish American youth, was now dead. At the same time, the powerful message of identity and empowerment known as Black Power was gaining popularity and would soon spread among not only Filipinos but also Chicanos, Puerto Ricans, American Indians, other Asian Americans, and even white Americans. Rooted in various civil rights, antiwar, and other struggles, many of these groups founded militant organizations that provided the basis for what historian Max Elbaum calls the "New Communist Movement."[3]

Meanwhile, as President Richard Nixon began withdrawing troops from Vietnam, President Ferdinand Marcos, supported by Presidents Lyndon Johnson and Nixon alike for backing the US Vietnam War effort, was wearing away at the foundations of constitutional government in the Philippines.[4] A new generation of Filipino nationalists young and old had caught on to Marcos's ambition for dynastic rule. In the late 1960s, they began to organize an anti-Marcos movement that challenged not only his dictatorial ambitions but also his collusion with the US empire's war in Vietnam and interference in Philippine politics.[5] The revolutionary wing of this nationalist movement, led by English professor Jose Maria Sison, who founded Kabataang Makabayan (Nationalist Youth) in 1964, gradually adopted Marxism, especially as filtered through the experiences of the Chinese Cultural Revolution. Working within the confines of the old Partido Komunista ng Pilipinas (PKP, or Communist Party of the Philippines), Sison and his loyal followers struggled against what they perceived as the PKP's revisionism— its abandonment of armed struggle and embrace of strictly parliamentary politics. After a tempestuous internal struggle, Sison's urban youth group broke away from the PKP and established a new Communist Party of the Philippines in 1968.[6] In the following year, peasant revolutionaries from the PKP joined the new Communist Party and provided the basis for establishing the New People's Army (NPA) and the communist insurgency.[7]

The anti-Marcos movement failed to stop the country's drift toward authoritarianism, and after what appeared to be a series of staged bombings, Marcos baldly declared martial law in September 1972, turning thousands of political dissidents into political prisoners while sending hundreds more into exile, especially in the United States.[8] Most Filipinos in America looked the other way at these usurpations of civil and human rights. Perhaps as recent immigrants, they were more concerned about surviving in their new country. Or perhaps they were convinced of Marcos's promise of restoring peace and order and crushing the private armies of the oligarchy and the communist rebels. Moreover, Marcos seemed bent on modernizing the Philippines through a revolution from above (in characteristically Asian and authoritarian style, such as in Singapore or South Korea).[9]

In light of Marcos's repression of political freedoms, a fleeting coalition of students, politicians, and intellectuals came together in the United States, momentarily unified around the demand of restoring civil liberties in the Philippines.[10] But the coalition soon revealed the tensions of vastly different political philosophies, social-class outlooks, and generational experiences, which led to disbanding the group and founding three separate anti-Marcos or anti–martial law organizations. These were the Movement for a Free Philippines (MFP; made up of exiled elite politicians and professionals), the Friends of the Filipino People (FFP; made up of Filipino and Euro-American anti-imperialists), and the Katipunan ng mga Demokratikong Pilipino (Union of Democratic Filipinos), known simply as the KDP.[11]

While this US anti-Marcos movement was coming into full swing in the early 1970s, a Filipino American movement in the United States was simultaneously emerging. Local efforts at organizing Filipino Americans around social issues such as youth delinquency, care of the elderly, and discriminatory professional licensing examinations gradually led to large-scale annual meetings. Beginning in Seattle in 1971, instigated by the Seattle organization Filipino Youth Activities (FYA), various Filipino groups gathered annually in Far West Conventions all over the West Coast, drawing hundreds of students, labor leaders, and community organizers into discussions and strategy sessions about issues facing Filipinos in the United States.[12] Some of the most active members of these conventions would eventually join the KDP. Indeed, the KDP's growing numbers constituted a challenge to the older guard in US Filipino communities because of the former's aggressive promotion of anti-Marcos activities and their revolutionary, internationalist perspectives on domestic issues. For such stances, the older guard would come to regard the KDP as usurpers. But KDP members, more numerous and better organized, would prevail and set the agenda for future conventions and other community settings.[13]

THE UNION OF DEMOCRATIC FILIPINOS

While various Filipino groups in the United States advocated for *either* a domestic agenda for social change *or* an international struggle against the

Marcos regime, only the KDP was poised to lead organizationally and ideologically on both fronts.[14] Founded near San Francisco in July 1973, the KDP achieved the seemingly impossible feat of bringing together the best-educated activists among recent immigrants and some of the most talented and dedicated activists of the American-born and the 1.5 generations (those who came to the United States at an early age). In doing so, the KDP bridged vast differences of social class and cultural experience, combining immigrants from the upper crust of Philippine society with working-class, American-born Filipinos as well as the descendants of current Philippine intellectuals, politicians, and professionals with the descendants of the pioneering First Wave Filipino laborers to America known as the *manongs* (older Filipino men).[15]

The KDP called itself a "revolutionary mass organization." Its members were among the hundreds of thousands of Americans of the New Left, young and old, who rejected the Establishment and increasingly embraced Third World Marxism and a militant style of politics lacking in the Communist Party of the United States (CPUSA).[16] Seeking to represent the contradictory binational pressures faced by Filipinos in America—between assimilation and the pull of the homeland—the KDP advocated a "dual-line" program, which simultaneously called for establishment of socialism in the United States and supported a national democratic movement for the Philippines led by the Communist Party of the Philippines (CPP).[17] In order to carry out this agenda, KDP members adhered to a strict discipline and organizational structure known as democratic centralism. Moreover, they paid substantial dues, provided childcare for each other, and adhered to decisions about transfers to other parts of the country. They took the business of revolution seriously, even religiously, often incurring great personal sacrifice.[18]

In its public pronouncements, the KDP took a bold stance in supporting the New People's Army, the CPP's armed wing.[19] (Unlike the much weakened CPP of today, the CPP of the 1970s and 1980s was an inspiring phenomenon, having thirty thousand NPA troops and a support base numbering in the millions, which was represented by the National Democratic Front.)[20] Throughout much of the 1970s, the KDP enjoyed a close relationship with the CPP that found expression in mutual support, binational travel, and theoretical exchange, even as the CPP began to increasingly rely on Philippine support groups in western Europe. This vital connection to the Philippine Left, which for complex reasons ended in the early 1980s, not only provided a concrete link for US-based Filipino activists committed to the Philippine revolution but also endowed the KDP with indubitable cultural capital as the authentic Filipino revolutionary group among progressives in the United States.[21]

Such capital allowed the KDP to spearhead efforts against martial law in the Philippines and to combat the Philippine state's efforts at intimidating Filipinos in the United States. During the 1970s, the KDP established an anti–martial law coalition that sparked numerous mass actions against the Marcos regime while successfully lobbying the US Congress to cut military aid to the Philippine government.[22] In the early 1980s, Gene Viernes and Silme Domingo, two KDP labor activists from Seattle, succeeded in proposing a resolution criticizing Marcos's repressive labor policies in the Philippines. The resolution passed at the annual convention of the powerful International Longshoremen's and Warehousemen's Union (ILWU), despite objections of a corrupt union leadership that was closely tied to Marcos and had long resisted efforts at union reform.[23] Viernes and Domingo successfully connected the struggles for union reform in the ILWU with the anti-Marcos movement. For these efforts, they were gunned down in 1981 in the Seattle ILWU union hall. (Proving the assassinations' connection to Marcos and obtaining justice for Viernes and Domingo became a decade-long battle for the KDP.)[24]

In 1983, the exiled former senator Benigno Aquino Jr., Marcos's principal political rival, was also assassinated upon his return to the Philippines. In the wake of this brazen act, world opinion turned against the Marcos regime. In coalitions with a plethora of new anti-Marcos groups inspired by Aquino's martyrdom, the KDP helped channel this increasing mass sentiment against Marcos in the United States and in doing so contributed to the "People Power" revolution that led to Marcos's ouster in February 1986.[25]

The KDP would become synonymous with the campaign against Marcos, but this was just one facet of the group's agenda. Just as important, the KDP led struggles against discrimination, urban renewal, and job exploitation faced by Filipinos in the United States during a period of recession, corporate restructuring, and increasing racism. The KDP was also at the forefront of opposition to discriminatory licensure exams for foreign medical graduates.[26] Moreover, as historian Catherine Ceniza Choy writes, the KDP defended Filipina Narciso and Leonora Perez, two Filipina nurses wrongly implicated in several unsolved murders in a Michigan hospital, a case that interwove racism, sexism, and the long colonial relationship between the United States and the Philippines.[27] Finally, KDP activists were prominent in opposing corporate and government efforts to demolish the International Hotel in San Francisco's Manilatown, which had provided low-cost housing for retired Filipino and Chinese laborers as well as a space (in its basement) for various Asian American revolutionary groups.[28]

During the mid- to late 1970s and early 1980s, during an increasing right-ward drift in American politics, the KDP participated in discussions with other left groups interested in building a new communist party. These efforts led many KDP leaders to join the Line of March (LOM), a Marxist-Leninist organization, and to expand their activities to anti-imperialist and antiracist struggles outside the Filipino community.[29] Like many other mergers of US left groups, the LOM expressed concern over the country's rightward political drift, the resurgence of racism, and the United States' overseas adventures, including those in Libya, Grenada, Nicaragua, and El Salvador. As Max Elbaum writes, the LOM was among the bevy of left groups energized by the presidential campaign of the Reverend Jesse Jackson in 1984, under the banner of the Rainbow Coalition.[30]

Both the Marcos overthrow, which ended the rationale for an anti-Marcos movement, and the increasing complexity of US political struggles, which strained the organization's resources, led to a decision to disband the KDP in 1986.[31] Afterward, former KDP members continued their activism in a variety of ways. Some redoubled their efforts in the LOM, which would continue until 1991. Others returned to the Philippines to join the CPP or other socialist alternatives, struggles for political transparency, or alternatives to globalization and environmental degradation. Most former KDP members decided to remain in the United States to advocate for Philippine issues. Still others have devoted their energies to building labor unions, the social service sector, and various advocacy groups or have become academics, journalists, lawyers, or elected officials. (Indeed, two former KDP members have been elected to office in the State of Washington.)[32] Even two decades after KDP disbanded, most former members continue their associations with each other, tied together by deep political, familial, and social bonds, stamped with the indelible experience of life inside the KDP.

THE AUTOBIOGRAPHY OF A MOVEMENT

During the first reunion of the KDP in 1998, former members decided to write their own history, impelled by the needs of a new generation of Filipino and Asian American youth for an account of the earlier period and by new writings about the Asian American movement. Instead of compiling a definitive political or social history, which they felt would have plunged them into interminable debates about the past, former KDP members chose to write autobiographical sketches, reminiscences, and personal histories, which we have assembled here. Rene Ciria Cruz's panoramic and reflective introduction nonetheless provides a strong ballast for these first-person accounts. The KDP editors provide background in short introductory essays and footnotes, but the individual voices are the central story. Altogether, this collection brings together forty-two personal accounts of the 1972–86 period. Some narratives cover several years; others remember one day, or one hour, or one moment. Fifteen accounts are by men and twenty-seven are by women, reflecting the powerful role women played in the organization.

In these narratives, instead of ideological debates, we see the inside of a movement, the emotional and deeply felt experiences of a group of young people dealing with difficult situations, some involving great personal risk, others requiring courage to challenge the status quo or disrupt the familiar, and still others the ability to respond to loss or sudden change. If there is an underlying theme, it is perhaps suggested by the root of the KDP name in the late nineteenth-century organization the Katipunan (meaning "gathering" in Tagalog). The Katipunan was a secret society that ignited the Philippine revolution against Spain. Its goal was *kalayaan*, translated simply as "liberty" but embodying corresponding desires for independence, social justice, and a return to a childhood state of bliss.[33] The Katipunan, inspired by José Rizal's writings and earlier protest movements, would itself inspire subsequent Filipino protest movements.[34] The US invasion of the Philippines in the late nineteenth century in fact curbed a moment of independence from colonialism, seen as the unfinished revolution, that Filipino nationalists have been trying to recapture ever since.[35]

The KDP in part saw itself as a co-inheritor (along with the CPP) of this history of political and social protest, this unfinished revolution. Indeed, the word *katipunan* not only names KDP but also its newspaper, *Ang Katipunan*. Moreover, the Katipunan logo, the letter *K* written in the pre-Hispanic alphabet, adorns not only the KDP's newspaper but also its internal documents. The KDP also celebrated June 12, the traditional date of Philippine independence, as Philippine National Day, honoring Andres Bonifacio, the plebeian founder of the Katipunan, instead of Emilio Aguinaldo, the president of the first Philippine Republic.[36]

While the KDP sought to appropriate the Katipunan tradition in the Philippines, it also attempted to connect with the Filipino progressive political tradition in the United States. Many KDP members found inspiration in proletarian author Carlos Bulosan, whose *America Is in the Heart* reflected their family histories and political aspirations. Alongside labor leaders Chris Mensalvas and Ernesto Mangaoang of ILWU Local 7, Bulosan was also a role model because of his close association with the Communist Party of the United States, which was at the forefront of many struggles for immigrant and labor rights that were so important to Filipino old-timers.[37] The KDP also had some contact with surviving Filipino CPUSA members. In this volume, Romy Garcia's "How My Life Changed" mentions old-timer "Mang" Mario Hermoso, a former party member who joined the KDP, while Ermena Vinluan's "A Cultural Gypsy" highlights the inspiring role of Josephine Patrick, Bulosan's common-law wife, on KDP members.

Still, despite these important encounters, the KDP's connections to the Philippine and Filipino American past were at best limited. The old Left in both the United States and the Philippines had been decimated by red scares, state repression, and its own internal weaknesses by the time KDP came on the scene in the early 1970s. And there were thousands of miles of ocean, not to mention the archipelagic nature of the Philippine revolution, that prevented regular contacts with the new CPP under Sison.

KDP members were, however, deeply embedded in the social movements of the United States. More than a few members had participated in antiwar activities while others, like Romy Garcia, whose brother had died fighting in Vietnam for the United States, had additional motivations for opposing the war. Several KDP members in this volume record their encounters with the black, Chicano, Puerto Rican, Asian American, and gay and lesbian movements. Still others highlight the unique institutions of the time, such as San Francisco Newsreel, an anti-imperialist media collective, or alternative schools that emphasized political and ethnic empowerment.

These movements for political power in the United States have also been labeled identity movements because of the significant cultural impact they had on the youth of the time. While too much has perhaps been made of the politics of identity, the Filipino progressive movement represented by the KDP was undeniably a powerful motor for cultural and personal change, although tied to a project of political transformation. Estella Habal, a former KDP member from San Francisco, relates the powerful impact of KDP on her life in "I Have Not Stopped Dreaming":

> The KDP changed my perspective and my life. On the one hand,
> I was always attracted to seeking out my roots as a Filipino,
> because so much of my history was kept secret from me and
> other Filipino youth. But sentimentally looking to the Filipino
> past was not enough. My identity had to also be forged in the
> direction of the future. And the future I found was full of promise
> and optimism, revolution and Marxism. The risks were great and
> some of the sacrifices were heavy, but I was convinced I was
> dedicating my present life for a better future, not just for me, but
> for humankind. In some ways, my faith in the revolution was

somewhat idealistic and utopian, but I have not stopped dreaming.

Habal's words nicely blend the search for roots, history, and Filipino-ness with a rejection of sentimental nativism and embrace of an alternative future provided by Marxian revolutionary ideals. Romy Garcia tells a similar story of the challenges faced by a 1.5-generation Filipino American—gang life, prison, and the deaths of young relatives in senseless violence—and the transformative role the KDP played in his life. US-born or 1.5-generation youth like Habal and Garcia were joined by idealistic Philippine youth, many from middle-class backgrounds, like Jeanette Gandionco Lazam and Ma. Flor Sepulveda (the pseudonym of Christina Araneta), who would develop their political and cultural identities in the KDP. Lazam hastily fled the Marcos dictatorship in the Philippines, sent to the United States by worried parents.

How did the KDP succeed in this balancing act of bringing together first-generation migrants and 1.5- and second-generation Filipino Americans? Certainly, the organization's dual-line strategy provided the atmosphere for this kind of internationalism, as did the liberal ethnic environment in the United States at the time. Yet, in this collection, we see little discussion of that dual-line perspective. Instead, we see other responses. One thing that helped galvanize the KDP was its rich cultural work, expressed in various ways, from a recorded album of revolutionary songs; to a KDP book of recipes; to Sining Bayan (People's Art), a theater group inspired by the University of the Philippines' Sining Bayan, Teatro Campesino, and the San Francisco Mime Troupe. Moreover, we cannot underestimate the key role of cultural and linguistic translators like Cynthia Maglaya, an immigrant and cofounder of the KDP, whom Estella Habal credits as being a mentor to second-generation Filipino Americans.

We should also factor in the commitment of KDP activists—the nonsectarian, nonracial unionizing practices of Viernes and Domingo in the Pacific Northwest—that attracted people of different immigration, generational, and even racial backgrounds, evidenced in Emily Van Bronkhorst's account, "Initiation from Hell." Or perhaps we should consider the KDP's appeal to young progressives as a vanguard organization, succinctly articulated by Elaine Elinson in "They Won't Know What Hit Them": "We'll use every toast as an exposé of Marcos's crimes, every Marine salute as a platform to oppose the US military bases in the Philippines. We're going to turn the whole thing around, because we're armed with all the information, we have *the analysis*, and we're *disciplined*. That really is the power of Leninism" (emphasis added).

Finally, there is the steely determination to end martial law in the Philippines for which KDP members became famous (or notorious, depending on your perspective). This is visible in Sorcy Apostol's and other KDP activists' creative action at the Honolulu International Airport in the 1970s to disrupt Marcos's arrogant speech—all the more humorous for Apostol's code-switching between English and Tagalog in her cursing of the dictator, which was captured by television news stations. And nearing the end of Marcos's reign, as the People Power revolution was in full swing in February 1986, we see the simultaneous and resolute act of empathy by Fely Villasin and other anti-Marcos activists in the United States, described in "One February Night in San Francisco":

> For almost a week before this night, we have been demonstrating in front of the consulate [in San Francisco], the crowd growing larger each day. On the first day, a thunderstorm sent many of our friends scampering for cover, thinning our picket line. I panicked at the thought that our action would prematurely end. We were left to sustain the protest, continuing our circle. We doggedly held up wilting placards and shrinking banners against the pouring rain, shouting louder, "Marcos dictatorship has to go!" Then, one by one, some sheepishly, those who sought cover, came back to the picket line. No rain was going to keep anyone away from this vigil until Marcos was gone for good.

This idealism was made possible not only by the commitment of individual KDP members but also by a developed organizational infrastructure designed for revolutionary change. This collection of essays is replete with references to the daily lives of KDP members, whether this involved paying dues, or providing childcare for other activists, or socializing at "HQ" (headquarters). KDP members were encouraged to participate and take leadership roles on the national, regional, and local boards and working committees of the organization. And the KDP's transfer policies made possible the easy relocation of members. Indeed, many examples in these accounts tell of KDP activists transferring from one city to another, even from one country to another, in response to the changing needs of the organization. This was especially important as the challenges and demands of local chapters increased—as in the aftermath of the assassinations of Viernes and Domingo, which resulted in the influx of KDP members from all over the country into the Seattle chapter.

The frequent transfers of KDP members speak to the organization's mobility, which prefigures a kind of counterglobalization strategy, perhaps be dramatized in the story of Ka Linda (a pseudonym). Ka Linda, a recent immigrant who had participated in founding the KDP, returned to the Philippines in 1982 to talk with the CPP leadership about political differences. However, the CPP "center," as a test of her loyalty, assigned her to the New People's Army and the mountains and remote villages of the northern Philippines, where she wandered for months before she was able to make her way back to Manila and then the United States. Similarly, Michael Withey's visit to the Philippines in 1986 highlights the interconnectedness of Philippine and Filipino American politics. Withey, along with former KDP leaders Rene Ciria Cruz and Cindy Domingo, visited the Philippines after Corazon Aquino became president, and they sought Marcos's files on the murders of Viernes and Domingo. All were surprised at the seemingly warm reception they received from General Fidel Ramos, Marcos's former chief of staff.

Even within the United States, KDP members were in constant movement. The itinerant Sining Bayan of the KDP, for instance, toured the country at various times. In particular, as narrated by Ermena Vinluan, the group visited Hawaii's remote Molokai Island in 1981. They were the entertainment for the whole island. And they did not disappoint, providing the pioneer farm laborers and their families with a performance that spoke to their racial and class experiences.

With this constant restlessness and mobility, it is perhaps not surprising that a kind of global consciousness developed among KDP members. One sees a glimpse of this in Elaine Elinson's near sensual experience of doing daily propaganda work. "I loved the sound of it: National Propaganda Commission. We might be in a dingy two-bedroom house in the Oakland Hills, but *we were just like our comrades on propaganda teams in Manila or the mountains of Morazan in El Salvador*, preparing broadsides and broadcasts for the revolution" (emphasis added).

Ultimately, however, despite all these outstanding qualities, it is the KDP's participation in the crucial mass struggles of the day that determines the group's social and historical importance. Out of so many political struggles, this collection highlights two: the International Hotel struggle in San Francisco and the fight for labor reform that began with Viernes and Domingo and ended in a campaign for justice for their murders. While Estella Habal's "Between the Personal and the Political" gives a sense of how the KDP may have misread the struggle for the International Hotel and failed to devote the necessary resources to the anti-eviction struggle, Jeanette Gandionco Lazam's " 'Is This What You Call Democracy?' " takes us directly inside the hotel.

Lazam, like many Filipino American youth, saw the old-timers' fight as part of her own parents' struggle (her father had come to the United States in the 1930s to attend college). Her account of moving into this all-male hotel gives the vivid detail of life inside with the old-timers, in particular the modicum of comfort they desired, which provides an ironic counterpoint to the callous efforts of capital and the state to evict them. As she writes,

> My decision to move into the hotel was both uncomfortable and easy at the same time. For sure I had to stretch out of my comfort zone. . . . The rooms at the International Hotel were postage-stamp size, ten-by-fifteen square feet. And although the place had been painted and refurbished through years of voluntary community efforts to try to make it more like a home, it also still remained home to roaches and multicolored rats. The bathrooms and showers were in the hallways, which helped you get to know our neighbors real fast! There was a common kitchen, which also served as a kind of community gathering place, although everyone had illegal hot plates in their rooms too. Of course, there was not a washing machine in sight, and the neighborhood laundromat served an eight-block stretch, making it almost impossible to do laundry no matter what time of day or night.

Lazam befriended the leader of the tenants' association, the charismatic Wahat Tampao, whom she was assigned to protect and through whose eyes she would witness the inevitable eviction: "Wahat and the rest of the tenants would soon witness the more ruthless and destructive face of capitalist democracy—that in the grand scheme of things, democracy often fails and disappoints the poor." Lazam, like the tenants, would suffer the eerie sounds of sledgehammers breaking down the International Hotel's walls and bathrooms. She would witness the old-timer Filipinos and Chinese weeping as they were forced from their homes.

The Domingo and Viernes struggle likewise occupies a substantial portion of this collection of reminiscences, perhaps for good reason, because the struggles of these two labor activists were of signal importance—indeed, someday, historians might write that their work was the KDP's most significant contribution to the political struggle of the times. Much was at stake, as Thomas Churchill's novel *Triumph over Marcos* dramatically narrates.[38] The essays in the present volume take us to the day of the murders and their immediate aftermath, the reactions of comrades inside the union whom Viernes and Domingo had recruited or trained to become part of the KDP and to fight the powers that conspired to maintain racial discrimination and class exploitation in the Alaska canneries. In these accounts the murders become ineluctably connected to the Marcos regime.

What these reminiscences convey is the terror of those days and the uncertainty of what was to come, for indeed the guns that had fired on Viernes and Domingo might next be trained on their family and friends. But as Terri Mast, Domingo's widow and fellow labor activist, would say, courage comes not from the absence of fear but from the ability to continue to act even when one is afraid. Indeed, in the aftermath of Domingo's and Viernes's deaths, Mast and other KDP members did not withdraw from the struggle but took up the cudgels for union reform even more fiercely, fired by a desire to see justice done in the names of her fallen husband and their comrade. In "We Had Already Lost Too Much to Turn Back," Mast describes one union meeting in which she bristled at ILWU Local 37's president Tony Baruso attempt to silence the voices of reform, which had long been intimidated by the threat of violence and by gang members, and his attempt to appropriate the legacy of the dead men whose ideals Baruso had despised:

> I could hear my own voice as though someone else was speaking.
> "You're not going to stand up here and tell people to shut up anymore. We're tired of that bullshit and we're not putting up with it. This is our union and everyone has the right to speak and be heard. And another thing, I'm not going to let you stand up here and claim credit for Silme's and Gene's years of hard work."

This collection is made of such wonderful human qualities, perhaps all the better for those who seek to understand this movement and those of the 1960s and 1970s, which conservatives have vilified and even liberal historians tell from a predominantly white male perspective.[39] For these activists, gathered in their own *katipunan*, displayed their commitment and determination in every action, whether participating in campaigns for democracy in the Philippines, struggling for the Filipino minority in America, or simply selling the KDP's *Ang Katipunan* newspaper or distributing the *Taliba* newsletter in the streets of San Francisco or among Filipinos working in the World Bank in New York.

Still, as varied as this collection is, it provides but a glimpse of the KDP's extensive political work, a full history of which remains to be written, if Rene Ciria Cruz's panoramic introduction is any indication. The organization was involved in important lobbying efforts in the US Congress, struggles against discrimination against nurses and other health professionals, anti-Marcos activities in the wake of Benigno Aquino Jr.'s assassination, and exciting electoral work that find little expression here. Much of the internal life of the organization, particularly its complex relationships with the Philippine revolutionary movement and party-building groups in the United States, also awaits further elucidation. Nonetheless, this autobiography of a movement provides a tantalizing beginning to what we hope will be further projects of retrieval and reflection of relevance to the experiences of immigrants, people of color, and working-class people, as much as to discussions of the meaning of youth, ethnicity, activism, gender, and nationalism. There is a desperate need to shed light on this crucial moment in the intertwined histories of the United States, the Philippines, and Filipino America, especially as 1.5-generation, second-generation, and recent immigrant youth continue the search for their identity in the United States.

NOTES

1   Janelle Wong, S. Karthick Ramakrishnan, Taeku Lee, and Jane Junn, *Asian American Political Participation: Emerging Constituents and Their Political Identities* (New York: Russell Sage Foundation, 2011), 80 (emphasis added).

2   See Steve Louie and Glenn K. Omatsu, eds., *Asian Americans: The Movement and the Moment* (Los Angeles: Asian American Studies Center Press, 2001); Lucy Burns, "Coup de Theatre: The Drama of Martial Law," in *Filipinos on the Stages of Empire* (New York: New York University Press, 2013), 75–106; Catherine Ceniza Choy, "Trial and Error: Crime and Punishment in America's 'Wound Culture,'" in *Empire of Care: Nursing and Migration in Filipino American History* (Durham, NC: Duke University Press, 2003), 121–65; Max Elbaum, *Revolution in the Air: Sixties Radicals Turn to Lenin, Mao and Che* (New York: Verso, 2002); Augusto Espiritu, "Journeys of Discovery and Difference: Transnational Politics and the Union of Democratic Filipinos," in *The Transnational Politics of Asian Americans*, ed. Pei-te Lien and Christian Collett (Philadelphia: Temple University Press, 2009), 38–55; Jose V. Fuentecilla, *Fighting from a Distance: How Filipino Exiles Helped Topple a Dictator* (Urbana: University of Illinois Press, 2013); Estella Habal, *San Francisco's International Hotel: Mobilizing the Filipino American Community in the Anti-eviction Movement* (Philadelphia: Temple University Press, 2007); Geraldine Pratt, *Families Apart: Migrant Mothers and the Conflicts of Labor and Love* (Minneapolis: University of Minnesota Press, 2012); and Mark Thompson, *The Anti-Marcos Struggle: Personalistic Rule and Democratic Transition in the Philippines* (New Haven, CT: Yale University Press, 1995).
      These new perspectives join essays on or by former anti-Marcos activists, including Prosy Abarquez-Delacruz, "Holding a Pigeon in My Hand: How Community Organizing Succeeds or Falters," in Louie and Omatsu, *Asian*

Americans: The Movement and the Moment, 56–63; Yen Espiritu, "International Medical Graduates Are Tested Every Step of the Way: Edgar Gamboa," in *Filipino American Lives* (Philadelphia: Temple University Press, 1995), 127–42; Estella Habal, "How I Became a Revolutionary," in *Legacy to Liberation: Politics and Culture of Revolutionary Asian Pacific America* (Chico, CA: AK Press, 2000), 197–210; Rose Ibañez, "Growing Up in America as a Young Filipina American during the Anti–Martial Law and Student Movement in the United States," in Louie and Omatsu, *Asian Americans: The Movement and the Moment*, 74–79; Abraham Ignacio, "Makibaka, Huwag Matakot: A History of the Katipunan ng mga Demokratikong Pilipino," *Maganda Magazine* 7 (1994), www.flashpoint-design.net/images/KDP-Ignacio .pdf; Gil Mangaoang, "From the 1970s to the 1990s: Perspective of a Gay Filipino American Activist," *Amerasia Journal* 20, no. 1 (1994): 33–44; Carol Ojeda-Kimbrough, "The Chosen Road," *Amerasia Journal* 20, no. 1 (1994): 64–73; Helen Toribio, "We Are Revolution: A Reflective History of the Union of Democratic Filipinos (KDP)," *Amerasia Journal* 24, no. 2 (1998): 155–77; and Kent Wong's essays, "Luisa Blue" and "Amado David," in *Voices for Justice: Asian Pacific American Organizers and the New Labor Movement* (Los Angeles: UCLA Center for Labor Research and Education, 2001), 5–18, 45–54.

3   Elbaum, *Revolution in the Air*, 3.

4   Daniel B. Schirmer and Stephen Shalom, eds., *The Philippines Reader: A History of Colonialism, Neo-colonialism, and Dictatorship* (Boston: South End Press, 1987), 225; Raymond Bonner, *Waltzing with a Dictator: The Marcoses and the Making of American Foreign Policy* (New York: Times Books, 1987), 52–53.

5   Schirmer and Shalom, *Philippines Reader*, 160–61.

6   Patricio N. Abinales, "Jose Maria Sison and the Philippine Revolution: A Critique of an Interface," *Kasarinlan: Philippine Journal of Third World Studies* 8 (Third Quarter 1992): 17–22.

7   Schirmer and Shalom, *Philippines Reader*, 160–61, 204.

8   Thompson, *Anti-Marcos Struggle*, 68–70.

9   Madge Bello and Vincent Reyes, "Filipino Americans and the Marcos Overthrow," *Amerasia Journal* 13, no. 1 (1986–87): 73–83. See also Belinda Aquino, "The Politics of Ethnicity among Ilokanos in Hawaii," in *Old Ties and New Solidarities: Studies on Philippine Communities*, ed. Charles J.-H. Macdonald and Guillermo M. Pesigan (Quezon City, Philippines: Ateneo de Manila University Press, 2000), 100–116.

10   NCRCLP, "Report of the National Committee for the Restoration of Civil Liberties in the Philippines," in *Marcos and Martial Law in the Philippines*, ed. David A, Rosenberg (Ithaca, NY: Cornell University Press, 1979), 253–85.

11   Bello and Reyes, "Filipino Americans and the Marcos Overthrow," 76–78.

12   "Third [Fourth] Far West Convention: Filipinos Call for Unity," *Ang Katipunan* 1, no. 1 (October 1–15, 1973): 5.

13   Catherine Tactaquin, KDP National Executive Board, "What Is the 'Price' of Unity? FYA Withdraws Support from FWC" (editorial), *Ang Katipunan* 2, no. 8 (November 20, 1975): 5.

14   For instance, anti-Marcos groups like the Friends of the Filipino People and the Movement for a Free Philippines concentrated on developments in the Philippines. Meanwhile, Filipino Youth Activities of Seattle and Los Angeles–based Search to Involve Pilipino Americans (SIPA), which took on the character of local civic organizations or social work, concentrated exclusively on the American scene. See Fuentecilla, *Fighting from a Distance*, for accounts of the MFP; Joann Natalia Aquino, "A Conversation with the Cordovas on *Filipinos in Puget Sound*," *International Examiner*, October 20, 1010, www .iexaminer.org/2010/10/conversation-cordovas-filipinos-puget, for the FYA; and Royal Morales, *Makibaka: The Pilipino American Struggle* (Los Angeles: Mountainview Publishers, 1974), 100–101, for an account of SIPA.

15   *Ang Katipunan* 1, no. 1 (October 1–15, 1973): 1.

16   Toribio, "We Are Revolution," 163.

17   *Ang Katipunan* 1, no. 1 (October 1–15, 1973): 1.

18   "Democratic centralism," as Elbaum explains, was the working mode of the "party of a new type" advocated by Lenin and the Bolsheviks in early 1900s Russia. Against any form of erratic, spontaneous organization, Lenin advocated democratic centralism. That is to say, "Once open debate and then a vote had produced a party position, all members had to maintain unity in action." Moreover, the new organization theory emphasized centralized control over other party committees. Elbaum, *Revolution in the Air*, 150–52.

19   Toribio, "We Are Revolution," 157.

20   The numbers are from a Senate Select Committee on Intelligence study of November 1, 1985, cited in Schirmer and Shalom, *Philippines Reader*, 315, 316. The best accounts of the CPP's and NPA's periods of growth are William Chapman, *Inside the Philippine Revolution* (New York: W. W. Norton, 1987); and Gregg R. Jones, *Red Revolution: Inside the Philippine Guerrilla Movement* (San Francisco: Westview Press, 1989).

21   See my essay "Journeys of Discovery and Difference: Transnational Politics and the Union of Democratic Filipinos," in Lien and Collett, *Transnational Politics of Asian Americans*, 38–55.

22   *Ang Aktibista*, August 26, 1975, 1–2.

23   Helen Zia, *Asian American Dreams: The Emergence of an American People* (New York: Farrar, Straus and Giroux, 2000), 149; David Takami, "Marcoses Found Liable for Seattle Cannery Workers Union Murders," *International Examiner*, March 6, 1991, 125–28. Note also Zia's painstaking account of the congressional debate and the important US Supreme Court case of the cannery workers, *Ward's Cove v. Packing, et al.* (pp. 142–65).

24   Takami, "Marcoses Found Liable for Seattle Cannery Workers Union Murders," 125–28.

25 See Bello and Reyes, "Filipino Americans and the Marcos Overthrow," for this account of the KDP and overseas Filipinos' role in the overthrow of Marcos. For other perspectives on overseas Filipinos during the Marcos period, see Linda Basch, Nina Glick Schiller, and Cristina Szanton Blanc, *Nations Unbound: Transnational Projects, Postcolonial Predicaments, and Deterritorialized Nation-States* (New York: Routledge, 1994), 225, 227, 255–56, 273–74; Espiritu, *Filipino American Lives*, 127–42; and Fuentecilla, *Fighting from a Distance.*

26 For reference to these antidiscrimination struggles, see Toribio, "We Are Revolution," 171–73.

27 See Choy, *Empire of Care*, 123.

28 See Habal, *San Francisco's International Hotel*, 20–25.

29 Elbaum, *Revolution in the Air*, 242.

30 Ibid., 278, 280–81.

31 See Toribio, "We Are Revolution," 155, 176.

32 These include Velma Veloria, former member of the Washington State Legislature, and David Della, former Seattle City Council member. See Seattle Civil Rights and Labor History Project, http://depts.washington.edu/civilr /veloria.htm and http://depts.washington.edu/civilr/della.htm; and Ligaya Rene Domingo, "Building a Movement: Filipino American Union and Community Organizing in Seattle in the 1970s" (PhD dissertation, University of California, Berkeley, 2010), 62.

33 Reynaldo Ileto, *Pasyon and Revolution* (Quezon City, Philippines: Ateneo de Manila University Press, 1979), 87–88.

34 José Rizal is a Philippine national hero who emerged in the anticolonial struggle against Spain. As an author, Rizal became a key member of the Filipino Propaganda Movement and used his writings to advocate for the freedom of the Philippines from Spain. He was executed by Spain in 1896 after being court-martialed for rebellion, sedition, and conspiracy.

35 See Reynaldo Ileto, "Reflections on Agoncillo's *The Revolt of the Masses* and the Politics of History," *Southeast Asian Studies* 49, no. 3 (December 2011): 496–520. For the "unfinished revolution," see pp. 499, 500.

36 The long history of the old Communist Party of the Philippines, the Partido Komunista ng Pilipinas, heir to the Katipunan and its early labor-organizing efforts, is left out of the KDP's understanding of Philippine political history. This perhaps reflects the *new* Communist Party's influence on the KDP, in particular Amado Guerrero's diatribe against the PKP, *Philippine Society and Revolution* (Manila: Pulang Tala Publications, 1971). (Amado Guerrero is Jose Maria Sison's nom de guerre.)

37 Ironically, Bulosan portrayed the party in unflattering terms in *America Is in the Heart* (Seattle: University of Washington Press, 1973). See page 293 for criticism of the party as run by "stupid little men" who were "anti-Filipino" during its first phase of organizing among Filipino workers.

38 Thomas Churchill, *Triumph over Marcos* (Seattle: Open Hand Publishing, 1995). The book's title page gives this description: "A story based on the lives of Gene Viernes & Silme Domingo, Filipino American cannery union organizers, their assassination, and the trial that followed."

39 See Glenn Omatsu, "The 'Four Prisons' and the Movements of Liberation: Asian American Activism from the 1960s to the 1990s," in *The State of Asian America: Activism and Resistance in the 1990s*, ed. Karin Aguilar-San Juan (Boston: South End Press, 1999), 22–24.

ACKNOWLEDGMENTS

A Time to Rise: Collective Memoirs of the Union of Democratic Filipinos (KDP), like all efforts of the KDP, is a collective project. It has taken twenty years to produce and along the way many people have made significant contributions.

Thank you to Edwin Batongbacal and Abe Ignacio for their support and research; to the late John Stamets, who chronicled the work of the Committee for Justice for Domingo and Viernes through his photography; to the Alaskero Foundation and Jack Storms for use of their photographs; to David Spohr for his proofreading skills; to Ces Rosales for last-minute extensive formatting; and to May Lim and Teresa Ojeda for invaluable assistance in completing this book.

Our introduction to the University of Washington Press would not have been possible without the assistance of UW professors Vicente Rafael, Moon-Ho Jung, and Rick Bonus. A special thanks to UW professors Mike McCann and George Lovell for their ongoing encouragement to finish this collection and, who along with Conor Casey, found a home for the KDP archives at the Labor Archives of Washington, UW Special Collections.

Others served as editors of this anthology at different periods, including Geline Avila, Jaime Geaga, Mila de Guzman, and the late Helen Toribio. Sincere appreciation goes to Legacy of Equality, Leadership and Organizing (LELO) and the Domingo Viernes Justice Fund for their financial and administrative support.

Lastly, thank you to all the contributors who shared their stories and the members of the KDP, without whose work and commitment to radical social change this book would not be possible.

A TIME TO RISE

INTRODUCTION

A Snapshot—The Life and Times of the KDP

RENE CIRIA CRUZ

Rene Ciria Cruz is originally from Manila, where he became a member of the Samahang Demokratiko ng Kabataan (SDK, or Democratic Association of Youth) at the University of the Philippines. In 1973, as an immigrant in New York City, he joined the Support Committee for a Democratic Philippines, precursor to the city's KDP chapter. He was a founding member of the KDP and was in its national leadership until the group's dissolution in 1986. He was also national coordinator of the Anti–Martial Law Coalition (later the Coalition Against the Marcos Dictatorship) from its founding in Chicago in 1974 until 1983. From 1973 to 1980, he was the KDP's East Coast regional coordinator. In 1980, he joined the KDP's National Executive Board (NEB) and moved to Oakland, California, becoming editor in chief of Ang Katipunan *in 1981. Starting in 1983, he simultaneously chaired the NEB, which guided day-to-day operations of the organization. This snapshot of the KDP's history is Rene's personal reflection on the collective experience of the organization and is partly based on his shorter article summarizing the KDP's first decade, published in* Ang Katipunan *in September 1983. (For a view of KDP history by a local activist and chapter leader, see the late Helen Toribio's "We Are Revolution: A Reflective History of the Union of Democratic Filipinos [KDP],"* Amerasia Journal 24, no. 2 [1998]: 155–77.) *Rene became editor in chief of* Filipinas Magazine *in the 1990s and a Pacific News Service editor. He is currently US bureau chief of* Inquirer.net, *the official website of the* Philippine Daily Inquirer, *the Philippines' largest-circulation daily broadsheet.*

I T may not be readily apparent in the very personal stories in this collection that a dispassionate revolutionary consciousness made the Katipunan ng mga Demokratikong Pilipino (KDP, or Union of Democratic Filipinos) a unique political phenomenon in the Filipino American community in the 1970s and 1980s. The secret to the organization's viability was its constant, detached analysis of the conditions that defined its community, in order to change them through progressive political activity. Although adherence to Marxism was not a requirement for KDP membership, Marxist theory shaped the group's collective consciousness. It was the lifeblood that sustained the organization for nearly two decades, through times both inspiring and dispiriting. With this consciousness, the young KDP activists were able to move in concert in the United States, wage and actually win political battles for reform, and establish an undeniable leftist presence in what was a conservative post–World War II Filipino American community.

However, the KDP also flourished in no small measure because the world's political temper was so different at the time. For many members of the baby boom generation, it was a time to rise. Capitalism, even in the United States, looked vulnerable, besieged by surging armed movements for national liberation worldwide and shaken by unrest at home. Political theorists both revolutionary and establishmentarian considered the wave of national liberation struggles to be the motivating forces for the global expansion of socialism as capitalism's rival. The existence of the Soviet bloc, China, and Cuba—combined with the revolutionary ferment in Latin America and Asia and the anticolonial guerrilla wars in Africa—made it seem possible that capitalism could collapse within the postwar generation's lifetime. Imminent revolution, to young minds, was conceivable even in the United States. This international zeitgeist inspired radical left movements worldwide.

Though fully aware of their ambitious aims, KDP founders could not foretell the marked impact their work would have on their community in more than a decade of activism. The new group became instrumental in keeping alive a broad, US-based opposition to the Ferdinand Marcos dictatorship in the Philippines, while also mobilizing Filipinos based on steadfast advocacy for their rights as a minority group in the United States.

The KDP had fairly sophisticated operations: a centralized national leadership; chapters in San Francisco, Los Angeles, Honolulu, Seattle, New York, Chicago, Philadelphia, Washington, DC, Sacramento, San Diego; and affiliated organizations in Canada (Toronto, Vancouver, and Montreal). Its newspaper, *Ang Katipunan*, projected the group's politics, even after the KDP's dissolution in July 1986. The newspaper continued operating until 1991 as *Katipunan* (whose masthead read, "A Socialist Newsmagazine").

The KDP's emergence as a self-described revolutionary organization was a provocative event in a relatively small but growing community then known for its political timidity. Traditional community leaders, ensconced in often-redundant councils and associations, or in openly reactionary publications, now faced a highly organized challenge, a polarization that was both ideological and generational.

FAVORABLE CONDITIONS

Important historical trends influenced the KDP's birth. By the early 1960s, postwar generations everywhere were confronting the established order and upsetting political and cultural truisms. The United States itself was in the midst of an internal upheaval against long-standing racism, the American war in Vietnam, and imperial intervention elsewhere. An all-sided culture war raged, in which American youth were overturning conservative values and lifestyles. The Philippines too was convulsing, wracked by a deep economic and political crisis for the first time in its life as a young republic.

In Marxist parlance, therefore, the external conditions favored the rise of a radically progressive force in the Filipino American community. So did the internal conditions. The overwhelming majority of Filipinos were working people, recent immigrants, most of whom may have come with college degrees, professional skills, and facility with English but became wage earners who integrated into the labor force. The entrepreneurial sector was small and would remain so compared with the higher profile of its counterparts in other immigrant communities. Filipinos shared the conditions of wage earners in general, but as immigrants they faced discrimination because of their national origin as nonwhites. These realities tended to dispel, over time, some their most treasured illusions about America.

Furthermore, radicalism was not a new phenomenon among Filipinos in the States. It had emerged before among the pioneer immigrants in the 1920s and 1930s, brought to Hawaii and the West Coast by a US agribusiness greedy for cheap and unorganized labor. Exploitative working conditions and open racism led to periods of political ferment. In the face of antimiscegenation laws, denial of citizenship, and physical attacks by white racists, many among these First Wave immigrants set up mutual-aid societies, Masonic organizations, antidiscrimination committees, and labor-organizing groups.

Some of their leaders still held remnants of the nationalism that had fed the revolution against Spain and the resistance to American occupation of the Philippines early in the twentieth century. A number joined or were influenced by the Communist Party USA—immigrants like the writer Carlos

Bulosan or labor leaders like Ernesto Mangaoang, Chris Mensalvas, Mario Hermoso, Pablo Valdez, and Jorge Frianeza. (Frianeza later became a Central Committee member of the Partido Komunista ng Pilipinas—Communist Party of the Philippines—and was killed in the Southern Tagalog mountains by Philippine soldiers.) Strains of radical anticlericalism and socialism circulated among the more organized circles of the First Wave.

The first progressive current among Filipinos, however, had serious limitations. The pioneer immigrants were mostly itinerant manual laborers who followed the farming and fish-canning seasons on the West Coast. Their lack of opportunity to establish families generally kept stable communities from taking root, while racism blocked their full integration into US society. Even the US communist movement failed to pay particular care to their status as nonwhite and foreign-born workers. Relatively isolated, largely without stable and multigenerational communities, the progressives could not ensure the continuity of their influence. While historically an important source of political lessons for future activists, the First Wave experience would be overshadowed by the conservative impact of the Second Wave of Filipino immigration.

The Second Wave qualitatively altered the community's social and political profile. Younger First Wave immigrants who had served in the US military during World War II were granted American citizenship and came back from the Philippines with war brides. US Navy enlistees recruited from the Philippines and other service veterans later swelled their ranks. With US citizenship, new families, government jobs, and military benefits that buffered them from economic pressures, these Filipino Americans quickly formed stable communities on the West Coast. Soon, the Second Wave's regional and religious groups, councils and veterans' posts dominated the community's social life. A particular strain of conservatism held sway in the postwar community. Colonial mentality and gratitude for the return of American forces during World War II consolidated a nationalism that included loyalty to the American "liberators." The stabilization of Filipino family life occurred amid the McCarthyite anticommunist hysteria of the period, further hardening the community's conservatism. Parents pursued assimilation with illusions and ideological blinders. Being "good Americans" as quickly as possible was the reflexive response to racism in the military, the neighborhoods, and the civilian workplace: children must learn English without any trace of a foreign accent; Filipinos must prove themselves more deserving of trust than other nonwhites; they must steer clear of trouble and suffer slights in silence.

Conservatism among Filipinos, however, had important vulnerabilities. The community was by no means well off; Filipinos largely held modest-paying jobs and were not completely immune to economic pressures. In addition, the Second Wave produced a baby boom generation whose illusions were more fragile than their parents.' They were coming of age as nonwhites in America at a time of rising militant cultural challenges to white supremacy. The community was not hermetically sealed from the political upheavals in the larger society. Thus, when the political and cultural explosions began rocking the United States in the 1960s and 1970s, a significant segment of the Filipino community, mostly from the postwar generation, readily became critical of the prevailing conservatism in their community.

The civil rights movement and protests against the war in Vietnam fueled the radicalization of American youth, and words like *imperialism, revolution,* and *socialism* became part of the political vocabulary. Soon, many second-generation Filipino Americans were joining protests, marches, sit-ins, and strikes against racism and the war or for ethnic studies in colleges, questioning their community's implicit acquiescence to second-class citizenship. A search for one's roots led to an identity movement that retrieved the narrative of the First Wave's struggles. It also inspired examination of the United States' colonial domination of the Philippines. The arrival of Third Wave Filipino immigrants helped accelerate this latter inquiry.

For five years beginning in 1965, the United States eased its immigration policy to respond to domestic needs for certain skills and to propagate a Cold War image of internationalism and benevolence. Thus began the entry of "anchor" Third Wave immigrants, starting a chain of immigration that continues to this day. Included in this largest wave of Filipino immigration were college graduates deeply frustrated with the deterioration of Philippine society, at a time of ascendant Filipino nationalism and anti-imperialism. Soon, the political explosions in the Philippines in the late 1960s resonated among Third Wave immigrants, and study groups emerged on the East Coast and in the Midwest, often leading to academic conferences and protest demonstrations in front of Philippine consulates. Some immigrants formed the National Association of Filipinos in the United States, while others in New York and Philadelphia organized as the Support Committee for a Democratic Philippines; still others formed the Philippine Study Group in Chicago to study the meaning of national democracy, the program of the new Maoist Communist Party of the Philippines (CPP).

Second-generation Filipino American activists—especially on the West Coast—also followed Philippine events with enthusiasm, particularly the emergence of the New People's Army (NPA) and a new Communist Party. Ferment spread among young Filipinos in the San Francisco Bay Area, Los

Angeles, San Diego, Honolulu, and Seattle. Eventually, Filipino American leftists and their newly arrived counterparts found one another.

THE LEFT ORGANIZES

In 1971, a handful of identity movement radicals and immigrant activists from the Philippines formed the Kalayaan collective in San Francisco and published a newspaper of the same name, in honor of the periodical published by the Katipunan, the secret society that had led the revolution against Spanish rule in the Philippines in the late 1890s. The *Kalayaan* newspaper articulated the antiracist and anti-imperialist perspectives of the identity movement and called on Filipino Americans to support the revolutionary armed struggle in the Philippines. Many Filipinos in the United States were first introduced to the CPP, the NPA, and the national democratic cause through *Kalayaan*.

Growing political tensions in the Philippines, heightened further by Marcos's suspension of the writ of habeas corpus, drove home the need for greater coordination among supporters of the Philippine Left. Thus, in September 1972, Kalayaan hosted a conference in San Francisco to set up a nationwide anti-imperialist network. Just as the conference was taking place, Marcos declared martial law and seized dictatorial powers. Electrified, the conference called for nationwide protests and launched the National Committee for the Restoration of Civil Liberties in the Philippines.

Marcos's power grab polarized the Filipino community and fused the concerns of both Third Wave and Filipino American progressives into a single movement. On one side were the progressives and radicals; on the other were conservatives from both the Second and Third Waves who supported Marcos. Within the broad identity movement, some organizers claimed that opposition to the dictatorship was irrelevant to the concerns of the community and a distraction from "real" community issues. In the movement against the Marcos dictatorship, anticommunist elements avoided the Left and later consolidated with exiled former government officials and prominent politicians. They would gravitate to the Movement for a Free Philippines led by former senator Raul Manglapus.

The Kalayaan radicals and their allies across the nation saw a long-term challenge as more disenfranchised politicians began arriving as exiles, bolstering the anti-Marcos movement's conservative flank. While legitimate opponents of the Marcos regime, these elite personages also actively intrigued against the Left and tended to obscure the role of US military and economic interests in propping up the dictatorship. How were the emerging leftists going to navigate the complex demarcations within the community while advocating for the concerns of Filipinos in the United States? The answer led directly to the founding of the KDP.

Kalayaan activists, after consultation with some key leaders of the Philippine Left underground, began laying the groundwork for a national revolutionary organization that would bring together, train, and guide the most progressive and militant elements of the Filipino community. Its dual task was to promote and defend the politics and program of the national democratic movement in the Philippines as well as the democratic and anti-imperialist agenda of the still largely spontaneous US socialist movement.

Finally, on July 27–28, 1973, some seventy representatives from various study groups around the country convened in Santa Cruz, California, and founded the KDP on the basis of a "dual-line" program of supporting national democracy in the Philippines and promoting socialism in the United States. The KDP Founding Congress instituted a centralized leadership structure: a National Council that met every six months, a National Executive Board for day-to-day leadership, Regional Executive Boards, Chapter Executive Boards, and a National Congress of members every two years.

CONSOLIDATION

After the KDP's formation, the task of uniting and training nearly three hundred activists across the United States fell to a nine-member National Council, whose National Executive Board provided day-to-day guidance to national operations. This included supervising nine chapters, with the help of a National Secretariat. At its height, the National Secretariat had up to thirty activists working in it. The subgroups included the National Propaganda Commission, which published the newspaper *Ang Katipunan*, successor of *Kalayaan* and later simply named *Katipunan*; the National Organization Commission, which conducted "chapter checkups"; the National Finance Commission, which collected chapter dues and raised money and supplies sent to the movement in the Philippines; the National Education Commission, which planned and coordinated theoretical studies throughout the organization and conducted an annual summer school for activists; and the Cultural Commission, which guided the cultural group Sining Bayan (People's Art) and prepared cultural material for use in propaganda work and distributed by its Pandayan publishing arm.

At this juncture, key individuals played a crucial role in steering the organization through its growing pains and building up its capabilities: Bruce Occena, Melinda Paras (both US-born Filipinos), and Philippine-born Cynthia

Maglaya composed the National Executive Board in the KDP's early years. Occena was a veteran of the ethnic studies student strikes at the University of California, Berkeley; Paras, who joined the Kabataang Makabayan (Nationalist Youth, the leading left youth group in the Philippines), was deported back to the United States shortly after Marcos imposed his dictatorship; Maglaya was a Kabataang Makabayan activist who was instructed to build a support movement in the United States (she later passed away from a debilitating illness).

This first National Executive Board spent a tremendous amount of intellectual energy consolidating the KDP, drawing lessons from other revolutionary movements and training activists in the rudiments of methodical organizing and political work. The most immediate task of the national leadership was to consolidate the new organization based on a revolutionary standpoint and orientation, begin the theoretical training of activists, and begin political and organizing work in the Filipino community. This included winning over or winnowing out some individuals, who wanted to dilute the activist and leftist character of the new organization, and eradicating bureaucratic styles in the leadership bodies.

The National Congress met every two years to discuss and approve a One-Year Plan, and the National Council met every six months to evaluate the progress of its implementation (and formulate a new One-Year Plan between congresses). Based principally on this plan, national campaigns on both Philippine and US issues broke new political ground in the Filipino community. For systematically training activists on the science and mechanics of coordinated campaigns, the National Council summarized lessons from political work, disseminated through an internal theoretical bulletin called *Ang Aktibista* (The activist) and discussed by the chapters. National leadership conferences in the San Francisco Bay Area deepened these lessons. While the influence of Maoism unleashed activists' enthusiasm and dedication, ideological work based on Marxist theoretical education sustained KDP activists through the years. National Congresses were combined with a national theoretical school that educated activists about basic Marxist philosophy and methodology. The express purpose of this education, as Occena explained during an early theoretical school, was "to learn not strictly what Marx wrote and said but to master his process of thinking." Activists highly valued this theoretical training; it gave them confidence, sharpened their practical organizing skills, and reinforced their commitment to the cause. Theoretical training contributed greatly to the resilience of the organization.

In the beginning, the KDP was significantly influenced by the foundational tenets of the Maoist Communist Party of the Philippines. The KDP adopted the party's National Democratic Program as the transitional stage toward socialism in the Philippines. KDP leadership also initially embraced the CPP's and the Communist Party of China's denunciation of "Soviet revisionism and social imperialism." In later years, however, while still adhering to the economic features of the National Democratic Program for the Philippines, the KDP became receptive to the possibility that the CPP's strategy of classic peasant-based people's war was not the only option for the Left's seizure of power in the Philippines. Specifically, when mass unrest erupted in 1983 after the assassination of opposition leader Benigno Aquino Jr. and the Marcos dictatorship faced a crisis of rule, the KDP recognized urban insurrection as a distinct option for the Left, as well as the necessity of adopting transitional forms of struggle that could facilitate that option. This could include, for example, a broad anti-dictatorship (as opposed to anti-imperialist) front, peace negotiations with the Corazon Aquino government, and participation in the parliamentary arena. (By the end of its existence in 1986, the KDP also had adopted a gentler view of the Soviet Union and the socialist bloc, influenced by former leaders like Bruce Occena and Melinda Paras who had left to help form the Line of March [LOM]; this organization initiated a spate of theoretical activities, including a critique of Maoism and reexamination of the legacy of the international communist movement.)

Theoretical training from infancy helped the KDP achieve independence in its relationship not only with the Communist Party of the Philippines but also with the US New Left. The application of theory as a practical tool in concrete political work helped activists avoid the trap of dogmatism, which prevailed in the many "pre-party" formations in the broader left movement. KDP independence was also helped by the group's rule against dual membership with other democratic centralist groups of the US Left and its refusal to get embroiled in polemical, often infantile leftist debates. (The KDP changed its no-dual-membership policy only in the late 1970s, when some leading KDP members, mostly US-born, began transitioning out to form the Marxist-Leninist Line of March, in a serious attempt to help change the orientation and direction of the US Left. Many Filipino Americans eventually joined the LOM while remaining in the KDP. Even then the KDP remained, as a matter of policy, a nonparticipant in the broader theoretical struggles of the US Left.)

The results of the KDP's early consolidation efforts showed very quickly. Throughout the 1970s, the KDP drew the Filipino community into a sustained flow of political activity. Publications like the now-defunct *Ningas Cogon* called the 1970s "a decade of awakening and action," and even the anticommunist *Philippine News* begrudgingly recognized the role of the KDP in the unexpected eruption of Filipino grassroots activism. The KDP evolved into a relatively tight and disciplined organization, capable of deploying committed activists to different parts of the United States when the need arose. Often, a handful of activists could mobilize scores, even hundreds of Filipinos in political activity.

CONSISTENT OPPOSITION TO DICTATORSHIP

One of the KDP's immediate political successes was consistent and cumulative exposure of the Marcos dictatorship's crimes and the self-serving support the regime received from the US government. This meant organizing a well-oiled network of grassroots opposition that included non-KDP anti-Marcos individuals and organizations. A national conference in Chicago in December 1974 founded the Anti–Martial Law Coalition (AMLC) (later the Coalition Against the Marcos Dictatorship, after the nominal lifting of martial law in 1981).

Although the newly established Movement for a Free Philippines led by former senator Raul Manglapus refused an invitation into the coalition, the AMLC went ahead. For the rest of the decade, it launched nationally coordinated campaigns, educating the community and non-Filipinos on the plight of political prisoners, US motivations for propping up Marcos, and the regime's various maneuvers for legitimacy and its multifarious crimes, from corruption to human rights violations. These campaigns took the form of petition drives, both planned and emergency demonstrations, Christmas caroling, speaking tours of secret delegations to the Philippines and deported or exiled critics of the regime, and fund-raisers for the Philippine labor movement and refugees of government anti-insurgency campaigns. In 1977, AMLC activists even occupied Philippine consulates in four US cities to protest the regime's sentencing to death by firing squad of key opponents: Benigno Aquino Jr., NPA chief Bernabe Buscayno, and Lieutenant Victor Corpus, a defector to the NPA.

The AMLC (which in 1981 became the Coalition Against the Marcos Dictatorship, or CAMD) produced and disseminated books, pamphlets, photo exhibits, slideshows, posters, and a monthly broadsheet called *Taliba*, which regularly featured exposés of the Marcos regime's abuses. The KDP also helped organize the Friends of the Filipino People (FFP) and with the CAMD set up the Congress Education Task Force in Washington, DC. This task force gave Marcos a scare by successfully pushing to cut aid to the regime during the Carter administration. As a result of years of consistent work, the coalition was the only organization capable of coordinating a quick nationwide campaign of protests during Marcos's state visit to the United States in September 1982.

Amid a reinvigorated anti-Marcos grassroots movement, the KDP independently popularized the Communist Party of the Philippines' National Democratic Program as well as the party's leading role. The KDP also independently organized medical and financial aid drives for the Philippine Left underground. The KDP as a matter of policy responded to every major intrigue against the national democratic Left fomented by the regime's operatives as well as by exiled elite oppositionists.

ANTIDISCRIMINATION CAMPAIGNS

Pursuing their dual-line program, KDP activists also initiated political mobilizations around domestic US issues, politically activating Filipinos who might have been hesitant to join the anti-dictatorship movement.

In 1975, the KDP led a successful campaign to stop the deportation of Filipino doctors trapped by the technical and bureaucratic maneuvers of the American medical establishment and the Immigration and Naturalization Service (INS). This was immediately followed by a similar campaign in 1977 that prevented the deportation of hundreds of nurses victimized by licensure tests slanted against graduates from underdeveloped countries. Activists organized a community nurses coalition known as the National Alliance for Fair Licensure for Foreign Nurse Graduates, which successfully negotiated with the INS under the Carter administration for a halt to the deportations.

Meanwhile, also in 1977, attempts to frame and make scapegoats of two Filipina nurses, Leonora Perez and Filipina Narciso, for mysterious deaths in a Michigan veterans' hospital sparked outrage among Filipinos everywhere. The KDP stepped in, sending activists to Chicago and Ann Arbor to systematically build defense committees nationwide that raised funds, organized the first nationwide protest of Filipinos against racial and national discrimination, and circulated petitions for the defendants, who were acquitted in 1978. (A similar campaign in 1979 defended US Navy physician Bienvenido Alona when he was framed for the malpractice of white doctors.) Also in 1977, activists stirred up a hornet's nest over the exploitative treatment of Filipino 4-H trainees on US farms, putting pressure on both the Philippine government and the 4-H Foundation to institute program reforms.

These national campaigns gave activists new skills in organizing, mobilization, and mass communication. They also gave the KDP a recognizable profile as a militant advocacy group for the Filipino community. Regional and local campaigns soon flourished as Filipinos brought cases of job discrimination or police misconduct to the attention of KDP chapters. In 1975, activists led an education task force that challenged the racist depiction of Filipinos in California's school textbooks. Drawing allies in the community, the KDP also campaigned for low-cost housing in Seattle's International District, even while initiating efforts to reform Local 37 of the International Longshoremen's and Warehousemen's Union (ILWU; the Alaska Cannery Workers Union), which was under the control of corrupt leaders and their goons. Meanwhile, in San Francisco, activists mobilized a broad citywide coalition to stop the eviction of the elderly tenants from the demolition-bound International Hotel, demanding low-cost housing for the displaced. The city had to send riot police to yank demonstrators from the hotel and evict the tenants they were defending.

KDP activists moved to the center of the annual Filipino Far West Conventions on the West Coast, bringing to the agenda of community organizers and leaders such topics as busing, bilingual education, immigrant rights, the Philippine political situation, and even such broader issues as nuclear disarmament and US military intervention in Central America. Deliberately challenging the conservatives' consulate-centered exclusive gala festivities on June 12, Philippine Independence Day, KDP chapters built local coalitions to mark the date as Philippine National Day—"a day to commemorate the Filipino people's continuing desire for independence," as described in a One-Year Plan, and the Filipino minority's struggle for equal rights in the United States and Canada. The KDP coalitions hosted community-wide celebrations that dwarfed the conservatives' events.

Using cultural activities for political education, activists organized a specialized drama group called Sining Bayan, which toured nationally, staging original productions that portrayed the Moro people's fight for self-determination in the Philippines and the experiences of pioneer Filipino immigrants and the postwar Second Wave. The group toured Hawaii, dramatizing the contributions of Filipino workers to the labor movement in the islands. But even before Sining Bayan was organized, the KDP in 1976 produced a record album of revolutionary songs from the anti-dictatorship underground resistance, which circulated widely in the States and the Philippines.

REACTION FROM THE RIGHT

Conservatives in the community responded with alarm to the rising tempo of activism, issuing reactionary warnings like "Don't bite the hand that feeds you" and "Don't rock the boat." Seeing that these had no appeal among even recent Filipino immigrants—especially as the broader US political scene encouraged protest and militant advocacy—conservatives switched to paying lip service to "relevant issues." Aware of the growing links between anti-Marcos activism and the antidiscrimination ferment, the Philippine consulates and their allies in community councils and pro-Marcos publications began using antidiscrimination rhetoric while trying to isolate "red infiltrators" and "radical troublemakers."

Some KDP detractors were self-declared progressives, even leftists, who refused to give the organization credit for any accomplishment and were often the sources of political intrigues. Some attacked the KDP's role in the Friends of the Filipino People in 1979, precipitating an open split in the latter. The incident provided those who had axes to grind the opportunity to initiate the first major anticommunist attack on the KDP. The *Philippine News*, the unofficial publication of the Movement for a Free Philippines, spearheaded this attack. Its publisher, Alex Esclamado, openly declared that he opposed communists more than he opposed Marcos.

Meanwhile, the Marcos government stepped up covert actions in the Filipino community in the United States, using its own agents as well as allies in conservative circles. A plan later uncovered, called the Philippine Infiltration Plan and in operation since 1973, involved not only spying on activists but also phoned threats, attempts to disrupt public events, and even an arson attempt on the KDP office in Chicago. These intimidation efforts culminated in the assassination of KDP activists and ILWU Local 37 union officials Silme Domingo and Gene Viernes on June 1, 1981, in Seattle. The two had just successfully linked up with the resurgent labor movement in the Philippines and were mobilizing support from US trade unions when hoodlums connected to a local Marcos operative gunned the men down in cold blood. (Their families later won $23.3 million in damages in a wrongful death suit against the Marcos estate and other defendants.)

Through Freedom of Information Act files, the KDP confirmed that US government agencies such as the FBI and US Naval Intelligence conducted secret surveillance of KDP activists, even coordinating information gathering with Manila. The Reagan administration and the Marcos regime also attempted to push through an extradition treaty, in which Marcos named key opposition leaders among moderates, elite exiles, and the KDP as prime targets.

The KDP experienced growing pains and, along the way, made avoidable mistakes. Particularly in the early years, some activists' resort to ham-handed maneuvers for influence, as well as dogmatic and sectarian tendencies, alienated potential allies, some irreparably. But activists were by and large open to self-criticism, and the "ultra-left" mistakes in rhetoric and action steadily gave way to flexibility.

In 1976, misunderstandings about the KDP's dual-line program led activists in the Chicago chapter to split away, according to the chapter's statement, "to focus solely on Philippine support work." The National Council sent a small team of activists (Rene Ciria Cruz from New York, Geline Avila and Nena Hernandez from San Francisco) to Chicago for an indefinite period, both to implement the full program and to start a dialogue with the breakaway group. The leadership of the Philippine Left underground intervened and discouraged the split, stating, "There's more that unites us than divides us." The underground was acting on the mutual understanding between the first generation of CPP leaders and key KDP founders that Filipino leftists in the United States would be recruited and trained in a single revolutionary organization—the KDP. The potentially injurious schism was healed after a yearlong process of reconciliation.

One split was never resolved. In the early 1980s, a vicious intrigue divided the Friends of the Filipino People from the KDP, and some of the latter's internal documents appeared in a red-baiting attack by the *Philippine News*. The FFP would gravitate to the orbit of the new Philippine-support center set up secretly in the United States by the National Democratic Front and the CPP when they jointly withdrew support for the KDP.

One KDP error that was never corrected was the tendency to demand a commitment of "all or nothing," particularly from leading activists who may have found themselves wavering, not willing to take on a more challenging assignment, or wanting a break from the hectic lifestyle of the organization. As a result, some key members were relegated to the sidelines or allowed to quietly drop out altogether, for fear that they would set a bad example for other activists. Yet, ironically, the organization's policy of "everyone has something to contribute to the movement" regardless of current limitations was applied to nonactivists that the organization was trying to organize. By the time the national leadership identified the error of requiring all or nothing from key activists, it was too late to rectify: the KDP was already on its way to dissolution.

DECLINE AND DISSOLUTION

Just as historical factors led to the KDP's birth, a confluence of developments led to the group's gradual decline and then abrupt disbanding in 1986.

By the mid-1980s, the US political scene had begun a rapid cooling. Progressive ferment had started receding with the end of the Vietnam War in

1975, but it ebbed further in the face of the Reagan counterrevolution against the legacy of Vietnam, meaning the politics and values of the civil rights and antiwar period. The KDP continued despite the changing political climate, although it began clearly encountering increased difficulties in expanding its membership and political work. Meanwhile, dislocations and discontinuities in the leadership of the Communist Party of the Philippines, resulting from arrests and deaths, had seriously weakened mutual understandings and previous working arrangements with the KDP leadership.

The CPP and KDP had mutually agreed that, in the interest of preserving forces and facilitating training, all Filipino left activists would be concentrated in one organization—the KDP. However, it was also understood that this was an expedient and temporary arrangement, that eventually activists strategically oriented toward the US Left would leave the KDP to take up responsibilities in the US Left. Indeed, by the mid-1980s many veteran Filipino American KDP activists began transferring to the broader US pre-party Marxist-Leninist movement, particularly into the Line of March organization. Although activists who remained in the KDP benefited from access to the LOM's theoretical activities, the Philippine "center" began objecting to the departure of mostly Filipino American activists at a time when the CPP was also trying to boost armed struggle against the Marcos dictatorship and obtain necessary material aid from abroad.

The resulting pressure moved the CPP leadership to fundamentally question the KDP's dual-line program, essentially demanding an exclusive focus on Philippine support work. The CPP refused to accept the KDP's argument that mobilizing support for the Philippine revolutionary movement and rallying Filipinos to fight for their democratic rights in the United States were not mutually exclusive; rather, each strengthened support for the other. The KDP's fragile relationship with the new leadership of the Philippine Left entered a troubled phase.

Overlapping this tension were long-standing but formerly nonantagonistic differences over the "international line" of the CPP, in which the KDP leadership advocated reexamining the Philippine movement's Maoist orientation. But China's invasion of Vietnam and the Philippine Left's official support for China's action sharpened this disagreement. Simultaneously, as their theoretical capacity developed, KDP activists became critical of some of Maoism's simplistic interpretations of Marxism and nationalistic anti-Soviet revisionism, which among other things tended to divorce Philippine revolutionaries from the long history and rich experiences of international Marxism, beyond various national liberation movements. The CPP's close identification with Maoism, the US activists argued, also alienated the

Philippine movement from the mainstream of international socialism, unnecessarily costing the Philippine movement vital support from the then-existing socialist bloc, which refused to break with the Soviet Union based on Maoist critiques of revisionism and social imperialism.

Angry and suspicious of the KDP, the Philippine Left's leadership finally sent organizers to build its own operations and mass organizations in the United States that were to be exclusively oriented toward Philippine support work. It demanded that the KDP dismantle itself and, by eschewing joint activities, refused to legitimize the US group's Philippine support work. This left the KDP in an untenable situation of continuing to support the Philippine revolutionary movement while the CPP leadership no longer welcomed its efforts and, in fact, viewed them with hostility. The new Philippine support groups briefly flourished, buoyed by the flow of mass opposition that resulted from the assassination of Benigno Aquino Jr., while many KDP activists felt disowned and demoralized.

The conflict with CPP leadership deepened further when the KDP independently decided to support Corazon Aquino's presidential bid during the 1986 snap election decreed by Marcos. Instead of following the CPP's policy of boycotting the election because it was merely a contest between the movement's ruling class enemies, the KDP saw an insurrectionary situation developing; win or lose the election, the regime could no longer rule in the same way and its US supporters could no longer wholeheartedly support it. Marcos could only win by cheating or by preventing an opposition victory with arbitrary force. Either development would only escalate popular resistance and worsen the regime's crisis while rendering continued US support politically untenable. The KDP correctly predicted the emergence of a revolutionary crisis that could prove fatal to the regime and presented an opening for the Left's intervention. (Appendix 2 excerpts from the April 16, 1984, issue of *Ang Aktibista*, the KDP's internal theoretical organ, detailing the group's analysis of the Philippine political situation and US-Philippine relations two years before the snap election.)

With this independent position, the KDP cemented its ties with the moderate oppositionists in the United States who were mobilizing support for Aquino; but the position sealed the group's alienation from the national democratic Left in the Philippines. Sadly, the Left's boycott of the election that led to Marcos's ouster, and its refusal to support Aquino during the campaign, rendered it politically marginalized in the aftermath. The Left's considerable national influence quickly shrank, and breakaway formations critical of the party's leadership decimated the party's ranks.

The fall of the Marcos dictatorship and the return of bourgeois democratic institutions in the Philippines presented a challenging historical juncture for the Philippine Left. In the United States, Philippine-oriented political activity as a whole, including the KDP's, ebbed following the removal of the polarizing dictatorship. The CPP's hostility proved incapacitating for the KDP's Philippine work, which was now informed by a dissenting analysis of the historical juncture in the Philippines. The KDP leadership tried to reconfigure its Philippine support work by establishing alternative relations with non-CPP forces in the Philippines, but another crisis hobbled the KDP's struggle for continued viability.

Leftist political ferment in the United States had begun cooling with the end of the war in Vietnam and further chilled with the emergence of the Reagan counterrevolution. Further, the fall of existing socialism and the consequent doubts about the soundness of Marxist theory demoralized revolutionary forces worldwide and put them on the defensive. The collapse of international socialism punctuated the end of the time to rise. The remnants of the Marxist US Left disintegrated, including the Line of March, which had many former KDP activists in its ranks. Alienated from the main body of the Philippine Left and unmoored by the collapse of the socialist paradigm, the remaining members of the KDP finally voted to disband the organization in 1986.

PART ONE

BEGINNINGS

THE KDP was militant and well organized, and it could seem to a distant observer a relatively homogenous grouping. In reality, the organization was made up of very diverse individuals who had very particular personal experiences (both in the Philippines and United States) that drew them to the group. They came from different walks of life. Some were from privileged backgrounds in the Philippines, while some came from the lower classes. Many had been influenced by the radical youth movement before dictatorship was imposed in 1972, and a number of immigrants who joined the KDP a bit after its founding had been active in the left underground in the Philippines. Most Filipino Americans had working-class origins; they were baby boomers who became active in the civil rights and anti–Vietnam War movements. Some KDP members, even leading ones, were not of Filipino descent but were politicized by their association with Philippine politics or Filipino activists in the United States. Part 1 of this collection provides a glimpse into the political life histories of some activists—Filipino Americans, immigrant Filipino nationals, and non-Filipinos—and how their awakening came about.

TO TEACH THE MASSES A LOVE FOR BACH, CHOPIN, AND BEETHOVEN

THERESE R. RODRIGUEZ

Therese R. Rodriguez joined the KDP New York chapter and became a member of the Chapter Executive Board and, eventually, the Regional Executive Board. Part of Therese's work was leading the organizing of Philippine National Day, the Narciso-Perez Defense Committee, and the Anti–Martial Law Alliance (AMLA). She also built community coalitions to prevent the deportation of foreign medical graduates and to oppose the unfair licensure process for foreign nurse graduates. Following the assassinations of KDP activists Silme Domingo and Gene Viernes in Seattle, she was assigned to Washington, DC, to do congressional education and lobby for hearings on the collaboration of US intelligence agencies with agents of the Marcos regime operating in the United States. When Marcos was overthrown in 1986, Therese joined other opposition forces in the newly created Philippine Commission on Good Government (PCGG) to locate the wealth stolen by the Marcos family. Therese is now CEO of the Asian and Pacific Islander Coalition on HIV/AIDS (APICHA) Community Health Center, which serves people living with HIV/AIDS, members of the LGBTQ community, and immigrants of limited English proficiency.

I LEFT the Philippines for the United States in July 1972, unsure if I was just trying to run away from getting too involved in the social ferment of the period.

Back in the Philippines during the late 1960s, I cut most of my classes during my last year at Saint Theresa's College, a private Catholic school.

Members of the Kabataang Makabayan (KM, or Nationalist Youth) and Samahang Demokratiko ng Kabataan (SDK, or Democratic Association of Youth)[1]—including Lori Barros (who later died as a leader of the New People's Army), Richie Benavidez, and Aimee Laurel (a Saint Theresa's classmate who would marry future KDP leader Rene Ciria Cruz)—and radicals from the University of the Philippines would come to our campus in Quezon City. They would hold "DGs" (discussion groups) and skits in our cafeteria and other function rooms.[2] Once, a well-known movement personality at the time, Sixto Carlos (a leading figure in the SDK), was allowed to use a classroom. I remember that he drew a pyramid on the blackboard, showing how the few on top were ruling over the many, and described the three evils of Philippine society: feudalism, imperialism, and fascism. At the end of the presentation, he drew an inverted pyramid. That was the ideal world, where the many would rule over the few.

I frequented the cafeteria. Between a class in statistics or a discussion on the class analysis of Philippine society, I chose the latter. It was really the heyday of student power. Along with sympathetic lay teachers and nuns, we rode Saint Theresa's school buses to a huge demonstration in front of the Philippine Congress on January 26, 1970, when President Marcos was to deliver his state of the nation address. It resulted in a police riot, with cops brutally attacking students with truncheons and tear gas. That began the season of massive student marches. I would soon join marches with a few Theresians, who became chapter members of those radical student groups.

Where I lived was not far from Manila, the center of the political storm. Many students from the city resided in Paranaque, a suburb south of Manila proper. Student activist chapters soon got formed in our town and local actions began to take place.

I stayed more intellectually involved than anything else, but somehow I ended up being asked to set up meetings in our home. On one occasion, farmers belonging to the group of Luis Taruc (a leader of the armed

---

1   Both the KM and SDK were militant, revolutionary student organizations based principally at working-class colleges and the state university, the University of the Philippines, whereas Saint Theresa's College was a private girls' school widely viewed as elite.

2   DGs were a major venue for recruiting new members to the revolutionary movement. These groups usually involved eight to twelve people; discussion centered around some short reading with questions and answers, led by a couple of more experienced or knowledgeable activists.

communist Huk Rebellion[3] in the 1950s who later became an anticommunist reformer) held a DG on our lanai. The group stayed the night and slept in our home. On another occasion, a commuter jeepney strike was called and the aim was to prevent all vehicles from taking the road. The strategic location was the Paranaque Bridge. It had to be blocked! Our house was located by the river and had a perfect view of the bridge from the second-floor balcony. My younger brothers and I decided to provide support to the SDK. Following the lead of James Gatus, a local activist, we lay down on the bridge, along with others, to block traffic.

My mother, who belonged to the landed class, was already upset over the Huks sleeping in our elegant living room. So she was beside herself with fear when she saw us from the balcony. Under the intense tropical sun, she strode over to the bridge carrying her umbrella, followed by Ansang, our longtime domestic helper, and pulled my brother and me out of the ranks.

In my nighttime dreams, however, I would be in fear of the revolutionary masses marching with red banners and declaring the end of elitist rule. I knew we were not of the masses. I was truly afraid of becoming too closely tied to the activists. As soon as I suggested leaving for abroad, all arrangements were hurriedly made.

I was living with my cousins in Elmhurst, Queens, in New York when I read a small item in the inside pages of the *New York Daily News* that Marcos had declared martial law. I remember clipping the article. A few days later, I got a call from Nonoy Marcelo, creator of the popular Tisoy cartoon character in the Philippines.[4] He was an acquaintance of a writer from my hometown. He informed me of an anti–martial law demonstration being organized in front of the Philippine consulate in Manhattan.

Drifting in New York, guilty about leaving the Philippines, aware of my own inner conflict and reservations, I decided to join the demonstration. The organizers were very fearful of Marcos agents. I tried to establish some connection with them by dropping names of activists I had known in the

---

3   The Hukbalahap, or Huks, were the communist-led guerrilla army that fought the Japanese invasion of World War II. Taruc was one of its prominent leaders. However, after a long imprisonment, he renounced Marxism and became a leading figure in the Catholic Church–backed reformist social movement of the day. He later became a supporter of Marcos.

4   Tisoy, also slang for *mestizo* (a person of mixed blood, usually European and Indio, the latter a colonial name for native Filipinos), was a popular cartoon character published in one of the Manila daily newspapers that spoofed the lifestyle of shiftless student youths.

Philippines. (They later admitted that they thought I was an intelligence agent trying to trip them up.) At the time, I could not understand why these supposed representatives of the masses were snubbing me and literally walking away from me.

Thus, still stricken with angst, I went back to the relative comfort of drifting along, until one day I was invited to a party at Peter Cooper Village, a huge housing complex in Manhattan, where we moved later that year. Peter Cooper is a maze of red brick buildings on the east side of Manhattan, from Fourteenth Street to Twenty-Third Street, from First Avenue to Avenue C. Buildings rise up thirty floors. It is a housing development for middle- and upper-class families. Doctors, nurses, and medical professionals who worked at nearby Bellevue Hospital, New York University Hospital, and Beth Israel rented apartments there. When my cousin and my cousin's spouse (both were doctors) moved from Queens to Manhattan, I moved in with them. They had an apartment on the twentieth floor with a view of the East River and its tugboats and, farther upriver, of the Queensboro Bridge.

At that party I met Leni Marin, a former University of the Philippines student. She seemed such a party animal. For the longest time she was leaning against the piano, a glass of wine in hand, singing Cole Porter and Erroll Garner songs. Later in the evening she came over to me and asked, "What's your ideology?"

Leni became my self-appointed tour guide in Manhattan. She introduced me to the jazz clubs and cafés of the East Village. We would hang out at her sister's apartment in the Chelsea area; she would play (and as usual sing along to) records of Bette Midler, Melissa Manchester, and Billie Holiday. Leni was also the sole link to my short-lived political past. One day she learned of a DG at the apartment of a certain Amador. She suggested we go. I was not enthusiastic, so she said, "Let's go get hamburgers at McDonald's." I could never have enough of McDonald's when I first came to the States. She knew that. We went to the McDonald's on Twenty-Third Street and First Avenue. When we were done with our burgers, she pressed on, "Why don't we just observe, because well-known student activists in Manila like Nelson Navarro, Aimee Laurel, and Rene Ciria Cruz will be there," tempting me with the celebrities of the Philippine movement. "And by the way," she said, "Amador's place is just across the street."

So I relented. We went to the DG. We entered an apartment full of people. As soon as we came in, Aimee looked alarmed. She motioned for me to go into a room with her. Looking at me with her big sharp eyes, she said, "Do you know who you're with?" referring to Leni. "She's with that revisionist

MPKP!"[5] Confused, I said, "Ha? Revisionist what? I didn't bring her, she brought me. Besides she's not a revisionist, she's just an observer!"

The DG began. One of the participants, Aleli, with a professorial voice and hand motions, read a passage from Mao's Little Red Book and explained the concept of working-class standpoint and the term *proletariat*. She asked me later what I considered myself to be when I told her that I just got hired as a billing clerk for Native Textiles Inc. After thinking about the question, I said that I was not a worker, that I did not consider my job the same as the work I would like to do. When she pressed for my definition of work, I answered, conviction and all, that work to me would be to teach the Filipino masses a love for Bach, Chopin, and Beethoven through classical guitar!

Many DGs, ideological struggles, and years later, much of the guitar playing I did was strumming C, G, D, and A-minor chords and the bridge refrain F–G while singing the marching song "Ang masa, ang masa lamang ang siyang tagapagligtas" (The masses, only the masses are the saviors) and the dirgelike "Ang buhay ng proletaryo'y nakabulagta" (The proletarian lies prostrate).

---

5   The Malayang Pagkakaisa ng Kabataang Pilipino (MPKP, or Free Association of Filipino Youth) was the youth arm of the old Communist Party of the Philippines that had led the Huk Rebellion of the 1950s. In the late 1960s, the Philippine Left was sharply polarized between the old, revisionist Communist Party that was ideologically aligned with the Soviet Union and the new, rectified Communist Party that was aligned with the Maoist Communist Party of China. The revolutionary Philippine student movement of the 1960s was principally aligned with the new Communist Party and its military arm, the New People's Army.

"WHO IS MARSHALL LAW?"

JEANETTE GANDIONCO LAZAM

*Jeanette Gandionco Lazam joined the KDP San Francisco chapter in
1975 and was assigned to the Filipino People's Far West Convention
preparations and anti–martial law work in the Filipino community.
In 1976 she took up organizing with the International Hotel Tenants
Association, working against eviction from the very beginning to the
end. After the eviction in 1977, Jeanette worked as part of the Regional
Executive Board that guided the Bay Area KDP chapters until she
resigned from the organization in 1990. Jeanette has logged over
forty-five years of activism on Filipino, LGBTQ, women, and race
issues, with her most recent interest being Palestine and the Middle
East. She has written about her experiences as an activist and about
the KDP in several anthologies, including* Seven Card Stud with Seven
Manangs Wild *and* Beyond Lumpia, Pancit and Seven Manangs
Wild. *A retiree, Jeanette continues to express her creativity through the
arts, such as acting, charcoal and pastel or pen and ink drawing, as
well as Facebook.*

I WAS in the barrio of Biasong, Leyte, in the Visayan Islands of the Philippines when martial law was declared. I hadn't known that Marcos had declared martial law, because there was no radio or newspaper where I was staying. I do remember that morning though. I had set out early for Ormoc, en route to Cebu City. An eerie quiet had descended on the town. The usual hustle and bustle that started around 4:00 a.m., with fishermen, vendors, and housewives washing their clothes—none of that was happening. I took a cab to the pier to buy my ticket back to Cebu. The lines were unusually short, and the tempers among the passengers were unusually mild. I boarded the small, not-so-crowded boat around noon and reached Cebu at 5:00 p.m. that evening.

Meeting me at the dock were our maid and her son. The pier was unusually quiet. We unloaded my luggage and swiftly took a cab back to Espiña Village. Jumping out of the cab and running into the house, I asked my mother if something was wrong? Before she could answer, the phone rang. It was my aunt, who calmly told me that Marcos had declared martial law! I was blown away.

At first I didn't believe her because she told me in a rather joking tone. I asked if she was kidding, and she responded, "No." She said Marcos had planned a national broadcast for 8:00 p.m., when he would explain why he declared martial law and explain the full text of presidential Proclamation 1081, which imposed it. I was in a state of shock. As I reflected back on the day's events, it clicked why there were hardly any people on the streets, on the pier, or in the marketplaces.

Martial law had been declared and the lockdown on democracy and political dissent would be complete by eight o'clock that evening. For the next three hours, the Filipino people held their collective breath and waited.

I took a bath, ate a light dinner, and headed over to cousin Millie's house to listen to Marcos's statement. He didn't come over the airwaves until almost 9:30 p.m. During the long wait, Millie, to break the ice, joked about "Who is Marshall Law?" I didn't think she was so funny. Finally, the radio crackled and Marcos began to speak . . . not in Tagalog, but in English!

Starting with his opening statement—"I am ordering Proclamation 1081, the imposition of martial law, to go into effect upon completion of my statement"—I honestly could not believe that he was saying what I thought I was hearing. It was too unbelievable, too much like fiction, too fantastic to comprehend. Never in my wildest dreams did I think I would ever be in a situation where democracy, as I had come to know it, would end. I had read in history books about different countries, mainly in Latin America, where martial law had been imposed. But I never thought it could happen in the Philippines. I have to say honestly that I was scared shitless.

The next morning, only one newspaper reached the newsstands, and it was a Marcos-controlled paper. By the time I got there almost all the copies were gone. Clearly, the population of Cebu City had already descended on every newspaper stand, as well as every supermarket, buying out the canned goods, meat, candles, and batteries. Cars lined up at gas stations, and the telephone wires were burning up with calls to relatives and friends all over the islands and abroad.

In the streets, tanks and armored vehicles positioned themselves. The Philippine armed forces camps were on red alert, and the Philippine Constabulary, the national police force, manned every corner and alley. Roadblocks were set up on the major highway. The entire island of Cebu was now an armed encampment.

Radio and television stations, the national and local press, universities, and all interisland and overseas travel stopped operating. Each island was left unto itself, rife with anxiety and chaos as citizens scrambled for whatever provisions they could get their hands on. By noon, the streets of uptown and downtown Cebu City were deserted. Everyone stayed home, close to radios or television sets, waiting for the next government announcement. No midday announcement came.

By late in the evening, the Marcos government aired a progress report. The government had successfully raided safe houses, universities, churches— anywhere they suspected communist activists and sympathizers might be hiding. Thousands of people, all over the Philippines, were arrested and sent immediately to trial or torture or swiftly to their deaths.

My mother knew that I had a long and active history with the struggle for civil rights and social justice in the United States, where I had grown up. She also knew that I was not one to just sit idly by and watch as the Marcos fascist machine bore down on the population. She made a decision. I had to leave the Philippines immediately. But all interisland and overseas travel had ceased. She made me promise not to do anything rash or stupid to cause the authorities to take notice of me. I complied with her wishes so as to not place my immediate family in jeopardy.

After one week, Marcos allowed interisland and overseas travel to resume. It was thought that by doing this he would not appear to be a ruthless dictator in the international press. As he lifted the travel ban, he also announced that no one who was peace-minded, who complied with Proclamation 1081, and who held foreign passports (provided they did not offer support to the communist insurgency) would be arrested or detained. This was the signal my mother needed. She immediately made travel plans to Manila; there, she would purchase my ticket back to the United States.

Early the following day, I was ready to leave. Packing all through the night, I managed to fit everything I needed in two medium-size suitcases. In the afternoon, we headed for Mactan Airport, where my mother and I boarded a plane for Manila.

Arriving two hours later, we were met by my aunt. We stayed there for another two days while my mother arranged for my flight back to the United States. I made several phone calls to friends I had known in the States, who had since returned back home. One person in particular, Luz, arranged to meet me at Manila International Airport. She had a small, inconspicuous envelope she wanted delivered to a mutual friend in San Francisco. I agreed to take it.

Manila International Airport was under construction at the time, so it was completely enclosed by cyclone fencing and looked more like an armed camp than an airport. Luz and I met in the main restaurant. We exchanged pleasantries, talked briefly, and then she gave me the envelope. My mother didn't want to enter the airport, so she stood outside, waiting for my plane to take off. At last it was ready, and one last search of carry-on baggage was conducted.

When I got the envelope from Luz, I divided the contents. I placed some papers inside the jacket of one of the record albums I'd packed, putting the more bulky papers inside an envelope labeled "flight insurance," which I then placed in my passport folder. I decided to take the bag of record albums on board with me so they wouldn't get broken or chipped in the general luggage compartment. When it was time for the inspector to check my carry-on luggage, he fumbled around, looking between and inside each album. As he came close to the one that contained the envelope, my heart raced. Sweat had begun to form on my brow and nape and roll down my back. I knew he would find it. I knew I was going be in trouble.

When he finally reached the album, he opened it up and found the papers. He took them out and started to read them. Bunched in his hands were newspaper clippings and articles from magazines Luz had managed to cut out the day before martial law had been declared. There was also a letter addressed to John and the Kalayaan collective in San Francisco, a group of radical Filipino Americans and immigrants, which was a precursor to the KDP. It was my unfortunate luck that since martial law had been declared, the definition of contraband had changed and now included any and all pieces of propaganda written against the regime.

The inspector looked at me long and hard. He immediately summoned representatives from the armed forces. All in all, fifteen men with rapid-fire machine guns surrounded me. I could barely move. Next, a government official came and seized my passport folder. He rifled through it, taking my passport. I knew at that very moment that he was about to ask me what was inside the envelope labeled "flight insurance." By this time I was an absolute wreck.

I quickly got my wits about me and demanded to know why they were detaining me; after all, I was an American citizen. They explained that they had found antigovernment propaganda in my carry-on; they wanted to know who had given it to me and why I was in the Philippines. All the while my mother stood outside the gates of the airport wondering why my plane hadn't taken off.

Stalling for time, I demanded to speak with American embassy officials and have them present during my interrogation. The inspectors denied my request. I again insisted that I be put through to the American embassy. And again they refused. By now I thought for sure they were going to arrest me and send me off to Camp Crame or Muntinlupa.[1] Instead, they brought me to a small room with a little lamp and proceeded to ask me more questions. It was the same thing over and over, only each time they asked, the questions were rephrased in an attempt to get me mixed up and confused. But I held my ground. By this time, my plane was already delayed two hours, and I knew the other passengers were pissed.

Flinging my passport folder on the table in front of me, one inspector asked me what was in the envelope labeled "flight insurance." For a split second I thought I should just give up, but I quickly dispelled that thought and decided to bluff him. I responded, "What do you think is in that envelope? It says flight insurance. If you want to look inside, just open it." He slowly picked up the envelope and pressed it against the light of the lamp. He could only see my flight insurance forms, which I had wrapped around the papers Luz had given me. So all the inspector was able to discern from the shadow of the envelope was precisely what I had told him. He placed the envelope back in the folder and gave it to me. I breathed a slow and heavy sigh.

In the meantime, other inspectors took my luggage off the plane and proceeded to rip it open, looking for other papers or perhaps some secret compartment. They found none. I was then released, given some rope to tie my luggage together and told to board the plane.

As I ran down the tarmac; I took one last, long look at the Philippines and my poor mother standing outside the gate. I cried out, fearing that I would never see her or my brother again. That was the longest seventeen-hour ride back to the States.

When I arrived I immediately contacted John. We met at the United Filipino Association office, where I handed him the envelope.[2] He opened it and

---

1   Camp Crame became the main detention facility for political prisoners during martial law. Muntinlupa, on the other hand, is Manila's main prison and principally holds criminal detainees.

2   The United Filipino Association was a community-based self-help organization in Manilatown, San Francisco. Its office was located in the International Hotel. It initiated the struggle to save the hotel from demolition.

placed the contents on the table. I'm glad those inspectors never opened the envelope, for inside was a summation of the armed struggle in the Philippines, written by the Communist Party of the Philippines (CPP). Also inside was the latest printed copy of *Ang Bayan*, the news organ of the CPP. Could you imagine what those officials would have done if they had found those documents? I shiver to think.

The association allowed the Kalayaan collective to use its back office for meetings and layout space for publishing the *Kalayaan* newspaper.

HOW MY LIFE CHANGED

ROMY GARCIA

Romy Garcia joined the KDP San Francisco chapter in 1980 and routinely distributed informational flyers and sold the KDP paper, Ang Katipunan, *in the community and at local churches. He was briefly involved with immigration rights organizing and the production of* Ang Katipunan. *In 1984, Romy was transferred to the Seattle chapter to bolster its Filipino community work in the aftermath of the Benigno Aquino Jr. assassination. Romy went back to school and received his degree in social work. He continues to do grassroots organizing for workers' and human rights through the Legacy of Equality, Leadership and Organizing (LELO); his union (Local 843 of the Washington Federation of State Employees, or WFSE); the Asian Pacific American Labor Alliance (APALA); and his Buddhist faith community, Soka Gakkai International (SGI).*

A SUMMER NIGHT, 1977

I T must've been close to midnight. The sky was restless, with patchy clouds drifting across a full moon. I was with some of my *barkada* (clique), prowling the side streets around Lake Merritt in Oakland, hoping to find a car we could break into and hot-wire. Suddenly, flashing streaks of red and blue lights were everywhere; someone yelled, "Oh shit, the *parak* [cops] are here!" We bolted in different directions. I headed for some bushes and then crawled under a car. The footsteps of the police officers became louder and louder and suddenly stopped. With a vice-like grip around my ankles, a cop pulled me from beneath the car, read me my rights, handcuffed me, and shoved me into the back of his patrol car. A couple of my other friends were also caught; the others got away.

This was a lot what my life was about back then; the only difference was this time I got caught. When I was arrested, I had run away from home. I was living on the streets with some friends, smoking weed and drinking a lot and, of course, not attending school. It must've been several months earlier, before this incident, that my *barkada* had formed itself into a gang. We called ourselves the Sino Na Gang, which translates to "Who's the Gang?" It was half a joke, but we were easily able to get a "backup" gang if we really needed one, because some of my homeboys had cousins who were members of older, more daring Filipino gangs. I met most of my *barkada* through different junior high schools I attended; in many ways they were a lot like me—born in the Philippines, dragged to America by our parents, stranded in a strange land where we felt out of place, "less than," and pissed off.

Like many of my Filipino friends, I was confused and felt alienated from my parents who were also struggling to sort out what Filipino traditions and values we should maintain in America and which ones we should eliminate. I was a very angry young man. My father was a retired military man, a strict disciplinarian, who always had to have the last word. I, on the other hand, hated authority. We clashed and didn't communicate very well with each other.

In 1967, I arrived in the United States with my mother and seven siblings. I was about seven years old. My father had already retired from the US military and had come to America three years earlier with my oldest sister and three older brothers. My father worked as a janitor at the General Services Administration in San Francisco. Between that job, his pension, and the earnings of my older brothers and sister, they managed to save enough to bring the rest of us to America. Initially my father didn't want my mother to work but to stay home and care for us kids. However, with such a large family we could hardly make ends meet. Eventually my mother started working in a cafeteria at the Presidio military base. Later, she had a string of other jobs, ending up as a dietary technician at Laguna Honda Hospital. My mother was more open to changing some of her ways, but because of the difficulty of trying to raise several unruly children in a very different culture, she resorted to having my father discipline us. My father's punitive approach didn't work well. Most of us children took turns running away from home as we tried our best to adjust to the realities of growing up as immigrants in this country.

On really bad days I would find myself thinking about the Philippines, missing it a lot and wishing somehow that we could go back. The more

America hurt, the more I romanticized our life in the Philippines. Our family comes from Santa Rita, Pampanga, not too far from Manila. It seemed to me that everyone in our home barrio was connected to us through family or friendship ties—we truly belonged there, it was our place. My mother oversaw the household. We had regular househelp to care for us children and do most of the cooking and housework. It seemed that all my feelings of warmth and protection got tied up with memories of back home—the festive Christmas season, the church gatherings, and Apo Seshia, my great aunt, whom we lived with, who cared for me and spoiled me. But here in America, it seemed our family had become isolated, with no support or security.

During the first few years in San Francisco we moved around, which didn't help with getting adjusted to the new country. Initially we lived in the Western Addition district. All of us were crammed into a two-bedroom house, kids ranging in ages from three to twenty-two. Later, we moved to the Bernal Heights area. I went to lots of different schools. I started in Paul Revere Elementary. Then I went to Portola, where I remember getting jumped by some black kids who stole my milk money. I went home and told my older brothers what happened to me. The next day they kicked some ass; then an even bigger fight broke out. I was moved to Giannini Junior High. There I had a few incidents with white kids who were making fun of my accent. I got suspended for bringing nunchuck sticks to school to smash the white kids' heads open. So I was sent to Everett. By this time I had a chip on my shoulder. It wasn't a question anymore of whether I'd get into trouble, just how and when. My Sino Na Gang began to develop at Everett. Most of us then went on together to Mission High. My future was already looking pretty bleak.

Some of my Filipino American cousins were sensitive and accepting of us and were pretty cool. But I felt that most Fil-Ams looked down on me (and people like me) because we spoke with Filipino accents or didn't dress right. At the same time, my older brothers embarrassed me too because they remained too immigrant in their ways, with their flashy clothes and all. My older brothers didn't seem to have the same identity conflict. Because they had grown up in the Philippines, they were just Filipino; that was all there was to it. I can remember telling them about how kids at school would make fun of my English, and they would just say, "Tell them that they can only speak one language, but that you can speak two." Their advice would help me for a little while, but then I'd begin feeling bad again. It was like I couldn't go forward or backward but was just trapped in the middle.

I think it was about a year or so after our entire family had settled in America when my parents were informed that my nineteen-year-old brother,

Marcial, had been killed in Vietnam by friendly fire. I was still very young, but I remember that feeling of fear and doom that gripped my heart that day I came home from school to find our house filled with relatives and my mother crying hysterically. I remember the funeral. I remember, too, that my father had not wanted Marcial to join the Marines and had refused to sign the permission paper, not because he opposed the war, but because he wanted Marcial to continue working to help out the family. But Marcial talked to some sergeant and managed to get himself in anyway. Although some of the edges of this memory are blurred, I'm sure the whole incident marred our family's transition to America. For me, it increased my feeling that nothing but harm and disaster awaited me here.

COMMIT THE CRIME, DO THE TIME

I was sentenced to ten months at Log Cabin Youth Detention for that night of vandalizing cars around Lake Merritt. I was sixteen years old at the time, steadily working my way closer and closer to the state penitentiary. When I arrived at Log Cabin, I discovered that my identity as a Sino Na Gang member was known to the other youths in the camp. Probably because I wanted to somehow prove myself, I decided to have the symbol of our gang tattooed on my front left thigh. I felt proud of my tattoo, especially because I was one of the initiators of the gang. It was my way of telling the world, "Hey, I'm here. Don't mess with me because I don't have anything to lose."

People in the detention camp were from all backgrounds. But race dominated the scene. Most of the Asians, including myself and the other Filipinos, hung together. The Chicanos hung with the Chicanos. The blacks hung out with the blacks. No big fights between the groups broke out while I was in detention, although at times tensions ran high. I had an African American counselor, Alexander, who took the time to get to know me. He challenged me to take myself seriously and invest in my future by completing high school. It was also during this time that I began rebuilding relations with my mother and siblings during their regular visits. Their visits showed me that they cared about me. Lots of the other kids in juvie never had people come to see them. I think all these things helped to slowly change my attitude toward the options I could have in life. After a couple of months of detention, I slowly weaned myself from smoking weed and took to running as my favorite pastime. Gradually I was nudged along a more positive path.

Before I left the detention center, my probation officer recommended that I attend an alternative school so that I would have a better chance of finishing. I agreed, thinking that maybe I needed a break from my *barkada* and that I should try to at least graduate from high school. I had already been kept back a year. Ironically, the alternative school was named Opportunity II High School. And indeed, this was probably my last opportunity to get a diploma. This was also where my initial politicization began.

It was a small school, so there was much more time for students to interact with teachers. Most of the teaching staff, including the principal, were politically progressive; some openly shared their leftist and socialist politics with us in classes. The students, as well as the teachers, were very racially and culturally diverse. There were only a handful of Filipinos: me, my first cousin, a close friend, and a couple of others. Both my cousin and close friend didn't stay too long because of conflicts with other students in the school. Most of my other classmates were African Americans, some Caucasians, and a few Latinos.

We had lots of school assemblies with speakers like Angela Davis, representatives of the Sandinista revolution in Nicaragua, members of the African National Congress fighting to overthrow apartheid, and organizers opposed to the California state initiative Proposition 13.[1] It was during these assemblies and the classroom discussions that followed that my mind was opened, my biases challenged, and my ignorance exposed concerning many important social and political issues like racism, classism, the oppression of gays, capitalism, and imperialism.

As students we were also encouraged to become politically active and involved in the issues that affected our lives, aside from learning the basic schoolwork. Several of us took the lead in organizing our classmates to protest US investments in apartheid South Africa, to support the Nicaraguan revolution, and to oppose Prop 13. I remember mobilizing fellow students to attend a statewide march in Sacramento against Prop 13. Although the initiative ultimately passed, the process of coming together with classmates, teachers, and community people was incredibly enriching for me. In hindsight, it was these experiences at Opportunity II High that contributed to my growing interest in politics. And slowly but steadily, I gained confidence in both my academic and leadership skills.

---

1   Proposition 13 was passed by California voters and implemented in 1978. Prop 13 declared that property taxes were to be assessed at 1975 values, and it restricted annual increases to an inflation factor, not to exceed 2 percent. Reassessment of property tax could only take place when ownership changed or construction took place. This legislation has had devastating impacts on state and local budgets, resulting in huge cuts to programs that serve low-income and people of color communities.

It was a clear, sunny day, and I had graduated from high school a week earlier. Restless, with nothing to do, I decided to take a walk with my dog, Tanya. With Tanya on her leash, I began my casual daily walk, which on that day would lead me toward a life of political activism. I had no particular destination in mind, and I made my way to the Mission district, the warm belt of the city where most of the Chicano/Latino community resides. I headed toward Dolores Park, across the street from my former high school. When I arrived, I noticed a gathering of nearly three or four hundred people huddled around colorful booths and an elevated stage at one end of the park. From a distance, I saw a huge banner across the stage with the words "Philippine National Day (PND)."[2]

My curiosity rose quickly; I had to get closer. I strolled down to the event and realized it was a gathering for the Filipino community. I was impressed because the only other time I had ever seen this many Filipinos together was when I attended church functions, which was not too often anymore. I found myself surrounded by Filipinos speaking English and various Filipino dialects, eating *inihaw* (barbecued meats), adobo, *lumpia* (egg roll), *leche flan*, *halo-halo* (a shaved ice dessert), and more.

I felt a surging sense of belonging and pride. I strolled around the information booths; one booth in particular caught my eye. It displayed newsletters, some books, and a variety of posters, some of which depicted frail Filipinos living in poverty and Filipino prisoners peering from behind bars. A banner hung across the booth with bold letters, "Anti–Martial Law Alliance, San Francisco Chapter."[3]

At the time, I didn't know much about the Philippines politically, except what I heard from my relatives. They told me that the Philippines was a

---

2　June 12 is officially Philippine Independence Day, which Philippine consulates in the United States and their allies in the Filipino community celebrated with fancy, elite balls, often in first-class venues. The KDP launched a national campaign to mark June 12 as Philippine *National* Day instead (because the Philippines was not truly independent from the United States), to be marked with picnics and fiestas in public parks, open to everyone. Philippine National Day celebrations were attended by hundreds, often thousands of Filipinos, and soon overshadowed the elite official Philippine government commemorations of June 12.

3　Each local chapter of the Anti–Martial Law Coalition (AMLC), founded in Chicago in 1975, was called Anti–Martial Law Alliance (AMLA).

Catholic country, that we gained independence from Spain and eventually from the United States. I also knew that most of my relatives were poor, like most other Filipinos, but that there were several extremely wealthy Filipino families who could actually be identified by name. All I knew about President Marcos was that he was a rich and a powerful person who was to be feared.

Several people were sitting behind the tables at the anti–martial law booth, and one of them asked me if I had any questions about what was happening in the Philippines. Her name was Wilma, and she introduced me to Paulette, Chuck, Raddy, Pilar, and others. I don't exactly remember our discussions, but I must have given them my name and phone number. After a week or so, I began receiving phone calls inviting me to meetings. I attended some meetings and volunteered to take on small tasks. Through meetings and discussions I learned about the anti–martial law movement in the United States and the revolutionary situation in the Philippines. After attending several discussions groups, I began to take interest in the KDP because it seemed so clear about its role in supporting the movement in the Philippines and fighting against national and racial discrimination here in the States.

The KDP activists' level of revolutionary commitment was astounding to me. They seemed to have the ability to attend all-night marathon meetings and then go to work the next morning. It was difficult to picture myself going to meetings almost every day and night and not spending time socializing with my friends. I wasn't sure I could make such a commitment, since I was just a reformed gang member who had experienced only a little bit of politics in my last year of high school. However, the folks in the KDP assured me that I was up to the task and could handle the commitment. (I discovered after joining the KDP that the work at times was exhausting and the time commitment tremendous!)

But I think what mainly drew me to the organization was the respect and ease in which Filipino immigrants and Filipino Americans interacted and worked with one another. Given the chauvinism I'd experienced in most of my dealings with Filipino Americans, I could hardly believe my eyes as I observed the way KDP activists worked together. I imagined that this had something to do with the politics of the organization. It was a powerful magnet for me. Once I joined, I also discovered I needed to quit smoking. I'm not talking about cigarettes. Whenever I smoked marijuana, my mind wandered aimlessly and I would forget tasks I had volunteered for at previous meetings. It reached a point where I had to decide between my old lifestyle of just hanging out or becoming an activist. I chose the latter.

One of my favorite assignments was *Taliba* distribution.[4] We would hand out the *Taliba* at Sunday mass, where there were lots of Filipinos. I got my first chance to meet many Filipinos and find out where they stood on the Marcos regime. Many did not stop to talk with us at all, but their overwhelming nonverbal support for the *Taliba* was apparent in the way they'd reach out for it and begin reading it immediately on the way into church. Many would say, "Salamat para sa balita" (Thanks for the news), or "O, ano na bang nangyayari?" (What's happening over there now?), or "Ano na ba ang ginagawa ni Macoy?" (What did Marcos do now?). Then, of course, there were some *kababayan* (compatriots) who were disturbed by our presence. Some would say, "Kung walang martial law, maraming gulo sa atin!" (Without martial law there would be trouble), or they would attack our credibility with, "Papano mong alam kung ano nangyayari sa atin, kung nandito kayo?" (How do you know what's happening there when you're over here?).

At times I found myself unprepared to respond to pro-Marcos comments. What really helped, though, was that afterward we would always share our experiences back at headquarters. Often we'd repeat word for word what was said, how we responded (or didn't know how to respond), and then *kasamas* would give each other feedback and suggestions about how to respond better the next time. This was a very effective learning process; much of our activism was learned this way, learning from doing.

One person who remains sharp and clear in my memory is Mang Mario Hermoso (*Mang*, or *Manong*, signifies respect for an older male). He had already been a member for a few years when I joined the San Francisco chapter of the KDP. When I first met him at Wilma's house, he was seventy-seven years old. Mario was a shade less than medium height, with a compact build and shaped like a thick box. You got the impression that he must have been very strong in his younger days. His eyesight was going quickly, so he would

---

4   The *Taliba* (Herald) was a monthly leaflet distributed nationally by the Anti–Martial Law Coalition to analyze developments in the Philippines or explain the dictatorship's latest political maneuvers. The coalition's national coordinator in New York City wrote these pieces, and camera-ready facsimiles were air-expressed to local chapters, which produced copies for distribution. (This was before the age of picture faxes and e-mail). Occasionally, chapters produced their own issues to address a local concern related to martial law. On average, 25,000 to 30,000 copies of each issue were distributed nationwide, filling the information gap about the Philippines, which was under the dictatorship's heavy press censorship.

come close to address you, with a twinkle in his eye and a soft, gentle voice, almost a whisper. He was gracious and polite in a very Filipino way. But his hands were strong and his fingers were knotted from years and years of hard manual work. His brown skin was no longer taut against his face but showed the many lines of a man who had aged beautifully.

Mario was from the Visayas, in the Philippines' central islands. He came to America as a young man in his late teens. He did what most Filipinos did back then—worked in the fields, went to the Alaska canneries, did kitchen work in the cities, and the like. But Mario was also very different. He was one of the few Filipinos of his generation in the United States to become a Marxist and a revolutionary. He and Mang Pablo (who also joined the KDP) were in the Communist Party of the United States (CPUSA) in the late 1930s. In its heyday, the CPUSA successfully broke through the color line and aggressively drew minority people into and around it. In California, Mario was one of the CPUSA's best "street propagandists." They say he could sell more copies of the *People's World* newspaper than anyone else. Mario remained fiercely loyal to the CPUSA through thick and thin, despite the personal hardships he endured during the anticommunist McCarthy period. Even after he adopted the KDP as his new family, he could not be budged from his support of the CPUSA, which the Maoist Communist Party of the Philippines considered a "revisionist" party allied with the Soviets. Mario would listen patiently to our criticisms of the CPUSA but would never change his position. When he got tired of listening to us, he'd sometimes raise one hand and ask with a sly smile on his face, his eyes half closed, his head tilted slightly, "Why do you think I really joined the CPUSA?" After a pause in which he had everyone's attention, he'd answer himself: "So I could meet beautiful women!" This was Mang Mario's way of ending the discussion.

Mang Mario lived at the Vincent Hotel on Turk Street. His room was an absolute fire hazard (fortunately, he didn't smoke). It was cluttered from floor to ceiling with books and papers. Despite his poor eyesight, Mario remained an avid reader and carried a huge handheld magnifying glass around to help him read. He was also very active in the North of Market Seniors' Group and always sported a large blue "Senior Power" button on his lapel. His dark clothing always seemed to hang loosely on his body, emphasizing the smoothness and flexibility of his motions. In the pocket of his wrinkled shirt, there was always a pad of paper and four or five pens of different sizes and colors. And, of course, he always wore his black beret, tilted to one side, highlighting the roundness of his face and the silver of his hair. He was quite a sight to behold.

Mario and I teamed up to distribute the *Taliba* and sell *Ang Katipunan* in front of Saint Patrick's Church on Sunday mornings. Sometimes I would pick him up at the Vincent Hotel; other times he'd make his way down to the church on his own. After we'd finish our "propaganda assignment," we'd often go to McDonald's to grab a bite to eat. He would talk to me about many things related to philosophy, political economy, socialism—deep issues that I was just beginning to understand. He had confidence in my ability to think, and he showed respect and patience for my opinions, even when I knew they were muddled and confused. Like many other KDP activists, I felt like Mario and I had a special relationship. Mario had a way of making everyone feel that way, which was important because Mario was our link to the past. He would inspire us on a regular basis. He especially used one metaphor often: "You know," he'd say, "you may have gas and pistons and rods in your car, but all of these things don't matter unless the spark plug gives off the spark—that's the KDP's role, to be the spark for change in the Filipino community, the spark to move it forward."

My preoccupation with the past was tragically interrupted when events in the present threw parts of my own past in sharp relief. My nephew Nicolas was shot dead in the San Francisco Bay Area in drug- and gang-related violence. Before my family could finish grieving, my cousin Rickie was killed in a similar fashion and circumstances in July of the same year. Then nine months later, another nephew, David, was set up and executed, gangland style, just a few blocks from my parents' home.

The emotional toll on me was tremendous. My mourning was deepened by the sober recognition that if I had not changed my life years earlier, I would have surely found myself in the same crossfire that claimed my family members. I'm also saddened by the fact that so much of the discrimination and violence that framed my youth still plague our community—there's still so much left to do.

WHAT'S IN A NAME?

MA. FLOR SEPULVEDA (CHRISTINE ARANETA)

*Ma. Flor Sepulveda is the pen name of Christine Araneta, whose
political involvement was greatly influenced by the Diliman
Commune student strike and pre–martial law activism at the
University of Philippines, before immigrating to the United States
in 1971. Once in the States, Christine sought out other Filipino
American community activists in the Bay Area and became involved
in the International Hotel struggle and the Kalayaan collective,
focusing on publishing the* Kalayaan *newspaper. When the KDP was
formed, Christine was assigned for a number of years to the KDP's*
Ang Katipunan *newspaper, primarily covering Philippine events.
She would later be transferred to the KDP San Francisco chapter,
where among her major responsibilities was helping organize the
protests against the San Francisco leg of the Marcos state visit in 1982.
Having spent a good part of her life dedicated to the overthrow of the
dictatorship, Christine eventually resumed her interrupted college
education in 1984. She later trained as a physician assistant and
has been practicing as a midlevel clinician. Her early activist years
informed her outlook as a clinician and she continues to practice
in culturally underserved, uninsured, low-income communities.*

HOW IT BEGAN

T was January 26, 1970, the National Day of Condemnation protest called
by student activists, in front of the Philippine Congress in Manila. Masses
of students crowded the grounds, and more prepared to debark from

buses from as far south as Laguna Province, south of Manila. The stifling heat, exhaust fumes, and sheer numbers of bodies packed into the square threatened to overwhelm my little patch of the demonstration. In front and flanking me were taller, boisterous college students. Behind me were faculty members of my high school. And above, as I craned my neck upward, red banners blazed against the gray Manila sky.

The police and soldiers were there too. In full riot regalia, they stood at attention on the edges of the demonstration and on the roof of the capitol, ready to shoot should the command come down. And that's exactly why we were all there. My mother, sisters, brother, and I had ventured beyond the safe confines of the university community to protest the murder of three university students only a fortnight ago on Mendiola Bridge.[1] These were no longer faceless, nameless peasants embroiled in some provincial land struggle. Each of these latest victims was one of us, the "enlightened middle class," who were engaging in peaceful protest. When the shots rang out on Mendiola Bridge, the tenuous peace of the middle class began to shatter. The right to protest, a presumed right, could be crushed on the street, suspended, branded subversive. We were not radical or unreasonable. The presence of nuns, priests, distinguished academics, and journalists spoke volumes about the realignment of Philippine politics taking place.

And so there I stood—all of thirteen years old—shoulder to shoulder with thousands of others on the precipice of history, hoping to turn back the fascist tide. I understood fully that despite my aching back and sweat-soaked uniform, this was the only place to be.

BERKELEY, CALIFORNIA, 1971

A blast of cool bay breeze hit my face as I pulled up the handlebars to do wheelies. There was a perfect place and time to execute this maneuver—Saint Joseph's Convent driveway at 6:00 p.m., the first stroke of the Angelus. Only now, I didn't stop to pray. I pedaled faster, racing to the Co-op, a Berkeley new age–type supermarket, to buy a quart of milk, and then to Walt's Drugs to buy a *Tiger Beat* magazine. In this neighborhood of small stucco

---

1   The murder of unarmed student protesters by government troops at Mendiola Bridge in Manila sent shock waves throughout the country, and overnight the social base and militancy of the anti–United States, anti-Marcos movement broadened and increased.

bungalows, my family was building a new life in the United States. And like all uprooted and transplanted immigrant kids, I found the experience exhilarating, confusing, and painful at the same time.

"Free George Jackson," "Free Angela Davis," "Free the San Quentin Six," "All Power to the People." I whizzed by the radical graffiti every day. "Cool," I thought to myself, "there are political prisoners in the US too." But I didn't understand why the students at the University of California who were routinely smashing storefront windows and occupying People's Park never ended up at San Quentin. I wondered why only black people, Indians like those at Wounded Knee, and other nonwhites were the ones who got really hurt in all the turmoil. In a way I was pleased to be nonwhite, from a Third World country oppressed by US imperialism. Somehow this was a chic and radical identification at the time. Yet I could see that for most of my black and Chicano co-students huddled in the back of the classrooms at Berkeley High, being nonwhite didn't seem to bring much benefit at all.

Where I fit in this new class, race, and ethnic picture, I wasn't sure. No question, I was Filipino. I guess I was FOB (fresh off the boat), but because this implied unsophisticated provincialism, I resolved, in usual teenage fashion, to be as hip as possible and to distance myself from those who seemed unapologetically FOB.

Cutting classes was especially appealing. I was dislocated and alienated, and what better way to pass time than on Telegraph Avenue? On the Ave, incense and musk mingling with roasting smells of gyro lamb and curried lentils. There were tie-dyed T-shirts, bell-bottoms scraping the sidewalk, ranting radicals, Hare Krishna chanters, wasted hippies, and Berkeley High boppers—wannabes like me. To the cadence of beating bongos, the limping Bubble Lady blessed us all, her benedictions floating like luminescent orbs above our heads.

Occasionally, a shiver of guilt passed down my back; I should be in class. In my head I rationalized that revolution was more important than studying biology. Wasn't Cambodia being carpet bombed? What if this domino theory really worked? Would the Philippines be the next target of the B-52s? Mao Tse-tung's Little Red Book, the *Communist Manifesto*, *To Serve the Devil*, *Mother Jones*—these formed the substrata of my fourteen-year-old mind.

And so I threw in my lot with those who seemed clearest on who they were and what they stood for: Filipino exile students at UC Berkeley and their Filipino American radical counterparts. They seemed to understand the connections between the Philippine situation and the Southeast Asian war, between racism and imperialism. At fifteen, I joined the Kalayaan collective, which later evolved into the KDP.[2]

What's in a name? Soon, the burgeoning movement claimed all my waking hours. Evenings were spent in discussion groups about the war in Indochina, militarization in the Philippines, domestic repression of the Black Panthers, racism, and much more. New activist exiles from the Philippines joined our ranks, and progressive-minded community people gravitated toward the *Kalayaan* newspaper.

And ten thousand miles away, the Philippines was joining the ranks of newly militarized police states. Like Park Chung Hee of Korea, Augusto Pinochet of Chile, and Nguyen Van Thieu of Vietnam, Ferdinand Marcos was destined to take his place in the company of US-supported puppet dictators.

I vicariously participated in the events called the First Quarter Storm through letters from my sister, who had remained in the Philippines and had deepened her involvement in the revolutionary movement over the course of two years. Evidence of her participation came through in the new manner in which she communicated with us—in cryptic, small letters, coded messages, and assorted pseudonyms. "Amy Moraleda" was how she signed off to me. I understood that observing clandestine procedures was a matter of life or death under martial law, because the military routinely inspected the mail and midnight raids on private homes were common. In the United States, too, COINTELPRO surveillance of exile groups required tighter security procedures.[3]

In fact, the allure of changing one's name held so many romantic possibilities in my teenage mind. Even Patty Hearst had reinvented herself as Tania. And on a whim, white hippies became Rainbow, Sunshine, and Wavy Gravy. Besides, I hated my name. It was so Western, bourgeois, and landlord-sounding. Christine, so froufrou. Even worse, Araneta. Whenever I introduced myself to a fellow Filipino, the requisite rejoinder would be,

---

2   The San Francisco Bay Area–based Kalayaan collective was formed in 1970 and published a newspaper of the same name. Members included student activists who had recently come to the United States from the Philippines as well as Filipino American radical students involved in the Third World Strike movement on various campuses.

3   COINTELPRO was a comprehensive FBI operation during the late 1960s and early 1970s directed at "radical" groups (including left-wing "exile" groups). The operation entailed surveillance, infiltration, misinformation campaigns, and the like.

"Araneta—as in Coliseum, *aba*, you're rich!" Of course, we were not, except in a historical *ilustrado* (intelligentsia) sense. I descended from the branch of the family that had more stock in academic achievement than in the Manila Stock Exchange.

My search for a new name assumed urgency because the head of the Philippine news section of the *Kalayaan* could no longer tolerate living in "the belly of the beast" and resolved to return to the Philippines. So the editorial responsibilities fell in my fifteen-year-old lap. "Heroically," I shouldered the burden. Who was I to complain? I wasn't being asked to join the New People's Army and go to the mountains. Besides, I was flattered. Up until then, my tasks had amounted to clipping newspapers, sorting them out into categories, bundling the *Kalayaan*, or selling the paper on weekends.

Somehow, I thought that as soon as I decided on my pseudonym, the more difficult task of writing would magically fall into place. My nom de guerre had to meet certain criteria. It had to sound Filipino and *masa*,[4] but it also had to redress an old psychological grievance. Raised in a Catholic country, I was always self-conscious of the fact that I was not baptized with the requisite Maria, abbreviated "Ma." before my given name. Instead, my mother had named me Christine. Growing up I felt incomplete. Every other girl seemed to be named after Mary and a saint, Ma. Luisa, Ma. Concepcion, Ma. Teresa, even Ma. Dulce, though I doubted there was such a saint. During morning roll call, the nuns would presumptively pronounce, "Ma. Cristina?" "Present, Sister, but, ah Sister, it's Christine only." By the fourth grade, I was convinced that the only other Christine I ever heard about was the promiscuous Christine Keeler, the British Mata Hari of the Profumo affair.

So, Maria . . . what? By way of an underground newspaper, I learned of the murder of a student activist, Flordeliza something. The plagiarism would be too patent, so I decided to shorten it to Flor. Ma. Flor, a good start!

A RITE OF PASSAGE

Because I was the youngest of the revolutionary lot, I always felt I had to prove myself, to show that I could make up with zeal and bravery what I lacked in knowledge and experience.

In 1973, the United Farm Workers' second Grape Boycott was in full swing. The union's table outside the Berkeley CO-OP always attracted the largest crowds, and the Aztec eagle beckoned. Little-known then, and now, was that

---

4   A Tagalog term referring to "the masses," the workers and peasants.

Filipino farm laborers started the strike in the grape fields of Delano, California, which gave rise to the boycott. The *manongs* (older Filipino men) had begun the early efforts to unionize farmworkers and now, in tribute to them, a retirement village was being constructed in Delano.

Delano. Watching the massive farmworkers' demonstrations on TV idealized the strike and boycott in my mind. "Maybe Delano is like Yenan," I thought.[5] Volunteer crews from all over the country were being organized to construct the retirement housing. Mostly young people—college students from the East Coast, activists from the Los Angeles area—converged on the sleepy, dusty town. For me, it meant spending a month in a farmworkers' camp, living among the *manongs* and union organizers.

It was my first long trip by myself anywhere. Early on a Saturday morning, I packed a duffel bag and boarded a Greyhound Bus bound for the Central Valley. It didn't hit me that I was taking a giant step toward the unknown until I took my seat in the middle of the bus. There were biker types with tattooed arms, army guys, a few rowdy derelicts carrying on in the back of the bus, drinking and smoking. In the front of the bus were some Mexican women with their young children and a couple of older people.

Seven hours is a long time on a bus. A haze of cigarette smoke hung in the air, mixed at times with pungent whiffs of marijuana. Long-distance passengers eyeballed one another and wondered what each other's stories were. "They probably think I'm a runaway," I thought as I slouched deeper into my seat. Those who averted their glances upon eye contact, I was reasonably assured were merely curious. But one biker returned a cold, steady stare. Him I feared, and I felt a dry lump in the middle of my throat. What was he? The Zodiac Killer, a Klansman, a Hells Angels rapist? My palpitations were almost audible. I knew no one in the Central Valley, except the name of United Farm Workers' Filipino leader Philip Vera Cruz, and that was only because he was well known.

I passed the time staring out the window, reading road signs, and distracting myself by memorizing political formulations: "Imperialism," the highest stage of capitalism; "feudalism" . . . dah da ta tah . . . "bureaucrat capitalism" . . . it worked. Surveying the wide expanse of California countryside, the rolling hills, the spacious uninhabited lands, I pondered why the United States would venture beyond its borders to claim new territories, markets, and raw

---

5   Yenan, China, was where communist forces, led by Mao Tse-tung, were headquartered. From there, they built up their strength for eventual revolutionary victory nationwide.

materials. There was such abundance right here. Why were peasants in the Philippines being driven off their lands to make way for US-owned export agriculture? Did agribusiness giant Castle & Cooke know about the Central Valley? "Of course," I said to myself, "silly girl, they probably already own the damn place!"

My reveries were interrupted by the whiff of beer breath. Imagined or real, I felt the biker's cold stare on the back of my neck. Was he sitting behind me, next to me, across the aisle? I shuddered at the possibilities but refused to face them. I was freaking myself out. Twilight descended on the dusty highway. My mind was getting desperate. What if nobody picked me up at the bus depot? What kind of address was this anyway, "Schenley Camp, Delano"? I swallowed hard.

The bus turned and lurched to a stop. The sign read "Sepulveda: Pop. 850." The door swung open. I remained transfixed on the sign: "Welcome to Sepulveda [some vegetable] Capital of the World." Lettuce or avocados—I forget. I heard trudging steps down the center aisle. The now-familiar foot stomps sounded like the biker's boots. He walked past me and alighted from the bus. I sighed in deep relief.

For whatever reason—that moment of dread, that surreal summer experience in Delano, my rite of passage, whatever—the town of Sepulveda became burned into my memory. I chose it as my new surname—my revolutionary pseudonym was complete.

My first headline in the *Kalayaan* read "US Imperialism, the Root Cause of the Central Luzon Floods," by Ma. Flor Sepulveda. A persona was born. My maiden article was a dissection of the disastrous 1972 central Luzon floods. True, torrential rainstorms had caused the deluge, but nature was not alone in wreaking havoc on peoples' lives. Indiscriminate logging by lumber exporters and the slash-and-burn techniques of the *kaingineros* (mountainside slash-and-burn farmers) had magnified the damage. These activities caused erosion and runoff, and the denuded forests became made to order for mudslides and flooding. And who did the loggers sell the famous Philippine hardwoods to? Foreign markets. And why did the *kaingineros* have to eke out a living on the mountainside? Because semifeudal landlordism made subsistence agriculture impossible on the plains. (It seemed all so clear-cut back then.) This ecological disaster was tied up with imperialism because the once pristine forests were now bound up with and directed by international market forces.

The logic was elegant, tidy, flawless, so I thought. I cut my teeth on the central Luzon floods, but many similar articles indicting imperialism as the source of human misery would follow over the years.

Ma. Flor Sepulveda's true identity was a guarded secret, known only to the *Kalayaan* editorial board and a few staffers. The Marcos blacklist made everyone paranoid and edgy for good reason. Families of known and exiled activists in the United States pleaded with their kin to keep a low profile.

One day, years later, a *kasama* (comrade) working on the bilingual curriculum project for the Oakland schools rushed to the national KDP headquarters and reported that an FBI agent had paid her a visit at work. She was working then as a ward clerk at the French Hospital in San Francisco. She reported: "He asked me who was this Ma. Flor Sepulveda? I said I didn't know because, *talaga naman* [really] I don't know!" Her implied query was met with concerned but stony silence.

"Well, well," I thought, "it seems the persona Ma. Flor Sepulveda represents a threat to the US-Marcos dictatorship." Whatever the origins, intent, or true identity of Ma. Flor Sepulveda dissolved into irrelevance. I smiled to myself in silent triumph.

RUNNING AWAY TO LIFE

ESTELLA HABAL

Estella Habal was in the San Francisco–based Kalayaan collective before she became a founding member of the KDP in 1973. In the early years of the KDP, she was in the National Secretariat, assigned to develop the organizational structures of the Regional Executive Board of the San Francisco Bay Area as well as the San Francisco chapter. In 1975, she was assigned to the KDP team supporting the International Hotel tenants and the mass anti-eviction movement. By 1979–80, she had joined the Line of March (LOM), working in the Marxist-Leninist Education Project. Estella returned to college after a three-decade hiatus; she completed her bachelor's degree at San Francisco State University in 1991 and her doctorate in history at the University of California, Davis, in 2003. Her book, San Francisco's International Hotel: Mobilizing the Filipino American Community in the Anti-Eviction Movement, *was published in 2007 and is based on her direct experience in that well-known struggle. She taught courses in Asian American and women's studies at San Jose State University and other universities in the Bay Area for over twenty years. She is Asian American studies professor emerita at San Jose State University and continues to do research and writing. Estella has four grown children: Anthony and Don Alonzo, Kalayaan Habal, and Isaac Obenzinger. She has eight grandchildren and two step-grandchildren and is married to author and educator Hilton Obenzinger.*

As I raised my wine glass in a toast to Patty Hearst, I was enjoying, along with my friends and children, the best cut of roast beef in my life. We dubbed it the "Patty Hearst Roast Beef." The group responsible for the food giveaway that had brought us the meat was the Symbionese Liberation Army, or SLA. They had made front-page news for weeks by kidnapping Patty Hearst, granddaughter of the newspaper magnate. In a bizarre twist, she later reportedly joined the group and assisted them in holding up a bank or two in the early 1970s. Society was so polarized that these were the type of revolutionary events we lived with day to day.

The SLA demanded that Randolph Hearst pay for the free distribution of good-quality food to poor people. One of the groups identified in the group's "manifesto" to receive and distribute the food to the community was none other than the Kalayaan, the "underground" revolutionary Filipino collective and newspaper of which I was a member. The whole thing was so strange, but I must admit that the idea of forcing rich people to give good food to poor people had a tremendous appeal. And perhaps partially because of that, the Patty Hearst Roast Beef was so tender and succulent that only a fork was needed to cut it.

Of course, when I look back on it, eating that free meal did not change my life. Neither did the SLA's treatise and its isolated terrorist actions. It was, however, my membership in the Kalayaan collective (which later became the KDP) that led me into more than a decade of political activism in the Filipino community—and that did change my life. Of course, the SLA incident illustrated the excitement of those revolutionary times we lived in—when people thought they could make a fundamental difference in society and build a movement that displayed endless optimism, youthful exuberance, and confidence.

For some reason when I sat down to write this piece, I remembered that particular event, the Patty Hearst dinner, so vividly. And I recall thinking at the time how exciting my new life was compared with my miserable existence in Los Angeles, just one year before.

Moving to San Francisco was a turning point, the beginning of my commitment to revolutionary politics and a new life. I had literally run away from a five-year marriage that was the product of two teenage pregnancies and a lot of ignorance. I felt the whole world had opened up to me. Feeling both empowered and scared, with two baby boys to raise on my own, I knew that life would be hard. But my experience as young mother and college student had already somewhat prepared me for the adventures ahead.

Twelve days before my sixteenth birthday, I had given birth to my first son. I had pleaded with my father that I did not want to be married. He told me I had no choice. Marrying the father of my baby was the only way to save the family name from the disgrace of pregnancy out of wedlock. So, at a tender young age, I married a Filipino boy who was only two years older than me, in what was called in those days a shotgun wedding. A year later, I gave birth to another baby boy.

Years later, my father tried to convince himself that my husband's family had probably planned our match because our family was supposedly more prestigious in the community. In fact, there was not much difference between the two families. Although my family was a bit more assimilated, both were poor, working-class families struggling to survive in the Filipino barrio of the small town of Seaside, California. Both of our fathers were World War II veterans, both families were large, and both mothers and siblings had to work to make ends meet. My sisters and I, as teenagers, worked in the Salinas fields, just like my husband's brothers and sisters. Nonetheless, my marriage was not a match made in heaven. As a young teenage wife, and mother of two children, I felt trapped and deeply unhappy.

Graduating from high school was an early test of my perseverance and strength. My ninth, tenth, and eleventh grades were spent in a special high school program that allowed young girls like me to continue school at home by telephone. Many of the other girls were like me, shunned by their schools because they were pregnant or teenage mothers or physically disabled. By the time I reached twelfth grade, luckily, birth-control pills had become popular and I was able to keep from being forever pregnant. I was able to enroll in the normal high school with other kids my own age. I excelled in school, made the honor roll, joined the debating club, and spoke about social issues at the local Lions Club luncheons. I longed so much to be like the other kids, but I knew I was different; I was already a mother with two children. Not surprisingly, my senior classmates at Carson High School voted me "the most serious."

Part of my feeling trapped had to do with my aspirations to become something other than a farmworker or housewife. After high school, I worked for several years but felt a yearning to learn more. I wasn't even sure what. I decided to go to college. I remember that my husband couldn't understand why I would be interested in attending college, especially since I was already making a decent living as a clerical worker. I had a white-collar civil-service job at Harbor General Hospital in Carson, California. By my husband's standards, I had already achieved my goals. He viewed graduating from high school as more than enough and going to college an excessive luxury. Besides, all hands were needed to work. Without his trust and support, I knew he could never understand me, and our estrangement deepened.

Fortunately, I had the support of my own family, which saw college as a big step for everyone. I was the first of my generation to attend college. Both my parents came from poor peasant backgrounds in the Philippines, and none of my siblings had the level of academic achievement or desire to go for higher education at the time. My mother was willing to babysit my boys while I began to attend classes.

I was intellectually curious and enjoyed the bustle of activity at Long Beach State College (now California State University, Long Beach). At the time, the campus seemed to teem with revolutionary fervor and youthful activities. Students for a Democratic Society (SDS) had a chapter, but Filipino students like me (there were only a handful of us back then) were more attracted to the other minority student organizations rather than groups monopolized by white males. There were also very few black students on campus. I remember seeing Angela Davis on campus once; she was already famous with her wide, wide Afro. Although I didn't believe for a minute the newspaper claims that she had tried to smuggle a weapon (inside her hairdo) into San Quentin in the ill-fated attempt to spring George Jackson and others of the San Quentin Six out of prison, her appearance still frightened me.

My first introduction to revolutionary Marxist politics was by Chicano students in an organization called MEChA (Movimiento Estudiantil Chicano de Aztlán). The Mexican revolutionary style did not scare me much. I donned the beret and *bandolera* with ease. Perhaps because of the similar Spanish colonial history, Catholic background, working-class status, and immigrant culture, I felt an affinity for Mexican students (the term *Chicano* came later). They taught me about popular Mexican historical figures, such as Emiliano Zapata. I knew so much about the father of the Mexican Revolution before I even learned about Filipino contemporaries who fought against both Spain and the United States.

After my exposure to revolutionary politics, campus life shrank and felt like small potatoes. Although I don't remember the exact moment, somewhere inside me I decided to drop out of school and embark on a new life. Opportunity knocked when I got the chance to run away. Fleeing an oppressive marital situation, I hooked up with another man, packed up my kids, and left for San Francisco. When I arrived I went immediately to the International Hotel, which was at the time a mecca for Filipino activist youth throughout the West Coast. Only a year before I had visited the hotel with a group sponsored by Search to Involve Pilipino Americans (SIPA), from Los Angeles, which I had helped start. We had spent the weekend painting and cleaning the hotel. Those were defiant times. The Filipino old-timers had already organized themselves in the face of eviction notices and refused to move. And young radicalized students from all over descended on the hotel every weekend and volunteered to renovate the building to show their support.

It seems my fate was sealed the day I returned to the International Hotel. I met Rodel Rodis (who would be a founding member of the KDP and is today a prominent community leader). He was a revolutionary from the Philippines who was both a novelty and a mystery to me, since I had known only assimilated first- and second-generation Filipino Americans most of my life. He was the first young immigrant I met who had only recently arrived from the Philippines. I remember how dashing he looked in his black leather hat and jacket, like the TV hero Zorro. And he seemed to always have a group of young girls following him around like puppies. He was an exiled student activist who came to the United States in the face of the increasing repression of the Marcos regime (this was a year or so before the declaration of martial law). He was something of a celebrity, even within American progressive and left-wing circles, because he embodied the first real link to the revolutionary movement in the Philippines.

Rodel helped me get my first job in San Francisco. I joined San Francisco Newsreel, an anti-imperialist film collective. This was my first real entry into organized left-wing politics. Through the medium of revolutionary documentaries and films, I became aware of many other people's movements, both in the United States and throughout the world.

I stayed with the Newsreel collective for about two years, during which time my main responsibility was film distribution. It was the height of the anti–Vietnam War movement. We'd get rental orders from all over the country, mostly from radical student groups. The most popular films were about Vietnam and Cuba, the Black Panthers, Young Lords, and Detroit Revolutionary Union Movement (DRUM). I processed the orders, shipped out the films, and did routine maintenance to ensure that the films were in good working condition. Another part of the collective concentrated on actual film and documentary production. While I was with Newsreel, the film *Revolution until Victory* (about the Palestine liberation movement) was in the making. Unfortunately, I never got my turn to be trained in film production. Looking back, this was in part because I was young and had no filmmaking experience; but I'm sure it was also because I was a mother and woman of color.

The Newsreel collective participated directly in the antiwar movement, and although it considered itself an educational arm of the movement and not a political organization, it was widely known and respected in movement circles. I remember representing the collective in the Spring Mobe (Mobilization) of 1971 or 1972. It was the first time I helped organize anything that big—tens of thousands of people showed up on the day of the march. The end-point rally was at the old Kezar Stadium (renamed Martin Luther King

Stadium) in Golden Gate Park. We had secured a large auditorium up the hill at the University of California and showed films all afternoon to hundreds of folks who had marched that day.

Collectives back then were a total experience. For example, members of Newsreel tended to organize themselves into household collectives as well. The household collective shared everything (in theory anyway)—members pooled money, shared cooking and chores, and set weekly house meetings for criticism–self-criticism over household tensions. I and another woman were mothers, so all in the collective took turns doing childcare. I gave birth to my daughter while living in the Newsreel collective, which gave the household four young children, in total, to deal with—quite a task!

Throughout this experience, I felt a need to center my political growth and development closer to Filipinos and the Filipino community. Whatever reservations I had were resolved when I met Cynthia Maglaya (an immigrant from the Philippines who would become a founding National Council member of the KDP), and we became close friends. I first met Cynthia during a planning meeting for an anti–Vietnam War demonstration. I played the Vietnamese woman in a skit displaying the atrocities of the American military. After the meeting, Cynthia asked me to come to a meeting of the *Kalayaan* newspaper collective. Although she explained the politics of the organization, I didn't fully understand what she said. All I needed to know was that it was a Filipino revolutionary organization, and I was ready to join.

Cynthia's appeal was her warm and winning personality, her knowledge of Philippine politics, and her indomitable faith in the human race. Back in the Philippines, she had been in the National Council of Kabataang Makabayan (KM, or Nationalist Youth), and like a number of other student activists she gave in to family pressure and went into exile (at least temporarily) in the face of mounting government violence and repression.

Her honest, straightforward style and political astuteness convinced many Filipino Americans to join the movement, especially the women. She used to address every one of her comrades *mahal* (meaning "love" or "sweetie"), which endeared her to many of us. And soon afterward we were all calling each other *mahal*. Cynthia was always curious and willing to learn about American ways. She'd often ask me about the mannerisms or habits of certain Filipino Americans or other Americans we knew in common. My explanations about what she viewed as our weird and strange ways would sometimes help her and often amuse her. I can still see her at times, throwing her head back, placing her hands over her mouth, and repeating over and over *gaga* (fool), laughing hysterically at the things I told her. But it was done in such a good-natured way, I found myself laughing with her. I began to appreciate our cultural differences and how strange Americans can appear to other people. For her part, she also tried to fit. One particular habit she developed was excessive swearing, both in Tagalog and English. Almost every one of her sentences included some kind of profanity. This had a certain shock value because of her demure appearance.

To me, Cynthia's greatest influence and contribution within the KDP was her ability to bridge the political and cultural differences between recent immigrants and Filipino Americans. She laid the cornerstone that allowed us to build a truly integrated organization of Filipino immigrants and Filipino Americans. Most of the Filipino Americans came from relatively poor, working-class backgrounds, while the majority of the exiled student activists from the Philippines were from more privileged backgrounds. The class chemistry between the two groups was often not good, and at times the chasm seemed unbridgeable. Yet the confidence of the KDP that we could work with this contradiction and overcome many of the differences in pursuit of our common goal was due, in no small part, to the role Cynthia played in the early, formative years of the organization.

A LITTLE RED BOOK

DAVID DELLA

*David Della joined the Seattle KDP chapter at its founding in
September 1974, immediately after his third season working in the
Alaska salmon canneries at Ward's Cove Packing Company. As a
student at the University of Washington, David participated in the
campus- and community-organizing work of Filipinos for Action
and Reform. As the KDP work in Local 37 of the International
Longshoremen's and Warehousemen's Union (ILWU; the Alaska
Cannery Workers Union) advanced, David was assigned to the team
for union elections in 1978 and 1980 and became part of the Seattle
KDP leadership. After the 1981 murders of Silme Domingo and Gene
Viernes, David took over Silme's role and led the Local 37 reform work.
David then went into public service, working under a Seattle mayor
and two Washington State governors. Eventually, David was elected
and served one term as a Seattle city councilmember. After his city
council service, David went into the private sector, first consulting in
the areas of clean energy and sustainability and then working as
municipal contracts manager for an environmental services company.*

R EAD this while you're gone," my friend Angel Doniego said as he handed
me the little red book titled *Philippine Society and Revolution* by someone named Amado Guerrero.[1] This was right before my departure to

---

1   Amado Guerrero is the nom de guerre of Jose Maria Sison, founder of the new
    Communist Party of the Philippines (CPP).

Alaska in the summer of 1974. I had no idea what the book was about; and besides, I would probably be working in the cannery twenty hours a day, with two hours' sleep on workdays and partying on the days off.

"Oh, all right," I said as I hastily put the book in my bag before I left for the union hall, where I'd meet my crew and board the bus for the airport. Funny thing, though, I took the book out of my bag during the flight to Ketchikan and started trying to read it half seriously. Its content flew over my head the minute I looked at a page. What in the world was this? Such big words and complicated ideas. I wondered why Angel would give me this book, when I could very well just thumb through the many picture magazines on the plane, or simply look out the window and not have to think about a thing.

I remembered that Angel had returned from the Philippines recently, where he'd seen what had been happening since the imposition of martial law. And when he got back to Seattle, he'd met some white guy with round granny glasses. This guy was leafleting Filipino and Asian community events with information about the Philippines and news about a new San Francisco Bay Area organization called by three funny initials, KDP, or the Union of Democratic Filipinos.

Was this a labor union? What type of workers did this Union of Democratic Filipinos represent anyhow? And why was this white guy with an old Volvo stirring up things about the Philippines—even more so than Sabino, our local Filipino radical? I got suspicious. At any rate, Angel was involved and trying to get Silme and me involved in this group. Whatever Angel was interested in stirred an interest in me as well, so I took the book to see what the hell he was so passionate about these days.

For some reason, I took the book out again and continued to read it whenever I had a chance at the cannery, even though I initially grasped very little of its meaning. I wrote to Angel and Silme to ask if they were part of the new organization and what this had to do with our student and community organizing. For some time I got no response, until Angel finally broke down and wrote me a letter. He informed me that our community work now had to be linked to a revolutionary change in this country, the United States, and that this had been confirmed for him when he went back to the Philippines and saw what was going on there. He encouraged me to persevere and continue reading the book and said he would talk to me about it more when I returned to Seattle after the fishing season.

As for Silme, Angel admitted he still had to do some more convincing to get him involved. Silme was very much tied up with the cannery workers' antidiscrimination lawsuits and the Alaska Cannery Workers Association (ACWA).[2] He wasn't giving Angel any commitment yet. Angel felt that recruiting Silme was key to bringing a lot of new people into the organization, given Silme's stature in the Asian community. Angel wrote that the white guy, whose name was Dale Borgeson, was going to invite him and Silme over to his place for dinner. It all seemed very strange to me.

Upon my return from Alaska, Silme contacted me for a debriefing following the canning season and to say that he was now part of the KDP's new Seattle chapter. He invited me to a party that Dale was having at his place, complete with food and booze, to talk about the new organization. At this so-called party, I saw Angel, Shari, Rick, Glen, Mario, and many others with whom I had been associated in the Asian movement. They all had copies of that same little red book and talked of building a KDP chapter in Seattle. Supposedly, one of the jobs of this new organization would be to pass out information about what was going on in the Philippines with martial law, as well as work in the Filipino community on issues of discrimination and fight for revolutionary change in the States.

That night everyone agreed to hold a demonstration in front of the Seattle Philippine consulate on September 22, the day martial law was imposed in the Philippines. The party ended with everyone singing a Philippine nationalist song, "Ang bayan ko" (My country). I was amazed to see even the non-Filipinos in the crowd, like Shari and Rick (Chinese American and Japanese American, respectively), singing loudly. Even Silme was singing as though he

---

2   ACWA formed in 1973, before the formation of the Seattle KDP chapter. In an attempt to redress the blatant and long-standing discrimination against Filipino workers in the Alaska fishing industry, ACWA filed three class-action suits under Title VII of the 1964 Civil Rights Act. Over the years, two of the suits were settled in favor of the Filipino cannery workers. The third, against Ward's Cove Packing Company, went to the US Supreme Court, which on June 5, 1989, ruled 5-4 that to prove discrimination, the salmon cannery workers had to do more than present data showing numerical imbalance ("disparate impact") among the races in different jobs. Congress effectively reversed the decision with a bill that restored an easier-to-prove discrimination standard. But to ensure passage, the Senate agreed to Alaska Republican senator Frank Murkowski's provision preventing the Ward's Cove plaintiffs from pursuing their remaining claims under the looser standard. ACWA also collaborated closely with similar antidiscrimination suits involving farm laborers and black construction workers.

knew the song. "Is it possible they even understood what they were singing?" I thought. I know I didn't; it was all in Tagalog. So I just pretended to sing, in order to fit in. I said to myself, "Shit, a lot has changed over the summer I've been away!"

NOT THE USUAL PATH

BO APOSTOL (AS TOLD TO HIS DAUGHTER
REBECCA APOSTOL)

*Misael "Bo" Apostol joined the KDP in 1979 as a student 4-H trainee
from Bataan, Philippines. Soon after joining, Bo became an activist in
the KDP's San Francisco and Sacramento chapters, organizing fellow
students and trainees to protest unjust conditions and the absence of
educational access that the 4-H program had promised. He performed
with the KDP's cultural arm, Sining Bayan (People's Art), which
toured the West Coast and Hawaii with productions such as* Ti
mangyuna *(Those who led the way),* War Brides, *and* Isuda ti imuna
*(Those who came first). Bo is married to fellow activist Sorcy, and
together they have two talented daughters, Rebecca, a present-day
activist herself, who wrote down his story, and Rinabeth, a talented
actress and singer.*

CAME to the United States when I was seventeen years old. I did not come
as a tourist or on a student visa, as most Filipinos who are from the middle
class do. I came from a poor farming family in the town of Orani, Bataan
Province. We were not rich, not even middle class—we got by.

I learned from a young age the truth about farming: work is hard and it
never ends. I worked side by side with my father and siblings to plant rice
twice a year. In between rice-planting seasons, we grew fruits and vegetables. I would wake up before dawn to go with my mom and take a jeepney
(jitney bus) to town so she could sell produce at the market. I would then
work the fields before going to school. After school, I would return to the
fields to finish up the day's work. Although life was hard, I enjoyed working

with my father. From my father I learned the dignity of even the most menial work.

Being the sixth of eleven children, I knew that the money to send me to college would run out by the time it was my turn. So when the 4-H Club coordinator in Orani invited me to apply for the Philippine Training Agricultural Program (PTAP), I jumped at the chance.

The 4-H organization in the Philippines was modeled after the one in the United States. It was a social club and training program for young farmers. PTAP was a 4-H-backed program that sponsored young Filipino farmers for agricultural training in the United States. Although PTAP was highly competitive, requiring interviews and tests on the municipal, provincial, regional, and national levels, I was admitted. It was the proudest time of my life. I was proud to represent my town, my family. I had great expectations, excited that I was going to learn all the modern techniques and technologies in farming in the United States.

In the two-week orientation for the trainees in Manila, I was surprised to learn that some of the people selected for the program were not really farmers at all. A number were professionals trying to find a way to go to the United States: a government employee who resigned from his job two days before the trainees were to leave; a teacher, an older man, who was a *barangay* (village) captain. I was disappointed to find out that even the 4-H program was not immune to Philippine-style corruption, that things could be "arranged" if you knew the right people.

There were nineteen in my group. We landed in San Francisco, where we were put on a bus and driven around the city. I remember seeing the Golden Gate Bridge and being told it was where millions of people passed through, dreaming of the golden opportunities that awaited them in this land.

We were then taken to a Motel 8 room in Santa Rosa. After a week, the American farmers came. They divided the trainees, each taking a group. There was no explanation of what was going to happen and who was going where. Later, I would liken it to a slave auction. The American farmers came and took their slaves away.

I was in the group that was sent to Oregon. I and another trainee flew to Portland, where a Mr. Tamura met us at the airport. He was a Japanese farmer who owned Tamura Farms outside of Portland, in a rural area called Troutdale. The farm was in the middle of nowhere—no buses, the nearest neighbor miles away. When we arrived at the farm, Mr. Tamura took us to a small, rundown house that was filthy. The other trainee, Pablo, and I spent two days cleaning the place to make it livable.

A number of trainees had preceded my group and were about to go back to the Philippines. They told Pablo and me the reality. There was no training, no school (unless you could find someone to drive you to town to enroll in the community college), only backbreaking work in the fields. I then realized with a sick heart that the "training program" was a farce.

The next day, we were taken to the fields, where we started to pick vegetables. The first vegetable I picked was rhubarb, which I had never seen before. I worked with an old farmhand who drank while picking.

Work was seven days a week, sunrise to sundown. In the summer, we worked almost sixteen hours a day. In the winter, with temperature below thirty degrees and frost all over the ground, we continued to pick vegetables. I would pick the cauliflower, scraping frost off the leaves, folding the leaves together, wrapping them with a rubber band, and covering the head to keep it white. We were not paid for our work. Instead, we were given an "allowance" of one hundred dollars a month, which was supposed to be for our food.

After my first week on the farm, I wrote the 4-H program in the Philippines. I warned them not to send any more people to the United States, as the program was no good. I was told to be patient and things would get better. I continued to complain. At the first 4-H meeting in the States that I attended, I spoke up and protested our conditions. I said, "We are supposed to be exchange students, agricultural scholars, yet we have never even seen a classroom." My complaints went unanswered.

Two incidents led to my decision to escape. One day, very early in the morning, when the night frost was still on the ground, Mr. Tamura insisted that we go out and work. I protested. Mr. Tamura became angry and yelled, "You came here to work!" I responded, "We are not slaves, we are exchange students." When Mr. Tamura threatened me, I pulled a knife. I knew at that moment that if I was not careful, I might wind up in jail because of my frustration at the situation.

Another incident made me realize that I could not count on the program's being reformed. One morning, two officials from the Philippine PTAP came to visit us on the farm, supposedly to check in on the trainees. I knew from the previous group of trainees that these officials came only to enjoy themselves. The farmers paid for these officials' plane tickets, meals, and hotels. I complained to these officials, but I knew it was futile.

Having made my decision to escape, I put my plans into action. First, I called my brother who lived in California. My brother had immigrated to the United States in the 1960s. Although I was ashamed to admit it, I told my brother about my unbearable situation. My brother promised to send me a plane ticket to come to California. Then I called my friends whom I had met at church in town and told them my plans. The next day, they picked me up from the farm, supposedly for church services; but they brought me to the airport where a plane ticket awaited me at the airline counter. I was able to make my escape because, unlike the other trainees, I refused to hand over my passport to the 4-H officials in the States. With my passport to identify me, I was able to board the plane.

A few days later, the 4-H coordinator from Oregon came to my brother's house. He offered me another farm and said that if I refused, I would become deportable for violating my visa. I demanded to be sent back to the Philippines and compensated for the work I'd done at Tamura's farm. The coordinator refused. A few days later, immigration agents came looking for me. So I became undocumented.

A short while later, I was contacted by activists from the KDP. They told me they had become aware of the 4-H trainees' plight and were trying to help them by reforming the 4-H program. There was already a group of 4-H trainees in Stockton, California, that the KDP was organizing. The KDP activists invited me to attend a meeting of the 4-H trainees in Oakland.

Despite my precarious legal status, I decided to attend. During the meeting, I realized that my experience was not unique. The other trainees shared the same stories of long hours of unpaid work and no training.

The KDP worked with the 4-H coordinator in Modesto, California, to find another farm for me. I moved to a farm where I worked with Mexican laborers. One day, a low-flying plane went by, and I was surprised to see the group of Mexican laborers running, shouting, "La migra!" I realized then that they had no papers. At that moment I thought, "When would my time be to run and hide?"

I lasted on that farm for only two months. The host farmer did not like my attending meetings and speaking up about the injustices of the 4-H program. Soon I started becoming more active in the KDP's organizing efforts to reform the program. I attended meetings in Oakland and Stockton. I even traveled with KDP activists to North Carolina to help organize East Coast trainees and encourage them to join the West Coast trainees in a nationwide campaign to expose and reform the 4-H exchange program. I became the spokesperson for the campaign, speaking out on the exploitation of the trainees, the Philippine 4-H officials' corruption, and their complicity with the farmers.

It was at this time that I became educated about the political situation in the Philippines. I knew martial law had been declared but did not understand what it meant. I remembered one friend in my hometown who talked about the violence and the torture of some friends during martial law. But it wasn't until the car rides with KDP activists to the organizing meetings that I understood the US-Philippine relationship, the corruption of the Marcos regime, and the need for systemic reform of Philippine society.

So it was that I finally realized my dream of hands-on training, not in the field of farming, but in the field of organizing and fighting for justice.

THE ACCIDENT

DALE BORGESON

*Dale Borgeson was a founding member of the KDP and the pre–
martial law organization the National Committee for the Restoration
of Civil Liberties in the Philippines (NCRCLP). Although of Swedish
descent, Dale's involvement in the Philippine issue followed his
experience as a conscientious objector and organizer during the
Vietnam War. He was editor of the* Lewis-McChord Free Press, *an
antiwar newspaper with a monthly circulation of forty thousand on
US international bases. From 1970 to 1972, Dale served as a GI
organizer in Asia (Japan, Okinawa, and the Philippines). In 1973, he
was sent to Seattle by the KDP National Executive Board to establish
a KDP chapter, which he successfully did in 1974, with Silme Domingo
and Angel Doniego. The Seattle chapter became the largest, most
ethnically diverse KDP chapter and was very influential in Seattle
Filipino community politics. Dale was a member of the KDP National
Executive Board from 1978 to 1982 until he joined the Line of March
(LOM) to help head up the Peace and Solidarity Alliance. Dale
returned to school after LOM disbanded, earned an MBA, and
became an emergency medicine administrator at University of
California, San Francisco, before moving to the University of Arizona
Medical Center, where he still works. Dale is married to leading KDP
activist Geline Avila and together they have two grown activist
children, Isabella and Eugene.*

BY historical accident, I was an initiator although not the main organizer of the Seattle KDP chapter in 1973. My role gave rise to much
ribbing about the "multiracial" character of the chapter because it

included a Swedish guy from Minnesota. I had been an activist in the anti–Vietnam War movement, and I spent a year and a half in the Philippines in 1971–72 working with Filipino activists and organizing GIs against the war. Before going to the Philippines, I had been drafted in the US Army upon graduating from the University of Minnesota in 1969. I spent only eight months in the army before being discharged as a conscientious objector at Fort Lewis, Washington, in October 1970, just as I received orders to report to Vietnam. I was lucky—my friends' conscientious objector applications were denied, and several of them then refused orders to go to Vietnam. They were court-martialed and sent to Leavenworth Prison.

I stayed in Seattle to help with the defense of these friends, who became the Fort Lewis Six. I then volunteered to go to Asia to do antiwar work with American GIs as part of the Pacific Counseling Service and the National Lawyers Guild Military Law Project. We set up GI coffeehouses outside US bases in Japan, Okinawa, and the Philippines, where we published and distributed antiwar newspapers. We also provided GIs with American civilian lawyers and conscientious-objector counseling. In November 1971, we helped organize and mobilize for Jane Fonda and Donald Sutherland's Free the Army (FTA) tour of US bases in Asia (*FTA* meant something else to the troops—"F—k the Army"). The show was the antiwar movement's answer to the prowar, promilitary Bob Hope show. We worked with Elaine Elinson, the advance publicist for the show, and Francine Parker, the director. The FTA show received an enthusiastic welcome from thousands of GIs outside US bases in the Philippines and elsewhere in Asia as antiwar sentiment built among the largely draftee military.

Repression by the US and Philippine military against our GI project increased, especially after we got US soldiers to testify before Senator Benigno Aquino Jr.'s Philippine Senate Foreign Relations Committee in May 1972 that the bases in the Philippines were violating the US-Philippine Military Bases Agreement because of their use in direct aggression against Vietnam. The Philippine Constabulary raided our GI coffeehouses, and I was arrested while playing basketball in Angeles outside Clark Air Base for not having my passport on me. The police took me to Camp Olivas in San Fernando, where the officers accused me of being a terrorist, responsible for a recent bank robbery in Los Angeles. Fortunately, our project lawyers intervened, and I was released and driven back to the GI coffeehouse by the officers.

One of the activists who worked with our project was Melinda Paras, a Filipino American from Madison, Wisconsin, who was attending the University of the Philippines and playing on its women's basketball team. Melinda served as liaison to the Philippine revolutionary movement, educating US soldiers about the Filipino people's struggle. In May 1972, historian Renato Constantino interviewed Melinda and me, and he wrote a favorable column in the *Manila Chronicle* about the GI antiwar movement.

When Marcos declared martial law in September 1972, the Philippine Constabulary raided our offices again, this time smashing our printing machines and arresting and deporting our staff, including the civilian American lawyers. I had left the country to attend a peace conference in Japan, so I missed the action. Marcos and his US backers were in no mood to tolerate dissent, whether from Filipinos or Americans. We were fortunate to have received favorable press coverage, including from US newspapers such as the *New York Times*. This publicity protected us from harsher reprisals by the regime and its US supporters. I often think of how fortunate we were compared with American activists in Chile at the time of the Pinochet coup just a year later. The military there summarily killed many American activists alongside their Chilean comrades in the US-backed coup.

Melinda was at her grandfather's home in Manila, where the police found and arrested her. Her grandfather was a retired chief justice of the Philippine Supreme Court and her uncle was commissioner of immigration. Despite these connections, martial law officials swiftly deported her to the United States along with all the American project activists and lawyers. Upon hearing of the martial law declaration in Japan, I returned to San Francisco. There, in October 1972, we established the National Committee for the Restoration of Civil Liberties in the Philippines (NCRCLP) to challenge the legitimacy of the regime and oppose US support.

I stayed in San Francisco for several months, working with the Pacific Counseling Service to support the remaining GI counseling projects abroad. In February 1973, I took the train to Seattle to rejoin friends from my Fort Lewis antiwar movement days. Melinda Paras and other activists—including Bruce Occena, Cynthia Maglaya, and Rodel Rodis—gave me a grand going-away party at Mabuhay Gardens Restaurant, adjacent to the International Hotel in San Francisco's Manilatown. One of my going-away gifts was Carlos Bulosan's *America Is in the Heart*, which I read on the train to Seattle. This was my first exposure to the history of the First Wave Filipino immigrants who arrived in Seattle in the 1920s and 1930s and worked in West Coast agricultural fields and Alaska canneries, where they organized a labor union to fight for their rights.

My friends also gave me a list of contacts in the Seattle Filipino community so that I could work to organize an NCRCLP chapter there to spread the anti–martial law message. I didn't know then that I was establishing the trajectory of the rest of my life.

IN THE NAME OF LOVE

MARIBEL SALOMON

*Maribel Salomon had been living in the Midwest for more than a
decade when a high school classmate invited her to attend the Filipino
People's Far West Convention in Los Angeles in 1978. Maribel had been
working as a nurse but was restless for adventure, so she accepted.
She ended up staying in Los Angeles, joining the campaign for fair
licensure of foreign nurse graduates being led by the KDP, and then
signing up with the Coalition Against the Marcos Dictatorship
(CAMD) and, later, with the KDP itself. She returned to Indianapolis
after Marcos was overthrown. There, she helped organize celebrations
of the "People Power" uprising and Philippine National Day. Maribel
later settled in Guam. She is a highly trained nurse with both a
bachelor and master of science as well as a doctorate in nursing from
Indiana University; she spent twenty-two years working as a registered
nurse, eight years as a nurse educator, and seven years as director of
nursing at the University of Guam. She is currently a nurse
practitioner at a family and urgent-care clinic.*

B ORN of health professionals who immigrated from the Ilocos region of
the Philippines in the late 1960s, I lived in the Midwest for eleven years
in what seemed an aimless life of moving from one nursing job to
another. Then, the blizzard of January 1978 finally pushed me to leave for
warmer places. Single, naive about politics, and totally skeptical about the
Philippine struggle, I was adventurous enough and homesick for other Filipinos. I responded to a high school classmate's call to come west and experience the Filipino People's Far West Convention. I don't remember knowing
that my friend belonged to the KDP. I loaded my ten-speed bike and everything

worth hauling into my car and took the scenic route to California. I must have known that my adopted free and rugged individualist days were going to end—so I took the long and slow route.

Three weeks later, I reached Los Angeles. It was September, just before the twenty-second. My welcome to LA was an initiation to an exciting and challenging experience. I was picked up after dark from an uncle's house in San Gabriel and taken to KDP headquarters to pick up some things and people. Then, packed in the car, we drove to Temple Street, where we wheat-pasted posters for a demonstration in front of the Philippine consulate, and the rest is history. I learned after the event that postering was something of an extralegal activity, but it had to be done. More than that, I learned that there is more to a demonstration than just looking out for Marcos spies and carrying the laboriously hand-painted placards that screamed "Down with Marcos!" It felt radical to simply march in a circle and chant slogans calling for the dictator's downfall. I was bold because I wanted to be one of the radicals. It was my romance with controversy. It felt good to be needed by the movement.

But it took more than boldness and romantic notions to understand what everything we did meant. It could just as easily have been for love, the power of collective love for a homeland and its people—a love fueled by each *kasama*'s (comrade's) capacity to give of the self. The KDP became my family. The group wanted to help me struggle to unleash my potential to think, organize, and lead. I was in the organization for about six years. I learned. I was in awe of the leadership. They were friendly, down to earth, committed, intelligent, and young. Despite the fact that many *kasamas*, myself included, faltered in our commitment, I learned passion for politics and I learned personal and collective struggle for accountability, responsibility, and excellence, whether it was my turn to cook at HQ or prepare for a press conference.

It is still difficult for me to "mass line" dialectical-historical materialism (i.e., explain it to the "masses"), but I will never forget how easily Therese did it in the Marxist-Leninist Education Project.[1] I remember being criticized for my "anti-masses" approach, and I'm a better person because of it. I wish I had never left the KDP—I guess I never really did. It's like a love affair. Even when you think you've left it, it hasn't left you. When I feel like telling

---

1   The Marxist-Leninist Education Project was a standard course on historical materialism, political economy, and Marxist philosophy taught by activists of the Line of March (LOM), a "pre-party" organization, for its members and those of fraternal organizations like the KDP.

someone her attitude is for the birds, I always think of comrade Maria, who used to say, "It might be good to . . ." When faculty meetings become emotionally charged, I remember to suggest that we should be more "objective" and "demystify" things.

When I think of our struggles with the Filipino American Community of Los Angeles (FACLA),[2] I remember the night one of the opposition's men got stabbed outside the community center, and I happened to be there to patch up his wound. I remember telling one community leader that she did not have any principles. Then a *kasama* told me that I had stopped a fight between the *kasama* and a certain Boy Daza. I also think of leading KDP activist Aimee Laurel and the team of the National Alliance for Fair Licensure for Foreign Nurse Graduates (NAFL-FNG) negotiating successfully with the Immigration and Naturalization Service commissioner not to deport nurses who failed their licensure test. And I remember confrontations with the Queen of Angels Hospital administration for its English-only policy.

Maybe our boldness was always there, but the KDP certainly had the discipline.

So how can one not miss the KDP? Years of discussion groups, committee meetings, FACLA election campaigns, Philippine National Day events, selling *Ang Katipunan*, leafleting, networking, phone follow-ups, banner making, postering, fund-raising, Christmas caroling, singing, having children, falling in love, falling out of love, writing press releases and letters to the editor, speaking for the Far West Convention on TV, Sal making fun of me twiddling my thumb on the TV news, the time we could not light the Marcos effigy and so we had to stomp on it. Who can forget Los Angeles chapter leader Greg Santillan and his Juan dela Cruz graphics? Vince's jokes. Florante's dad. Living at HQ. Watching some of the activists' kids—Veronica, Gabriella, Andrei, and Andy—grow up. Naming my son Diego after the Philippine hero Diego Silang, who led an early rebellion against Spanish colonists.

The KDP days will definitely live on for me. The romance is not over as long as the love continues to burn for those who pulled me into the struggle, those who taught me how to love.

---

2   FACLA was a community center run by competing conservative factions; its elections usually featured vote buying and lawsuits. Activists tried to initiate reform but later decided it was too difficult.

DIFFERENT ROADS HOME

VELMA VELORIA

Velma Veloria joined the San Francisco KDP chapter in 1977. Velma helped organize and mobilize many demonstrations against the Marcos dictatorship, cultural events reflecting Philippine colonial history, and educational forums against racism and for social justice. She also helped organize Filipino nurses in the city. In 1984, she was transferred to Seattle, along with other members of the KDP, to work in the Committee for Justice for Domingo and Viernes (CJDV) and was assigned to the team at Local 37 of the International Longshoremen's and Warehousemen's Union (ILWU; the Alaska Cannery Workers Union). In 1992, she was elected to the Washington State House of Representatives, becoming the first Filipina American and the first Asian American woman to hold a seat. While in the legislature, Velma sponsored House Bill 1175, which made Washington the first state in the nation to criminalize human trafficking. Since HB 1175's enactment, forty-eight states have passed similar legislation. Velma continues her work on domestic and international human trafficking. She works as a government relations representative for several nonprofit organizations in Washington State.

I T was a gift that changed my life.

I was eleven when my family left the Philippines in 1961. I would not return for a visit until 1976. In the intervening years, my mother died, and I was busy helping my father raise my three siblings.

When I graduated from San Francisco State University, I gave myself a graduation present: a trip back to Bani, Pangasinan, my hometown. I visited family, friends, everyone who was still there. One visit in particular had a lasting impact on my life. I met up with my cousin Carlos. Carlos was tall, lanky, good-looking, and smart. He brought me to his friend's house, and I remember we ate *kilawin* (raw fish or meat steeped in vinegar, like ceviche). During my time there, we would have all sorts of discussions, about many things I never thought about. Kuya Carlos (*Kuya* is a term of respect for an older brother or relative) talked about something called US imperialism. Later on, I found out that Kuya Carlos was a member of the New People's Army.

As soon as I got back to San Francisco, I wanted to find out more about the Philippines and its connection with the United States and this thing called US imperialism. The KDP had a chapter in San Francisco. One of its members was my friend Nonie Briones. Nonie was a medical technologist like me. Nonie started inviting me to KDP events. First, it was to cultural events, typically plays or concerts that connected some part of Philippine history and the Filipino people's struggle for freedom. Then, she started bringing me to the KDP education forums. At the forums, a political point of view was presented and the audience was invited to interact with one another and discuss the idea. I also started attending the barrio fiestas (Philippine National Day) organized by the KDP, where we all had a good time eating, listening to music, and just spending time with friends. Finally, Nonie invited me to the KDP discussions groups (called DGs by the members).

At the time, the KDP was already starting to study the impact of the exodus of many medical personnel, particularly nurses, from the Philippines. At one such discussion group, we discussed the push and pull factors that resulted in Filipinos leaving the Philippines for the United States. I learned that what pushed Filipino professionals to leave was the country's inability to provide living wages to its college graduates, and what pulled them to the United States were the job opportunities and historical, economic, and cultural ties between our two countries that made the United States so appealing to Filipinos in search of a better life.

At the end of this multilayered process, I was recruited into the KDP.

During this time, many of my friends who had been drafted to fight in Vietnam were returning home. Some lost a limb or two; some came home paralyzed. Others never came home at all. I was already angry at the US government for the draft, for going to war. But I was even angrier when I learned about how this thing called US imperialism worked, how it exploited Third World countries in search of profits for multinational corporations. Finally, I understood why the United States was fighting a war in Vietnam—it was really a war against the Vietnamese people. I also understood why my parents had to leave the Philippines. They had no choice but to leave so they could provide a better life for their daughters and sons.

LEARNING TAGLISH IN NEW YORK

Just as my involvement in the San Francisco KDP chapter was ramping up, I decide to move to New York City. The KDP had ten chapters in the United States and three in Canada. There was a KDP chapter in my new home.

New York was totally different. Most of the *kasamas* (comrades) there were recent immigrants who were activists from the Philippines. They all spoke Tagalog; I spoke Ilocano because my family came from the Ilocos region.

In New York, my political education continued. At our weekly discussion groups, I learned more about the class struggle—the bourgeoisie, the working class, the peasant class. I would ask questions in English and someone would answer in Tagalog. One day, a *kasama* told me, "Velma, if you are going to organize Filipinos, you need to learn to speak Tagalog." Thus, I learned how to speak Taglish, a hybrid of Tagalog and English.

At this time, the case of Filipina nurses Filipina Narciso and Leonora Perez was getting a lot of press in New York. The city is full of Filipino nurses. These two nurses were accused of murdering patients in a Veterans Affairs hospital in Chicago. The KDP New York chapter decided to study the case, and it became apparent to us that the VA hospital was scapegoating Narciso and Perez for patients' unexplained deaths. Because of biased reporting, the two nurses had already been tried and found guilty in the media. We launched a campaign to defend them; it became a national KDP campaign, in coalition with various community organizations. I learned the structure of a campaign—organizing efforts, propaganda in support of the organizing, and mobilization of the community. Soon I was writing leaflets to educate people about the plight of Narciso and Perez. After producing the leaflets, we developed plans for their distribution the next day. Our campaign to free the women publicized the injustice being done to these two immigrant nurses and put a spotlight on the flimsy, circumstantial evidence against them and the racism that pervaded their trial. Although Narciso and Perez were found guilty of conspiracy to poison three patients, even though the murder charges were dropped, the judge ruled that the prosecution was guilty of misconduct and so the verdict was overturned. The case was never retried and Narciso and Perez were released. We celebrated our victory by holding potlucks in the community.

A few years later two KDP activists were murdered on June 1, 1981. Gene Viernes and Silme Domingo were members of the Seattle chapter. They organized Filipino workers in Seattle and in Alaskan canneries. Gene had just returned from the Philippines, having attended a labor conference and presented a resolution condemning the Marcos dictatorship. Gene and Silme were gunned down in the union hall of Local 37 of the International Longshoremen's and Warehousemen's Union. There was no doubt in our minds that their killing was politically motivated, that their deaths were tied to the work KDP did. Years later, we were not surprised to learn that their killers had been hired by the Marcos regime. The murders of these two *kasamas* affected me profoundly. They made me question being an American. Since Marcos was a US puppet, I started questioning the complicity of the US government in the murders of these two American citizens.

Our anguish and anger pushed us to redouble our efforts. We studied, organized, and mobilized harder. The KDP base and its influence grew nationally and internationally. We formed alliances with other national struggles—in Central America, Haiti, Cuba, South Africa, and Southeast Asia. We also started working with the peace and social justice movement here in the United States.

Just as the KDP was stepping up its work in the States, the *kasamas* in the Philippines were escalating efforts to overthrow the Marcos dictatorship. Aside from the military campaigns in the countryside, *kasamas* were forming united fronts with the middle class, the clergy, students, and other sectors of Philippine society to politically isolate the dictator.

FROM BLOOMINGDALE'S TO THE ALASKA CANNERIES

It was around this time that the KDP national leadership asked me to move to Seattle. The deaths of Gene and Silme had left the Seattle chapter understaffed, and several of us from the East Coast were being transferred. Once in Seattle, I was asked to do some work in the Alaska canneries, where many of the Filipino workers were Ilocanos. My knowledge of the Ilocano dialect became valuable.

To say I was out of my comfort zone is an understatement. King Cove, Alaska, is as far west from New York City as you can get without being outside of US territory. The experience was surreal. One day I was shopping at Bloomingdale's, and the next day I was shopping at the company store in the canneries. One month I was organizing Filipino professionals, and the next month I was organizing Filipino cannery workers. I had gone from working in a medical lab in a New York hospital to working in a cannery, gutting fish. My work in the canneries helped hone my skills in building different types of relationships with different kinds of people. These interpersonal skills would come handy one day.

In 1986, the Marcos dictatorship was overthrown. Corazon Aquino became president through the "People Power" uprising. The work that KDP did in the United States and internationally was an important part of the people's movement that led to the downfall of the dictator.

A DIFFERENT ROAD

With Marcos gone, the focus of the KDP's work came into question. It was a period of self-examination. Many *kasamas* decided to go back to school; others restarted careers that had been put on hold. I myself did not know what to do with my life. I went through an identity crisis and spent the next few years searching, moving from job to job. Nothing held my interest.

Then I met Ruth Woo, Dolores Sibonga, and others like them who were involved in electoral politics. The discussions I had with these women were intense; this time, however, we weren't talking about how to launch a revolution but how to get positioned to be a delegate to the Democratic Party national convention.

For me, the struggle had now moved to the legislative arena.

PART TWO

IN THE THICK OF THE STRUGGLE

K DP activists in various local chapters had many different areas of "mass work" (work with the masses). Each activist was assigned to a propaganda-organizing team (POT) with at least three members and led by a member of the Chapter Executive Board. Day to day, the POTs engaged in propaganda, organizing, and coalition building, often localizing a national campaign on an issue of discrimination against Filipinos, responding to a local issue in the community; for example, a Philippine POT did anti-dictatorship work from within a local chapter of the Anti–Martial Law Coalition (AMLC), which included non-KDP members. Each KDP activist was also assigned internal committee work, such as collecting dues, fund-raising, and preparing discussion groups for recruitment purposes. Part 2 of this collection provides a peek into the KDP's varied day-to-day political operations as recalled by some of its activists.

THE BIRTH OF A KDP CHAPTER

DALE BORGESON

A RRIVING in Seattle in February 1973, I linked up with old friends. I got hired at Bethlehem Steel, joining the industrial working class. This work and my neighborhood in West Seattle left me in very bad position to make contact with the Filipino community. My section of West Seattle, in fact, was fittingly named White Center. When Cynthia Maglaya, who became my contact in the Kalayaan collective, called from Oakland to ask how the work was going, I had to admit that I was making little progress. Her call prompted me to pull out my contact list and start phoning around.

Luckily, I called a University of Washington (UW) student, Norris Bacho, who knew my friends in San Francisco. Norris graciously invited me to attend parties of Filipino students at his Capitol Hill apartment. He was an officer of the UW Filipino Students Association (FSA) and had attended minority student rights conferences in California. His family in Seattle had already dared to speak out against martial law in the Philippines, displaying a rare courage for the time. Norris introduced me to his fellow students as an activist just returned from the Philippines. This gave me a chance to talk about building opposition to martial law.

Gradually, a group formed and we developed a small campus chapter of the National Committee for the Restoration of Civil Liberties in the Philippines (NCRCLP), precursor to the Anti–Martial Law Coalition (AMLC). The chapter included Flora Lopez from the FSA and Julia Laranang, who was a member of the Filipino Youth Activities (FYA) group. In the spring, at the UW Ethnic Cultural Center, the chapter staged a presentation of Filipino activist songs and a slideshow exposing martial law. Cynthia came up from

See "The Accident" for contributor biography.

San Francisco for the event and met the students. She brought word that a conference was being planned for July in the San Francisco Bay Area to establish a national Filipino activist organization. This would become the KDP. Cynthia invited me to attend and to recruit participants from Seattle.

Julia Laranang from FYA encouraged me to call Fred Cordova, another name on my list. Fred and Dorothy Cordova were older professionals who had founded Filipino Youth Activities. The FYA was a cultural and recreational organization in Seattle's Central District that sponsored an award-winning Filipino drill team with a drum and bugle corps. Fred was originally from Stockton, California, a center for Filipino agricultural workers since the 1920s. In 1973, Fred was communications director at Seattle University. I met him at his office and we talked about common friends in San Francisco. He invited me to his home, where I met his wife, Dorothy, who headed the Demonstration Project for Asian Americans (DPAA), an affirmative action group. Fred and Dorothy were different from the much more conservative leaders of the Filipino Community Center (FCC).

The Cordovas saw themselves as part of the civil rights movement and were strong advocates for Filipino rights. Fred was fond of characterizing the Filipino community as "a minority within a minority within a minority" (immigrant, nonwhite, Asian). He had played a leading role in launching the first Filipino People's Far West Convention (FWC) in 1971, which had sought to promote cultural identity, "Pinoy pride," and affirmative action as a ladder to American middle-class status.

Despite their advocacy of Filipino rights, I could never convince Fred and Dorothy to join the anti-Marcos struggle. Marcos's declaration of martial law in 1972 further polarized the US Filipino community. Philippine consulates nationwide, including in Seattle, were energetically spreading propaganda about martial law, claiming it necessary for "peace and order." They carefully lined up community leaders to support the regime. The propaganda had its effect and, combined with fear of speaking out and endangering family in the Philippines, it succeeded in silencing many community leaders such as the Cordovas. It was important for Marcos's credibility in the United States that the Filipino community be perceived as supportive of him.

Fred's position was that martial law should not be discussed at all. Further, he believed that any activity opposing it would weaken and divide the struggle to unite Filipinos around important cultural and affirmative action issues. After several attempts to convince him of the Filipino people's suffering under martial law, I had to cross this big name off my list. Later that fall of 1974, after we had organized a KDP chapter in Seattle, our first planned activity was attending a presentation by the former Philippine peasant leader

Luis Taruc, who was touring the United States to tout Marcos's so-called land-reform program. To my dismay, Taruc's Seattle appearance was sponsored by Fred Cordova, who now worked at the University of Washington. Fred moderated Taruc's presentation at the UW Ethnic Cultural Center Theater. We mobilized a significant number of Filipino and Asian American students and community members to expose Marcos's land reform as a sham and to criticize Taruc for selling out his peasant community. Fred was outraged by our actions, accusing us of "mau-mauing" (attacking to intimidate, after the Mau Mau anticolonial insurgents in Kenya). He never forgave the KDP for "humiliating" him on his home turf.

It was becoming clear that raising criticism of Marcos in the Seattle Filipino community was not going to be easy. Many Filipinos, including First Wave *manongs* who formed the base of the Alaska Cannery Workers Union, hailed from Marcos's home Ilocos region. Many of them took pride that a fellow Ilocano was now president. And the leaders of the post–World War II Second Wave immigrant organizations, such as the Filipino Community Center, were socially conservative and had close ties to Seattle's Philippine consulate. The regime even initiated "Balikbayan" tours and mobilized Filipino Americans to visit the Philippines so that they would return praising Marcos's "New Society."

Luckily for me, veteran Filipino labor leader Philip Vera Cruz, who was vice president of the United Farm Workers (UFW) union, came to Seattle to promote the UFW Grape Boycott in the spring of 1973. Philip was a progressive who was not afraid to speak out against martial law. He would later openly criticize UFW president Cesar Chavez for his endorsement of Marcos's land-reform program. I attended Philip's talk in Seattle's Chinatown, where he linked the farmworkers' struggle for a union with international labor-rights issues, including those in the Philippines, where unions were being repressed under martial law.

At the reception, I made contact with other progressive Filipino American labor leaders, including Nemesio Domingo Jr., who was a UW graduate and member of Local 37 of the International Longshoremen's and Warehousemen's Union (ILWU; the Alaska Cannery Workers Union). He was a founder of the Alaska Cannery Workers Association (ACWA), an organization that operated separately from Local 37 and was organizing cannery workers to file class-action discrimination lawsuits against the canneries in federal court. The suits challenged the racism that consigned Filipino workers to the hardest, most dangerous jobs in the canneries, including cleaning and packing salmon, where many accidents resulted in worker injuries. The higher-paying skilled positions, such as machinists and quality control, were always reserved for whites. Filipino workers were relegated to separate and inferior bunkhouses and mess halls. Unfortunately, ILWU Local 37 had fallen under the corrupt leadership of Marcos crony Tony Baruso and opposed the efforts of younger rank-and-file workers such as Nemesio Jr. to challenge the canneries' racist, exclusionary practices.

Nemesio Jr. and I visited Wapato in the Yakima Valley, where ACWA was trying to sign up cannery workers as plaintiffs. We met two young Filipino American activists, Andy Pascua and Gene Viernes. Andy and Gene had been working summers in the Alaska canneries since they were teenagers. Andy was an ethnic studies teacher at Yakima Valley Community College. While still a college student, Gene had organized a successful food strike at Ward's Cove cannery that won Filipino workers a better diet, including fresh fruit and vegetables previously enjoyed only by white workers. Gene impressed me immediately as someone eager to learn the history of the labor movement and to join the fight for better conditions. Together we spent a day talking to workers under the hot sun. Later, we went to a trailer for beer and burritos. When Gene began asking about news from the Philippines, his father's homeland, I began to tell him about the repression of labor unions and the people's resistance to Marcos. Gene was excited and said he really wanted to visit the Philippines and meet union leaders. Eventually he did go, in May 1981, on an investigative visit that put him in the crosshairs of the dictatorship.

Back in Seattle, as I considered whom to invite to the upcoming KDP congress, I met Nemesio Jr.'s younger brother Silme, an instructor of Philippine history in the UW Ethnic Studies Department who was emceeing the standing-room-only Filipino Students Association cultural show. The show included skits and stand-up comedy routines that satirized the sacred cows of the Filipino community, such as the *terno* (Filipina gown) balls and queen contests of the Filipino Community Center. Some routines expressed Filipino American youth attempts to find an identity distinct from their families' immigrant roots, highlighting their own experiences with racism and national discrimination in the United States. Many comedians satirized vestiges of colonial mentality. Others lampooned their parents' nagging advice on how to blend in and achieve success in America. The students were very perceptive about the racial dynamics of American society. Unlike their parents, they did not ignore what they saw but rather lightheartedly asserted their resistance to racism. The performances were wildly popular, drawing thunderous applause and raucous laughter from the crowd.

After the show, Silme, who was receptive and curious about my Philippine experience, invited me to the after-party at the Four Seas bar in the

International District, where we drank whiskey, ate garlic ribs, and played Pong. I told Silme that Filipino activists were meeting in California in July to organize an activist group to fight racism and discrimination in the States and to support the nationalist struggle in the Philippines. Silme was interested but was leaving soon on an investigative tour of Alaska canneries to promote the ACWA suits. To take his place, he suggested I contact Angel Doniego, a Filipino immigrant labor activist. Angel, however, was visiting his home in Cagayan Valley in the mountains of northern Luzon that summer. I promised Silme an update from the conference when he returned from Alaska. Silme's personality and style were very different from his brother's. Whereas Nemesio Jr. was serious, thoughtful, and soft-spoken, Silme was jaunty and fun-loving. What they shared was a commitment to the community's struggle for justice, the courage to speak out, and natural leadership talent.

Both Nemesio Jr. and Norris Bacho came to California to what became the founding congress of the KDP in Santa Cruz in July 1973. The congress not only drew individuals from across the United States but also brought together Filipino activist collectives from San Francisco, Chicago, and New York. At the concluding meeting, I was shocked to be elected to the National Council of the new organization. Returning to Seattle by train, I was now faced with a bigger and more difficult responsibility—establishing an activist organization in the Filipino community.

My first step was to quit my job at Bethlehem Steel and move from West Seattle to the Asian community of Beacon Hill. I went to work part-time at Swedish Hospital, which employed large numbers of Filipinos, especially in its dietary department. By this time, Angel Doniego had returned from the Philippines and Silme was back from Alaska. We got together to talk about the KDP congress and how to establish a chapter in Seattle. We organized a series of house parties and invited students from UW and Seattle Central Community College.

We soon learned that there was an Asian student conference planned for September at Beacon Hill Methodist Church, focused on Asian student activism, ethnic studies, and affirmative action programs. Silme used his UW ethnic studies instructor position to invite prominent Asian American activists from Los Angeles—Russell Valparaiso and Warren Furutani—as keynote speakers. Russell was, like me, a member of the KDP National Council. Each night after the conference, we retired to Angel and his girlfriend Mitsue's home on Beacon Hill with many of the student activists who would become founding members of the Seattle KDP chapter. Amid the partying, we sang Filipino activist songs and talked about what we could do in the United States to challenge the Marcos dictatorship.

By the time Russell and Warren returned to LA, we had recruited four-teen activists into a Seattle chapter of the KDP. Among the founding members were leading activists from the student and youth movements, the housing and social services movement in the International District, and the labor movement. There were Filipino Americans, immigrants, and other Asian Americans. We even had a cultural group, Pagbabalikwas (Uprising), composed of youth who passionately performed activist songs like "Ang bayan ko" and Philip Vera Cruz's immigrant anthem "Profits Enslave the World."

Over the next several weeks, we organized discussion groups on the KDP political program. The group's dual-line program—fighting for democratic rights in the States and opposing Marcos in the Philippines—proved popular with our chapter of Filipino Americans, immigrants, and other Asian Americans. Contrary to conventional thinking, the Fil-Ams were very interested in the Philippine struggle, and the immigrants were very interested in the experience of Filipinos fighting for their rights as a minority in the United States. This flew in the face of later criticism from some in the Philippine Left that getting involved in US democratic rights issues diverted resources from Philippine solidarity work. Likewise, it disproved the assertion of people like the Cordovas that raising the Philippine issue divided the Filipino American community's struggle for equality. Once our discussion groups were meeting regularly, we turned our attention to finding a political headquarters. We finally chose a big two-story house located between the International District and the Central District and near Saint Mary's Catholic Church, which had a large working-class Filipino membership. We used the main-floor rooms for chapter business and meetings and the second-floor rooms for activist bedrooms. We could pack fifty people into the combined living and dining room downstairs for educational and cultural presentations.

Now came the hard part—figuring out how to organize the community. Cynthia Maglaya and Bruce Occena, from the KDP National Executive Board, came to help us analyze the Seattle Filipino community and develop a strategy for our work. We studied the three waves of Filipino immigration to the United States to learn how they each played a role in the Seattle community. The First Wave had been composed of workers and students who left the Philippines in the 1920s while it was still a US colony. They came to the United States to find work in the fields and canneries of Hawaii and the West Coast. Their wives or girlfriends could not join them because of immigration restrictions, and they faced anti-miscegenation laws on the West Coast that prevented them from marrying whites.

The First Wave *manongs* in Seattle distinguished themselves by fighting to build unions in the fields and canneries, and many also supported the nationalist movement in the Philippines. They had progressive leaders like Ernie Mangaoang and Chris Mensalvas Sr. of the Alaska Cannery Workers Union as well as the distinguished writer Carlos Bulosan. In the 1950s, these progressive leaders had drawn the wrath of anticommunist McCarthy-era government officials. Attempted deportations followed. I was fortunate to meet labor leader Chris Mensalvas Sr. while organizing at the International District hotel where he resided in the 1970s. I spent hours in Chris's room talking about the KDP and listening to his stories about union organizing in the Alaska canneries. By the 1970s, most of these leaders were dead or no longer active, and ILWU Local 37 had been taken over by gangster elements first led by Gene Navarro and then by Tony Baruso, who had been Marcos's ally since World War II. As union president, Baruso headed a system that took bribes for dispatching workers and ran the gambling rackets at the canneries, which sucked up the workers' wages.

The Second Wave of Filipino immigrants arrived after World War II, composed largely of military veterans who had fought alongside the United States to defeat the Japanese. With their military background, Second Wave immigrants were predominantly conservative and pro-America in their political views. Some worked at major military contractors like Boeing. They brought their wives and families to the States and formed a stable core of a growing community, establishing conservative social organizations like the Filipino Community Center of Seattle. FCC president Sylvestre Tangalan was typical. He worked at Boeing along with Tony Baruso and was an avid supporter of the Philippine consulate and Marcos's martial law. The FCC traditionally celebrated July 4 with a big ball and a formal visit from the mayor and consul general. At that time, FCC leaders did not recognize discrimination as a problem for the Filipino community.

The Third Wave immigrants began arriving after liberalization of US immigration law in 1965. They were mainly professionals with high levels of education: doctors, nurses, lawyers, engineers, social workers, and so on. As a group they were more critical of Marcos's martial law because they understood the dynamics of poverty and repression they had left behind in the Philippines. This group was a ready target for recruitment to the KDP program of fighting discrimination in the United States and martial law at home. Professionals like Dr. Vilma Santos, social worker Vicki Claraval, and newspaper publisher Diony Corsilles became reliable allies in these struggles.

The Seattle KDP chapter elected our local leadership: Silme, Angel, and me. Once we had studied the community, we deployed our activists to organize it. In most cases this was easy, because we had recruited activists already engaged in many issues. We set up the following teams:

The Student Team aimed its efforts at Filipino student organizations at the UW and Seattle Central Community College. Some KDP activists already held leadership positions in the Filipino Students Association and the Asian Student Coalition at the UW. The UW Ethnic Cultural Center became a focal point for our organizing and educational work on that campus. Leaders such as David Della, Jacque Agtuca, and Rick Furukawa put us at the center of Filipino and Asian American student life. The KDP eventually joined with other minority student organizations, such as MEChA (Movimiento Estudiantil Chicano de Aztlán), to defend and expand ethnic studies programs.

The Youth Team worked with the International District Youth Council, which soon put us in touch with Filipino immigrant youth whom we mobilized to defend low-cost housing in the International District for Filipino and Asian seniors and various democratic rights struggles.

The Housing Team was deployed to the fight for low-cost housing for Asian immigrant elders, a campaign that had long centered in the International District housing nonprofit InterIm CDA, which had already achieved significant gains. Hundreds of Asian elderly, including Filipino *manongs*, were living in the cheap hotels in the International District. Many hotels were demolished to build a sports stadium, the Kingdome. Activists failed to stop construction but successfully won low-income housing guarantees from the King County Council.

The Labor Team focused on building a democratic caucus to fight for reform within ILWU Local 37. Tony Baruso hated the Alaska Cannery Workers Association and its lawsuits and accused the KDP of "dual unionism." We clarified that ACWA was not a union but an organization for filing anti-discrimination lawsuits, which the union should be supporting. Silme and Gene emerged as leaders of the rank-and-file caucus and recruited other leaders, including Terri Mast and Emily Van Bronkhorst. In 1980 union elections, Silme was elected as secretary-treasurer and Gene as dispatcher. Immigrant activists Sabino Cabildo, Mario Suson, and others played a leading role in organizing the heavily Filipino workforce at Providence Hospital into the Service Employees International Union. Although some on the Philippine Left claimed that these activities were a distraction from solidarity work, our presence in the center of these labor struggles gave us influential standing in the community when we raised the Philippine human rights issue.

The Community Team hosted the Filipino People's Far West Convention (FWC) at the UW three years after the KDP's founding. Though they had helped initiate the FWC in 1971, Fred and Dorothy Cordova boycotted the Seattle convention because of the KDP's leading role. Given their influence both in the community and at the UW, their boycott was a major challenge.

We argued that nobody owned the FWC—it belonged to the whole community. We did careful organizing work with key individuals and organizations and built a broad coalition and active steering committee that included Third Wave professionals, Filipino students and youth, and community leaders from Seattle, Tacoma, and the Yakima Valley.

In 1976, the Seattle FWC was a major success and positioned us to launch the reform ticket for Filipino Community Center elections in the fall. With the help of Ade Domingo, Reme Bacho, Vilma Santos, Diony Corsilles, Vicki Claraval, and many others, we succeeded in ousting longtime FCC president and pro-Marcos mainstay Sylvester Tangalan, replacing him with a reform candidate, Vincent Lawsin. As a result, the FCC became open to Third Wave professionals and to educational, cultural, and political programs. Instead of the previous stilted July 4 celebrations, the FCC became a center for organizing June 12 Philippine National Day celebrations, which advocated for true national independence from US dependency.

The Philippines Team built the local anti-dictatorship movement through the Anti–Martial Law Alliance (a local chapter of the Anti–Martial Law Coalition, or AMLC). We combined leafleting at churches and Christmas caroling to reach thousands of Filipinos. One of our most enjoyable and politically effective activities was caroling for political prisoners. The KDP and AMLC made this activity a national campaign in the mid-1970s. We wanted to raise awareness and raise funds for the families of the thousands of political prisoners of Marcos's martial law regime. Christmas caroling was popular in the Filipino community, so organizing the singers was easy. Alliance member Emma Catague got us into many homes. Besides singing carols in Tagalog, we sang patriotic songs like "Ang bayan ko." We used these holiday gatherings to let people know the human cost of martial law repression. We encouraged people to adopt political prisoners by pledging support for their families. The caroling sessions were uplifting and emotional and often had surprising results. One evening, we were caroling at a home in industrial West Seattle. After we finished singing, the host asked if we knew his son. The son turned out to be Rene Ciria Cruz, a KDP National Council member from New York and AMLC national coordinator who would become the editor of the KDP newspaper, *Ang Katipunan*, in Oakland. It was truly a joy to meet Rene's father.

On Sunday mornings, the Philippines Team faithfully leafleted at Catholic churches that had large Filipino immigrant congregations. We handed out the *Taliba*, news bulletin of the AMLC, and sold *Ang Katipunan*. This hawking became so regular that parishioners soon began to rely on us for the latest news from the Philippines. In exchange, they shared the latest news from their workplaces or community organizations. Many offered advice on how to expand our leafleting to reach a broader audience.

The Cultural Team, through the group Pagbabalikwas, entertained and educated Filipinos, combining immigrant songs like Philip Vera Cruz's "Profits Enslave the World" with Filipino patriotic songs. The cultural group was especially effective in performances at area campuses.

The Seattle KDP chapter was fortunate to have skilled leaders in all these areas. They quickly won support and built a base for a progressive political platform that broadly reflected the KDP program of fighting discrimination and opposing the US-backed Marcos dictatorship. Silme Domingo was at the center of all this. He was a natural leader who also hailed from a family central to the Filipino community. Silme's father, Nemesio Sr., was a First Wave immigrant who had joined the US military and fought in the Philippines during World War II. He then married Ade and returned to Seattle after the war to raise a family. Nemesio Sr. was an officer of ILWU Local 37. Ade was one of the women who ran the Filipino Community Center. Nemesio Jr. was a founder and leader of the Alaska Cannery Workers Association that filed the class-action discrimination suits. Nemesio Jr. and Silme were both active in Local 37, combining organizing in the canneries with signing up workers as plaintiffs. Sister Cindy was a student activist who got her master's degree in Philippine history at the Goddard-Cambridge School in Social Change, studying with Daniel Boone Schirmer, and then joined the National Education Department of the KDP. Silme had close ties to leading activists in the Asian American student movement as well as at the *Asian Family Affair* newspaper. His style was open and engaging, and he thrived on a swirl of activity, social and political.

Although Gene Viernes was quieter, his leadership style was characterized by strong conviction, tireless energy, and eagerness to learn and organize. He also read voraciously about Philippine history. One night, Gene literally saved my life at a KDP fund-raising party in Oakland, applying the Heimlich maneuver when I was choking on a BBQ rib. Gene came from a working-class family in Wapato, Washington. He had gone to work in the Alaska salmon canneries at an early age. He well understood Filipino workers' exploitation and had a knack for creatively organizing to oppose it, such as the successful food strike at Ward's Cove cannery. Gene was also eager to visit the Philippines and learn about the labor movement there, which he eventually was able to do right before his death in 1981.

Silme was in the middle of so many things that his pace was dizzying. Angel Doniego and I worried that he would lose focus on priority areas. As a result, Angel asked the KDP chapter's leadership to ensure a disciplined approach to political work in each of the issue-area teams. Meanwhile, I worked to link our teams' efforts to the larger effort to win influence for our progressive program within the Filipino community. Angel's participation was invaluable. He brought courage, toughness, and resolve to our work, refusing to give in to obstacles and standing up to threats. He was at his best when he brought his righteous anger to bear, as he did when confronting Luis Taruc at the UW forum on Marcos's sham land-reform program. For my part, I did my best to provide political education to the chapter, to facilitate liaison with the KDP National Executive Board, and to coordinate outreach work on the Philippine issue.

The Seattle KDP chapter had many key leaders, including Terri Mast and Mario Suson in the labor struggle; David Della, Jackie Agtuca, and Mike Kozu in student and youth work; Elaine Ko, Andy Mizuki, and Shari Woo in the International District housing struggle; Emma Catague in Philippine solidarity work; and Alonzo Suson, Abel Borromeo, and Sissy Asis in cultural work. We were fortunate to have strategic allies who were formidable leaders, united behind a progressive program in all our issue areas. Among these were Bob Santos of InterIm; Nemesio Domingo Jr. and Sabino Cabildo in labor work; Ade Domingo, Reme Bacho, and Vilma Santos in Filipino Community Center work; Vicki Claraval and Diony Corsilles in anti–martial law work; Donnie Chin in International District youth work; and Andy Pascua in student and labor work.

By 1978, the Seattle KDP chapter was on firm footing and had significant influence in the Filipino community. The progress we had made in five short years was remarkable. We headed the reform caucus within ILWU Local 37 that would soon win election of Silme and Gene as secretary-treasurer and dispatcher, respectively. We had ousted the pro-Marcos president of the Filipino Community Center and broadened the center to reach out to the whole community. We had opened the community to real news from the Philippines and broken the consulate's attempt to use fear and propaganda to silence voices of dissent.

NO ALOHA FOR MARCOS

SORCY APOSTOL

*Sorcy Apostol was introduced to the KDP in November 1973 when
someone handed her an anti-Marcos flyer at a San Francisco
performance of the Philippines' dance troupe Bayanihan. She
immediately sought out the KDP and joined its discussion groups and
mass protests. This became the avenue to continue her former student
activism in the Philippines. Sorcy led the local chapter's Anti–Martial
Law Coalition campaign in support of the seven activists arrested and
jailed after staging a sit-in and takeover of the Philippine consulate in
San Francisco (this campaign was called AMLC 7). In 1980, with a
six-month-old baby in tow, Sorcy was transferred by the KDP to
Honolulu to help organize No Aloha for Marcos protests against the
dictator's first attempt to set foot on US soil and legitimize his martial
law rule. After the KDP disbanded in 1986, Sorcy continued to
organize in the Filipino American community in Sacramento around
education issues and Philippine National Day celebrations. She
retired from the University of California, Davis, and continues to
teach at Sacramento City College.*

F ALL 1966 was the last official state visit that President Ferdinand Marcos made to the United States. After he declared martial law in 1972, he
was not invited back. This was an insult and source of discomfort for
him, since the United States was his main political and military backer. Then,
in 1979, he made his first post–martial law attempt to revisit the States when
he attended the American National Publishers Association convention in
Hawaii. The visit was a trial balloon to test both the reaction of the Filipino
community and American public opinion.

At the time, I was working in the KDP National Secretariat in Oakland with *Ang Katipunan* newspaper staff. I hadn't yet been transferred to Hawaii—that came later. The KDP National Executive Board decided to send a team to help the Hawaii chapter organize a protest of Marcos's visit. Three or four of us went—Rene Ciria Cruz, Jeanette Gandionco Lazam, and I. And because I was nursing my daughter, RB, who was only six months old, my husband, Bo, came with us too. (Fortunately, World Airlines had a sale going on—sixty dollars each way. Of course, we had to sleep at the airport in order to get a flight out.)

In Hawaii, the popular front that had been pulled together around Marcos's visit was very broad, including the Movement for a Free Philippines (MFP), led by former Philippine senator Raul Manglapus. The leftist groups in the coalition included the Committee for Human Rights in the Philippines (CHRP), Friends of the Filipino People (FFP), and of course, the KDP. The coalition called for holding a counter-convention in the same hotel, at the same time as the publishers' convention that Marcos was scheduled to attend. In fact, the counter-convention was supposed to be directly across the hall. Meanwhile, outside the hotel, the coalition would also maintain an educational picket line for the duration of the convention.

In the coalition's planning meetings, the left-leaning groups saw the need for more disruptive tactics, arguing that Marcos should be confronted with militant protest at every stop of his itinerary. However, we couldn't persuade the MFP. They especially didn't like the idea of protesting in front of churches where Marcos was scheduled to visit. To everyone's credit, the coalition didn't fall apart. The MFP just agreed that the KDP, CHRP, and FFP would organize militant protests throughout Honolulu. (Interestingly enough, in the course of Marcos's visit a number of MFP individuals joined our more militant protests.)

Planning the protests necessitated lots of social investigation and intelligence work. First, we had to find out the details of Marcos's itinerary. Fortunately, we had good detectives in the community. Julie, a CHRP member, was assistant to the lieutenant governor of Hawaii. Other anti–martial law politicians (like future governor Ben Cayetano) helped us piece together the times and places of the official state functions. We also had good ties with several newspaper folks who received a lot of press releases and advance notices about Marcos's activities. Even our friends in the International Longshoremen's and Warehousemen's Union gave us information overheard from bragging pro-Marcos union members. Jeannette and I were in charge of organizing the "flying picket lines," so we tried to refine our standard chants to match the different audiences and circumstances of Marcos's planned appearances. It was quite a challenge to organize all this.

It's also important to appreciate what we were up against. In Hawaii, the Ilocanos' regionalistic loyalty to Marcos remained strong, and the pro-Marcos Filipinos spearheading the "community welcome" had a lot of money to work with—most of it straight from Marcos himself. Marcos wanted to show America that he had the complete support of Filipinos. The main pro-Marcos effort was focused on staging a massive "spontaneous" airport welcome when Marcos arrived. Buses were chartered from every corner of the island. Filipino radio stations and newspapers gave the schedule of times and pickup places. There were promises of T-shirts, flags, and free lunches. Of course, culturally, this whole approach to politics is very familiar to Filipinos—it's common in the Philippines around election time—so we knew that many Filipinos would take advantage of this opportunity, even if they weren't firmly pro-Marcos. The real danger was that the American public might not be able to see through the sham.

Marcos's other tactic was to try to intimidate the opposition into silence. Rumors circulated that a number of boxing matches had been scheduled to coincide with the Marcos visit. This created a cover for him to deploy an advance team of thugs from the Philippines. These thugs attended all the public planning meetings of the anti-Marcos coalition. They stood in the back of the room and looked mean, saying nothing, just listening to our plans. Their presence was very obvious and unnerving. Because of this, the atmosphere in meetings was extremely tense. Everyone pointed out the agents to each other with their heads, eyebrows, and lips—the way Filipinos do—"Oy, agent doon!" (Look, there, agent).

This was the context in which we decided we had to somehow disrupt Marcos's airport welcome, the planning for which couldn't be conducted in public meetings. We went to case the airport, to study how Marcos's arrival would be staged and figure out the best way to disrupt it. Again, we were lucky to have supporters who worked at the airport. They were able to give us the setup plans, so we knew exactly where the stage would be, the direction it would face, where the press would be, where Marcos's plane would taxi to, and so on. We discovered there would be a big cordoned-off area on the southwestern side of the airport. Marcos's plane would taxi to right next to the stage. The press area would be at the backside of the stage, separated off by glass walls. Stage security would be very tight, according to our friends.

In surveying the area, we were pleased to discover that there were ornamental planters some twenty feet away from where the stage would be. We decided to try to stand on these planters so that our banners could be seen more clearly. It would be the perfect place for our protest, because the banners would be almost as tall as Marcos's stage. We also noticed that the elevated freeway ran so close to that part of the airport that a huge banner hung there would be clearly seen by everyone. Timing, however, would be important. That banner couldn't be set up beforehand, or it would be taken down. So the plan called for comrades to time their ride on the freeway just as Marcos began to speak, pull the car over, and run to the railing and unfurl the large banner. So we would have two levels of banners, the ones inside and the one hanging off the freeway.

The key to it all was how to sneak inside among the "welcomers" without getting detected. We decided that women comrades were better suited for the task. Our thinking was that the Marcos goons would be less likely to harm the women (in public) and that women would look less suspicious boarding the buses. I think five women from the KDP and the local anti-Marcos coalition were selected—Lee, Davi, Julie, Marvie, and me. We weren't just assigned, however; we all had to voluntarily agree, because each of us had to accept the risk that we may be beaten up by Marcos agents or some over-zealous Marcos supporters. The men had the easy job of unfurling the banner on the freeway—Moy Tacazon and Gigi Coquio, among them.

Other women in the KDP, CHRP, and FFP were too well known by pro-Marcos people to be able to board buses in Kalihi (the Filipino district of Honolulu). They had to go to outlying towns to get on the buses. I was the only one able to board the bus in Kalihi. My face was new in town, so I could pass for just another ordinary Filipino wanting to see Marcos at the airport. Besides, because of my very light complexion I don't look very Filipino.

Just the thought of this action made me both so excited and scared at the same time. I'd been shouting anti-Marcos slogans for so many years, but golly, to shout them when Marcos would be so close! Back in the Philippines I never saw Marcos close-up. Now he would be right there. Would I have the courage to push through with this plan? What if something happened to me? Bo would be a widower right away and RB an orphan.

The big day arrived. We all had to get to the pickup points early so we could blend into the crowd and not raise suspicions. But I was scared because I was all alone. In my handbag was the banner "Free All Political Prisoners." I sat down and pretended I was reading a book. Then I looked around and realized I was the only one reading and I looked too academic. So I put my book away and began making small talk in Tagalog with those around me. When we were given permission to board the buses, I almost panicked. I saw that the Marcos thugs were inspecting everyone as they boarded the buses. I kept chattering away in Tagalog to anyone close to me (not even knowing what I was saying anymore)—it worked! They looked at me from head to toe, up and down, and let me pass. Once on the bus we got our T-shirts, flags, balloons, and of course, our free chicken lunch. Then off we went to greet "our president."

At the airport I had another scare. I sank with terror when I realized security was searching bags. One checkpoint was airport security—no problem; they were looking for metal weapons. But the other was special Philippine security. They were making everyone bring out the contents of their bags. Oh, my Lord—again, I almost panicked. My anti-Marcos banner was nicely folded. I placed the welcome flag inside the banner and wrapped the T-shirt with it, hoping that all mixed together they would appear like official welcoming materials. As I approached the checkpoint, I tried to look excited and dumb at the same time. Again, it worked! They let me pass.

Once I realized I had succeeded in getting inside, I felt good—but then I felt scared again. In the course of planning, we had agreed that once we got inside we were each on our own. We weren't supposed to recognize or stand near each other. And once one of us began the commotion, then the rest had to join in, support each other, and play off one another's protest.

I had to muster up all my courage. I looked around me and couldn't tell which Filipinos were just curiosity seekers and which were truly pro-Marcos and might try to lynch me once I started to protest. I realized how different this was from demonstrations in the Philippines, where you had to keep a close eye on the police but you felt safe with the people around you because they also opposed Marcos. I tried hard to spot the other comrades but couldn't. I began to fear that maybe they hadn't made it through security, and I was all by myself. I looked and looked but couldn't find them. Perhaps I was so scared that I was looking straight at them but not seeing. I decided to make my way to my assigned position, near the front, next to one of the planters. Marcos's advance men were already on stage, teaching the greeters how to chant and wave our flags on signal, what to sing, and the like. So I had to do all of that, pretending to be happy and excited, while at the same time having so much anger in my heart.

Finally, Marcos's plane arrived, and then there he was, right in front of me! This dictator that I had hated for so long. "Hitler!" I mumbled to myself, "Smile . . . smile ka pa . . . bastos, demonyo!" (How dare you smile, boor, demon!). Marcos began his speech in Ilocano and then switched to Tagalog. He was interrupted again and again with cheering—all orchestrated from the front of the stage. So I also had to wave my flag and yell. He went on for five minutes or so. I kept thinking, "Bola! Bola lahat!" (All lies!).

None of the other comrades had begun the protest yet. I think we were all waiting for an appropriate time. Plus, we couldn't see each other to even signal. I became frightened—what if Marcos ended his speech abruptly and we lost the moment? Timing is so crucial in actions like this, but I was so agitated I could hardly concentrate on what Marcos was saying. I tried to refocus. Marcos was talking about all the good things he was doing for the country, how he had changed the Philippines for the better. He was speaking Taglish, making sure that all his "accomplishments" were said in English for the press to pick up. After each accomplishment, he paused for the crowd to applaud and wave flags. I thought to myself, now or never! How could I get up on the planter without being dragged down by security? It was about three feet high. I needed to look innocent and spontaneous or else they might think I was trying to shoot Marcos. Again, I acted as though I was so carried away with love and excitement for Marcos that I needed to make myself higher so as to see him better. When I got up, I held my breath for a few seconds. Nothing happened—security left me alone.

From that height, I looked around and spotted Lee in the front and activist Rick "Totoy" Rocamora in the press box; just seeing people in my team emboldened me. Slowly and casually, I got the banner from my bag while Marcos was declaring yet another one of his accomplishments. I was still scared, unsure if any sound would come out of my mouth. There was a short pause between the orchestrated applause, and Marcos started to speak again. I unfolded my banner and began shouting, "Marcos, Hitler, dictator, tuta!" (Marcos, Hitler, dictator, puppet!) and "Free all political prisoners"! Only then did I discover that all the other comrades were at their posts. I could hear them shouting similar slogans.

I kept chanting and chanting at the top of my lungs. We had succeeded in making a commotion. There was a buzz throughout the whole audience, and security began moving on us from all corners. Because I was standing on the planter, I was the most noticeable. Marcos looked straight at me and then, gesturing to the crowd, said, "Paano ba yan, mga kababayan?" (What is this, my countrymen?). He went on to discredit us in Tagalog: "Even if I wanted to debate them, they can't even speak our language, they're Americans!" I became so angry. I shouted back, "Putang ina mo! Sinong may sabi sa iyo? Sino ang Kano? Pilipino ako!" (You son of a bitch! Who said that? Who's American? I'm a Filipino!)

Marcos was visibly shocked. I was so close I could actually see his face register confusion as he tried to recompose himself. All throughout this exchange, the other comrades kept chanting and chanting. And just then, we looked up to see the *kasamas* on the freeway above unfurl the large banner "Down with Martial Law!" The media caught all of it—everything! Marcos said a few more feeble things—he pretended he was not affected and tried to go on with his speech. But I knew he had lost it. My heart was jumping with joy! I felt so triumphant, so victorious that I wasn't scared anymore. It was a joyful, ecstatic moment that I will never forget.

Meanwhile, airport security started taking us away, but by that time we didn't care. We had broken through the sham and made our point—the Filipino people did not unanimously support the Marcos regime. As it turned out, the personnel that approached us were not Marcos security. They were polite—"Come on miss, please come down." That was it. We just followed them out of the assembly. But the whole mood had changed dramatically—the fiesta atmosphere had evaporated. Everybody knew, the whole world knew, that there would be no aloha for Marcos!

That same afternoon, all the mainstream media wanted to know what the shouted exchange between Marcos and me was all about. They translated it into English, substituting blanks for the curse words, but the Filipinos all knew exactly what I'd called him There it was, boldly printed in the next day's newspapers and aired on all the major TV stations that night.

Of course, we were only able to surprise Marcos once this way. For the rest of his stay in Hawaii, his security knew us and blocked us from entering other events. So we had to stay outside. But our pickets were very militant and spirited. Many people joined us and, as a result of our disruption of the Marcos airport welcome, the major newspapers and TV stations wanted to interview us all the time during his tour. This threw a long shadow over Marcos's entire stay.

Even now, almost thirty years later, when we talk about the Marcos times, I always wonder how I found the courage to do that. Every time I think about it, the airport images flood my memory. I smile and say, "That's what being an activist was all about—we dared to speak the truth against incredible odds." I'm still so proud of that moment. I think I want it on my epitaph: "She called Marcos a lying son of a bitch to his face and lived to tell the story."

BETWEEN THE PERSONAL AND THE POLITICAL

ESTELLA HABAL

THE Kalayaan collective's headquarters was in the back of a storefront in San Francisco's International Hotel. Originally conceived as a propaganda-organizing team, Kalayaan's main purpose was to nationally distribute a Filipino newspaper with an anti–US imperialist, antiracist, and anti–national discrimination perspective. After a year of propaganda work, we decided to become a more all-sided and disciplined underground collective. I didn't bat an eye at this development. In fact, I thought it exciting that I could participate in a movement that championed the working class and poor in both the United States and the Philippines. I remember quoting Marx to myself: I had "nothing to lose but my chains."

I was still with the San Francisco Newsreel collective when I began attending early meetings of the Kalayaan organization. I remember experiencing both the pains of pregnancy and the anticipation of revolutionary activity in the Filipino community. My daughter was due in the fall, and I decided then to name her Kalayaan Guerrero, which literally translates as "freedom fighter." When friends asked how Kalayaan was, I always answered, "Getting bigger every day." You can imagine their shock when they discovered later that I was not talking about the newspaper!

But how was I going to deal with being a mother in a movement, which was primarily composed of young people without children? I knew I was different, but that did not deter me. Taking my inspiration from stories about Communist China, I knew that childcare could and should be taken into account to encourage women's full participation. After all, even Chairman Mao said, "Women hold up half the sky," and in those days that was enough

See "Running Away to Life" for contributor biography.

to settle any argument. At first I sought childcare in a Chinatown day care organized by leftists for their children and those of other working people in the community, but this did not work out for me. My persistence paid off, though, when my comrades in Kalayaan (and later the KDP) helped with childcare while I did my political work.

I never entertained utopian ideas that the "collective" or that even "socialism" could fully take care of children. I knew that as the primary caregiver the burden of responsibility for raising my kids would remain with me, regardless of how much help I received. Deep down I knew that being a mother would limit my political activity, no matter what. Difficult decisions regarding where to place my time and attention were before me every day. At times I resented that others didn't have to confront the same problem. The tensions created by the demands made by my leadership in the movement versus the needs of my children would remain a constant thread throughout much of my life, a contradiction that had to be negotiated and renegotiated again and again.

The first major decision in which my family responsibilities affected my participation was at the first KDP National Council meeting in 1973. We had just finished our founding congress, and I was elected to the National Council. I was then nominated to become a member of the new National Executive Board, the day-to-day national leadership body. I thought intently about my revolutionary tasks and how exciting it would be to build a national organization from the ground up. However, after much soul-searching, I realized that the responsibilities would be too encompassing for a mother with three young children. So I declined. The council reluctantly acknowledged my conditions and chose someone else to fill the position, a young Filipino American woman who had working-class credentials similar to mine, but no children. I was then assigned to help build the local KDP chapter in the Bay Area.

Ironically, my political work in the local San Francisco area over the next ten years may have been even more time-consuming than a national-level assignment, which had a more methodical and controlled aspect to it. At any rate, I worked in many different leadership bodies—the San Francisco chapter leadership, the northern California Regional Executive Board, a special team assigned to lead the work at the International Hotel, and finally in the National Education Department. My life was filled with a constant flurry of activities, with "mass work" (community organizing) as well as internal leadership responsibilities. At times I could hardly keep my head above water. I'm saddened to say that I was constantly slipping in my responsibilities to my children.

The leadership responsibilities on a chapter level were separated into internal work and mass work. For internal chapter building, the leadership met once and sometimes twice a week. This involved particularizing KDP national campaigns to local conditions, and due to our inexperience, the task often found us meeting far into the night. Internal duties also included meeting with prospective members for two to four weeks to orient them on the political program of the organization. We also had biweekly chapter meetings to study new documents or educational materials from the national leadership. And there were dues to collect, reports to write, and on and on.

Chapter leaders were also expected to participate directly in community organizing efforts. The activities and campaigns were so numerous that they blur in my memory as I grow older. As an example, I remember organizing support for Filipina Narciso and Leonora Perez, two nurses in the Midwest who were wrongly accused of murdering their patients. We distributed flyers at churches, hospitals and workplaces where Filipinos were concentrated. We organized mass meetings with our contacts to discuss the issue and circulated petitions. Sometimes our activities went beyond the expectations and capabilities of the KDP. For example, for two to three years I helped a Filipina registered nurse who worked at the Blue Shield insurance company to launch a class-action suit on behalf of Asian Americans, probably one of the first of its kind. A few years later, a strike ensued at the same company, and the KDP was enlisted to do support work for the strikers. We set up a community support team.

In addition to this mass work, we also had propaganda work, which typically meant selling the KDP newspaper, *Ang Katipunan*, early on weekday mornings at work sites where there were lots of Filipino workers, at Saturday farmers' markets, on Sundays in front of key churches or during special community events. Last but not least, we were all on call to do occasional cultural work, mainly singing, at demonstrations.

When I worked on the Regional Executive Board, I traveled constantly between San Jose, Sacramento, Oakland, and San Francisco to meet with chapter leadership bodies in those cities and assist in developing their local plans. Many times this meant attending their organizing functions as well as their internal recruitment meetings. I was engulfed in these activities daily, for years. While it was exhilarating, it was exhausting and life-consuming as well.

By this time, childcare had become institutionalized within the organization, and I lived in a collective household especially designed to help me with my responsibilities to my children. By now, however, my boys were about nine and ten; they had started to get into trouble with the police, mainly mischief and petty stuff, but terrifying for a mother nonetheless. I personally could not find the time to help them with their homework. They were beginning to be regular truants at school. Although my comrades often helped, they could not, of course, deal with the teachers and the schools. I felt that no one really understood my emotional crisis and the stress of attempting to raise two adolescent boys in the Mission district barrio, who already had juvenile records before they reached their teenage years. I felt increasingly alone and in despair.

To top it all off, the crisis at the International Hotel was mounting. The decade-old stalemate between the housing needs of the elderly Filipino and Chinese tenants and the forces of capital and private property was coming to its inevitable showdown. Our strategy was to attempt to forge a broad alliance, what in those days we called a popular front. This would force the city to accept responsibility for providing low-income housing while simultaneously organizing the tenants and their staunchest supporters to resist eviction to the very end. It was easier said than done, but that's another story altogether.

The International Hotel assignment was probably the most difficult political task I had been handed so far, both in scope and depth. Burdened by the nerve-racking round-the-clock demands of the struggle, intimidated by big capitalist interests, harassed by other leftist groups as being "centrist reformists," we felt stressed to the breaking point. But the final straw for me was the failure to get support from the KDP itself. The KDP I-Hotel team members were criticized for being "maverick and elitist veterans" not accountable to the local and regional KDP. We were essentially browbeaten to accept additional responsibilities in the chapter on top of all the hotel campaign tasks. The San Francisco leadership in particular seemed to have no appreciation for the significance and scope of the I-Hotel struggle. This contradiction became evident during a KDP regional conference in which the hotel was not even considered an area of work to be reported on or analyzed. This contradiction made it difficult to utilize the KDP organization to provide all-around support during the peak of the struggle, which was a bit of an embarrassment. The style of browbeating comrades into submission was tolerated for a while until it ran into other political problems, and the KDP national leadership stepped in to repair the damage. That type of behavior was later targeted as ultra-left, but for me, by that time, the damage had already been done.

I was extremely demoralized politically, and my personal life left me drained, unable to struggle. Meanwhile, during the last months before the I-Hotel tenants were evicted, my life fell apart. Overwhelmed and unable to get help for myself, I considered suicide as an escape. But this was too dras-tic, and believe it or not, what kept me from it was the gnawing question, who would take care of my kids? Feeling guilty about quitting in the middle of the struggle, I limped along in my political work. I could not concentrate on anything. I closed myself off and went around almost in a trance. Today I would know to call this depression; back then we termed it "vacillation."

Finally, after the I-Hotel eviction in August 1977, I quit everything for the sake of survival. People at the hotel thought I had abandoned them, and in a way I had. Except for a few close friends, the KDP chapter leadership did not seem to care about my crisis. In fact, they refused to accept my resignation. I no longer went to meetings, I did not answer my phone, and I tried slowly to repair my life. I started to work again (I had been on welfare for years) so that my kids could have a somewhat stable life, a few material goods, some good food on the table, and a mother to help them with homework.

For a year I went on this way, restoring my life. But I could not stay com-pletely away from politics. So, finally, I asked the KDP to transfer me to politi-cal work that was not so demanding. The National Education Department needed someone to lead its education work, which was considered a very important task in the KDP. The education program consisted of Marxist-Leninist classics and readings from other revolutionary movements, as well as developing our own study guides. The KDP put a premium on learning the Marxist method of historical materialism as well as gaining a common theoretical language in the organization. Unless KDP activists had gone through this type of education and training, they were not considered all-around activists. I enthusiastically embraced my new assignment and was also glad to no longer have to be in the local chapter. This new assignment probably saved me from becoming an embittered reactionary.

But then my physical health took a precipitous turn and I lay sick with an ulcer, probably suffering from a nervous breakdown. My saviors were close friends and my family, especially my new husband, Hilton, who knew my quiet despair and gave me stability and support. (He also gave me my fourth child and youngest son, Isaac, a few years later.) For a year, I could manage little more than tending to my health and personal life. After I became well again, I never returned to the KDP.

TRANSFER TO PARADISE . . . NOT!

WALTER YONN

Walter Yonn became politicized during the Vietnam War and joined the KDP in the Bay Area in 1974. From 1977 to 1980, Walter was assigned to the Honolulu chapter, organizing the Committee for Human Rights in the Philippines (CHRP). Eventually, Walter joined the Line of March (LOM) and focused on the Central American nonintervention and aid movements. Walter worked with union staffs for thirteen years. Since 2000, he has been an employer representative in Kaiser Permanente's Labor Relations Department on the regional and national levels. Walter also eventually returned to school and received a master's in public administration from California State University, East Bay, and is currently director of labor relations in Kaiser's National Labor Relations Department in Oakland.

THERE were live chickens underneath the house, perhaps crawling with lice, perhaps dying or dead for lack of food and water. I heard an occasional half-hearted cackle, but mostly silence, which seemed to confirm my worst fears. When I asked Dean Alegado why we needed to use live chickens for a fund-raising barbecue, he said because they were really, really cheap. Supposedly our friend Boy's uncle in Pearl City had sold them to us for a dollar each. "But who's going to kill them, pluck them and clean them?" I asked. Dean, ever the optimist, assured me this wouldn't be too hard. I didn't say anything at the time, but I had already decided it would be a cold day in hell before I'd be killing chickens when there was a supermarket right up the street.

This was one of the first lasting memories of my new life in Hawaii. It had been only days since we had stepped off the plane from the mainland in December 1977. I still couldn't believe I was in Hawaii. I was convinced I had condemned myself to the farthest frontiers of American political life. In the San Francisco Bay Area, I had been serving on the KDP's northern California Regional Executive Board along with Sorcy Apostol and Josie Camacho. I had just been starting to feel good about the KDP and the related developments in the broader left movement. Of course, we never took vacations in those days, but I was beginning to enjoy reading the journals of competing Marxist sects as a strange form of recreation.

Actually, no one in the KDP ever seemed interested in transferring me anywhere in particular, including Hawaii. I was sort of an optional afterthought to the transfer of my wife, Cathi Tactaquin. Cathi, who was on the National Executive Board, told me she'd accepted an assignment from the national office to go to Hawaii—and I could choose to come along if I wanted. It was more like an ultimatum than a negotiation, and there wasn't much time to make up my mind. My life in California wouldn't be the same without Cathi, so I found myself packing my meager possessions. I was Honolulu-bound.

To make things worse, my Regional Executive Board comrades alerted me that my going-away party would also be an ad hoc criticism session, an opportunity to point out some of my stubborn ideological shortcomings, which I'd still need to work on when I got to Hawaii. For some reason, I always seemed to be stumbling into big ideological mistakes, ever since my earliest days in the KDP. I'd once been called on the carpet by either Bruce Occena or Melinda Paras of the National Executive Board, because I was caught making fun of leadership and questioning their competency (I'm still not sure who reported me). Then, of course, there was my offensive tendency of nominating myself for leadership positions in the organization, another no-no. Apparently, you were supposed to wait until your merits were observed and tested and you were chosen for promotion. I knew that wouldn't work for me because I'd be waiting a long time!

My most recent blunder had been some curt comment I'd made during a hectic moment at a Narciso-Perez rally. This sparked a discussion regarding the reemergence of my elitist tendencies, which were apparently latent in my personality. There seemed to always be more weeding out to be done in the struggle for ideological perfection. My problem was that I never had much patience for weeding. Needless to say, I skipped my going-away party. It was bad enough that I was going way off to Hawaii; I didn't need another remolding session to see me off.

When tourists arrive at Honolulu International Airport, they usually take cabs or buses straight into Waikiki along the Nimitz Highway. There is a stretch on the western outskirts of the city that you pass through, consisting of mostly galvanized metal industrial buildings, with small cinder-block apartment buildings tucked in between and behind them. Well, that's Kalihi, and that's where we were going to live. Believe me, you have a whole other first impression of Hawaii when your destination is Kalihi and not Waikiki. If you shut and open your eyes quickly, you'd think you were in some provincial town in the Philippines. On the neighborhood street where the KDP chapter headquarters was located, there were no sidewalks; there were wire and wrought-iron fences, wooden and concrete-block houses with galvanized roofs, and an occasional rooster crowing. Ilocano or Tagalog was spoken everywhere.

In a week or so, I found a housekeeping job at the Holiday Inn in Waikiki. It was a nonunion hotel, and I worked the graveyard shift. The woman who headed housekeeping was a tyrant and seemed to enjoy firing someone every morning to get her juices flowing. It seemed to me that her choices for termination were completely random, which didn't give me much incentive to work harder to prove myself. So I adopted the habit of being in the front lobby every morning when she arrived for work. Slowly, in zombie-like fashion, I'd be polishing the wooden signs, without the slightest display of either fear or bravery on my face. She would scowl at me each morning, wanting to fire me, but she'd soon lost interest, perhaps thinking it would have little impact on the other workers because I was obviously someone with limited mental capacities. Every morning when one of my coworkers dropped me off near home, I'd be glad to have survived one more day, thinking, "This is going to be a long, long stay in Hawaii!"

As I approached our house, if I was unlucky (and I usually was), the old woman next door would greet me and follow me up to the front door, shouting, "Hey you! You no-good son of a bitch, I see you, I see you!" And she would continue cussing me until I got through the front door and shut it behind me. That's how everyone knew I was home. Then, as I tried to get some sleep, the blistering morning sun would shine through our curtainless windows until I thought I'd suffocate. Just as I'd be managing to doze off, the son and daughter-in-law of my old-woman friend next door would begin their loud, daily fight over some bullshit, right outside my window. It made a Tennessee William's play seem like an upbeat comedy in comparison.

Unable to sleep one morning, I got up to find Dean in the kitchen experimenting with one of the previously live chickens that lived under the house. Having cooked some part of it in a normal way, he found it impossible to bite into its flesh, which had the consistency of leather. Now he was trying to pressure-cook it, hoping to somehow make it become chicken. After several hours of this, and using a green papaya for tenderizer, he invited me to give it a try. I couldn't remove one bite of flesh from the bones. Suddenly, I had more respect for this chicken in death than in life. Even Dean had to give up the idea of killing the rest of them, and I wouldn't be asked to help kill and pluck them. Later, it came out that, in fact, Boy's uncle sold eggs! These poor chickens were old retired hens that had given many years of loyal egg-laying service. There were fryers and roasters and even stewing chickens in the market, but the USDA would have had to figure out a new grade for Boy's uncle's inedible Pearl City chickens, which resembled various man-made materials. I think we were eventually able to give the chickens back to Boy's uncle, but for a slight additional charge.

Three years later, these first days in Hawaii were a dim memory. Our KDP chapter actually became quite proficient at *huli-huli* chicken fund-raisers. We bought the chickens wholesale (dead and from a market), seasoned them with sea salt and paprika, and cooked them over the barbecue pit we had built from an old steel drum and wire. Eventually, we also moved our headquarters to the other side of King Street, near Farrington High, still in Kalihi but a little more upscale. Davi and Dean, their delightful baby girl, Rosie, and Cathi and I lived on Farr Lane. A friendly family who lived just behind us rented a nice house to us. Mr. Almida, our landlord, was a retired shipyard worker who was fond of casting his net in the Ala Wai Canal (not the cleanest body of water in Hawaii). His dog, Chico, always accompanied him. Mr. Almida regularly gave us tilapia, a fish that thrives in the polluted rivers of countries in the Southern Hemisphere and is often, sometimes unfairly, maligned because of that. Out of politeness, we'd always accept the fish and then throw it away later when he wasn't looking. One day, Mr. Almida thanked us; he said he was glad we liked the fish, because he wouldn't eat it himself!

My last year in Hawaii, I managed to land a job at the Hilton as a gardener. I worked by myself for the most part and got a pay increase all the way up to five dollars an hour. In my former job, I'd grown really tired of the silly debates among my Filipino housekeeping buddies. These debates ranged from the magical qualities of albino house lizards to whether or not the ability of certain birds to speak meant that they also had the ability to think. Pedro told a tale of a man from his hometown in Ilocos, who had a bird he taught some words to. The bird then told his owner one day about the visits of another man to his wife while he wasn't at home. So the man killed his wife in a fit of jealousy. Then the bird supposedly reported the man to the investigating police. This story was repeated again and again with a straight face. Pedro swore it was true.

My coworkers Pedro and Romy always greeted me with "Hey, Marcos" or "Good morning, martial law," as an accepting kind of support for the political work I was always trying to do with them around the Marcos dictatorship. We'd grown fond of one another, and when they discovered I'd gotten a new job, they insisted that I pretend one last time to fall down the exit stairs of the ballroom, while they shouted "Industrial!"—even though our supervisor, long ago, had stopped thinking this was funny.

On one of my last days in Honolulu, Gigi Coquio invited us out to visit his current work in a youth diversion project on the Waianae coast of Oahu. If I thought Kalihi was a poor neighborhood, the Hawaiian communities on Oahu had things even harder. Gigi once again demonstrated why no one in her right mind would lend him a car a second time, as he proceeded to drive us up a hill over large rocks in the road, not even attempting to avoid them, while cussing at the VW's inability to make headway. He showed me the *kalo* (taro) terraces he and the kids were rebuilding, their fava beans and cassava. He gave me two large cassava roots, which I smuggled back to California to my Filipino grandmother. She made delicious *suman* (cassava tamale) from them, steaming them in banana leaves from my mother's backyard.

Gigi, an Italian ex-priest, was the best Italy has to offer. He worked for years in the Philippines and in the US anti-Marcos movement. He was also filled with strange and interesting stories. I remember Gigi asking me if I'd noticed how the coconut trees in the parks were always kept trimmed of their fruit. Of course, I said I had no idea and hadn't even thought about it. He told me that the woman who had donated the new mimeograph machine to us had been watching a baby one day in Kapiolani Park, and a coconut fell from a tree and hit the child. This resulted in a large lawsuit by the child's family and established the city practice of trimming all the coconuts off the trees before they ripened.

I must admit, in my third and final year in Hawaii, I became almost stir-crazy. I watched an inordinate amount of public television and learned a couple of lifetime's worth of knowledge about different turtles and tigers and tadpoles from all over the world. I also developed some strange mainland fantasies, like driving for hours, seventy miles per hour, on Interstate 5, in one direction, just because I could! But years later, after my return to

California, I still read the Honolulu newspapers online. And I'm always very glad to see comrades from the old Hawaii chapter whenever Cathi and I go back for vacation, or when they visit us in the Bay Area. In a way, Honolulu will always feel like my adopted hometown.

HITTING THE HIGH NOTES

GIL MANGAOANG

Gil Mangaoang, descendant of the great Filipino labor leader Ernesto Mangaoang, was a founding member of the KDP's predecessor, the Kalayaan collective, and layout editor of its newspaper. In Gil's fifteen years in the KDP, he was involved in the San Francisco, Seattle, and Hawaii chapters as well as the northern California Regional Executive Board. Gil became chair of the National Secretariat, the national staff of the KDP that included the group's various departments and commissions—organization, finance, education, program, and Ang Katipunan. *Gil was also a member of the KDP's National Council and the organization's day-to-day guiding arm, the National Executive Board. Gil left the KDP in 1988 while in Hawaii and then moved to Los Angeles to be with his life partner, Juan Lombard. Returning to school, Gil graduated from Loyola Marymount University and continued the AIDS activism that he had begun in 1985. He retired in 2009 following complications with Kaposi's sarcoma, an opportunistic infection resulting from his exposure to HIV in 1989. He is currently writing a book on his family and life.*

THE room was warm and dank, with the dark green shade pulled all the way down to shut out the glaring noonday sun. From the room next door, voices could be heard and the smell of coffee and cigarettes crept under the door. I finished putting my last item of clothing on and was tying my shoestring.

Roberto Cruz had already begun fixing his side of the bed, so I joined in and tugged the sheets and blankets to make them smooth. I tossed him one of the pillows for his side and fluffed up the other one for mine. I looked around the room one last time to make sure we didn't leave any traces.

"Are you ready"? I asked Roberto.

He just smiled, standing there wearing his skintight jeans and T-shirt (he only wore T-shirts, but he had a great selection in different colors and styles). His left hand was on his left hip, elbow pointing out with his weight shifted onto his right leg, the good one.

"Any time darling," he crooned in his lilting, singsong way.

Outside I could hear the exasperated voices of females asking one another, "Where are Gil and Bob? We have to finish rehearsal before the next meeting."

At that, I turned toward the door; the old hardwood floor creaked under our feet as we moved. I took a deep breath and turned the doorknob.

Immediately, a flood of bright sunlight streamed into the darkened bedroom. The yellow kitchen walls were even brighter with the flooding sunshine. In front of the two tall, unadorned Victorian double-pane glass windows, against the glare of the sun, were three silhouetted figures (perhaps Christine Araneta, Letty Maglaya, and Thelma King—I can't remember precisely). They were in various poses, sitting or standing around the kitchen table, facing the bedroom door. The expression on their faces was wide-ranging, from awe and disgust to amazement and surprise.

Suddenly, it felt like we were in the spotlight as Bob and I stepped into the kitchen. He and I just looked at each other. I had a playful smirk on my face; he was deadpan.

From different voices came cries and rebukes, "Walanghiya!!" (Shameless!!), "Diyos ko!!" (My God!!), and "Animal!!!"

Bob was just oh so nonchalant and said, with exasperation, "Get over it already!"

In a composed voice I announced, "We were just clearing our throats. By your responses it worked well, because obviously you heard us as we hit the high notes rehearsing."

With that, Bob and I smiled sweetly. And we all went off to begin practicing "Alerta katipunan" (On the alert, revolutionaries), a cut on the KDP album *Philippines: Bangon! (Arise!)*.

The album was produced in 1976 by Paredon Records, a US Left record company. That's how San Francisco chapter member Bob Cruz happened to be at KDP national headquarters. The singers on the album were members recruited from the KDP national and the northern California groups. Bob and I sang tenor on the cut. The KDP hoped that through music and lyrics, the album would inspire those unfamiliar with events in the Philippines. The collection of songs was a call to action, and it was intended for use by the revolutionary movement there. The album had to be produced in the United States, though, as it was too dangerous to record it in the Philippines at the time.

In the mid-1970s, there were no gay role models within the KDP, or elsewhere for that matter. Nor was there any established gay code of conduct for how to come out. There was no experience with the concept of disclosure regarding one's sexual orientation. The theoretical foundation for gay sexuality was yet to be articulated. It had to be experienced and lived first, before any gay social norm could be established. At that particular time in history, the popular style was to come out in a very dramatic fashion: the more shocking and in-your-face the act, the greater the impact.

It took me some time to gather my strength to express my newfound sexuality in front of KDP members. So, being comfortable with having a liaison in the national HQ, right in the midst of a rehearsal break for a recording session of revolutionary songs, was my way of making a revolutionary statement at that time about who I was. Having sex in the national HQ seemed the appropriate way for me to declare, once and for all, and to set the record straight, that I was gay.

The move was not entirely deliberate, but one that was intuitive and spontaneous. It seemed to be the right place and with right person at the right time. Bob was working with the San Francisco chapter. I had known him socially at different gay clubs in the Castro district or other movement social events. We had flirted at times but never had the chance to "get it on." We both knew it would happen; it would just be a matter of time.

My decision to embrace my gay identity was actually traumatic. It was only in 1975 that Anne and I went through a wrenching emotional breakup in the midst of an ideological campaign against male chauvinism within the KDP. I was indirectly characterized as a villain. My self-esteem was shattered.

I had to figure out what to do next and how to survive the emotional free fall I was in. First of all, there were no openly gay men in the KDP. So here I was, perceived as a straight man who was in a live-in relationship of three years with Anne. Yet I was always suppressing my inner identity as a gay man. I was conflicted, tense, not knowing whether I would be accepted or rejected within the organization.

I also feared ostracism and potential organization discipline. But I said to myself, "What are they going to do, kick me out? I don't think so, I'm the master of organization." It was only a few months earlier that Melinda and Trinity had become known as an openly lesbian couple. When they came out, no one in the KDP made any disparaging comments. Their action was all I needed to begin my transition. I saw it as a clear signal that expressed, "Go for it!"

Up to this point, I had continued my straight act but lived in constant fear that I would be discovered. I was miserable living a lie. Don't get me wrong: I genuinely loved Anne and still do. It was a difficult decision for us to make the break. But it had to be done. I understood that I deserved to have a relationship with someone who was sexually attractive to me as a gay man, just as Anne deserved to have a relationship with someone who was attracted to her sexually.

All politics aside, though tragic in one sense, my breakup with Anne alone would not have led me toward my true liberation and freedom. There were still new pathways to explore and challenges to hurdle. I was yet to figure out how to integrate my newfound gay identity in the context of the KDP and how to interact with the burgeoning gay movement that tugged at my mind and soul. I was yet to be fully liberated; it would still take a few years

Around 1982 or 1983, I had started working with the northern California Regional Executive Board. Up to that point, I had been chair of the KDP National Secretariat, the staff responsible for the day-to-day operations of the national organization. The various departments and commissions of the secretariat facilitated the work of regional leaderships and local chapters. These activities could involve internal education, dues collection, materials production for recruitment, and the like. Depending on the political need to bolster different areas of work, members were transferred between regions, chapters, and the national staff. Such transfers were done in consultation with the leadership bodies and with the individual, sometimes under duress for the good of the political work. The decision to transfer personnel was no casual matter, since it often involved uprooting activists from jobs, living situations, and at times, from family, albeit temporarily.

But I had been in the secretariat for too long—ever since the founding of the KDP in 1973, in fact. My transfer to the northern California Regional Executive Board would give me the opportunity to grow beyond developing organizational plans and national guidelines for political work. Instead, I would gain valuable direct experience doing frontline organizing work.

"What is my bid for this record player?" I asked the audience. "Look at all its features—automatic changer, multispeed, detachable speakers, and it's portable."

"Twenty," came a male voice from the back of Saint Patrick's social hall.

"Come on folks, this player is almost brand new."

"Twenty five," came the bid from Monica, who was sitting right in front of me at the auction table. Her two daughters were sitting with her, the four-year old on one side and the seven-year-old on the other. I knew she wanted the record player for her girls. Before the auction began, the girls had gone to the display table and were fidgeting with the player controls. I heard them telling Monica that they really wanted it. I quickly moved to close the sale.

"Going once." Silence.

"Going twice." Silence.

"Sold!" I declared with a smile in Monica's direction. The sale of the record player to Monica was the last item for bid during the rummage sale.

"And with this last sale, ends our fund-raiser for the evening. Are there any announcements?" I asked.

No response.

I concluded, saying, "Thank you all for coming tonight and for your contribution to the Narciso-Perez campaign. Please remember to give your money to Raddy when you pick up your purchase."

People started gathering their belongings to leave the social hall. The church chosen for the fund-raiser was in the South of Market neighborhood, where a lot of recent immigrant Filipino families lived in a warren of alleys named Natoma, Tehama, Clementina, Clara, and Ritch. Saint Patrick's was where all the Filipinos went for Sunday mass. The nineteenth-century brick cathedral had survived the earthquake and fire in 1906.

Bo Apostol and I began removing the unsold items, packing them for the next sale and taking them to the door. It was getting late, and I wanted to get home before the rain started. People said their last goodbyes.

"Does everyone have a ride?" asked Wilma, a chapter leader, in her booming voice, to no one in particular.

"I'm not sure who's going to take me home," replied Monica.

Without hesitation, Wilma exclaimed, "Oh, Gil will give you a ride, since he lives in Oakland. Your house is on his way home."

I had avoided volunteering to take her home. "Thanks, Wilma," I said to myself in exasperation.

This wasn't the first time I'd had to take Monica back to her house. I cringed at the thought of going through the ordeal again. The last time had been awkward.

Monica was widowed and had been on her own for two years. Her involvement with the Narciso-Perez campaign was the result of her association with one of our activists, the late Nonie Briones. They had both been medical technicians in the same laboratory. Monica was all too familiar with the issue of unfair hiring practices experienced by foreign medical graduates. Before coming to San Francisco, she had been a registered nurse in Manila. When she applied for work as a nurse in the United States, she was told that her educational background and training were insufficient and not up to US standards.

The social hall was finally cleared out. I reluctantly approached Monica and said, "Are you and the girls ready to go?" She smiled at me and nodded. I picked up the portable stereo she had bought and carried it to the car. Monica and her daughters followed me.

I walked slightly ahead, with Monica behind me holding the hand of each daughter on either side of her. The older one on her right was skipping along. Her sister was tired and cranky but too heavy for Monica to carry.

We reached the car just as the first drops of rain began to fall. Monica's girls clambered into the rear of my two-tone blue Datsun 200SX. They were small enough to not feel cramped in the tiny backseats. Monica was sitting shotgun up front.

As I maneuvered out of the parking space and into traffic, the rain began a steady rhythm. *Swish, thunk, swish, thunk, swish, thunk*, went the wipers. Other than the steady patter of rain on the car roof, the only other sounds were from the girls yawning.

"Can I ask you something personal?" Monica asked quietly but with a sense of urgency. "Are you married?"

This caught me off guard.

Monica was a strong-willed woman and single again with two small girls. She was also important to the KDP's work, so I had to be careful with my response. I didn't want to embarrass her or hurt her feelings, for fear that she would withdraw from our political work completely. She was one of our most reliable second-sphere supporters—people who were not as active as the core group of a campaign but could be counted on to render some form of support.

The rain made the asphalt streets shimmer, like the jumble of my thoughts. We were at a stoplight. I searched and searched for the appropriate reply. I didn't want to lead her on, knowing that I appeared to her as an eligible catch, the usual impression of women outside the KDP. But the reality was that, for at least the last six years, I had been cohabiting with Juan Lombard, in a committed relationship. I already had a "spouse" and had no intention of changing my sexual orientation.

When the light turned green, I thought, "Don't respond, just a few more blocks; pretend you didn't hear her."

Panic! What do I say? The silence was deafening. Finally—her apartment building's front entrance. Before she got out of the car, I looked at her and said, "I just haven't found the right one yet."

With that, she and the girls got out. Leaning down and through the open door, she smiled and said, "Maybe your search is over. Magandang gabi [Good night]." She closed the door and, a daughter on each hand, walked to the building entrance. I waited until they were safely inside.

Driving over the Bay Bridge and seeing the lights of the city, I reflected on what had just happened. I had encountered similar scenes so many times in the past: just change the woman's name and the political campaign.

Monica represented to me the sympathetic social justice–oriented individual in the Filipino community. Yet, many of those select few still held onto traditional views regarding homosexuality. There also was an operative sexual code of conduct akin to the old US military policy of "Don't ask, don't tell." Though generally denied, within Philippine culture it is not uncommon for some men to have a wife and family while simultaneously maintaining a gay lover.

I didn't want to assume anything about Monica's viewpoints. Instead, I chose to err on the more conservative side. I never felt comfortable with my sequestered gay identity while doing day-to-day organizing work. I feared rejection and didn't want to be the cause of damaging the progress of the KDP's political work in the Filipino community.

The future—when I could begin to live openly as a gay Filipino man—was yet to unfold.

FIGHTING US IMPERIALISM WITH
A MASTER'S DEGREE

CINDY DOMINGO

Cindy Domingo joined the Seattle KDP chapter in the fall of 1974 in the aftermath of her first visit to the Philippines. After attending the first conference of the Anti–Martial Law Coalition in Chicago, Cindy was assigned that arena of work. From 1976 to 1977, she attended the master's degree program in Philippine history at Goddard College in Boston and eventually was assigned to work at the KDP National Secretariat in Oakland, in the National Education Department, developing internal studies for the organization. After the murders of her brother, Silme Domingo, and Gene Viernes, Cindy returned to Seattle to become the national coordinator of the Committee for Justice for Domingo and Viernes, until the families won their landmark federal civil suit against the Marcoses in 1989. She continues to speak about the murders and the role played by the Marcos dictatorship and US intelligence. Cindy also continues her solidarity with the Philippines, working with the Akbayan Party and serving on two International Observer Missions during the 2013 and 2016 Philippine national elections. Cindy is active in many national initiatives, including the US Social Forum series, as well as international struggles, building solidarity with Cuba, Venezuela, and Latin American people's movements.

THE school doesn't exist anymore, the Goddard-Cambridge School in Social Change. However, every time I spend the night at my mother's house and sleep in my old bedroom, the dark wood–framed degree certificate bids me good night. I am reminded of my nine months in Boston, earning my master's degree in Philippine history. After almost forty years, the degree and my accomplishments over that period of time remain one of my greatest sources of pride. Even more important to me was the appreciation of history and confidence my professor instilled in me, which has had a lasting impact on my development as an activist, writer, historian, woman, and person. I know I learned more in those nine months at Goddard-Cambridge than in the six years I spent studying at the University of Washington.

In September 1976, I became one of four KDP members selected to attend the Goddard program in Cambridge, Massachusetts. The other students included Rose from the Los Angeles KDP chapter, Felix from the San Diego/ Los Angeles KDP chapter, and Maria from the San Francisco KDP chapter. The KDP National Executive Board selected each of us from the entire KDP membership. We were the third of four classes that would receive degrees from this school, with a total of sixteen students graduating. All but one of the students came from the KDP ranks. All the KDP students were expected to return to their home chapters and find teaching jobs at community colleges or universities.

The Philippine history program at Goddard-Cambridge was created in 1974 in an attempt to place KDP teachers in the Asian American studies departments of major campuses on the West Coast and in Hawaii, in cities with large populations of Filipino American students. Under the direction of Professor Daniel Boone Schirmer, the graduate program was within the Cambridge branch of Goddard College, a liberal arts school based in Vermont. Boone, as he was affectionately called, was well known in the Philippine solidarity movement as both a Philippine scholar and activist. He was most well known for his book *Republic or Empire: American Resistance to the Philippine War*, which documented the emergence of the first anti-imperialist movement in the United States in response to the US expansionist agenda in the Philippines.

My brother Silme was the KDP National Executive Board's first choice to attend the program from the Seattle chapter, since he was already teaching at the University of Washington's Asian American Studies Department. The KDP thought a master's degree could provide the credentials to keep him on campus, so Silme was the logical choice. However, after further discussion with the Seattle KDP leadership, it was determined that Silme was too important to Seattle's KDP work to leave, even for just nine months.

Silme was assigned to come and "struggle with me" to go to Boston. Deep down he was hoping I would say no, since he really wanted to go. My refusal would have placed his name back on the list, because there were no other candidates. Unfortunately for Silme, the choice was not very difficult for me, and after a little thought and discussion with my parents, I agreed to go.

Looking back, it was the right decision. Although I loved my political work with Asian American youth, I was having difficulty handling my newfound independence in a city where I grew up. Both my brothers, Silme and Nemesio, were prominent leaders in the Asian American and Filipino American movements, and it seemed I was always the little sister standing in their shadows. If I had stayed in Seattle, I would have had more difficulty coming into my own, both politically and personally. At twenty-two years old, I needed some new surroundings and direction.

Boone became surrogate father and mentor to us four students over those nine months. It was Boone who found our apartment and furnishings. He told us how to apply for food stamps and where to shop. As young Filipino Americans, we were not used to working so closely with older white people, but we quickly became very close to Boone and his wife, Peggy, just like the other previous students in the program.

Boone was an unforgettable character. He was tall and wiry, and his long, slicked-back gray hair would always fall forward onto his face as he emphatically made his political points in class. His graying mustache and beard, shaky voice, and wrinkled skin made you think he was older than his sixty-one years; but there was no doubt that his mind was crystal sharp and filled with a vast knowledge of Philippine history and Philippine-US relations. Boone was everything I'd imagined about "old, white, New England stock." He was a descendent of the real Daniel Boone, but he was certainly no run-of-the-mill Yankee. Boone was a Marxist and a tireless anti-imperialist activist.

Boone taught classes in his home, a half block away from Harvard University. Every Tuesday and Thursday night, regardless of the weather, we walked the twenty minutes to his house. We always went right to the kitchen to socialize a bit, get our tea and cookies, and greet Peggy. Our class was held in the living room, and Boone always sat in the same chair, with the branches of a potted avocado tree hanging over him, giving the room a nice ambiance.

Each student rotated in leading the classes according to the curriculum designed by Boone. To prepare, we'd do our research at the Harvard library, which contained a large section on Philippine history. Boone made special arrangements with Harvard to allow us to use the closed stacks, which included an incredible selection of original materials, such as reports from American colonial governors and pamphlets by the anti-imperialist movement based in Boston at the end of the nineteenth century. We spent hours and hours reading and researching. I found this type of intellectual and historical work very satisfying and a relief from the strain of activist organizing.

The subject of our master's thesis was collectively decided within the KDP National Executive Board: "The Use of Education as a Tool of U.S. Imperialism 1900–1940." As we stated in the introduction,

> This thesis will provide not only a concrete analysis of the US educational policy in the Philippines during 1900–1913, but [also] will supply evidence that the educational system was used as a tool for US imperialism. Furthermore, we feel our work will serve as a contribution to the West Coast Pilipino Teacher's Education Task Force (ETF). The ETF is currently investigating secondary and college-level history textbooks to expose their distorted perspectives of Philippine history. In addition to their research, the ETF is working towards providing alternative readings with a realistic approach to Philippine history.

It was our intention to provide a concrete analysis of the US educational policy and its implementation, to shatter the myth that the United States entered the Philippines, "not as invaders or conquerors, but as friends; that the educational system was geared to educate the people for self-government. . . . Furthermore, we will establish the educational policy as a key aspect of the colonial structure in the Philippines, which greatly affected the mentality and nationalist sentiments of the Pilipino masses and molded them into colonial subjects."

The thesis was divided into four sections, one per student:

- "The Educational System in the Philippines during the Spanish Colonial Period," by Maria Abadesco
- "The Implementation of the US Educational Policy to Maintain Political and Economic Control in the Philippines," by Felix Tuyay
- "The Organization and Implementation of the US Educational Policy as a Tool of Imperialism," by Rose Ibanez
- "The Reaction of the Pilipino People to US Education in the Philippines, 1900–1913," by Cindy Domingo

Every other week, Trinity Ordona from the National Executive Board would call us to track the progress of our academic work and any struggles within our collective of four. The board appointed Rose chair of our collective, suggesting that she was the most politically and personally stable. Unbeknownst to me until later, the board had summed up my personal and political practice to Rose, who shared it with the rest of the KDP Boston collective. Over time, as different personal struggles occurred with others in the collective, we were given tidbits of each other's summations, as relayed by the board.

Trinity would also follow up on the progress of our Philippine solidarity work with the small Filipino community, which included university students and some professionals. Boone and another woman in Boston who had cotaught the Philippine history course with him, Severina Rivera, were leaders of the Friends of the Filipino People, and so we also interacted with quite a bit of activity in Boston's non-Filipino communities.

Part of the agreement we all made before coming to Boston was to collectivize our money and expenses. Everyone was to gather as much money as possible to help pay for tuition and living expenses, using loans, savings, and family contributions. My parents gave me ten thousand dollars via my uncle and aunt in California, of which half went to pay my tuition. In addition, we were all asked to try to find jobs in Boston to help supplement our income. As I had secretarial skills, I was able to find a job fairly quickly. I worked for three months full-time as a Kelly Girl (named for the Kelly Agency) at Honeywell Corporation, to bring in extra money. The others weren't as successful in finding steady jobs but worked sporadically through temporary agencies.

As time went on, this system of collectivizing all our money began to lose its charm. As one of the people who felt that I was pulling too much of the load by working full-time and bringing in the biggest lump sum, I began to resent other people's spending priorities—buying organic food at higher prices, or contact lenses when that money could have been used for the collective. "What's the matter with glasses?" I thought because I wore glasses. Out of resentment, I started keeping the five and ten dollars that my dad would send me and spent the money on luxuries like ice cream, or eating out, or buying old books about the Philippines that I found while scouring the bookstores in Harvard Square.

At one point, I was asked to pool the travel money that my parents had sent for me to fly home during spring vacation and to take the cross-country bus with everyone else. By then I'd had enough of this Pol Pot experiment, so I refused and flew home and back round-trip. "Have your parents take a loan out like my parents did," I thought, because I wasn't about to spend half my vacation riding a stinking bus. I'm pretty sure my petty-bourgeois attitude was reported to the National Executive Board and added to my long list of criticisms for the year.

When springtime came around, we were all pretty tired of studying and staying home. We'd made a few friends, mainly from Boone's circles, and enjoyed the rounds of free dinners and appetizers in the Boston area. Since Rose was married, she felt restrained from going out dancing and partying, but Maria and I felt liked trapped animals. We'd sit around and tease each other that one of us would find a boyfriend, go out for dinner (on his tab, of course), call back to the house, and have our comrades meet us at the restaurant. Theoretically, the man would invite the rest of our collective to dine with us and pick up the tab and invite us all to go dancing! Yeah, sure—in our wildest dreams. The closest we got to that dream was going to one of those private after-hours black clubs in Mattapan with my boyfriend from another class in Goddard-Cambridge and getting one round of free drinks.

The best laid plans often fail. I never got to teach Philippine history, and I often feel I missed my calling. However, some of the other graduates from other classes did become Filipino history professors, including Felix from our class. Most of the historical details I once knew have faded in my mind, and every once in a while I look at my master's degree certificate hanging on the wall or pick up my thesis and think, "Sayang" (What a waste). But at other times I know it wasn't a waste. Through this experience, I gained a lifelong love of history and a confidence in writing that I have used in various projects over the course of my activism. The master's in Philippine history on my résumé has allowed me the credentials to move in academic circles with some credibility.

In my last talk with Boone, when I visited him and Peggy for three hours in the summer of 2002, he gave his last gift to me by telling me that he was proud of what I had done with my life and that I had remained an activist. And I thanked him for instilling in me the conviction that an appreciation and knowledge of history was key to changing the world. Boone passed away in 2006 at the age of ninety-one, but every time I sit down to write, I still think of him.

INFILTRATING THE WORLD BANK

JON MELEGRITO

Jon Melegrito joined the KDP Washington, DC, chapter in the mid-1970s. He led the capital's Anti–Martial Law Coalition (AMLC) chapter and wrote for Ang Katipunan, *the KDP's national newspaper, until it ceased publication in 1991. He retired in 2012 from the American Federation of State, County and Municipal Employees (AFSCME) after eleven years as a labor organizer and news reporter. Jon continues to be active in social justice advocacy work, notably in the campaign to secure benefits and recognition for Filipino World War II veterans, and is the Washington, DC, correspondent of the website of the Manila-based* Philippine Daily Inquirer, Inquirer.net.

S ECURITY at the World Bank wasn't always so tight, until the day Ding T., a chapter comrade, and I got caught distributing the Anti–Martial Law Coalition's *Taliba* leaflet inside the bank's cafeteria. The place has never been the same since.

Ding and I were assigned the task of leafleting at the World Bank, a complex of buildings only two blocks away from the White House. Ordinarily, we would just stand on one corner and hand out leaflets to Filipino-looking bank employees on their way to lunch. Some would accept them, and some would avoid us or simply look the other way. I've always wondered what was wrong with the ones who did that.

Anyway, Ding and I agreed to meet around noon that day in front of the main building on H Street. I was wearing a conservative tie and plain white shirt. I could easily pass for a bank employee. Ding, on the other hand, came straight from work and didn't have time to change from his US Coast Guard uniform. In fact, I don't believe he intended to wear something less obvious than a military uniform.

We met at the appointed time. Standing on each side of the front entrance, we started handing out the *Taliba*, whose headline story was about the upcoming visit of dictator Marcos. But only a few Filipinos were trickling out. We were getting bored just standing by the door, competing with each other as we rushed to give leaflets to people, sometimes overwhelming them with our lavish attention.

I don't recall now whether Ding or I suggested going inside the cafeteria to leaflet. In any case, we managed to get in, thanks to a very lax security system. In those days, we only needed to simply mention the name of someone who worked at the bank, and we were in.

Once inside, we went straight to the cafeteria, which wasn't hard to find. Like hound dogs, we sniffed and followed the smell. (After many years of being an activist and distributing all kinds of leaflets in the community, we learned how to sniff out the Filipinos as well.) There was a long line forming in front of the hot food section and another line by the salad bar.

Perfect.

Ding took care of one line, and I did the other. With a food tray in one hand and the *Taliba* in the other, bank employees were getting food for thought along with their roast beef and broccoli. I was elated to see so many Filipinos inside the building. "So this is where they've been hiding," I said to myself. It was like discovering a gold mine. Looking for them had been rather frustrating, and finding them all in the cafeteria was a bonanza. "There must be a God," I remember saying.

We were halfway through our stack of leaflets when a uniformed guard suddenly appeared from nowhere and asked what I was doing. "Nothing much," I said, "just handing out literature to my Filipino friends at the bank."

"Let me see it," he demanded. I demurred at first, but he grabbed a copy and after taking a cursory look, said, "Would you and your friend care to come with me to the office?"

I wanted to say, "Well, I'd really rather not, as I have work to do here." But he looked like he was going to do something to my face if I didn't do what he asked.

So I said, "Of course, officer, whatever you say." I looked around for Ding, but he was nowhere to be found. "Where's your friend?" the guard asked.

"What friend?" I said.

"You know who I'm talking about, the one in the white uniform."

At that point, I figured it was better to lie than jeopardize Ding's job with the Coast Guard. "I'm by myself, I swear!"

I followed the guard to the security office, all the while keeping an eye out for Ding. On one hand, I felt abandoned. On the other, I was glad he had disappeared.

"Who allowed you in?" a burly security chief inquired. I almost blurted out the name of a friend who worked inside. I pretended not to remember, and then I decided to make up a name. The chief opened the staff directory and looked through the names, but none matched what I gave him. Finally, he stopped looking. He wrote me up, asked for my name and address, and told me that what I was doing was illegal, that the World Bank prohibited such activity. He escorted me outside after confiscating the rest of the leaflets.

"And one more thing," the guard added. "I never want to see your face again."

Outside, I looked around for Ding, but he was gone. Smart move, I said to myself.

A week later, a friend from the World Band called to say that the bank had instituted new security rules at the front entrance. No one except those with official ID cards would be allowed in unless escorted by bank staff.

Of course, a month later we were back at the World Bank, standing on the same corner as before, handing out leaflets. Interestingly, more Filipino employees were accepting them. Apparently, the commotion inside a month earlier had made them more curious about what we were giving out. It seemed that our tiny scrape with danger had paid off after all.

MOVING TO GOTHAM

LOURDES MARZAN

Lourdes Marzan was swept into the Philippine pro-democracy movement when the government suspended habeas corpus before the September 1972 declaration of martial law. She first joined the KDP Philadelphia chapter and in 1979 was transferred to the New York chapter to become part of the Regional Executive Board for the East Coast. She was also elected to the National Council. After Silme Domingo and Gene Viernes were murdered in Seattle in 1981, Lourdes moved to Washington, DC, to join the Congress Task Force (CTF). As part of the CTF, she mainly researched and wrote op-ed pieces, education literature, and position papers for congressional lobbying. Lourdes recently retired as vice president in technology for a corporation in New York and continues to be a "progressive private citizen of the world."

T HE KDP leadership's words rang in my ear. "You already have a baby! Do you have to have another one? Can't you see? You have a role in history. Having another child would detract you from that role. It would be irresponsible!"

But nothing they said would convince me that I couldn't be an activist and mother at the same time. I gave birth to Victor, my second child. And he arrived with Down syndrome. A week later, I was out organizing for Philippine National Day (PND). I couldn't let my newborn saddle me. I had to start fund-raising for the PND.

Victor could not suck. It took two hours to feed him two ounces of formula. By the time he finished one feeding, it was almost time to feed him again. My husband, Frank, and Ma took turns while I attended meetings, leafleted the nurses at Temple Hospital, or went door-to-door in the Olney neighborhood to rev up interest for the upcoming PND—the one day when the community could forget its differences, come together, and show its unity.

Philippine National Day came and went that June. In July, Frank and I were spoken to by the KDP leadership. Maybe I was spoken to. It was at a National Council meeting in the Bay Area. I remember Bruce Occena holding me, expressing sorrow over my newborn with Down syndrome. In the next breath, he told me I was needed in New York right away. If it was too difficult to move my family on such short notice, I had to move without them and they could follow. Rene Ciria Cruz was moving to the West Coast to become part of the National Executive Board. Someone was needed to replace him immediately on the Regional Executive Board based in New York. I was the one who best fit the bill. The Philadelphia chapter would be dissolved and everyone had to eventually move to New York.

But we'd been in our house in Olney for only three months! Why didn't they think of closing down the Philadelphia chapter before they came up with the idea of "immersing ourselves in the Filipino community" in Olney?! When we'd moved from the University of Pennsylvania area to Olney, just Frank, Armin Alforque, and I moved our houseful of furniture and stuff. In fact, I think the move was why I had Victor five weeks early.

We couldn't live near the University of Pennsylvania because it wasn't a Filipino neighborhood. We'd had to sell our cozy town house with its hardwood floors and huge glass backdoor that looked out into a picturesque rock garden. We'd moved to the Olney section of North Philadelphia, into a small row house with ugly yellow, shaggy wall-to-wall carpet. We'd chosen Olney over a ghetto in South Philly only because it was more accessible to Temple University, where Frank worked, and was near the daycare center for our two-year-old, Chris. We'd spent a month settling in, scrubbing all the filth and exterminating the roaches. The place was adequate. At least we were now among Filipinos.

Philly chapter members Lina and Larry had also moved for the same reason we did. They had left their gorgeous turn-of-the-century stone house in West Philadelphia to live in a plain row house in Olney. Now they were also being asked to move to New York, or they would face charges of ideological vacillation. Larry had just given up a whole lifestyle for Christ's sake! He underwent ideological struggle so he could attend Friday-night meetings instead of shopping for groceries and going to the bank.

Now we were all supposed to drop everything and move to Gotham. This was just not fair. In fact, it was downright inhuman. I had always dreaded going to New York. I had already sworn never to live there.

What was I going to do with Victor? He was already in a home-based infant stimulation program in Philadelphia. The City of Brotherly Love took care of its infirm. God only knew if such services existed in New York . . . New York, which was then in the throes of a financial crisis.

And what about my career? I had been brought up to believe that I must always aim for the stars and that there was no limit to what I could do. Now I was being asked to give up my career, my vehicle to the stars.

But I had a historical role. I could see the KDP logic. I believed in the cause and its requirements. It was true. New York was, by far, more important than Philadelphia. Philadelphia did not even have a Philippine consulate. I was a rising and promising political leader and community activist. I was just getting good at it. I could really make a difference in New York. I could not possibly fail the movement.

By August, I had resigned my job, moved in with New York chapter members Amy and Romy in their apartment below chapter headquarters, and become a member of the East Coast Regional Executive Board. I was allowed to visit my family in Philadelphia every couple of weeks, when there was no important meeting or activity. Ma was always there, taking care of Victor, and I don't remember Frank ever complaining. And my son, Chris? Where was Chris all this time?

DEFENDING NURSES—I'D DO IT AGAIN

ESTHER HIPOL SIMPSON

Esther Hipol Simpson joined the KDP chapter in Chicago in 1976 and became one of its leading members. As a registered nurse and as part of her KDP work, Esther led local arms of the successful national campaigns to bring justice for Narciso and Perez, get fair licensure for foreign nurse graduates, and stop the deportation of H-1 visa nurses. But like other KDP activists, Esther also organized community events to support political prisoners and the labor movement in the Philippines and to oppose violations of human rights under the Marcos dictatorship. Esther was transferred to Seattle in 1982 and assigned to anti–martial law and Filipino community work in the aftermath of Silme Domingo's and Gene Viernes's murders. Esther retired in 2015 after thirty years at the VA Medical Center in Seattle and forty-seven years as an RN. She is married to fellow KDP activist Bill Simpson and together they have a son, Richard.

I AM Philippine-born and was raised with a strong Catholic background. I went to prestigious Catholic schools from the elementary grades through my nursing education. My superiors mistakenly thought that I was raised to be a nun.

After completing my bachelor of science in nursing from Saint Paul College in Manila, I got ready to go to America, which was everyone's goal. It was the most logical move for me because my auntie, also a nurse, was my role model, and she and my younger sister were already in Chicago. But my dad suffered a stroke when my papers were ready, and I decided to stay in the Philippines to take care of him and support my mom. I owed my parents everything, and it was only right that I take care of my family first rather than strangers in America.

I climbed up the nursing career ladder, from staff nurse to nurse manager, department head, nursing instructor, and so on within few years. I was respected at work and in my profession, especially as I was about to rack up another accomplishment: a master of science in nursing at the University of the Philippines. It was great to be a product of two of the most prestigious nursing schools!

Then my dad talked to me and gave me his blessing to go to America. My service to him was enough, he said; it was time to realize my dreams. So it was May 1973 when my life in America began in Chicago. I was welcomed by my relatives, who assisted in my acculturation and integration into the American way of life.

During the first year, it was a great. I felt free to ask questions, complain, and experience the independence to do what I wished. I felt this way because I had come from a Philippines that had been under martial law for six months by the time I'd left. You couldn't get reliable information, and people were afraid and exercised extreme caution in expressing ideas. But here in America there was free speech. The media freely disseminated the news—even what was happening in the Philippines that Filipinos back home didn't know.

I realized that what I had seen, felt, and concluded when I was still in the Philippines was superficial. I had even been selfish at times, resenting the traffic delays caused by the massive and frequent demonstrations in the streets of Manila before martial law was declared. Actually, why martial law had been declared was a big question in my mind.

My political reeducation soon transpired. I became exposed to some of the activities of the National Committee for the Restoration of Civil Liberties in the Philippines (NCRCLP), which later became the Anti–Martial Law Coalition and even later, the Coalition Against the Marcos Dictatorship. I began learning about the reality of life under martial law and that the long arm of the Marcos dictatorship reached the Filipino community in the United States. I was drawn to the NCRCLP because I was concerned about the violation of human rights.

Through discussion groups, I learned about the miseducation of Filipinos and the history of the Philippines and US colonization; I learned that my previous consciousness was a product of these processes. My first political activity was with the NCRCLP, and I was amazed at what I was learning about the symbiotic relationship between the US government and Philippine dictatorship at the expense of the Filipino people's freedom and well-being. This eventually led me to the KDP, which further deepened my new understandings.

As I matured politically, I became involved not only with supporting the struggle in the Philippines but also with organizing around the problems faced by Filipinos as immigrants in America. Our chapter in Chicago, like other KDP chapters, began studying the local Filipino community to prepare for work advocating democratic rights in both the Philippines and United States.

The Filipino community in Chicago is mainly from the Third Wave of immigration—doctors, nurses, medical technologists, and skilled professionals in other, nonmedical fields. Before the KDP was founded, the Philippine Study Group in Chicago had conducted a demographic survey that showed that forty thousand Filipino nurses lived and worked in Greater Chicago. They worked in hundreds of hospitals (the Yellow Pages had about a hundred pages of hospitals). The survey also showed zip codes where Filipinos lived in clusters. This survey served as a tool in our organizing work: studying the health-care sector enabled us to reach out to professionals in the field. Soon we were organizing not only against the Marcos dictatorship but also against discrimination faced by Filipino workers in the United States.

Filipino nurse graduates were receiving the lower pay of nurses' aides and technicians. Engineers were working as draftsmen, CPAs as clerks, dentists as dental hygienists, and on and on—all because of highly restrictive licensure processes. In the late 1970s, the KDP initiated a national campaign to stop deportation of H-1 visa nurses. The New York chapter investigated and found that hundreds of Filipino nurses were facing deportation for having failed their board licensure exams.

Many nurses were coming to the United States with H-1 work visas, sponsored by hospital employers. These nurses were mostly going to rural areas, where there was a continual shortage of medical personnel, and the foreign nurses received lower pay than their US counterparts. To finance their travel to the States, many nurses went into debt or sold family properties, only to find out upon their arrival that they had to take and pass the first available licensure exam. With little time for review and test preparation, many invariably failed. Without licenses to practice, they automatically lost their jobs and employer sponsorship—and their work visas. Although they might be willing to work as non-nurses, their visa problems remained unresolved, and they faced deportation.

Based on its investigation of the issue, the KDP national leadership determined that the Immigration and Naturalization Service (INS) would be the immediate target. Our campaign aimed to convince the agency to halt its policy of automatic deportation proceedings for the terminated nurses until the reason for their sudden unemployment—the arbitrary rule that newly arrived nurses had to take the next available licensure exam—could be resolved.

While we undertook petition campaigns, public education, and representations to the INS and lawmakers, we also started pressuring the National Council of State Boards of Nursing to reexamine and adjust its licensure procedures so as to not put H-1 nurses through undue dislocations. We also questioned the validity of the licensure test itself—its confusing language and cultural exclusiveness, for example. While we recognized that each country had the right to protect the safety of its citizens and ensure that care was given by qualified and competent nurses, we argued that H-1 visa nurses had to be given reasonable time to adjust to American culture and review for the board exams.

Our campaign forged local coalitions that included nurses—both H-1 visa holders and permanent residents—lawyers, community leaders, and people with relatives affected by the issue. The coalition was called the National Alliance for Fair Licensure for Foreign Nurse Graduates (NAFL-FNG). We organized local and national conferences and forums and learned to examine laws, regulations, and the flow of bureaucratic authority. The campaign made enough noise that the INS commissioner appointed under President Jimmy Carter's "human rights" administration agreed to meet and negotiate with us. We prepared a delegation, and the group became versed in the possible twists and turns the talks might take and united around our maximum and minimum goals.

Our negotiation resulted in victory for the nurses. The INS commissioner agreed to grant nurses who failed the board exams Deferred Voluntary Departure Status. This gave nurses time to adjust, review, and take the exam—even several times—while still earning money to pay debts incurred in fulfilling the dream of coming to America. Later, the National Council of State Boards of Nursing began conducting licensure exams in countries of origin like the Philippines, so that nurses who failed the test could avoid dislocation.

These victories, especially those won from the much-feared INS, sent a shock wave through the Filipino community. Community newspapers cheered the INS win in particular. When lower-level INS officers in New York who didn't like the arrangement raided the residence of NAFL-FNG national coordinator Aimee Laurel (Ciria Cruz) under the guise of investigating "the smuggling of nurses," she resisted them with legal arguments, and they had to back off. Our coalition raised a stink. Community newspapers denounced the harassment. We "anti-Marcos activists" gained the reputation of being fearless advocates for democratic rights and savvy negotiators who could bring about practical results.

These gains got the attention of Philippine consulates and their allies in the leadership of the Philippine Nurses Association. The latter in particular had refused to join the NAFL-FNG campaign; the association leadership didn't like the presence of "activists" and didn't want to make waves with the INS or the nursing establishment. This cast them in an unflattering light, because they had made no contribution to resolving a critical problem that had upended the lives of many of their professional peers.

In 1975, I got involved again in helping nurses in trouble. Two Filipina nurses, Filipina Narciso and Leonora Perez, were accused of murdering thirty-five patients at the Veterans Affairs hospital in Ann Arbor, Michigan. News accounts of the investigation infuriated Filipinos all over the United States, Canada, and even the Philippines—it was clear that the hospital administration and FBI were zeroing in on the two nurses because they were immigrants who, like most new immigrants, weren't aware of their rights.

The KDP again became central in this campaign to defend nurses. First, we had to have a reasonable belief that Narciso and Perez couldn't possibly be guilty. This was important because we wouldn't have defended likely wrongdoers just because they were Filipino. Then, after careful analysis, we began the sensitive diplomatic task of working with the defendants and their legal team. This was challenging because, unlike in the later campaign for justice for Silme Domingo and Gene Viernes, we were not internal to the defense team. We sent a national team to Ann Arbor and issued updates and dispatches from there to provide accurate reports and analyses of the trial proceedings. We were in constant communication with the KDP National Executive Board and local chapter leaderships. It was a well-oiled operation.

The KDP launched local defense committees in several cities and coordinated a national support movement for the two nurses, mobilizing the spontaneous sympathy within the Filipino community. Our message was this: the VA and FBI were scapegoating the two nurses for the shortcomings of the hospital administration, because the two women appeared vulnerable, being nonwhite immigrants. We held many forums, fund-raisers for the legal defense, and press conferences—even press conferences in Detroit, where the trial was being held, so the interpretation of the proceedings wouldn't be left to chance. At a key juncture in the trial, we held nationally coordinated demonstrations in front of federal buildings in several major cities. This was the first time in Filipino American history that the community held an orchestrated nationwide protest against a domestic injustice.

Local Philippine Nurses Associations this time helped build support and raise funds for the legal defense. KDP policy was not to insist that allies also oppose Marcos, but we also didn't allow suppression of contrary points of view about what was happening in the Philippines.

The Philippine government and its US supporters tried to gain a foothold within the Narciso-Perez campaign and sow anticommunist intrigue, but they failed miserably. Finally, in 1977, the federal judge ordered a new trial due to prosecutorial misconduct. The prosecutor never retried the case and Narciso and Perez were set free, much to the relief and joy of the Filipino community.

This effort was a great and noble experience working for democratic rights and justice. I would do it all over again.

THEY WON'T KNOW WHAT HIT THEM

ELAINE ELINSON

Elaine Elinson began her Philippine work in the 1970s during the Vietnam War, working with the Free the Army show (a traveling antiwar revue that entertained GIs stationed at US bases in Angeles and Olongapo). She was also a correspondent for the Pacific News Service. Upon returning to the United States, Elaine was introduced to Filipino anti-Marcos activists in New York and San Francisco and attended many of their events and meetings. Elaine did not officially become a KDP member until she moved back to San Francisco from England in 1980. She became an organizer of the Philippine Solidarity Network, mobilizing support outside the Filipino community for the anti-dictatorship movement and writing materials for national campaigns, including against the Marcos state visit and the US-Philippine extradition treaty. Elaine coauthored Development Debacle: The World Bank in the Philippines *with Walden Bello. She served as communications director of the American Civil Liberties Union of Northern California for twenty years and is now a freelance writer and editor, recently coauthoring* Wherever There's a Fight: How Runaway Slaves, Suffragists, Strikers, and Poets Shaped Civil Liberties in California.

I T was late, close to midnight, by the time we all got to the national head-quarters in Oakland. Geline Avila, KDP National Executive Board member in charge of Philippine work and national coordinator of the Coalition Against the Marcos Dictatorship (CAMD), had to finish phone calls to the

East Coast.[1] The late Maxie Villones, part of Geline's staff, was coming from a meeting with the San Francisco CAMD, which was going to bear the major responsibility for putting on the demonstration in Union Square on the day Marcos was to be handed the key to the city. Mayee Asidao, another team member, was still working the late shift at Children's Hospital.

Mayee and I pulled up to the wood and stucco ranch house within minutes of each other. I heard her behind me for blocks in that old black Ford with the broken muffler. We both had kids sleeping in the backseat, so luckily there were spaces in front of the house.

I shifted back into neutral and squeezed into the space in front of Mayee's car and behind the old red Datsun that had belonged to Dale Borgeson, then Edwin Batongbacal, and was now Rene's (Ciria Cruz). No one would imagine that this unassuming spot in Oakland's Dimond District housed a revolutionary organization. I smiled, pulling on the emergency brake.

I thought of the elaborate preparations being made in the White House and Malacañang Palace for Marcos's first official visit to the United States—state dinners and military bands, a planeload of press and two more planeloads of security. And here was our opposition, being launched from this old beige house in the low hills of Oakland.[2]

They won't know what hit them, I thought proudly. We'll use every toast as an exposé of Marcos's crimes, every Marine salute as a platform to oppose the US military bases in the Philippines. We're going to turn the whole thing around, because we're armed with all the information, we have the analysis, and we're disciplined. That really is the power of Leninism.

My son, Matthew, was sprawled out on the backseat, a stack of comic books for a pillow and a *Star Wars* figure clutched in his curled chubby fingers. Rene, my partner, had already gone to Washington, DC, to head up the

---

1 The CAMD, originally the Anti–Martial Law Coalition, was a community-based anti–martial law organization led by the KDP. The coalition functioned in a dozen cities throughout the United States and Canada. Although the CAMD included the participation of chapters of the Friends of the Filipino People and a number of local groups, the coalition did not broaden to include more conservative anti-Marcos elements, as originally anticipated. Over the years, the CAMD became associated with the more militant left wing of the anti–martial law movement.

2 In response to the 1982 Marcos state visit, the KDP and CAMD spearheaded a nationally coordinated series of militant demonstrations in every US city on the Marcos itinerary, including Los Angeles, San Francisco, New York, and Washington, DC.

national actions, so no one was at home. Childcare ended at 11:00 p.m. The American comrades, I thought smugly (ignoring that I was one of them)— they really couldn't fathom the demands of a flow like this. "Going toe-to-toe with the dictatorship," as Bruce Occena of the KDP National Executive Board would say. Never mind; we'd cope somehow. Mayee, Tessie Zaragoza, and I were used to bringing our first graders to sleep at HQ while we worked.

I pulled the front seat forward and stood in the darkness trying to figure out the best angle to get my son out of the car. "Need help, Inday?" Mayee, still in her white nurse's shoes, headed over to my car. She looked exhausted but still glamorous as usual, with her shiny cap of black curls and her long navy cape. "I'll help you carry Matthew and then we'll come back and get Lorena—she's conked out in my backseat. Better yet, I see Raffy's [Orpilla] car already. I'll go in and get him and Wicks [Geaga] and see if they can help us."

I stayed outside in the chilly street, keeping watch over both our sleeping kids. The night was clear. I could see the constellations in the sky and all the lights of the Mormon Temple—it looked like a frosted wedding cake in the dark Oakland Hills.

I thought of the deadlines that loomed ahead. I hoped Wicks, *Ang Katipunan*'s artist, was almost done with the poster he was working on—a circle of dictators with Marcos in the middle. There had been debate over whether Marcos should go in the middle or Reagan—he was, after all, the greater evil, the source of the Marcoses, the Shahs, and the Somozas—but then again, this was the Marcos state visit, and we had to focus people's attention on the Philippines.

Wicks had to finish that poster tonight, because we needed him to head up the layout of the special tabloid. He was a real graphic artist who could set the columns not only straight but with a sense of balance and eye-catching appeal. Raffy—really a bookkeeper for a deaf counseling service—had learned his layout skills in the movement, and Mayee's precision for laying down strips of copy was translated from her nurse's training in bandaging and measuring medicinal doses. They were good, but we needed Wicks!

The tabloid was eight pages long, and it would surely take us all night to finish. All the words were done—the history of US domination of the Philippines, the repression, the resistance, letters from political prisoners. No doubt we would lop off many paragraphs during the night.

We had all the graphics collected too—a gritty snapshot of three wide-eyed young girls staring out at the world from a cardboard shack in Manila's Tondo slum, juxtaposed next to a portrait of the glittery, bloated Imelda;

charts of World Bank loans; graphs of the debt owed by every Filipino baby as soon as it was born; and a startling pie chart showing the amount of arable land consumed by US military bases.

After we were done with layout, Maxie was going to drive the flats to Alonzo's Printers in South San Francisco, where we'd ordered a run of ten thousand copies—more than we'd ever printed before! It was going to be tight, but Geline insisted that the tabloid had to get to the chapters by Wednesday morning. And of course, we believed her.

Raffy and Wicks came outside and helped us get the kids into the house. They laid them down gently on the beige Naugahyde couch under the window in the living room; we covered them with quilts and an old army blanket. They hardly stirred; they were used to this.

Maxie and Geline were already at the table going over checklists and chapter reports. San Francisco, Seattle, Los Angeles, DC, and New York all had the same chants, the same mock-up for the leaflet, the banner and picket-sign slogans in English and Tagalog. Wherever the dictator dared set foot, we'd be ready for him. Tessie was on the phone. Mayee snooped in the kitchen for coffee. "Walang gatas?" (No more milk?), she asked slamming the refrigerator door, coming back empty-handed.

"All right, all right" Geline said, slightly impatient, "Let's goooo!"

We pulled up the secondhand metal office chairs to the green Formica table. Surrounding that humble table was the Marcos State Visit Team of the KDP National Propaganda Commission—us. Everyone had bags under their eyes. Like the rest of the *kasamas* (comrades), I had been at work all day, and later I had to deal with an active six-year-old, grocery shopping, dinner, and a PTA meeting at the elementary school.

But I was still exhilarated, and I loved the sound of it: National Propaganda Commission. We might be in a dingy two-bedroom house in the Oakland Hills, but we were just like our comrades on propaganda teams in Manila or the mountains of Morazan in El Salvador, preparing broadsides and broadcasts for the revolution.

"Everyone here?" Geline asked, looking around the table at the National Propaganda Commission (it sounded delicious, Soviet-like), and we had lots of work to accomplish before dawn.

WORKING THE CORRIDORS OF POWER

ODETTE POLINTAN

*Odette Polintan joined the Samahang Demokratiko ng Kabataan
(SDK, or Democratic Organization of Youth) in the Philippines as a
high school student and went underground when martial law was
declared in 1972. When she immigrated to the United States in the
mid-1970s, she met KDP activists in Oakland and Seattle. Odette
moved to Washington, DC, and joined the KDP chapter there. In 1982
she headed up the human rights lobby work for the Coalition Against
the Marcos Dictatorship (CAMD) and collaborated with other
anti-Marcos and international human rights organizations to shed
light on the abuses of the Marcos dictatorship and to pressure the US
government to withdraw its support. In the late 1980s, Odette moved
to Seattle and worked with the Committee for Justice for Domingo and
Viernes (CJDV). Odette returned to school and earned a bachelor of
arts in 1992 and a law degree in 1995. She is now in-house legal
counsel for a communications company in Seattle.*

M ANILA, *February 1986.* Throngs gather around Epifanio de los Santos
Avenue in front of the military camps. News spreads rapidly in the
crowd that Marcos has left Malacañang Palace. Old and young are
dancing in the streets. Some drop to their knees in thankful prayer—the
struggle against the dictatorship has finally ended, without much bloodshed.
I cry and hug my companion, Princess Nemenzo, wife of a University of the
Philippines professor and a renowned activist and intellectual within the pro-
democracy movement. I feel overwhelmed with joy and sadness all at once.
I cry because the moment we have been waiting for has finally arrived. But I
also feel a great sadness, thinking of the many comrades I worked with in

139

the movement who did not live to see this victory. It has taken us fourteen years to free the country of the dictator, many have fallen in the struggle, but the people have finally won.

I was in the Philippines on that fateful day to take Ramsey Clark, the former US attorney general in President Lyndon B. Johnson's administration and a human rights advocate, and several national church leaders to observe the historic Philippine election. Corazon Aquino, wife of slain opposition leader Benigno Aquino Jr., was challenging Ferdinand Marcos at the polls. Our "exposure trip" was one of the projects organized by the Congress Task Force (CTF) of the Coalition Against the Marcos Dictatorship (CAMD), which had joined with the Philippine Solidarity Network (PSN) in 1983. The CTF was the lobbying office of the CAMD. Its focus was to monitor all legislation in US Congress related to US-Philippine relations and to build national support for the anti-Marcos and pro–human rights movement in the United States.

For a left activist organization, the concept of the CTF was advanced at the time. Many US Left groups disparaged any form of work with governmental institutions, such as the Congress or state legislatures. But leaders and members of the KDP and CAMD thought it was important to have an office in Washington, DC, to study, interact with, and hopefully influence national debates on US-Philippine relations.

Although we in the CTF were physically based in DC, we also worked with national human rights offices and church organizations based in New York. The founding director of the CTF was Walden Bello, a newly minted sociology PhD from Princeton who had a keen grasp of Philippine politics and US-Philippine relations (he would later become an internationally known progressive activist and a left-wing legislator in the Philippine Congress). In 1982, when Walden ended his affiliation with us to join the new US operations secretly set up by the Philippines' National Democratic Front, Geline Avila, national coordinator of the CAMD, approached me about becoming the next CTF director. I still remember when Geline posed the question to me.

In my mind, I was an unlikely candidate to fill the post. Several years before that fateful conversation, I had been an activist in the Philippines and had since moved to the United States to reunite with my family in Seattle. I first became involved with the KDP in its Seattle chapter. When I married, my husband, Ding, and I moved to the East Coast and eventually ended up in the DC suburb of Oxon Hill, an enclave of Filipino immigrants. Throughout all the moves, I remained part of the anti-Marcos movement. When I arrived in the nation's capital, I joined the DC KDP chapter and focused on CAMD work.

My commitment was as strong as ever, but my experience with official Washington was very limited. I told Geline that there was no way I could do what Walden did. I reminded her, "For one thing, I don't have the credentials Walden has—for Pete's sake, I don't even have a college degree." I thought that without academic or political credentials, I would never be seen as an expert, especially in rarified DC circles.

Geline had a different point of view. She assured me that she had seen me work with Walden and thought that I interacted effectively with congressional aides, journalists, and DC-based progressive coalitions. She made me think again about what made an effective activist. She was right that I knew our issues; more important, I felt passionately about them. With a good working team, I could be just as effective Walden. Besides, Geline promised that the CAMD would bolster the CTF with two seasoned KDP activists who would move to DC from New York.

There was still one more hurdle. I was a legal secretary in a DC securities law firm, which paid very well. I was still married then and I needed a salary to help raise my two-year-old daughter, Silahis. I hesitatingly raised this concern with Geline. She told me what I already knew—the CAMD could not pay a regular salary, but she had come up with her own solution. Would my husband be able to support me? To myself, I thought, boy, that's a lot to ask Ding. After much thought and vacillation, I eventually agreed. I knew that this was my calling.

Walden showed me the ropes. He introduced me to key congressional staff members, press people, and other contacts involved with US-Philippine foreign policy debates. At first I was overwhelmed by it all. But I understood the importance of the task, so I buried my misgivings and forged ahead.

Soon after my conversation with Geline, Therese Rodriguez and Lourdes "Baby" Marzan arrived in DC, as transfers from New York. We immediately strategized and rapidly learned the congressional circuit. Therese covered the Committee for Justice for Domingo and Viernes (CJDV) front, working with the House Judiciary Committee to get a hearing on the political assassinations of our Seattle activists Silme Domingo and Gene Viernes, and I covered the area of Philippine human rights and democratic issues. Baby and Jon Melegrito were our writers. They produced our newsletters, press releases, and drafts of op-ed pieces. In addition, Jon also organized the Filipino community in the DC/Maryland/Virginia area to galvanize support for our human rights agenda. This was the core of our team. We were a powerful quartet because we were prepared to give our all. We were determined to leave the CAMD's mark on the nation's capital.

Our first step was to get our office and ourselves ready to be DC players. Our CTF office was on an upper floor in a row house that we shared with other organizations near Dupont Circle. We worked in one big room jammed with desks, file cabinets, and Selectric typewriters, state-of-the-art equipment donated by a supporter. We took the subway to the Capitol, where we would have meetings with staffers during the day; at night, we would meet with other organizations and hold internal meetings.

Of course, we had to get appropriate outfits. Baby and I would go shopping, and laugh that here we were, unemployed activists searching for suits, heels, and briefcases.

THE EXTRADITION TREATY

One of our team's major challenges came when the Marcos government attempted to push a bill through the US Senate to ratify an extradition treaty with the Philippines. The Reagan administration strongly supported the effort to boost its key ally in the Pacific. The Philippine dictatorship wanted to extend its tentacles in the United States to muzzle the growing and effective voice of all the Philippine opposition groups, including the CAMD.

The Philippine government had a list of names of people it wanted extradited back to the Philippines for supposed (and trumped-up) criminal acts. Our KDP members Rene Ciria Cruz and Walden Bello were on this list. So was opposition leader Senator Benigno Aquino Jr. who had been released from prison in the Philippines to receive medical treatment in the United States. In fact, many esteemed members of the opposition movement were on the list—and not a criminal among them. As it turned out, the release of this list was a blessing for us and damning for the Philippine government.

The CTF buckled down to analyze the proposed legislation. None of us had ever read a complex federal bill and we had no legal training. The language of this legislation was mind-boggling; it was so legalistic, it was like reading a foreign language. But we persisted. Our team read it line by line. We analyzed it section by section. We struggled to interpret the whole bill and its overall impact on established constitutional rights. Baby wrote a comprehensive summary. In the end, we were happy with our collective effort. To confirm our analysis, we shared it with Richard Falk, a professor at Princeton, a supporter, and an expert in international law and human rights. He agreed with our analysis. We were pretty proud of ourselves!

Once our understanding of the legislation was solid, the whole organization—from our CTF office in DC to the KDP and CAMD headquarters in Oakland to cities around the country—mobilized to devise a national campaign to defeat the extradition treaty. We had numerous phone meetings with Geline Avila to hash out detailed plans for lobbying, media relations, and grassroots organizing. We knew we needed nationally known personalities and influential organizations (such as churches, labor unions, and civil liberties groups) to speak out against this bill. We also needed an aggressive media campaign, flanked by grassroots efforts, targeting the Senate.

We had to alert the Filipino community in cities around the country about this dangerous legislation. The CAMD chapters were essential in keeping community leaders and opinion makers active in opposing this effort of the Marcos regime. From our office in DC, we identified our friends in the Senate who could hold the line.

We needed to boil down into clear and compelling points the complexities of the bill and the political persecution it would enable. We honed our principal message: the Reagan administration is opening the doors for repressive regimes, like the Marcos government, to extend and violate the democratic rights and liberties of people in the United States, especially people who legitimately oppose foreign governments.

The beauty of this formulation was that it allowed us to work with other organizations that had similar concerns. We won support from traditional civil liberties organizations such as the American Civil Liberties Union (ACLU); solidarity groups such as the Committee in Solidarity with the People of El Salvador (CISPES); and international human rights organizations such as the Arab American Anti-Discrimination League. Therese Rodriguez had worked in the "God Box" in New York, which housed the national leadership of Methodists, Presbyterians, and other denominations, and she helped us make connections in DC.

We found our allies in the Senate: Senator Ted Kennedy, the senior senator from Massachusetts; and the state's junior senator, Senator John Kerry. Kerry, a Vietnam veteran who had become a major spokesperson against the war, was then newly elected and perhaps looking for issues that he could become identified with. With our encouragement, he became very involved in US-Philippine policy issues.

We launched a letter-writing campaign. We urged our chapters to write or meet with their senators. We gave presentations at meetings of our supporters. We contacted the House Foreign Affairs Committee, which was already wary of the United States' huge financial and military support for the Marcos regime. Although the House of Representatives would not be voting on the treaty, we enlisted House members to write letters in opposition to the treaty and we released these letters to the press.

We looked for every opportunity to air our position. We wanted to use every platform available. We found allies among other US groups who opposed repressive foreign dictatorships and had been targeted by those regimes in this country, such as Salvadorans. We also worked with the other Philippine opposition groups and mapped out common strategies, especially in terms of congressional lobbying efforts.

We organized a national conference in DC that brought a lot of these groups together. Our speakers included professor and Arab American leader James Zogby, ACLU legislative advocate Wade Henderson, and our own Rene Ciria Cruz, who was on the infamous extradition list.

Our strategy was unprecedented in its scope. We had a national campaign—CAMD chapters from different cities (e.g., San Francisco, Los Angeles, Seattle, Chicago, and New York) actively participated at all levels to pressure their congressional representatives to oppose the treaty. In building broad support for the campaign, we made the issue not just a Filipino one but turned it to a broader question of civil liberties and human rights. With this wide array of supporting individuals and organizations, and with the growing notoriety of the Marcos government, we garnered a lot of media attention.

Then, a notorious event put a spotlight on our issue: Senator Benigno Aquino Jr., whose name was on the extradition list, was assassinated on the tarmac of Manila International Airport when he attempted to return home to the Philippines. That singular murder illustrated to the US government that the situation was too hot to explicitly help Marcos persecute his political opponents.

Our hard work paid off. We stopped the treaty in its tracks. In spite of the Reagan administration's strong support for the treaty, we successfully blocked the Marcos government's attempt extend its repressive tentacles in the United States. With this victory, our team familiarized ourselves with many of the congressional contacts and other lobbyists who had similar sentiments and agendas, and we established ourselves within DC foreign policy circles.

THE MARCOS VISIT

The contacts we used in the extradition treaty campaign had been developed in 1982, during Marcos's high-profile state visit to the United States, when his close friend President Ronald Reagan had invited him.

Knowing that both Reagan and Marcos wanted to use the visit as a showcase for the regime, the CAMD prepared long and hard for its campaign against it. We had numerous meetings to map out the national strategy as well as a local strategy for each city where Marcos was expected to visit. Many of our national leaders came to DC months before we expected Marcos to arrive.

Marcos had countless people in his advance teams—some of whom looked like they were here for no other reason than to physically harass the opposition. Soon, there was a series of frightening, unexplained incidents: some of us were "visited" in our homes by these thugs; our CTF office was broken into without anything valuable being lost or stolen; car windows were smashed; and one of our KDP activists in San Francisco was almost forced off the highway on her way home from work. But, collectively, we did not flinch. We implemented our plans.

On the one hand, the Marcos government spent millions of dollars to woo the overseas Filipino community by wining and dining community leaders. People were bussed to expensive hotels and given free food and T-shirts, among other enticements. There were extravagant programs with popular actors and actresses flown in from Manila to entertain and generate support for the Marcoses.

On the other hand, we used our organizations to build similarly broad-based opposition to the Marcos visit. Like Marcos, we also started with the Filipino community. We tried to ensure that the press would not get a picture of a community completely bought by extravagant dinners and shows. We broadened our support among churches, civil liberties groups, human rights organizations, and solidarity groups.

In Congress, support for human rights issues in the Philippines was almost always compromised by national security considerations; that is, the US military bases that were still functioning in the Philippines. The US military wanted unhampered access to these facilities; thus, the United States in its policy deliberations could not afford to antagonize the Philippine government. Nevertheless, through work in the CTF, we were able to get statements from several members of Congress to oppose the Marcos visit and Reagan's policy of unabashed support for the regime. We made sure these statements received coverage in the press.

In these types of campaigns, timing was very important, especially if one was trying to capture as much media attention as possible. In the CAMD's case, we were able to tie in the filing of a lawsuit against the Marcoses concerning the Domingo and Viernes murders in Seattle with the state visit. These murders were a stark example of how far the Marcos government would go to silence its opponents.

Therese Rodriguez and I joined forces when we explained the Domingo-Viernes case to congressional members and their aides. We literally knocked on each and every door in Congress to introduce people to this case, to let them know of this heinous crime committed by the Marcoses on US soil.

We had numerous long meetings with Congressman Ron Dellums's legislative aides. We were so paranoid about surveillance that many times we held these meetings away from Dellums's office, out on the lawn by the Capitol. One staffer agreed with us that even the congressman's office might be tapped. That staffer opened doors for us, especially with the House Judiciary Committee. We also met with the aides of two California members of Congress, Don Edwards and Pete Stark, and eventually with the congressmen themselves. At this stage, we were pushing for hearings on the case.

We also had a smoking gun. We had unearthed some classified documents that proved Marcos had been sending intelligence officers—in the guise of diplomatic personnel—whose mission was to "neutralize" opposition in the United States. We had to be careful, because it would be illegal for us to release these documents. We wanted the members of Congress to release them—it would be much more effective, much more of a media splash, and it would give us legal cover.

Trying to circulate these documents to members of Congress and verifying their authenticity took a while. Therese and I were overwhelmed with the enormity of what we had to do, but we persisted—door to door, office to office. It took a lot of hard work, not just on our part, but on the part of the whole CAMD organization. Our chapters in California were heavily lobbying Congressmen Edwards's and Stark's regional offices; both men were well aware that their constituents cared deeply about this issue of justice.

Finally, both Stark and Edwards agreed to release the classified documents. We decided to feed the documents to the *Washington Post* with an embargo (so the paper could prepare a good story) and then hold a press conference on the eve of Marcos's arrival in DC. At the press conference, Edwards and Stark unveiled the documents and linked them to the Seattle murders as a possible consequence of the Marcos government's policies. We did not get our full-blown hearing, but the press coverage served the same purpose. We considered this a coup, another piece of the puzzle that revealed the Marcos operation in the United States.

And, just in case the Reagan administration tried to clamp down on our efforts, we also lined up civil liberties groups and lawyers to defend us.

We were now a part of the DC scene and felt confident when we approached members of Congress about hearings on the Philippines. We helped organize a hearing on the US bases in the Philippines with Congressman Dellums's House Subcommittee on Military Installations Abroad. We had a hearing on human rights issues in the Philippines, overseen by the House Human Rights Subcommittee under the House Foreign Affairs Committee, chaired by Congressman Tom Lantos.

Every time the Philippine military arrested anyone, or if a person disappeared surreptitiously, we would publicize the abuse. Baby Marzan and Jon Melegrito wrote innumerable press releases, op-ed pieces, and newsletters. When the media wanted to get a clear picture about what was going on the Philippines, they came to us. We all worked nonstop trying to keep up with the demands for more information from our office. Even given the small size of our operation and budget, we made a substantial impact in DC during a very crucial period.

When Marcos announced the snap presidential election in 1986, the CAMD decided to tap our DC relationships to bring well-known observers to Manila. We anticipated that Marcos would rig the election, and we wanted powerful voices to witness that and speak out in the United States. We invited former US attorney general Ramsey Clark and several church leaders. Of course, Marcos did try to rig the election, but he never dreamed that the "People Power" revolution would overcome his treachery and deception. I was still in Manila when everything stopped: no one could get through the streets, and the airports were closed. That is why I was at the joyful celebration with Princess Nemenzo on Epifanio de los Santos Avenue in Manila, at the fall of the dictatorship. Our goal all along.

A CULTURAL GYPSY

ERMENA VINLUAN

Ermena Vinluan joined the KDP in the late summer of 1973 but was unable to attend the founding congress, as she was performing with Teatro Campesino, the Chicano theater group linked with the United Farm Workers. As an undergraduate at the University of California, Berkeley, Ermena was part of the KDP East Bay chapter's student organizing team. When the KDP formed its Cultural Commission, Ermena helped lead it, particularly as director of the KDP's theater group, Sining Bayan (People's Art). She also helped the Los Angeles, Seattle, and Honolulu KDP chapters form local Sining Bayan counterparts. Ermena has been a New Yorker for thirty years as an artist-activist involved in many causes, including the anti-apartheid movement, US-Cuba solidarity, racial justice, and recognition and equity for Filipino World War II veterans. Her award-winning documentary, Tea and Justice, *about police reform and the New York Police Department's first Asian women officers, aired on PBS in 2010 and is distributed by Women Make Movies. She is also producing a new documentary,* Fire in the Belly: Becoming Activists. *Ermena currently works on environmental justice with the Coney Island Mermaid Parade, the Filipino American National History Society (FANHS), the Sierra Club, 350.org, and the People's Climate Movement's Earth Day. She is also completing a Filipino American children's picture book.*

ERMENA is the eastern European version of the Spanish name *Herminia*. I was told that *Ermena* is a common gypsy name throughout eastern Europe and means "traveling troubadour of love songs." I'm sure my mother regrets giving me the name, because it must seem to her that I've tried to live up to it all my life. As a cultural activist in the KDP, I've lived around and about like a gypsy, organizing stage performances, poetry readings, recording sessions, house-to-house Christmas caroling fund-raisers, and more. And although very few of these have expressed romantic love, they did express another kind: love for Philippine music, my Filipino American heritage, and for the struggles of working people, democracy, and liberation.

My gypsy life in the political movement began without planning in the summer of 1973. I was an undergraduate in the Drama Department at the University of California, Berkeley, and was taking my first ever Philippine studies class. The teachers, John Silva and Bruce Occena, had asked me to coauthor *Isuda ti imuna* (Those who came first), a play about the history of the *manongs*, the Filipino "pioneers"—my own father's generation—who immigrated to the United States in the 1920s–30s. Their story was one that we in the tumultuous Third World student movements of the day were just uncovering ourselves.[1] We felt that the hidden history of our community had to be dramatized and popularized in some way: the blatant racism against Filipinos, the labor-organizing efforts, the Watsonville Massacre of the late 1930s, the writings of Carlos Bulosan, and so on. And from this inspiration came our first full-length theater production, *Isuda ti imuna*.

After two on-campus performances with standing ovations from the nearly 750 people in the audience, the cast and crew finished that school semester and took the show on the road. We would perform *Isuda* in Delano in the Central Valley, the very place where our immigrant forefathers had labored under the hot sun in the vast grape fields and fought over and over to build a labor union.

The *Isuda* caravan included a busload and several vans and cars, carrying more than fifty actors, musicians, dancers, and crew. We were mostly students from San Francisco State, UC Berkeley, and junior colleges around the Bay Area. Our numbers also included several Vietnam vets who were studying through the GI Bill, plus several high school students and a young grandfather (one of our choreographer-dancers). After our Delano performance, we stayed the weekend and transformed ourselves into a work brigade, donating our time to the construction of a medical clinic for members of the

---

1   On the West Coast, the student Third World Strikes of the late 1960s brought about Asian American studies programs at the university level. In the course of this struggle, a radical renaissance took place in which student activists uncovered and pieced together hidden aspects of Asian American history.

United Farm Workers (UFW) union. The Delano community was at the heart of UFW organizing, and there was still great conflict with agribusiness like the Gallo wine producers over contract negotiation and defending the union.

Our road trip was fun—a lot of laughing and chattering on the bus and a lot of singing. We sang songs from the play as well as other songs that many of us were learning for the first time: "Ang bayan ko" in Tagalog (My country), "Nosotros somos asiaticos" in Spanish (We are Asian), "Imperialismo lu tenemos avencer" in Portuguese (We will conquer imperialism), and songs from the civil rights movement. There was a lot of excitement and little sleep. We were young and carefree, on the road on our own, and doing something that felt meaningful—taking theater to the community.

Since that first highlight of my life as a cultural gypsy, I have taken my trusty, rusty, yellow 1967 Plymouth Barracuda on many road trips all over the West Coast, organizing activities as part of Sining Bayan (People's Art), the cultural arm of the KDP. For approximately ten years starting in 1974, Sining Bayan was the performing arts group guided by the KDP's Cultural Commission. It took its name, and much of its mission, from the Sining Bayan cultural group at the University of Philippines of the late 1960s. Our work was in the broad agitprop tradition, in which productions are designed to educate and politically activate the audiences. Sining Bayan also drew inspiration from contemporary US street theater troupes such as Teatro Campesino and the San Francisco Mime Troupe.

Sining Bayan drew from a mixed bag of genres, principally theater. And we always had music in our productions. Musical styles varied, ranging from Philippine to US folk, pop, Latin, and blues. Productions also usually incorporated dance or other choreographed movement. In all, we were simultaneously organizing to educate, mobilize, and involve people. "The play's the thing" was not enough; the networking of artists, students, and amateur cultural workers was just as important. Talent and experience were secondary considerations; if people were interested in the educational and political goals of Sining Bayan, we invited them to join. Rehearsals were hardworking affairs, as most performers had no previous stage experience. We paid attention to upholding high standards and developing performance skills. Extra rehearsals and individual coaching sessions were common.[2]

---

2   Sining Bayan put on twelve productions of seven different and original plays over a nine-year period: *Isuda ti imuna*, 1973; *Maguindanao* (a.k.a. *Mindanao*), 1974; *Sakada*, 1975; *Isuda ti imuna*, 1976; *Tagatupad*, 1976; *Isuda ti imuna*, 1977; *Mindanao*, 1978 (nine-city tour, 1979); *War Brides*, 1979; *Ti mangyuna*, 1981 (Hawaii interisland tour, twelve performances).

Another notable journey was in the summer of 1976. I was in the Cultural Commission at the time and was going to Seattle for the summer to help the KDP chapter write and direct *Tagatupad* (Those who carry on). I can still remember the beautiful ride north from San Francisco to Seattle as though it were yesterday. The play itself was a one-act drama about the housing struggle of Asian American senior citizens in Seattle's International District.

I have many sweet memories of Seattle. I recall befriending Jo Patrick, sweetheart of writer Carlos Bulosan; meeting Barry Hatten, former lawyer for Local 37 of the International Longshoremen's and Warehousemen's Union (ILWU; the Alaska Cannery Workers Union); and meeting Chris Mensalvas, one of Carlos's best friends and a former president of the cannery workers union. These three elderly comrades were a living part of Filipino American history, leaders in the heyday of radical politics in Seattle.[3] They regaled my friends and me with stories about the late Carlos Bulosan as we sat around the home that Jo and Carlos had shared, overlooking beautiful Lake Washington.

Jo took me and Kasamang Glenn, another KDP activist, on a pilgrimage to Carlos's grave. When we picked Jo up on that cold foggy morning, she was carrying something in a small brown bag. She told us of Carlos's often repeated request that, after he died, should his friends ever visit him, they were to bring a bottle of port wine to drink and then pour on his grave, so that they could drink together like in the old days. When we arrived at Mount Pleasant Cemetery, Jo had a hard time finding the grave, partly because the day was dark and the fog thick, but also, I think, because of the emotions she seemed to be feeling. She finally led us to the grave, and I was saddened to see that it was marked with little more than a small, humble concrete slab the size of a rolled-up newspaper thrown on someone's doorstep. We quietly and solemnly shared a drink, communed with Carlos, and then walked away. Jo referred to us as the children that she and Carlos never had. Despite dreary weather and the even drearier grave marker, it was a beautiful experience to pay my respects to Carlos Bulosan, whose literary legacy has helped plant Filipino American roots deep and strong in this land.

Seattle was steeped in Filipino American history that was still so visible, so tangible. That summer also showed me how daring the city's KDP chapter

---

3   Both Bulosan and Mensalvas were active in the Alaska Cannery Workers Union in the late 1940s and early 1950s. They were among the handful of Filipinos who were close to or members of the Communist Party at the time, when communists enjoyed substantial influence in the ILWU and a number of other trade unions.

was, especially the union-organizing work they were doing to clean up corrupt gangster influences in ILWU Local 37.

Later, in the winter of 1979, my troubadour travels included driving a rented U-Haul full of theatrical props, costumes, and lighting equipment across the frozen plains of Canada. This was for our performance tour of *Mindanao*, a contemporary drama about Muslim and Christian Filipinos banding together to save their farms and ancestral lands from land-grabbers and corrupt politicians backed by the Marcos regime.[4]

All in all, we staged a dozen productions of seven different plays in nine years. Whew! I should have carried a calling card: "Have cultural work will travel." However, after numerous cars, jeeps, trains, planes, buses, and trucks, I never expected to be a sea gypsy. Never did I imagine myself sailing on a catamaran to my next performance. But there I was in November 1981 on the *Aikane*, a Native Hawaiian double-pontoon boat, skimming over sparkling azure seas from one performance to another, with a company of about twenty actors and crew, from the island of Molokai to the tiny island of Lanai.

The ocean was as dangerous as it was beautiful throughout the Hawaiian Islands chain. You have to be an excellent sailor to navigate through the region's treacherous currents and rocky shores. That's why practically all of our inter-island travel had been by airplane. Our friends and sponsors, the ILWU, worried whether we could safely sail to Lanai's little dock. But flying to Lanai for a weekend performance was not possible. Lanai was the smallest of the five main Hawaiian Islands, and the Dole pineapple plantation was its one and only industry. And on weekend *pau hana*,[5] when work was over, everything in this company town shut down, including the airport. Back in 1981, Lanai had no tourist development—nary a hotel, let alone a golf course, to blight its pristine beaches. It was just one big pineapple plantation.

So we were on the *Aikane*, cruising along on fairly calm waters in beautiful weather. We were excited at this fantasy come true: lying on the deck in our shorts and tube tops, soaking up the sunshine, and breathing in the freshest air on earth. We briefly roused ourselves when the captain let us take

---

4   *Mindanao* underwent revision after the play was criticized for simplistically depicting the Muslim elite as equally responsible as the Christian settler elite for the land evictions that victimized indigenous Moros. Professor Aijaz Ahmed of Rutgers University, a friend of the KDP who had studied the Moro rebellion up close, protested that the play's original version obscured the national oppression of the Moros by the dominant Christian elite.

5   *Pau hana* is a Hawaiian term popularized by generations of plantation workers that connotes welcome rest after long, hard labor.

turns steering, and we scrambled to capture the thrill of that moment with our cameras.

Soon after, though, we caught sight of the little dock on Lanai and my sea-gypsy episode was over. My regrets were short-lived, because as we pulled closer to shore, I could see a small crowd of people welcoming us with the most heartwarming aloha we had yet encountered. Little Lanai, isolated from the rest of the world every weekend, was enthusiastically awaiting our arrival. We were what was happening that weekend; we were the only show in town. Lanai's community greeted and embraced us into the depths of its heart.

The plantation workers knew this was not just any other show; this was their show, a story about their lives and those of their parents and grandparents before them on the same plantations. And this was a show their own union was sponsoring. Our drama, *Ti mangyuna* (Those who led the way), depicted the 1937 Filipino labor strike on a sugar plantation at Puunene, Maui.[6]

This was the KDP's offering during Hawaii's seventy-fifth-anniversary commemoration of Filipinos' arrival in the islands. The anniversary saw a statewide celebration that included several events sponsored by the state legislature and various community organizations. Since most Filipinos had come to Hawaii as contract laborers for the sugar and pineapple plantations, we decided that *Ti mangyuna* would depict that almost forgotten history of the Filipinos' role in building Hawaii and its labor movement, which fought the racism and economic injustice of the plantation system. The production had a multiracial, but mostly Filipino, cast. Our Hawaiian choreographer used Hawaiian as well as modern and other dance movements. The dialogue was in English but was spiced with a lot of Ilocano and Hawaiian pidgin.

Audiences responded with great enthusiasm throughout Sining Bayan's entire Hawaii tour. Nearly every local family in Hawaii can trace part of its roots to the plantation experience. So it was not surprising that many, many families offered to be our hosts, housing and feeding us as well as holding festive receptions and luaus during our stay. On the island of Kauai, the community provided us with cots in a recreation hall. On Maui, our hosts sheltered us in a big, dark, haunted-looking lodge at a state park. We were a bit afraid to go to sleep, so we stayed outdoors as late as possible around a huge campfire while we sang, "talked story," played cards, or ran around the trees playing tag. When we performed on the Big Island in Naalehu and Honokaa,

---

6   *Ti mangyuna* was also the Ilocano-language edition of the *Honolulu Record*, a left-wing newspaper published during the 1940s and 1950s.

the ILWU members working at a newly opened tourist hotel in nearby Hilo got us rooms at a big discount. Some of Sining Bayan's members had never slept in a hotel before, let alone a nice one. Moy, one of our actors, had grown up in the slums of Manila. Another actor, Pio, was a college student who'd lived all his life back on Oahu's North Shore in old company housing on the Waialua sugar plantation.

And now here we all were at the end of our tour, on tiny Lanai. The only accommodations the community could hustle up for our sizable troupe was—get this—the former plantation manager's residence. The house was a real charmer: large, splendid, and set in a lovely garden on top of a hill. We whooped with delight and enjoyed the irony.

Demonstration in Washington, DC, 1982. *Ang Katipunan* file photo

Immigrant rights rally in San Francisco, n.d. *Ang Katipunan* file photo

Newsletter in Coordination With the Pacific Women's Resources

The Committee for Justice for Domingo and Viernes
UPDATE

July 21, 1981

Dear Friends,
This is our first issue of the Committee for Justice Update. Our intent is to keep you abreast of all related activities of the Committee for Justice in as timely a way as possible. Your impressions and input are wholeheartedly welcome.

Nemesio Domingo Jr.
Elaine Ko
— Co-Chairpersons

COMMITTEE FOR JUSTICE APPEALS TO THE COMMUNITY

Off the momentum following the slayings of Silme Domingo and Gene Viernes, over 100 persons recently launched the Committee for Justice for Domingo and Viernes (CJDV). In attendance were family, friends, members of the Filipino, Asian, and Black communities, and labor union representatives all concerned with justice in the June 1 murders.

"The loss has been tremendous for all of us," stated Nemesio Domingo, Jr. at the June 22 meeting. "But we must put our grief behind us and push forward the work which Gene and Silme dedicated their lives to."

Domingo and Viernes, union officials at ILWU, Local 37 were gunned down on June 1 while finishing a day's work. Two suspects have been charged with aggravated murder. A third suspect was arrested on July 13, held on $750,000 bail, and later released while investigation continues.

The Committee for Justice pledged efforts to counteract any possible fear and silence by persons who may have any information relating to the murders.

The Committee for Justice pledged efforts to counteract any possible fear and silence by persons who may have any information relating to the murders. Historically, a few petty criminal elements have kept people from assisting in solving crimes.

"It is only through an organized community-wide and city-wide effort that this fear will be overcome," stated Domingo. "The Committee for Justice encourages anyone with information related to the murders to courageously step forward with full confidentiality to the Prosecuting Attorney's office."

Immediately following the murders, an open Appeal for justice to the community was issued. This appeal for information related to the murders was endorsed by the families of Domingo and Viernes, several City Councilmembers, Congressman Mike Lowry, The Rev. William Cate, the ILWU Local 37 Executive Board and numerous community leaders throughout the city. While not all endorsers are members of the Committee, this represents an unprecedented display of support behind the mission of justice in the slayings.

Recently the Committee for Justice renewed its support to seek full justice — with additional endorsers — which targets getting to the bottom of the killings.

"We are gratified by the thorough investigation being conducted by the Prosecuting Attorney's office and Police Department," a recent Committee for Justice statement read. "We can confidently state that the intimidation and silence in our community has been intially broken. We fully expect more information to be forthcoming as to all parties behind these murders."

Due to the significance of Domingo and Viernes' work as union officials and Filipino Community leaders for social justice, outreach committees have been formed to speak to labor unions, Filipino, Asian, Black, women, and church communities about the work of the two slain leaders.

The Church Council of Greater Seattle recently endorsed a religious procession and program to be held in September on the weekend of the Filipino Peoples Far West Convention. Convention planners intend to dedicate this annual event to the lives and work of Domingo and Viernes to be held on labor day weekend. Labor unions are pledging funds and words of solidarity to the ongoing efforts started by Domingo and Viernes in Local 37. Womens groups are planning an educational evening around unionizing efforts particularly for women workers.

Memorial funds have also been established and work has begun around scholarships, and memorials in tribute to Domingo and Viernes.

Domingo and Viernes' deaths have clearly served as a catalyst for many who were touched by their relentless efforts for social justice.

Call 682-9767 if you can assist in the Committee for Justice.

●

LEFT: Committee for Justice for Domingo and Viernes (CJDV), first newsletter, July 1981. Courtesy of Cindy Domingo

BELOW: Rene Ciria Cruz, editor of *Ang Katipunan* and former national coordinator of the Coalition Against the Marcos Dictatorship. *Ang Katipunan* file photo

ang KATIPUNAN

SPECIAL ISSUE

VOL. VII, Number 6   Published by the Union of Democratic Filipinos (KDP)   FREE

SPEAK OUT AGAINST THE MARCOS VISIT!

No Aloha for Dictator

Marcos aims to reverse negative reputation. Whether he succeeds or not depends greatly on the ability of the anti-martial law movement to expose, oppose and frustrate his visit.

The past protest actions of the anti-martial law movement in the U.S., such as the one above, will assume greater importance in the upcoming period.

Protests Grow:
Militant Actions Readied

LEFT: Special issue, *Ang Katipunan*, September 1982. Courtesy of Cindy Domingo

BELOW: Philippine National Day in Seattle, June 12, 1982. Courtesy of Alaskero Foundation

Demonstration in San Francisco, September 1982, protesting Ferdinand and Imelda Marcos's state visit; organized by the National Committee to Oppose the Marcos State Visit and spearheaded by the KDP and Coalition Against the Marcos Dictatorship (CAMD). *Ang Katipunan* file photo, photo by Gary Reyes

Filipino People's Far West Convention in Seattle, 1981. *Ang Katipunan* file photo

ALL TO WHOM ..

BE IT KNOWN THAT LORA ALO y ROSARIO HAVING COMPLETED THE PRESCRIBED COURSE OF STUDY AND SATISFIED THE OTHER REQUIREMENTS OF THE UNIVERSITY HAS BEEN CONFERRED THE DEGREE OF

BACHELOR OF SCIENCE IN NURSING

WITH ALL THE RIGHTS, PRIVILEGES AND RESPONSIBILITIES THEREUNTO APPERTAINING. IN WITNESS WHEREOF, THE BOARD OF TRUSTEES HAS CAUSED THIS DIPLOMA TO BE SIGNED BY THE PRESIDENT OF THE UNIVERSITY AND THE DEAN OF THE INSTITUTE OF NURSING, AND THE UNIVERSITY SEAL TO BE HEREUNTO AFFIXED AT MANILA PHILIPPINES, THIS 3RD DAY OF APRIL NINETEEN HUNDRED AND SEVENTY-SIX.

DEAN OF THE INSTITUTE

LEARN MORE AND BE A PART OF THE FILIPINO NURSES STRUGGLES FOR FAIR LICENSURE !

FACT NO. 1 - Preliminary findings indicate that an average of 80% of FILIPINO NURSES taking the licensure exa- minations fail consistently. Does the high failure rate means that FILIPINO NURSES lack competence and educational background or the examination given is culturally biased and specifically designed to mini- mize the number of foreign nursing graduates admit- ted to the ranks of licensed nursing practitioners here in the United States.

FACT NO. 2 - FILIPINO NURSES "Nursing Skills" are utilized at a lower pay scale.

FACT NO. 3 - FILIPINO NURSES and other foreign nursing graduates are being subjected to unjust examination practices.

GET INVOLVED...... ATTEND ....

National Community Conference for Fair Licensure for Foreign Nurse Graduates

April 30 - May 1, 1977
New York City
****

Fundraiser/Program
April 16th 8PM St. Paul's Auditorium
1660 Church Street, San Francisco

For More Information CALL...

EAST BAY......
 Noni Espiritu - 655-8849
 Wevy Aragon - 530-5786
SAN FRANCISCO....
 Michael Manansala - 661-6729
 Wilma Cardona   - 826-8784

SPONSORED BY : NO. CALIFORNIA ORGANIZING COMMITTEE FOR FAIR LICENSURE OF FOREIGN NURSING GRADUATES

LEFT: Leaflet from Northern California Organizing Committee for Fair Licensure of Foreign Nurse Graduates, a national campaign launched by the KDP. Courtesy of Cindy Domingo

BELOW: Officers and board of ILWU Local 37 (the Alaska Cannery Workers Union), elected in 1982 after the murders of Silme Domingo and Gene Viernes. Courtesy of Alaskero Foundation

ang aktibista THEORETICAL BULLETIN OF THE K.D.P.

Vol. II No. 4   November 24, 1975   KDP Nat'l H.Q.

LIFT MARTIAL LAW,
HOLD IMMEDIATE ELECTIONS

INTRODUCTION

The new slogan, "Lift Martial Law - Hold Immediate Elections" has recently been put forward by the National Democratic Front in the Philippines. This slogan sums up the popular democratic sentiments of the vast majority of Filipino people, whose hatred for the Marcos dictatorship increases day by day. Undoubtedly, this slogan will "catch fire" and spread rapidly among the masses, uniting the people's voices in one clear demand and raising the popular pressure on the dictatorship to a new highpoint!

This slogan has also been adopted at the November Conference of the anti-martial law Coalition here in the U.S. This means that the representatives of the Marcos government overseas will also be confronted with the same unified demand that is being raised by the masses in the Philippines.

What does it mean for us that we now have a new slogan to popularize among people in the Filipino community? How will we proceed? What steps shall we take?

Some of our comrades might think that the first thing to do is to simply memorize it. But this would be an empiricist approach and the result would be merely mechanically "parroting" the slogan without having a firm grasp of it. This way neither benefits the mass movement nor the comrades involved.

Rather, the first step is to unfold careful study and discussion of the new slogan among all activists. In this way we can come to firmly understand the slogan and its significance; what the principal contradiction is which is being targeted by the slogan; and what are the strengths and limitations of the slogan. After we have done this, then we are in a position to take the slogan to the masses, explain it and popularize it.

The purpose of the short essay is to assist comrades in the struggle to grasp this new slogan.

WHAT'S THE PURPOSE OF A SLOGAN ANYWAY?

Before moving on, we should clarify a few points about slogans in general.

We have often heard the warning "No Sloganeering! No Rhetoric!" This is wise advice in conducting our day to day political work because it points out the importance of the "mass line", of speaking in the concrete, and in a language the people can understand. However we should be careful not to jump to wrong conclusions and think that slogans have absolutely no use and function within the revolutionary movement.

In fact slogans play a crucial role in providing direction and clarity to very complex mass movements. A slogan for example can serve to sum up the main point in a complex analysis; identify the immediate task at hand; point to the next stage

LEFT: *Ang Aktibista*, 1975; an internal KDP bulletin used to sum up important theoretical lessons and campaigns of the organization. *Ang Katipunan* file photo

BELOW: Memorial for Silme Domingo and Gene Viernes at ILWU Local 37, June 1981. Left to right: Emma Catague, Elaine Ko, Terri Mast, Leni Marin, and Cindy Domingo. Courtesy of Alaskero Foundation

OCT. 1982

TALIBA (News Flash/Commentary)

A Publication of the COALITION AGAINST THE MARCOS DICTATORSHIP
(formerly the Anti-Martial Law Coalition-Philippines, AMLC)

'Why did you let me bring so much baggage?'

The Christian Science Monitor

MARCOS VISIT:
A Political Fiasco

He came, he saw, he came to conquer. But he fell flat on his face. Ferdinand Marcos' grand visit to the U.S. was a multi-million dollar political fiasco. He and his entourage flew home rejected by U.S. public opinion and defeated by the U.S. based opposition.

Marcos came to the U.S. with three goals: to solidify his backing by Ronald Reagan; to reverse his image as a repressive tyrant; and to win support from the Filipino community. The dictator achieved his first goal but failed miserably with the rest.

MARCOS SHOWS TRUE COLORS

LEFT: *Taliba*, a leaflet-form newsletter, distributed by hand to inform the Filipino community of major political developments. This issue was used during the 1982 state visit of the Marcoses. Courtesy of Cindy Domingo

BELOW: March from the International District to the ILWU Local 37 union hall in memory of Silme Domingo and Gene Viernes immediately following their 1981 murders. Courtesy of Alaskero Foundation

Legacy of Equality, Leadership and Organizing (LELO) annual event, July 2011, commemorating the thirtieth anniversary of Silme Domingo's and Gene Viernes's murders and hosting a reunion of KDP activists in Seattle. Courtesy of Jack Storms

"IS THIS WHAT YOU CALL DEMOCRACY?"

JEANETTE GANDIONCO LAZAM

T HE year was 1975. I was involved in planning protest activities surrounding the US bicentennial. A lot of national hype and fanfare swirled around America's big two-hundredth birthday. But for many of us on the Left, the whole thing seemed obscene, so of course we had to try to pull off counterprotests in different cities. The KDP was a participant in these efforts nationwide.

In the midst of this, one of our comrades, Emil de Guzman, who had stayed with the International Hotel struggle through the thick and thin of it all, alerted the KDP regional leadership that the hotel was in the process of being sold to the Four Seas Corporation, a Thailand-based firm, headed up by Supasit Mahaguna, a reputed underworld figure.

A special KDP team was quickly formed to respond to this new threat. I was assigned to chair the team, composed of Emil, Estella Habal, Susan, Sylvia, and David. Emil was already living at the hotel, working with the Tenants Association, and I volunteered to move in as well. We divided the team responsibilities between internal and external. The two of us living in the hotel would concentrate on work with the Tenants Association, while the other four comrades would work on building community support.

The International Hotel was a very important struggle for many reasons. The anti-eviction fight had already gone through several stages since the late 1960s. Twice in the past, owners of the hotel had tried to evict the tenants, condemn the building, and have it razed in order to build parking facilities to meet the encroaching needs of San Francisco's Financial District commuters. Each time, the lawyers of the Tenants Association and supportive pressure

See "Who Is Marshall Law?" for contributor biography.

from the broad, citywide community coalition had successfully blocked the owners. So we geared up for yet another battle in a war that had been going on for years. At the same time, we knew that the bitter showdown with the forces of money and property would have to come sooner or later.

My decision to move into the hotel was both uncomfortable and easy at the same time. For sure I had to stretch out of my comfort zone quite a bit. The rooms at the International Hotel were postage-stamp size, ten-by-fifteen square feet. And although the place had been painted and refurbished through years of voluntary community efforts to try to make it more like a home, it also still remained home to roaches and multicolored rats. The bathrooms and showers were in the hallways, which helped you get to know our neighbors real fast! There was a common kitchen, which also served as a kind of community gathering place, although everyone had illegal hot plates in their rooms too. Of course, there was not a washing machine in sight, and the neighborhood laundromat served an eight-block stretch, making it almost impossible to do laundry no matter what time of day or night.

On the other hand, so much of my political growth had taken place in and around the International Hotel over the years; it was already like home to me. In many ways the hotel, and the struggle it represented, was the community cradle for a whole generation of Filipino American progressives in the Bay Area. Personally, I felt that my roots in that community went back to before I was even born. During the Depression my father had dropped out of Fordham University Law School, left New York, and headed for the fields of California and the canneries of Alaska. Like many of his compadres and the rest of the displaced, he searched for work, trying to make ends meet. Since he had no family yet, he joined the great migratory army, which Carlos Bulosan described so well in his writings, moving from city to city, state to state. My father's travels brought him back time and again to Manilatown, San Francisco, to the community in and around the International Hotel.

Many years later, I found myself at City College of San Francisco, involved in the burgeoning movement of Filipino students. In those days, the ultimate proof of your commitment was getting off campus and into the community. For many of us that meant the International Hotel, which had already become a symbol of the struggle against eviction and for low-cost housing. But for Filipino students it also represented an attempt to preserve what was left of Manilatown and our heritage.

I began my sojourn in Manilatown and the International Hotel working at the United Filipino Association (UFA), whose office was a storefront directly underneath the hotel. I worked with Mr. Joaquin Legaspi, Conchita, Bullet Marasigan, Jovina, John, Ed, John, Raddy, Reverend Tony Ubalde, and

Bullet's husband, Pete. Days were spent assisting the *manongs* (older Filipino men) who lived in the few surviving hotels along Kearny, Jackson, and Montgomery Streets with their Social Security applications or grocery shopping or often just providing some company. There were a million stories those old guys told—some would make your head spin and lots would make you cry. I started at 8:00 a.m. each day. I'd wait by the front door for Mr. Legaspi, and we'd spend the first half hour dusting, sweeping, and putting away paperwork from the previous day.

Mr. Legaspi was already in his seventies, but his memory and brainpower were as good as any twenty-year-old. He was still handsome, and I often thought he must have been quite a looker in his younger days. He spoke fluent Tagalog, Ilonggo, Spanish, and English. Mr. Legaspi had come to America in 1927, the same year as my father. Also like my father, he had come to continue his higher education, but with the Depression he found himself on the streets. He had been a merchant seaman, but more important he was a philosopher, a socialist, and an artist. I enjoyed his paintings and his poetry. Mr. Legaspi and I got along really well.

By 11:00 a.m., the UFA office buzzed with activity. The entire staff was present; the telephone was ringing off the hook and clients lined up for assistance. By 3:00 p.m., the staff work would wind down, but then the activity in the backroom would just be picking up. By the time 5:00 p.m. rolled in, a very interesting and weird mixture of folks who were in and around the Kalayaan collective and newspaper would begin to drift in. Then everything became a lot more serious and political. The Kalayaan folks were not the only reds on the block. A number of other revolutionary Chinese youth groups were moving into other International Hotel storefronts and setting up community programs as well. In many ways, the hotel became a communist stronghold, and there I was sitting in the middle of it, just trying to be relevant!

Of course, I was not merely surrounded by the Left, I was also attracted to it. I drew closer to the Kalayaan, went back to the Philippines for a while, came back after martial law was declared, began working with the National Committee for the Restoration of Civil Liberties in the Philippines, much of whose work was also organized out of the International Hotel. Eventually I joined the KDP, and I resigned and rejoined a number of times over the years. But through it all I found myself in and out of the International Hotel and back and forth to Kearny Street, over and over again. So in that sense, moving into the hotel was like moving home.

We had our work cut out for us this time. The Four Seas would prove to be a more formidable adversary than the former owner, Walter Shorenstein, who was a real-estate magnate in San Francisco with a lot of name recognition. He was also a big shot in the Democratic Party. Consequently, he was an easy target to be pressured, embarrassed, and hounded—tactics the Tenants Association became quite skilled at over the years. It would think nothing of throwing up a picket line in front of Shorenstein's residence in the exclusive Sea Cliff neighborhood, or barging in on a luncheon he was presiding over in the Financial District. Four Seas, on the other hand, was out of our reach in more ways than one. For one thing, it didn't recognize that the International Hotel residents had any rights whatsoever—even the idea of negotiating with the Tenants Association was foreign. In addition, the kingpin, Mahaguna, operated politically in Asia, not San Francisco. So throughout, his demand to the City remained more or less the same: "It's my property, I want the tenants out, now deal with it."

As the eviction threat loomed, we had a million things to attend to. The broadest possible support had to be built; friends and supporters accumulated over the years had to be alerted to the new eviction threat and reassembled to help resist it. The media work had to be stepped up. Elaborate eviction resistance plans had to be put in place, complete with a phone tree linking us to hundreds of people throughout the Bay Area. "People's security" teams, both inside the hotel and out in the street, had to be formed, as well as emergency first-aid teams, media support teams, even rooftop surveillance teams. And, of course, there had to be practice fire drills every day— quite a production, really! (In hindsight, some of it seems laughable, but at the time we were dead serious.)

All the while, the Tenants Association was still negotiating with the mayor, the Housing Authority, the Redevelopment Agency, and the sheriff's department to put a halt to the eviction by working with the tenants to develop a plan to save the hotel. Day in and day out, a small band of tenants—led by the president of the Tenants Association, Wahat Tampao, and its vice president, Emil de Guzman (a KDP activist)—would stump the corridors of City Hall, demanding an audience with the mayor or members of the Board of Supervisors; and then they'd cross the street to demand a meeting with the executive director of the Redevelopment Agency or the Housing Authority.

As the eviction date drew near, the doors of city officials and politicians who had previously found it popular to side with the International Hotel tenants began to close, the welcome mats withdrawn. I remember one last visit to Mayor Moscone. He refused to see us. And as we descended the steps of City Hall, I looked into the eyes of each tenant and I saw, for the first time, the look of despair. I think we all knew that this would be last time we would be walking up the steps of this building. We silently made our way back to the hotel.

Things were not all smooth and easy inside the Tenants Association either. There were divisions and struggles among residents over the best plan of action, how to respond to the twists and turns of the negotiations, where to stand firm and where to compromise, and so on. Tenant meetings were long and tedious and often emotionally charged. Everything was translated into two or three languages as well. When I look back on it now, I can appreciate how relatively inexperienced and immature we were politically. But we had to continually battle an even more primitive position, which amounted to "no compromises, no concessions"; easier said than done when dozens of elderly people's homes hung in the balance.

As the struggle wore on at this pace, I began to wear out. I was exhausted to the point of collapsing. I was working in a sweatshop at the base of Potrero Hill. I managed to get the job through one of the women tenants at the hotel. I had to be at work at 7:00 a.m., usually after an all-night meeting of the Tenants Association and the KDP team. I could barely keep my eyes open at work. Right afterward, I would rush back to the hotel to resume the political work left unattended from the day before. To top it all off, the pay was miserable, barely enough to make ends meet.

There were times I also felt very sad and lonely. Sometimes in the early evening I would visit Tino's barbershop, a longtime institution at the International Hotel. He would have his usual customers, as well as the *manongs* who regularly hung out there. One of them would whip out a mandolin, others would join in, and they'd have a complete *rondalla* band. Tino remembered my father. He would often say to me, "You're Frank's daughter alright, you look just like him." That recognition warmed my heart, but it also brought pain; I still missed my father terribly (he died in 1971). Being around the *manongs* brought back memories of my father I thought I had tucked away for good. I must admit, it was getting to the point that I just wanted to give up, because physically I could no longer keep up with the pace of events. However, before I could throw in the towel, the Tenants Association was placed on red alert.

In the past we had received inside word that the sheriff, police, and fire departments were preparing to evict the tenants. Twice, we had been able to mobilize citywide support, throwing up a massive picket line, five people deep, which surrounded the building, including the entire blocks of Washington, Jackson, Kearny, and Columbus Streets. On both occasions, we had been able to stall the eviction. But this time it looked as though the City law enforcement divisions were determined to move in and carry out the eviction. Word was sent out via our reliable phone tree, and within two hours thousands of people surrounded the hotel.

By three in the afternoon, the demonstrators outside took to chanting and singing songs, loud enough that you could hear their voices clear to Nob Hill. Inside, we began preparations to barricade ourselves by placing furniture and heavy items against the main door, nailing all the windows shut and placing lookout posts on every landing and the rooftop. In the hotel office, Wahat Tampao and other tenants took turns addressing the crowd outside. Wahat dared City Hall and the law enforcement community to "come on down and evict us!" In a loud, booming voice, he took the microphone and delivered an impassioned speech: "I cannot understand how this city, who claims to be progressive and caring of its citizens, can evict fifty-five elderly tenants and the community organizations housed in this hotel? I cannot understand why Mayor Moscone has turned his back on the very people who desperately need his help and support? Is this what you call democracy?"

Wahat was a beautiful man. He was small in stature but a magnificent specimen of a man. He was around seventy-five years old, but you would have never known that by the way he walked and even danced around the hotel. His hair was salt-and-pepper and thick and luscious. His forehead was smooth, as was the rest of his face; if he had wrinkles, they looked like small saltwater cracks etched into his face from his many years in the navy and as a merchant marine. He was a handsome man, full of vigor, with a few rough edges, but also soft, especially when he talked about his family back home.

Wahat was an Igorot from the Philippines, one of the few remaining minority tribes living high in the mountain regions of northern Luzon. Sometimes when I looked at him, I could actually envision him in his native environment. I guess I romanticized Wahat a bit, but years later I could still see him vividly in my mind's eye. Each morning he would leave the hotel around 5:00 a.m. with his fishing pole, bucket, fisherman's outfit, thermos filled with coffee, his lunch pail and head off in the direction of the municipal pier. Wahat never seemed to catch any fish, but the activity kept him occupied during the day.

By nine or ten at night, on that fateful day, the imminent danger of eviction was thought to have subsided; people were encouraged to go home and get some rest but stay on red alert. We all thought that maybe, just maybe, we'd succeeded again in averting an eviction. But Wahat and the rest of the tenants would soon witness the more ruthless and destructive face of capitalist democracy—that in the grand scheme of things, democracy often fails and disappoints the poor. We would all find out soon, around three in the morning to be exact.

I was assigned to guard and protect Wahat from any physical and verbal assaults by the law enforcers. Wahat was all over the building, making sure the tenants were okay, that the people watching over them were okay, and checking the rooftop to get the latest sightings of any police or sheriff movements. By two in the morning, I was dead tired and asked Wahat if I could lie down for a least an hour. He said fine.

No sooner had I placed my head on the pillow than the first general alarm sounded. The rooftop security people sighted a mountain of law enforcement personnel marching down Kearny Street. They came in fire trucks, station wagons, on horses, and on foot. They came with their fire hoses, nightsticks, hooks, and ladders. They came to forcibly evict the tenants.

Hearing the alarm, I jumped from my loft bed, quickly put on my clothes and shoes, and dashed out my door, looking frantically for Wahat. Finding him in the hotel office, I quickly grabbed his arm, pushing and shoving my way through the crowds of tenants and security personnel assigned to tenants, into our assigned room. It was chaos inside the hotel. Outside, the chanting got louder and louder, and the crowd began to sway side to side, looking like a coiled snake ready to strike. Inside the first-floor office, filled with at least ten other tenants and security, we watched as the police asked the demonstrators to move. They shouted back to the officers, "We won't move!" "Long live the International Hotel struggle!" The demonstrators closed ranks. The police, after some hesitation, began to bust through the lines.

Using a time-honored law-enforcement method, the officers lined up in V formation. As they surged forward, the demonstrators were thrown to the side by the wedge of swinging nightsticks. Behind the wedge were police on horses who charged into the crowd, sweeping aside the demonstrators with sheer force. Blood poured from the faces of protesters, many of whom were screaming in pain. Some were trampled underfoot; others were thrown back against the hotel wall, only to be shoved to the side again by charging deputies and police officers.

Inside the hotel, we heard the battering ram at the front door, then the crash, then footsteps of an army of sheriffs charging up the front stairwell. On the roof, fire fighters and cops using the long ladder from the fire truck had landed. Using an effective dragnet method, they rounded up all our security, handcuffing them to each other. We heard the footsteps of the firemen running across the roof, then the first eerie sounds of the third-floor bathrooms and shower fixtures being smashed with sledgehammers. Each time the sledgehammers pounded, the sound echoed throughout the building.

Inside a small room, a dozen of us waited. All we heard were the terrifying cries of tenants being evicted, the repeated sound of the sledgehammers pounding away at one door after another, behind which the tenants had barricaded themselves. Then came the voice of Richard Hongisto, city sheriff, moving closer and closer to our room, demanding evacuation at each door. Wahat turned to me, tears streaming down his face, "I've failed, I've failed everyone!" "No you didn't, Wahat," was my inadequate response. But before I was able to give him any further support, Hongisto was outside our door. In a loud voice he said, "This is Sheriff Hongisto, please unlock you door and come out!" I yelled back, "Okay, we're opening the door and coming out!"

I never had time to unlock the door. I guess with all the yelling and commotion Hongisto didn't hear me. Before I could reach the lock, a sledgehammer ripped through the door, showering us with splinters. Hongisto then yelled, "Stand back, please stand back!" The door to our room lay in a million pieces; the only thing remaining was a piece from the double bolt lock that hung pathetically from its hinges. Leaving the room, Wahat and I walked down the once colorful hallways toward the winding steps that led out the front door of the hotel. Dust was everywhere; wiring from ceiling lamps hung suspended, and porcelain from the bathroom and show fixtures was strewn all over.

I held Wahat's arm tightly as we descended the stairs to the hotel's front door, which also lay in splintered pieces. It was 5:00 a.m. Chinatown, normally quiet at night, had been harshly awakened by the eviction. The streets were filled with people, press, and anyone who wanted to watch the long anticipated event. As soon as Wahat and I collided with the cool San Francisco morning breeze, he fell to the pavement on his knees and cried. I cried with him and for him.

That evening, the national network news by Walter Cronkite covered the "eviction at the International Hotel." It was probably the most significant housing struggle of the decade, where the battle lines were drawn so sharply, the resistance and support so well organized and the eviction itself carried out in such a blatant and dramatic manner. For a brief moment, the democratic veil of bourgeois rule was ripped apart, exposing the clash of class interests underneath. But that morning, as I sat on the sidewalk with more than fifty forlorn and bewildered tenants, it was hard to see the big picture— it just felt like we had lost.

FAST-FORWARD TWENTY-TWO YEARS TO 1997

The Four Seas Corporation had managed to tear down the International Hotel and leave a huge gaping hole the size of a city block. It looked like a war zone, a no-man's land separating Chinatown from the Financial District.

For the next twenty years, that hole in the ground stood as a testimony to the International Hotel struggle and the issue of decent housing for poor people that it had come to symbolize. One year melted into another. The weeds in that lot gave way to trees. But none of the big-business interests, with all their money and power, could figure out how to construct a parking lot or an office building on that site, because although many of the tenants had died over the years, the issue hadn't died at all.

In 1997, plans were finally unveiled for a structure to be built on the old International Hotel site as a result of a broad-based community and City collaboration. Significantly, the plans called for two hundred units of housing, a school, a community museum and, of course, a parking lot. At various announcement ceremonies held at the site, former supporters, tourists, and curiosity seekers would be drawn to the cyclone fence surrounding the hole that was once the International Hotel because of red carnations laced into the fencing. As they came closer they'd notice a name tag next to each flower, with strange-sounding names of unknown people—Wahat Tampao, Joaquin Legaspi, Felix Ayson, Joe Diones, Louisa de la Cruz, Nita Radar, Katherine Knowles, Wing Liu, Fook Ling, So Chung, Suzzie Phong, and on and on and on.

WHY ME?

AMADO DAVID

*Amado David, as a child in Santa Ana, Pampanga, was exposed to
the historically strong political support in that province for the
revolutionary currents in the Philippines, from the Huk movement in
the 1950s to the New People's Army (NPA), founded in 1969. His
political education continued when, as an immigrant to the United
States, he was drafted and served nineteen months in Vietnam, seeing
the horrors of war. In 1974 Amado settled in Los Angeles, where he
joined the KDP chapter, serving on the Chapter Executive Boards of
the Los Angeles and southern California chapters. He then joined the
National Executive Board in Oakland, guiding Philippine support
work nationally. Like many other activists, after the KDP disbanded
Amado found a career in the labor movement, leading to more than
twenty years of organizing with the Service Employees International
Union (SEIU).*

WENT to the Philippines right before May Day 1982, the year after Gene
Viernes and Silme Domingo were assassinated. As part of our militant
response, the Coalition Against the Marcos Dictatorship (CAMD) organized a US trade-union delegation to visit the Philippines to make clear to
Marcos that we would not stop our organizing activities here in the United
States. I had only recently been assigned to the labor sector by the KDP, and
in fact, I was just beginning trade union activities myself. Back then I didn't
really know much about labor. When I was assigned to be part of the delegation, I was excited, because I hadn't been back to the Philippines since leaving as a child. But I was also so scared. Those were very tense times, and I
remember thinking, why me?

Before I went, Geline Avila and Inday Refi briefed me. We were in the middle of the "line" struggle with comrades in the Philippines and there were complicated security issues (not just worrying about Marcos's forces); for instance, how I was supposed to handle discussions of our differences.[1] The main thing I took from their instructions was that I should keep the trade-union hat on and make clear that I was not an official representative regarding the line struggle. They cautioned me to remember that people would be carrying guns! I don't think the warning meant that comrades at the "center" would kill me because I expressed different opinions; instead, Avila and Refi made me aware that there might be adventurist elements, maverick types, who might become overly passionate—*utak pulbura*, or "gunpowder brain," in the period's political lingo. But at the same time, they told me it would be okay to express my views about our work in the United States.

I think we were all very nervous because it had been only a year since Gene had been to the Philippines, and we were all convinced that Marcos's decision to have Gene and Silme killed had something to do with Gene's trip. I was married to Anne at the time, and we were living on Acton Street in Berkeley. We noticed a brown car parked in front of the house for three or four days, with some white guy wearing sunglasses. Anne was freaked out, and so was I. I remember reporting it to Geline; she looked concerned and worried, but the assignment stuck and I was told my trip was a go. Again, I thought, why me? I said nothing and packed my bags.

I was given a long list of security precautions for what to do when I arrived at Manila International Airport, what to do at the hotel, what to do in the countryside, and on and on. But almost as soon as I stepped foot in the airport, a guy wearing a barong shirt came within two feet of my face and took my picture. Right away, I forgot everything I was supposed to do. Luckily, a comrade met me and took me to the Tropicana Hotel. Soon after I arrived at the hotel, comrades from the International Liaison Committee of the Kilusang Mayo Uno (KMU, or May First Movement) visited me. This group included a European from Belgium or Holland, I forget, and a woman *kasama* (comrade) named Clarissa, who turned out to be my guide for most of my stay. Although I was part of the US trade union delegation, I was separated

---

1   The KDP was engaged in differences with its Philippine counterparts about what should constitute the primary work of the KDP, assessment of US-based Filipino communities, and analysis of conditions in the Philippines. For a more detailed description of these differences, see Ka Linda's story, "In the Armed Struggle," and appendix 2.

from the others right away and dealt with differently. I wasn't sure if it was because I was a Filipino, or spoke Tagalog, or was a leading member of the KDP or what—probably for all those reasons.

The next day, I was taken to one of the KMU headquarters. It was abuzz with activity—preparations for the congress, strike support, rallies. I felt right at home and fell into the rhythm of the practical work, working side by side with the other activists. We were producing leaflets and collating reports, picking things up, dropping things off—that type of grunt work. They had an old mimeograph machine. I hadn't used one in years. They also were silk-screening posters, something we used to do in the early years of the KDP, in the 1970s. I could see immediately that we shared the same movement culture. I felt for the first time that we were really the same movement, just working in different countries. It wasn't just that I spoke Tagalog; it was the common training and orientation we shared. It was actually very touching for me.

A lot of informal discussion took place about the line struggle over the next few days while I was helping at HQ. Whenever the question came up about our differences, I always qualified that I was not an official representative, that I was speaking for myself. But the discussions took place anyway. The biggest concern was why the KDP had two lines at all—why we were trying to contribute to a revolution in the United States instead of concentrating solely on the Philippine revolution? Much of the argument came down to repatriation: the KDP should focus its efforts on the Philippine revolution and, once it was victorious, we should all just come back home. I tried my best to explain that the Filipino community was a real part of US society. Even if individuals repatriated, families were rooted in America, and the community as a whole would probably not return to the Philippines even after the revolution. We went around and around on this issue. I tried to explain some the discrimination and economic issues we organized around in the KDP, but I don't think I convinced anyone.

Some good-natured joking had it that the KDP's real problem was that we were just "steak commandos"—we had become too comfortable in the United States and were rationalizing our fear of coming back to the Philippines, where life was too difficult. Comrades would refer to the fact that we all had our own cars—things like that. But there is always a message underlying Filipino humor, and the message here was about guilt, co-optation by American materialism, abandoning the homeland, and becoming American and thus allied with US imperialism.

I tried not to get defensive. I said, "Yeah, we eat steak once in a while, but nobody is really rich, and God, we work hard to be really comfortable. In fact, everyone in the KDP are workers—we do our movement work after we get home from our jobs." The discussion would end in laughter, but the issue wasn't settled.

Really, Maoism was at the core of our developing differences with our Philippine counterparts. The KDP had just begun to break with Maoism as a form of ultra-leftism; we were still conducting study groups ourselves. Even though I was educated about this, I didn't feel confident that I could conduct this theoretical debate without it somehow being reduced to a question of class stand, national loyalties, or "love for the masses." The Maoist approach emphasized the primacy of the subjective factor as the determinant of outcomes. Complex conditions and objective realities can bend to a political line, not the other way around. Applying this view to the Filipino American community, the Philippine movement regarded us as overseas expatriates who formed a rear guard for the frontlines in the homeland. We played a secondary, supportive role, which was mainly to provide material and human and moral support to the struggle. In this thinking, akin to the protracted war strategy, the urban centers had to support and supply the countryside because that was how the revolution would be won. Inch by inch, the countryside would be liberated until, finally, the city would be encircled, ending in revolutionary triumph. If armed struggle was the principal, if not the highest, form of struggle, then those revolutionaries and activists from the cities—or worse, from abroad—ought to be humble.

So I treaded very, very lightly whenever Maoism came up (my gut feeling told me that if I were ever to be endangered, it would be over Maoism). I could see that so much of the Philippine revolutionary movement was symbolically tied up with Mao Tse-tung thought—the name itself had incredible power—which said we must serve the people through simple living and hard struggle. This was the Little Red Book stuff we were all trained in. But for my own good, I decided not to push the point that the Communist Party of the Philippines (CPP) should drop Mao Tse-tung thought, even though that's what we believed in the KDP.

LIFE AND DEATH

After about a week, I hooked back up with the US trade-union delegation. We visited some striking workers. What struck me right away was how fierce the economic struggle was. The striking workers were camped out in shacks in front of the work site in order to deal with strikebreakers—it was really a life and death struggle. We got news of strikers getting literally run over by trucks that were ferrying scabs though their picket lines. This gave me a glimpse of the pressures facing Philippine comrades and why emotions ran so high. In the face of such urgent conditions, the spontaneous acts of heroism and sacrifice of the masses required unyielding support, the kind that only the CPP could provide.

The KMU congress seemed like it had over a thousand people in attendance. It was held at one of the Catholic schools in Manila. There were mainly speeches in a general-assembly format, with delegates speaking directly from the floor. All the Americans in the delegation wore shorts that day. It was a little embarrassing. I heard Filipino comrades snickering in Tagalog, "How are we going to put all these Americans up on stage in shorts? They look like vacationing tourists!" Luckily, I had enough common sense to wear long pants.

Already uncomfortable onstage, I became even more nervous when I wound up sitting next to KMU labor leader Rolando Olalia. I became paranoid: Was he going to talk to me about the line struggle? Or maybe he just wanted to sit with the Americans for a good photo op? Whatever the case, I had to take the opportunity to talk to him.

Frankly, I didn't find Olalia all that friendly or engaging. I tried to talk to him about Gene's and Silme's murders. He remembered Gene's trip but did not seem to put much weight on what had happened. He seemed to minimize it, almost dismissing it. I felt he also thought we were all just steak commandos who couldn't handle the kind of fascist violence that took place in the Philippines all the time. Whatever it was, I couldn't tell what was going on, but it didn't feel right.

Overall, I was impressed at how much space for legal activities the Philippine movement was able to force from Marcos. So much struggle and organizing was out in the open, even given the fascist dictatorship—rallies, pickets, even the KMU congress itself (although it was completely surrounded by police and heavily surveilled). And the economic struggles of the workers were completely politicized. I began to understand better why the AFL-CIO would be so scared of the KMU and view it more as a political organization than a traditional, narrowly defined trade-union federation. The national democratic line flowed through everything—explicit criticism of US imperialism and calls for the overthrow of the Marcos dictatorship. I'm sure there were differing political opinions among the rank and file, but the activist core of the KMU was definitely national democratic in persuasion.

The highpoint of our trip was the huge May Day rally in Manila. I'm sure this is an exaggeration, but it seemed like millions of people were there and that the stage was as big as a football field. I was supposed to speak. I was totally freaked out. I'd never seen a crowd that large in my life. And I'd never dreamed that I'd be speaking to that many people at one time! Besides, you can't imagine how passionate and fiery the Philippine comrades were. All the speakers would bring down the house. While I was waiting to go onstage, the comrades asked me, "Would you speak in Tagalog?" Though I spoke Tagalog, I could never deliver it the way they do. And the kind of Tagalog spoken was so deep, not the casual conversational talk I was used to. Somehow, I managed to get up there and speak. I remember mixing Tagalog and English together and getting myself fired up.

UNDERGROUND

As soon as I came off stage, I was whisked off. At the time, the comrades didn't explain what was happening, but later I was told it was because I was now very exposed to the enemy. Three comrades accompanied me—first we got into a jeepney, then we got off and boarded another one, then into a third one, and finally we ended up in a restaurant somewhere. There they told me I needed to go to the countryside to cool off. I still had some paranoia—I wasn't sure if I had displeased them and was in for big trouble. But I thought, what options do I have here? I couldn't really say, "Oh, no thank you, I don't feel like going today, just drop me off on the next corner." So, even though I wasn't sure what I was getting into, I had to trust them and follow instructions.

They took me north toward Baguio City in the highlands. I didn't meet formally with New People's Army (NPA) officials, but I'm sure I was surrounded by NPA all the time. I was given an exposure tour. I was taken to a lot of different activities in different barrios to get a sense of the grassroots organizing efforts going on—high schools, protest rallies, pickets. Usually, I traveled with a caravan of jeepneys, going from one location to another, giving support. Most of the time, I participated like everyone else; I wasn't introduced to a lot of people—I just sort of tagged along, blending with the crowd. That was the whole point. I was supposed to disappear from sight for a while.

Although I'd been active in the movement in the United States for a long time, this was my first direct contact with the underground in the Philippines. What struck me was that in different areas the comrades' names kept changing. For example, I'd be introduced to someone named Romy; then the same Romy became Pedro in the next town. (I remember thinking, I'm going to be in trouble when I get back home and am asked whom I met with.) Luckily, they let me keep one name for myself; otherwise I would have been really confused. I wasn't called Amado, but Abe. The only other person who kept the same name besides myself was Clarissa, my guide.

After a week or so in the countryside, I was taken back to Manila. I was supposed to do some things with the political prisoners before I left. I remember linking up with Satur Ocampo's brother and scheming a way to get inside prison to visit Satur, the leader of the National Democratic Front. I could tell he'd done this many times before. He made up a story—I think I was supposed to be some distant relative. I was nervous about getting past authorities, but strangely enough, once inside I felt okay. It all seemed normal to me—guns, revolutionaries in jail. That's the way I'd always thought it would be. So I felt safe in a sort of screwed-up way, but that's how I felt.

I spent a whole day inside with the political prisoners. It wasn't at all like prison scenes in the United States, with tight institutional controls. The comrades inside had their own community. People were cooking in clay pots, washing their laundry, studying. It was very relaxed. We sat around a big table and ate and told stories. I tried to explain a little bit about what we were doing in the United States around the political prisoner issue. At the time, the KDP was selling bone necklaces that the prisoners fashioned from the remnants of soup bones, to raise money for their causes.

Satur and I had a long talk just by ourselves. The atmosphere was very informal and relaxed. It's funny—it was like we could be more relaxed because we were already in jail. No one was coming for us. He wanted to know more about the KDP's work, how we were organized and what campaigns we were engaged in. We talked mainly about the Philippine support work. He was also very interested in understanding the KDP's socialist program for the United States and what it meant practically. He listened intently and was sophisticated politically. I didn't get a sense that he was dismissing us as steak commandos, or anything like that. Before I left, I even got a nice picture with him. When I got back to the States, I proudly showed my picture with Satur. But Geline was very upset because Satur was wearing a T-shirt with a very sexist message. They decided they couldn't run it in *Ang Katipunan*.

I sweated a little bit getting out of the Philippines. Any illusions that I had cooled off in the countryside were shattered when I got to the airport and another guy in a barong shirt came up and snapped my picture again! All I could remember were Geline's instructions: "Go straight to the gate and call comrades in Hawaii." Perhaps that was to give Marcos agents the idea that someone was waiting for me to get off this plane and I would be missed if I didn't. So that's what I did. I called Hawaii.

The flight to Hawaii seemed to take forever. I wasn't sure what was waiting for me at the other end. At the time we viewed Hawaii as a Marcos stronghold, so I was afraid something terrible might happen to me upon my arrival. The way Gene and Silme were gunned down in broad daylight was very real in my mind. When I got to Hawaii, Dean was waiting there for me, but I don't think I exhaled until we got away from the airport.

IN THE ARMED STRUGGLE

KA LINDA

Ka Linda, or Kasamang Linda, is a pseudonym for a leading KDP activist who joined the KDP chapter in New York shortly after the organization's founding. She became part of the chapter leadership assigned to lead Philippine support work, which included building the local anti-dictatorship coalition. She was later transferred to Washington, DC, to start the KDP chapter there and bolster efforts to isolate the Marcos dictatorship in congressional and religious circles. She was then transferred again, this time to national headquarters in Oakland, in preparation for her deployment to the Philippines. Ka Linda now lives in the San Francisco Bay Area.

THE BEGINNING

MY early political involvement in the Philippines was with the Kilusang Khi Rho ng Pilipinas (Christian Movement of the Philippines), a nationally organized youth group linked to the Federation of Free Farmers led by Jeremias Montemayor. I got involved in the late 1960s while still in high school, but soon after I began working with the Khi Rho National Secretariat in Manila. Agitating for genuine land reform was our main issue. Father Ed de la Torre, who would become a prominent left leader, was very active in Khi Rho at the time.

Broadly speaking, we were part of what might be termed the Catholic Left. We were on the reform end of the reform versus revolution debate. I had known of the new Communist Party of the Philippines (CPP) and its national democratic movement, and we joined together in some demonstrations during the First Quarter Storm (student protests in January–March 1970 against the Marcos government and the country's economic and political crisis). But mainly, our group worked and organized separately. We were opposed to armed struggle, not so much in principle, but we argued that it was not yet time and the farmers were not ready. Of course, the situation was very fluid, even then. And despite our opposition to armed struggle as a national strategy, Khi Rho was preparing militarily to respond to government repression and was studying the writings of Mao Tse-tung and liberation theology.

When we all felt that the declaration of martial law was imminent, my cousin and I were sent abroad. I left for Europe with the intention of garnering support for Khi Rho from the United Nations and other human rights groups. It was in Europe that the whole political landscape began to change for me. To begin with, there were very few Filipinos doing international solidarity work abroad at the time. I found myself mixing with support groups and official representatives from a number of African and Latin American liberation movements, from Zimbabwe and South Africa to Peru and Argentina. It was from those contacts that I first gained an understanding of the role and importance of armed struggle.

ORGANIZING IN THE UNITED STATES

When I came to the United States, I arrived in New York already sold on the idea of armed struggle. My first contact with the US revolutionary movement was with the Black Panther Party and the Young Lords Party, and I became peripherally involved in some of their support activities. In the beginning, I was not aware that there were Filipino support groups organized in the United States. When I discovered the existence of Support Committee for a Democratic Philippines (SCDP), I introduced myself as having been with Khi Rho back home. Unfortunately, Khi Rho was considered a reformist—or worse, clerico-fascist—group by followers of the national democratic movement, so I was not warmly welcomed at first. My dilemma, of course, was that I had no other way to identify myself, no other credentials. So I began mentioning the National Association of Filipinos in the United States (NAFUS), a group that was more flexible and less doctrinaire.

When Marcos declared martial law in 1972, it forced everyone to talk and cooperate. In fact, the SCDP and NAFUS jointly formed the National Committee for the Restoration of Civil Liberties in the Philippines (NCRCLP). Back in the Philippines by that time, Khi Rho had formally moved to the left and aligned with the national democratic movement. Father Ed de la Torre had reportedly joined the National Democratic Front and had gone under-ground. He wrote to me often about leading members of Khi Rho who had taken up assignments in the national democratic movement or had been recruited into the New People's Army (NPA) and Communist Party of the Philippines in Southern Tagalog, Bicol, the eastern and western Visayas, and Mindanao, all former strongholds of Khi Rho. My regular communication with Father Ed and others in the underground movement began to change US activists' reception of me. I learned later that Father Ed had sent word to leading members of the national democratic movement in New York that I was okay. Finally, they started to treat me nicely and welcome me into their ranks. Shortly after that, I joined the KDP.

In the early years of my political development, the idea of participating in the armed struggle had a certain degree of romance to it, of course. We con-sidered armed struggle as the highest form of the class struggle and the ulti-mate test of commitment to the revolution. So everything was in preparation for that day when we would be asked to join. Back in the Philippines, pro-gression toward participation in the armed struggle was a more structured affair. Leading comrades in the mass struggle who were known to the gov-ernment and its network of spies were routinely sent to the New People's Army.

At its peak, the national democratic movement in the Philippines sent scores of youth and student activists "inside" the liberated and semi-liberated zones every few weeks. But for those of us outside the country, it was not obvious how we would get to the point of ever being assigned to the armed struggle. We often discussed this among ourselves, and it was the source of our feeling frustrated at times, cut off from the "real struggle" back home. A few comrades resolved this by using their personal connections to return home and integrate that way. But for most of us, we continued to talk and stayed put and attended to the international support work in front of us.

For me, this feeling of being somehow disconnected from the struggle back in the Philippines was resolved a few years after I came to the United States. At the time, I was heading up KDP work in Washington, DC, focus-ing on lobbying Congress, exposing the existence of political prisoners under Marcos, opposing US aid to the regime, calling for the closure of US bases in the Philippines, and the like. I was approached by and recruited into the Communist Party (of the Philippines, of course). I can remember thinking, at last! This was the ultimate recognition of one's dedication to the revolu-tion and reward for years of service to the movement. In order to appreciate this, remember that in those days (the mid-1970s) we were absolutely con-vinced that the strategy of "people's war" would be victorious, and it was indisputable that the CPP was leading and directing that struggle on all fronts. Joining the CPP was synonymous with dedicating one's life for the victory of the Philippine national liberation struggle. It was that simple and that clear.

For me, once I joined the party, my work abroad and in the KDP gained new meaning. I felt more confident that our work in the United States was in fact linked to the revolution in the Philippines. I felt that if the party sent me back home to join the armed struggle, fine. If it instructed me to continue support work abroad until victory, that would be fine for me too. Of course, there was also a personal dimension to one's openness to direct participation in armed struggle. I realized that many party members outside the Philippines did not feel the same pull toward armed struggle as I did. In my opinion, the same dynamic operated inside the Philippines; but there, the pressure that sooner or later one would be sent to the countryside had the force of the inevitable.

CARRYING ON THE "LINE" STRUGGLE BY BEING IN THE PHILIPPINES

Years later, when I finally returned home to work with the New People's Army, a lot had changed for me—and that in turn affected my experience, for better or worse. My original romantic views regarding armed struggle had dissipated. Years of organizing and study, in the course of the KDP's work, had broadened my perspective considerably. I still viewed armed struggle as the most important arena for fighting the Marcos fascist dictatorship, but I no longer believed in principle that it was highest form of resistance, always and forever. I had begun to think that victory would lie in the party's capacity for utmost political flexibility in shifting to different forms and arenas of struggle, depending on changes in the international situation and the deepening crisis of the Marcos regime. Of course, this evolution was not mine alone. Many comrades working abroad in international work thought similarly.

Actually, it was these emerging political differences with the "center," more than anything else, that brought me back home. Those of us in the KDP realized we were not in step with the party on a growing number of questions. At the time these were mainly international issues, which began with our differences over the CPP's support for the Pol Pot regime in Cambodia and China's subsequent invasion of Vietnam. This escalated to more general differences over how closely the Philippine revolution should be identified with Maoism.

It was a very difficult period for us because we were so distant from the Philippines, and the fascist repression of the Marcos regime prevented a free and direct exchange of information and views with comrades in the Philippines. The CPP leadership was also beginning to accuse us of terrible things, such as abandoning our international responsibilities and subordinating our Philippine loyalties to the US movement. This was an especially hard charge to bear, since we had all given many years of our lives to building up—from scratch—an international support movement in the United States and Canada.

Personally, I held out hope that our differences with the center stemmed mainly from a communication problem that might be resolved by sending leading comrades back home, not just for a visit but for good—to be reassigned there and stay. From the inception of our work, certainly in the KDP, we held the position that Philippine nationals would and should repatriate back to the Philippines based on the shifting needs of the revolution. But in fact, over the years only a few of us went back. Without a doubt, life in the United States was more secure and comfortable, but I believe that people stayed mainly because the demands of our international work were so great and relatively few of us abroad had the necessary experience to direct that work.

As our relations with the center began to deteriorate, we needed to prove ourselves—to prove that we were willing and able to repatriate people. I volunteered to personify that commitment, even though I'm sure I wasn't the best comrade to take that assignment—especially when it came to joining the New People's Army! Unfortunately, by the time I got back to the Philippines, the center had solidified its opinion about us and we were under suspicion as to our true motives and agenda for returning. So I believe that my assignment to the NPA was more to test me than to actually place me.

When I met with the then-chairman of the party and the general secretary, they were very distant and formal. Even though they relaxed during our breaks, they remained guarded. We danced around our political differences and did not address them head on in these meetings. It's important to remember that our political differences at the time were not black and white; the tumultuous events that framed the collapse of the Marcos regime and the EDSA "People Power" revolution were still four years into the future.[1] I basically deferred to the unquestionable leadership of the CPP and to the overall correctness of the strategy of people's war.

However, I had a number of concerns regarding whether the party was too mechanical and dogmatic in its political thinking and analysis, whether

---

1   EDSA stands for Epifanio de los Santos Avenue, the street where people came for the People Power revolution.

it was paying enough attention to the political and theoretical training of the rank and file, and whether it was open to establishing closer ties and interactions with revolutionary movements other than China. At the same time, I was keenly aware that I had been out of the country for many years and had a lot to learn.

Some of the more spontaneous comrades in the party's national staff were curious and fascinated as to how I could have been away so long and still want to come back and participate in the hardships of the struggle at home. One told me that he had asked the same question "of our Dutch comrades." I was insulted, responding, "Yes, of course, you can ask that of the Dutch but not me—I'm a Filipino!" Nonetheless, it was a sincere question. But I'm afraid I've jumped ahead of my story.

I had not lived in the Philippines for twelve years. My first time back had been two years before, for a short official trip of meetings and hurried visits to the countryside and the underground in the urban areas. That short trip left me in awe of the level of organization and intricate nature of the underground network that extended as far as the Manila International Airport, where party operatives reportedly were able to watch me safely arrive and depart with the documents I was carrying intact. But this time, my repatriation did not have the official treatment of the first trip. I felt I was on my own.

As the plane landed, fear suddenly came over me: what if I didn't make it through the scrutiny of the military at the airport? I prepared by rolling up large amounts of dollar bills for bribes and by asking the elderly *balikbayan* (Filipino returning home) sitting next to me to claim me as his relative. Corruption and arbitrariness at the airport were well known; every traveler to the Philippines went through one or more hurdles. When my turn came, the immigration officer in military uniform, who was about to check my name against the government's blacklist, got distracted by a mother and her little girl, who was wailing from the intense heat, and he ordered me to quickly move on.

Once safely inside the country, I was moved from one house to another every few days—as was customary for security purposes—before being settled with a family in Quezon City where official contacts began. The family had children who were involved in the movement and were considered trustworthy. I was given my own room, separate from the main house. The house was next door to a NAWASA (the water company) station. There was a shrill, loud siren-like sound twenty-four hours a day—except for around three in the morning when, for some reason, it stopped for fifteen minutes. The sudden silence would wake me up and almost drive me crazy!

I remember there was a day-and-a-half-long debriefing with representatives from the CPP center. It consisted mostly of questions about where certain KDP activists involved in international support work stood individually on the various issues that divided us from our Philippine comrades. After this, there was no contact from the CPP leadership for a few weeks, which at times worried me. But I understood that a period of isolation was standard practice in preparation to meet with the center itself or to go inside the New People's Army zones. Eventually, meetings were arranged. By the second meeting, I was told I would be given a three-month "exposure" assignment to an NPA region. I wasn't sure why I was being given a temporary assignment and not a permanent one. I suspected it was in order to observe me and see if I could adjust to the demands of the armed struggle. I chose to keep my concerns to myself and just accept the assignment as it was given.

BEING AN NPA SOLDIER

I was assigned to the regional NPA command in Cagayan Valley north of Manila, which was responsible for several provinces, including Isabela, Kalinga-Apayao, Cagayan, and others. The long bus ride to Cagayan occurred mostly at night, and different escorts took turns at assigned stops, a procedure familiar to me. When we got to Tuguegarao at breakfast time, I walked into a large living room where a noisy mix of people from Manila had gathered. They were on an exposure tour to various locations. Among them was a physician, a religious leader, a health activist, an NPA soldier who was returning after being away for months to give birth in the city, and another pregnant comrade visiting her NPA husband. I was introduced as an activist from Cebu. I remember thinking what a clever cover, but I wished I had known about it before. I immediately picked up on what I believed was party instruction to conceal my US background and came up with some believable information about the work in Cebu.

We hiked for hours through dry, spiky rice paddies, crossed shallow waterways, and climbed what to me was an endless and harrowingly steep hill of very dry grass and thorny bushes. In the burning sun, my traditional getup of parachute pants and matching dark T-shirt got soaked in sweat and stuck to my skin. Many times I had to be pulled up by one of the local activists and pushed from behind by the pregnant comrade.

We reached the NPA command post set on the side of the province's mountain range and perfectly hidden by tall, overgrown bamboo trees. The regional leaders, who knew I was from the United States, thought I had been sent to beef up their staff, so they welcomed me with open arms. They immediately assigned me to their educational department, despite my feeble protests of "Are you sure? I don't think the center wants this." Days later a letter arrived saying that I should not be given major responsibilities; instead, I should be given only an exposure tour similar to the treatment for international visitors and media correspondents who had been streaming into the countryside to observe life in a "liberated zone" and record encounters between the NPA and Marcos's military. That instruction would have been easier to carry out had I not been a Filipino with a depth of knowledge and skills acquired through years of organizing. Not surprisingly, the press of the work was so great that I was soon integrated and given large responsibilities.

At the time, the NPA was very developed and strong, especially in the northwestern part of Luzon. The people's army had reached company strength to the point that "red fighters" were engaged in full-time military work covering an entire region. Full-time NPA soldiers were called to ambush and/or engage Marcos's troops in major encounters in order to take control of more territory. The full-time NPA also protected propaganda and organizing teams sent in to consolidate new territories; they patrolled the vicinity where provincial or regional CPP meetings were taking place; and they escorted party officials and their visitors. The Cagayan regional unit of the NPA had as many women as men. Most had started out as youth activists from local provinces and had become adept at military work. The NPA's structure, system of training, and basic rules were not unlike any other military organization. But because it was a people's army, it was flanked by a network of activists who did a wide variety of organizing, propaganda, and intelligence work for support and consolidation of the political base.

Whether or not one was a red fighter, everyone tied to the armed struggle was given basic military training. I was taught how to shoot, clean, and maintain not just my weapon but also other kinds of weapons—this was in case I had to quickly use another weapon in a battle situation or inherited a different kind of weapon from a fallen comrade. Of course, I was not very important militarily, so I was given only a handgun that didn't shoot very well; it was too old. Comrades told me it was *paltik* (a homemade gun) and originally from Mindanao. The last time it had been shot, comrades explained, it had only sprayed gunpowder stains on the target. I couldn't help thinking mine was not the most important life to spare. I played along with the joke that I'd probably have to kill the enemy by hitting him over the head with the gun!

I was not unfamiliar with the countryside. As a young student activist before I left the Philippines, I had spent time organizing farmers and peasant youth in rural areas. But everywhere I turned, I was struck by the profound difference that people's war and the NPA had brought to this work. Of course, peasants have been organizing themselves for generations, and intellectuals from the cities have been helping in that effort for a long time as well. Life is so hard and conditions so stark for the Filipino rural population that even a little bit of organizing and grassroots empowerment goes a long way. The relative benefits of mutual cooperation and assistance can often be seen quickly. The problem has always been that such organizing efforts are vulnerable to being crushed by the reactionary landlord forces or to petering out for lack of resources. But in the NPA zones, these organizing efforts were able to stabilize and accumulate because they were protected by the armed might of the people's army. These local organizing efforts were also seen as part of a nationwide strategy to seize power in the whole country. This made all the difference in the world.

On a more personal level, many activists preferred the relatively secure environment of the countryside compared with organizing among unarmed urban workers or students in the city, where activists were in fact more vulnerable without the nearby presence of the NPA. Most political prisoners were picked up from urban areas, termed "white areas" to distinguish them from "red zones." I too felt safer in the NPA areas, except for a few close calls, which comrades attributed to poor intelligence work or a possible tip-off by government spies. Because I was given a crash course in Ilocano, and my superiors were pleased with my quick command of the language, I joined a Sandatahang Yunit Pampropaganda (SYP, or Armed Propaganda Unit) to open up an area in a neighboring barrio about a day's hike from district headquarters.

Our team consisted of a veteran propaganda activist, two local youth activists, and myself. We were to meet another SYP team early the next morning to go into the assigned barrio. When it became dark, our NPA escort led us to a large empty house in the middle of a rice field about half a mile away from the barrio and then left, assuring us that the area had been sufficiently cleared of danger. After weeks of sleeping outdoors with only a makeshift roof as shelter from the morning cold (I had learned to assemble a parachute-like head covering by tying the fabric corners with nylon strings to tree trunks, branches, or big rocks), I looked forward to the luxury of sleeping inside four walls with a sheet-metal roof. Because I was distracted, I didn't follow the explanation about what had happened to the residents of this fine house. I was more interested in the privilege I was being accorded: as the only female, I had the pick of the only bedroom. Two other comrades each took a corner of the rest of the house, and the last one, who carried one of the "long" weapons, posted himself outside on the veranda. It was standard practice that weapons carried by a group were a combination of "longs" and "shorts," usually M16s and revolvers, in order to mount an adequate defense. I indulged in more luxury by helping myself to the straw mat rolled up against the wall of the bedroom, laying it over the clean, wide wooden floor.

At about three in the morning, shortly before the first rooster crow, the comrade outside burst in, his Armalite at the ready, kicking the wall of my bedroom and calling, "Sunog! Sunog!" (There's a fire!), code for enemy approaching. I only remembered grabbing my gun and putting on my rubber thong slippers. In a flash, I saw myself jump off the second-story bamboo platform that was part of the outdoor kitchen on the back of the house, my slippers flying in the air and my fingers firmly gripping the trigger of my *paltik*. The shots fired behind me and a couple of big explosions on the rice field just yards ahead only made me pick up speed. I no longer felt my bare feet touch the ground. It's funny how days later, after going through the usual group summation of the incident, I found myself participating in the light banter that characteristically followed the aftermath of difficult situations. We joked about them, even the ones with tragic elements. I enjoyed one comrade's exaggerated version of my "amazing leap" to safety.

Naturally, the strength of the people's organizations varied from one locality to another depending on several factors, not least the military strength of the NPA in the area. Nonetheless, there were organized cooperatives and collectivized childcare. The organizing teams provided basic-level educational and medical services, especially to the children. However, all of this was still at a very primitive level. People's lives in the red zones were not qualitatively improved in any material sense. Often what few material benefits were gained from organizing were given back to the NPA or used to feed and house more activists. Empowerment came more from being part of the larger struggle for power. The focus was on the future. Organizers would sometimes cut pictures from Manila magazines to show people electric ranges or dental clinics, to give some idea of the modern living that would come after the victory of the revolution. All in all, the scope and momentum of the people's war in the Philippines during that period was quite impressive.

Although I was with the NPA for a relatively short time, it was hard to treat me as a guest for long. I was given a number of important and difficult tasks. For example, I was asked to translate the military manual of Mindanao, the area that had the most advanced military experience at the time, and other documents from Cebuano into Tagalog, which later would be translated into Ilocano. As part of my SYP work, I conducted advance or intelligence work in areas not yet held militarily by the NPA. It was in this context that I was probably given my most difficult assignment.

Municipal elections were being held, and the position of the movement was to boycott them. For years Marcos had been trying to legitimize his dictatorship by staging such "elections." In the barrios where the NPA was strong, organizing the boycott was easier, but in Tuguegarao, the capital city of Cagayan, it was more difficult. Cagayan was the province of Defense Secretary Juan Ponce Enrile, and Marcos's military power was very strong there. The NPA goal in Tuguegarao was to foil the rigged elections by snatching as many ballot boxes as possible before government troops could pick them up. My job was to "convince" a local priest to cooperate by hiding several ballot boxes and turning them over to the NPA. The priest had to take the first risk, and although he was considered a sympathizer, he had never been tested.

NEW TASKS AND DIFFICULT DECISIONS

I came down from the mountains carrying my best skirt and blouse that I saved for my return to Manila, whenever that might be. It took a number of days—lots of walking and crossing small creeks and a river, sometimes on a water buffalo. Along the way I rested at the huts of sympathetic families who knew of my general destination but no details. Coincidentally, word had reached our district hideout that a spy for the Philippine Constabulary in Cagayan had been spotted in Tuguegarao. The NPA had implicated him in several recent actions; comrades in the district even suspected that he had something to do with one of my close calls. NPA armed partisans in the towns had been alerted. Later on I found out that this spy had been on the same bus that I took to Tuguegarao. This situation had created a dilemma for the town partisans: were they going to hit him then, while he was on the bus? Whatever political considerations the comrades weighed, I was glad they chose not to kill him that day on the bus!

A new identity had been arranged for me in case I was stopped and interrogated. A comrade who helped with preparations for my last stop in coming down from the hills told me that military spies were usually able to pick out movement leaders easily, especially those of petit-bourgeois origins from Manila, because of their youthful looks, their fairer and smoother skin, and the women's pierced ears. I was not worried, as I looked much older, having lost a lot of weight, and my skin had grown dark brown and was full of blotches, bites, scars, and cuts, some still bleeding. I thought all I need to do was untie my hair to cover my ears. The last few miles I was completely on my own. I changed to my city clothes, put on vinyl *tsinelas* (slippers), and hid my weapon underneath wrapped tomatoes and fresh vegetables inside an orange plastic market basket. I boarded the bus on the outskirts of the city that would take me right to the church, past the provincial headquarters of the Philippine Constabulary–Integrated National Police. Along the route I noticed disguised NPA comrades posted to watch and see if I got through successfully.

The priest was a bit nervous but very cordial and polite. We conducted our "business" over a nice lunch, as though we were acquaintances having a social visit. Another comrade, who was functioning legally aboveground, joined us. The conditions discouraged a free-flowing political discussion. Thus my task was more to coerce the priest than to persuade him. In many different ways he asked the same question: Did I speak for the NPA and did he have a choice? And in many different ways I answered: Yes, I was sent by the NPA, and no, he had no choice. In the end, he agreed to cooperate and later was successful in carrying out his part of the agreement. This meant that I had accomplished my assignment well.

This type of "political work" was completely new to me. For the many years I had worked in the United States, a very developed bourgeois democracy, persuasion was the only method used for moving a "middle force" like this priest into action. But I learned that the fine line between persuasion and coercion often got blurred in the course of the armed struggle. In the midst of these circumstances, the urgency, logic, and consequences were so clear. The class struggle was so polarized—to the point of ongoing armed conflict between the people's forces and the enemy. There was very little middle ground left. Yet forces like this priest, who was a good man, tried to occupy that slim middle ground as long as possible. And at the appropriate time they had to be pressed to take risks and cast their lot with the revolution. Although expediency framed my assignment as "gently" intimidating this priest into cooperation, I must admit I was into it and, given the situation, thought it was the necessary thing to do.

At the same time, some things I experienced caused me distress. For example, there had been an enemy raid on one of our army units and a comrade was hit in the stomach and hurt very, very badly. I was also in that ambush and helped the wounded comrade to escape. The suspected informer was an older peasant woman whose husband had been killed recently by the NPA for his collaboration with enemy troops. The decision was made to kill the woman too. I questioned the decision—actually, not so much the decision itself, but the process of arriving at it. I felt that the investigation was conducted rapidly and not very thoroughly, that the decision to eliminate her seemed to have been reached too easily, without exhausting other available options.

I realized that this was a difficult and complex issue. On one hand, the safety of the red zones was tied to making reactionary elements understand that they could not collude with enemy forces without facing the direst consequences. On the other hand, the sociological aspects of the situation were painfully evident and worrisome to me. The people in the position to make such life-and-death decisions were very young ex-students, relatively inexperienced in the practice of both life and revolution. It was difficult to compare their life experience with that of this suspected poor peasant widow who had spent her whole life in the fields, regardless of what her reactionary political views might be. To me, there might have been other ways to watch and control the woman, to neutralize her or eventually maybe even win her over. But the decision had been made, and I was informed that the "appropriate steps and process had been followed"—everything seemed so airtight and simple. Still, death is such a chilling and permanent sentence, and I couldn't help wondering if the life of this suspected woman collaborator might have seemed less expendable to the young commissars if she'd had social characteristics similar to their own mothers or aunties.

To be fair to the comrades responsible for this and similar decisions, many of these types of problems stemmed from the demands and hardships of the armed struggle itself. Imagine that while you're attempting to improve the country and people's lives, the enemy is tirelessly attempting to annihilate you, with far superior military resources. When you're in the middle of an armed struggle of this scale, there often seems to be little time for careful reflection, self-doubt, or consultation—all the things that seem to come naturally with long experience and wisdom. I guess it was this overall wisdom that I sensed was lacking at times, and it was unsettling to me. I felt I lacked it myself as well, and so although I voiced my reservations, I didn't pursue them because I wasn't sure how to reframe the issue. Also, in all honesty, I realized I was on thin ice—all my opinions and actions were being reported back to the center. If I became perceived as disruptive, my own personal safety could be in jeopardy.

As I was pulled deeper into the day-to-day work of the NPA, I felt like I impressed a number of comrades; there was even some competition as to where I would get assigned permanently. But there were moments that I would lie awake in the evenings wondering what I was really doing. After all, I did have an agenda for returning home to engage the center in discussions about the party's general line and strategy. While I could stay in this NPA region and learn a lot and be of some use, I was very removed from the center and its deliberations. More and more, I had the feeling that this was the center's way of dealing with me and that those discussions would not be available to me. Things were not adding up; the give and take and frank exchange of ideas with the center that we'd hoped for would not be forthcoming. I felt like I had failed my purpose for coming home, and it was overwhelming.

LEAVING THE NPA

I'm not exactly sure at which point I decided to leave the NPA, and no one incident precipitated the decision. However, once I decided, I was mindful that I needed to be extremely careful in planning my exit. I began to detach and minimize my opinions and bide my time. Fortunately, I could use the excuse that I had originally been sent for just an exposure tour (a fact that had long since faded in the minds of most comrades) and that I needed to return to the city to continue my discussions with the center and to ascertain if I would be reassigned back to Cagayan. I knew in my heart that I would not be returning, but I didn't feel like I could discuss this frankly, and it saddened me very much.

When I got back to Manila I felt stranded, with no support and no safety. I decided to return to the United States. I sent word to the center that my decision was due to "personal vacillation," which I felt was the only explanation they would be ready to accept and understand.

Four years later, the dramatic spontaneity of the People Power revolution brought the collapse of the Marcos dictatorship. This did not come about from the NPA's marching down from the mountains. And as the arenas of struggle shifted rapidly, the CPP was moved to the sidelines (though certainly not off the stage) and its leading role was no longer taken for granted. For me, this was a time to reflect on my earlier failed mission, the germ of an idea, the seedling of a discussion that I had attempted to bring back to the center. It was not a time to gloat but to sigh deeply. Despite our best efforts, I don't think we could have made a difference even if we had sent a steady stream of people back to the Philippines. The party's people's war strategy was too tightly embraced, its immediate accomplishments too tangible, its logic too airtight to be affected from outside the country by a group as small as the KDP.

PART THREE

THE TEST OF FIRE

O N June 1, 1981, two well-known leaders of the KDP were gunned down, gangland style, in the office of Seattle's Local 37 of the International Longshoremen's and Warehousemen's Union (ILWU; the Alaska Cannery Workers Union). The victims, Silme Domingo and Gene Viernes, were spearheading a reform effort to democratize their union and free its leadership from the gangster elements who used the dispatch system to chisel off money from Filipino workers and profit from gambling operations in the canneries. At the time of the murders, the activists had begun to make some headway. It appeared that the killings were a direct result of the reform efforts that were threatening the union's corruption. However, prior to their deaths, both Domingo and Viernes were actively gathering US labor support for the workers' movement in the Philippines against the Marcos dictatorship. It turned out that the Marcos regime, in addition to deploying its own intelligence agents to the United States, had links to gangster elements in Seattle via Marcos's fellow Ilocano, Tony Baruso, then-president of ILWU Local 37. Money from a secret Marcos slush fund bankrolled Baruso's murder conspiracy to stop both the union reforms and efforts to link the ILWU with the Philippine workers' movement.

These murders deeply touched everyone in the KDP. The organization initiated the Committee for Justice for Domingo and Viernes, which struggled for over ten years to bring the perpetrators to justice and to expose the role of Philippine and US intelligence in the assassinations. This effort spanned three criminal trials, resulting in convictions of the hit men and Baruso.

Moreover, the Domingo and Viernes families successfully brought a US federal civil suit against the Marcos family and other defendants, resulting in a $23.3 million judgment.

THE FALL

ALONZO GLENN SUSON

*Alonzo Glenn Suson, a longtime union and community organizer, was
born in Banga, Cotobato, and raised in Cebu City. He came to the
United States in 1970 at the age of sixteen. Alonzo became politically
aware when his father, Mario Parama Suson, was imprisoned by the
Marcos regime in 1972 for five years, as part of its disenfranchisement
of political opponents in the Liberal Party headed by Sergio Osmena
of Cebu. In 1974, Alonzo joined the KDP in Seattle and became a trade
unionist as a member of Local 37 of the International Longshoremen's
and Warehousemen's Union (ILWU; the Alaska Cannery Workers
Union). As a rank-and-file reformist, Alonzo was elected shop steward
by his coworkers in a cannery in Uganik, Alaska. He was then elected
to the executive board of ILWU Local 37. After the Silme Domingo and
Gene Viernes murders, he became one of the first organizers in
nonunion canneries in Cordova and the Kenai Peninsula. From 1991
to 2004, he was organizing coordinator for the Service Employees
International Union, leading campaigns to unionize health care,
public service, and janitorial services workers. He then spent six years,
until 2010, as country program director for the Solidarity Center
affiliated with the AFL-CIO in Cambodia. Since 2010, Alonzo has
been country program director for the Bangladesh Solidarity Center.*

Y OU got to breathe in through your nose and mouth, and suck it in.
Then exhale it from your mouth, man," said Gene, proceeding to dem-
onstrate. He was picking up his arms and legs, stepping up his pace. We
were jogging around Seward Park. Gene and I were practicing our run.

189

"Yeah, you got to do *this*," he explained, showing me the breathing-in and breathing-out motion. "Yep, my gym coach made sure we knew how to do the breathing; it's the only way you can gain some energy."

I was gasping along and following his instructions. "My legs are getting tired, Gene," I said.

"Just pick it up and breathe in and exhale out, until your diaphragm is empty," he insisted.

Gene Viernes, the jock, the wrestler, was giving me some pointers on jogging. On that spring morning, I could see our breath coming out of our mouths. We talked intermittently about our political work and the fine art of jogging. I used to teasingly call Gene the cowboy from Wapato, while he would throw back the tease that I was the cowboy from Cebu.

I first met Gene in his trailer house by some old railway tracks somewhere in Wapato, Washington. It was the fall of 1974. Dale Borgeson, David Della, Chris Mensalvas Jr., and I had to do a slide presentation about conditions in the Philippines under the Marcos dictatorship at the Yakima Valley Community College. Gene was unable to come to our presentation, so we decided to visit him. Gene was Chris's and David's friend and coworker at Ward's Cove Packing Company in Ketchikan, Alaska. Filipino old-timers up at the canneries considered him "one of those young buffaloes." They'd affectionately call young radical Filipino cannery workers *panggulo*, or "troublemakers."

Gene was a mestizo (his father was Filipino, his mother Caucasian) who easily bantered with Chris and David in pidgin Filipino. Since we were in our recruiting mode, Dale got into the rap about the KDP. In between beers and a joint from "his bush," as Gene called it, we really got into the philosophy of revolution and change. It must have made an impact with this brother; he promised to join us in Seattle for a meeting. And he was serious, because he showed up at our first KDP Seattle regional meeting in the spring of 1975.

Looking at him jogging by my side in his baggy blue sweatpants and cut-off sweatshirt over a white thermal, I thought, "Gene certainly has made his journey with the KDP." He had moved to Seattle to join the KDP labor team headed by Silme Domingo. Working in an office storefront on Eighth and King Streets in the heart of the International District (ID), Gene developed a good relationship with other activists in the ID. He volunteered at the community garden project, digging ditches and laying railroad ties to build terraces. He wrote articles about the history of Filipino labor struggles for the *International Examiner*. And he did his midnight fire watch at the Milwaukee

Hotel, a community project to provide low-income housing for people in the ID.[1] He was well liked by everyone.

Now, running beside me, here was Gene getting ready to make his first visit to the Philippines and trying to get in tip-top shape. Gene had that obsessive drive to push himself both physically and intellectually. The summer before, Gene had gone to work with the KDP National Secretariat in Oakland and to the University of California to study labor history.

As my feet began to ache, I thought, "Ha! What did I get myself into?" I had been babysitting Silme and Terri Mast's kids, Ligaya and Kalayaan Domingo, part of my chapter childcare responsibility. I was flustered when Kalayaan started to cry and bawl. I didn't have a clue about changing diapers. I called the house, and fortunately Gene, my housemate, was home. Being the middle child in a large family, he had taken care of his younger brothers and sisters and had experience changing diapers. So he came over and showed me how to do it. Kalayaan was the first child whose diaper I ever changed. Later that night, Jacque Agtuca and her friend Andrea stopped by. We got into a discussion about the importance of being in shape. As the discussion progressed, we challenged each other to a race around Seward Park: Andrea and Jacque against Gene and me.

Panting, sweat dripping from my face, I thought maybe it had been foolish to challenge Andrea and Jacque. They claimed to have been jogging a lot lately. "Are we going to make it around the whole park?" I asked Gene.

"Don't worry," Gene said, picking up his pace. "Look, just follow me!" All of a sudden as he sped up, he dove forward, crashed, and sprawled out on the ground. Feeling embarrassed because other joggers were coming by, he quickly picked himself up, dusted off his sweatpants, and started to jog again.

"Are you all right, Gene?" I called to him.

He looked back at me and gave me an embarrassed smile: "That doggone pebble made me lose my footing."

"Man, I'm getting tired let's just walk it for a while, okay?"

I sighed with relief when he said, "That's okay with me."

---

1   The *International Examiner* began publishing in 1974 as the newspaper of the Alaska Cannery Workers Association (ACWA); it became the main voice for the struggle to preserve the Asian community character of the ID from the encroachments of big-business development. It continues to publish to this day, more than forty years later. The Milwaukee Hotel was a community-initiated renovation project to help preserve the character of the community and encourage people to remain in the ID and fight for their rights.

As we walked up to his beat-up Datsun, Gene limping slightly, we laughed that even "jocks" fall once in a while. Somehow the race was forgotten and no one brought it up—especially me—since I think we might have lost to "the girls."

Breathing in and breathing out, closing my eyes while on the StairMaster, the sounds of Tower of Power pumping through my headphones, memories of Gene and his "fall" linger, bringing tears and laughter to my soul.

THE TERRIBLE BLOW

DALE BORGESON

I T's hard to believe it has been more than three decades since the assassination of Silme Domingo and Gene Viernes on June 1, 1981. I still feel
the raw emotions of shock, anger, and sadness that struck us all following
the murders. We did not have time or leisure to properly mourn our comrades because we were thrust into the maelstrom of activities against our
enemies.

I remember as if it were yesterday, sitting in the waiting room at Harborview Hospital and getting the word that Silme had succumbed to his wounds,
a day after Gene's death at the union hall. This was a terrible blow to all of
us. I was particularly shocked because I was not prepared to accept that there
was anything that Silme would succumb to. It was not in his nature to yield,
as I knew from my eight years of working with him. Indeed, even when mortally wounded, Silme had summoned the strength to give decisive clues iden-
tifying the murderers. His final actions led to a successful peeling of the
onion to reveal who was behind the conspiracy. Because of Silme's courage,
we would go on not only to win criminal convictions of the hit men but also
to trace the murder conspiracy back to its source in the Marcos regime.

At the end of 1978, I had left Seattle to join the KDP National Executive
Board in Oakland and to build the KDP's work in non-Filipino communities. My five years in Seattle had been an exhilarating period of personal and
political growth. My comrades threw a farewell party as I prepared to leave,
and Silme gave me a treasured political book collection.

From Oakland, I maintained ties with the Seattle chapter. Gene passed
through the Bay Area in April 1981 on his way to the Philippines to meet with

---

See "The Accident" for contributor biography.

progressive labor leaders. He came for a briefing by Geline Avila, who had just returned from a secret visit to the Philippines. US intelligence responded to Gene's trip by falsely reporting to Philippine intelligence that he was carrying big sums of money to fund the armed resistance. Not surprisingly, Marcos agents followed Gene everywhere he went in the Philippines. From the Philippines, Gene went directly to the International Longshoremen's and Warehousemen's Union (ILWU) international convention in Hawaii. There, our Local 37 reform caucus succeeded in getting the ILWU to pass a resolution to send an investigating team to the Philippines to assess labor conditions and rights under martial law. Pro-Marcos forces within the union fiercely opposed this resolution. ILWU Local 142 in Hawaii was the largest local affiliate in the entire ILWU and had thousands of Filipino members, so it played a central role in the community's politics. When it became clear that our resolution would pass, Local 37 president Tony Baruso ostentatiously offered to lead the team and have it hosted by Marcos in Malacañang Palace. But this desperate attempt to turn the investigating team into a Marcos propaganda coup did not win sympathy at the conference.

A few weeks later, Silme and Gene came to the Bay Area for a debriefing with Geline and to attend a national conference on racism at the University of California, Berkeley. On the night of their arrival in Oakland, Silme made his famous baked salmon for comrades at headquarters. He and Gene were exhilarated by the ILWU convention, both looking forward to the next stage—challenging Baruso for presidency of Local 37, the Alaska Cannery Workers Union.

But none of us were prepared for what happened next.

I was at the KDP national headquarters the evening of June 1, 1981, when the call came from Seattle that there had been a shooting at the union hall and that Silme and Gene had been shot. Bruce Occena of the National Executive Board; Silme's sister, Cindy Domingo; and I left immediately and arrived in Seattle later that night to learn that Gene had died and Silme was mortally wounded.

Silme died the next day at Harborview. We retired to the new KDP chapter headquarters on Beacon Hill and began analyzing what was behind the murders. We had to decide how to respond politically. We soon launched the Committee for Justice for Domingo and Viernes (CJDV), with Elaine Ko as head. Working with our attorney, Mike Withey, we began to peel back the layers of the murder conspiracy. Before dying, Silme had identified the hit men as Pompeyo "Ben" Guloy Jr. and Jimmy Ramil, members of the Tulisan (Bandits), a gang that ran the gambling at the canneries under leader Tony Dictado. A week later, Seattle police found the murder weapon—it was registered to Local 37 president Tony Baruso, who claimed the weapon had been stolen though he had never reported the theft.

Over the next three years, the three members of the Tulisan gang, including the head of the gang, Tony Dictado, were all convicted of first-degree murder and given sentences of life without parole. Baruso was called to testify in their trials and pleaded the Fifth Amendment to all questions. His protection from the Philippine and US intelligence agencies under Marcos and then–US president Ronald Reagan effectively kept him from being charged for several years. The FBI even floated the idea with Seattle prosecutors to give Baruso immunity in trade for testifying against gang leader Tony Dictado. Finally, after Corazon Aquino ousted Marcos in 1986 and Reagan left office in 1989, Baruso was charged with murder conspiracy by Seattle prosecutor Norm Maleng. He was quickly convicted and sentenced to life without parole like the hit men. The crowning achievement of the CJDV campaign for justice was the 1989 finding of the federal court in Seattle that the Marcoses were responsible for the murder conspiracy; the court levied damages of first $15 million and, in 1990, another $8.3 million, for a total award of $23.3 million.

We were not able to prove US involvement in Silme's and Gene's murders, but most of us remain convinced that they could not have happened without at least tacit approval by US intelligence. Most of us also believe that the CJDV's work remains incomplete until we peel away the last layer hiding the heart of the conspiracy.

In Quezon City on National Heroes Day, on November 30, 2011, I beamed with pride as Silme and Gene were the first Filipino Americans honored by having their names added to the Wall of Remembrance at the Bantayog ng mga Bayani (Monument to the Heroes [in the struggle against Marcos]). This is a fitting tribute to these leaders of the KDP, whose active solidarity with the repressed Philippine labor movement led to their martyrdom.

INITIATION FROM HELL

EMILY VAN BRONKHORST

*Emily Van Bronkhorst became an associate member of the KDP in
1979 after working with KDP activists at the Northwest Labor and
Employment Law Office (LELO) between 1975 and 1980. LELO was
cofounded by the Alaska Cannery Workers Association (ACWA), the
United Farm Workers of Washington, and the United Construction
Workers Association. (LELO later changed its name to Legacy of
Equality, Leadership and Organizing, to reflect its changing mission.)
Emily organized international solidarity and support for workers'
rights while in the KDP. In 1980, she became part of the reform
movement within Local 37 of the International Longshoremen's and
Warehousemen's Union (ILWU; the Alaska Cannery Workers Union),
and in the aftermath of Silme Domingo's and Gene Viernes's
assassinations she became a member of the team that ran the local.
She continued to work with the Rank and File Committee until 1987,
organizing cannery and freezer workers in Kenai, Alaska. After short
stints as an organizer with the United Food and Commercial Workers
and United Steelworkers, Emily was hired by SEIU Healthcare
1199NW in 1991. In 1998, she was elected as the union's executive vice
president, a position she continues to hold.*

I WAS twenty-one when I first met Gene and Silme in 1975 at the Northwest Labor and Employment Law Office (LELO), where I worked as part
of a community-involvement job tied to one of my university courses. In
the beginning, before I got to know them better, it seemed like they'd just
arrive at the office, have big arguments with the lawyers, and just as quickly
storm out.

My job at LELO was to do all the grunt work in data collection for the discrimination lawsuits against the canneries. To anyone who bothered looking, it was obvious that there existed a pattern of unequal treatment and racial discrimination against Filipino crews in the Alaska salmon industry—but we had to prove it in court.

Counting, counting, recounting, counting again! (Remember, this was before the age of computer spreadsheets, and it was all done using pencil and paper.) I was looking at different documents from about twenty-five canneries—things like employment applications, job listings, pay scales—as well as recording individual depositions. We were trying to show that whites systematically got placed in better-paying jobs, such as beach gang, tenders, machinists, machinist helpers, carpenters, and the like; in contrast, the Filipinos were stuck in the fish house, doing the line work—the butcher and slimmer jobs. The white women workers also tended to get the cushy jobs in the egg house, sorting roe under the careful inspection of the Japanese technicians. We also documented the differences between whites and nonwhites in terms of living conditions, sleeping quarters, and even the food served.

The canneries had gotten away with murder for so long, blatantly operating as though the civil rights movement had never taken place. My job was to document their crimes, quantify differentials, determine standard deviations, and so on. And just when I thought I was finished, the lawyers would always find something new to measure or a different way to examine the same data. Then I'd be off—recounting all over again.

Besides doing stats, I talked to a lot of folks informally and participated in some of the depositions that the Filipino workers gave for the lawsuits over the course of four years. I wound up knowing a whole lot of details about the industry without having any direct experience working in Alaska. For example, if you asked me about working a job like beach gang, I could tell you that you were likely to encounter a white male college student whose uncle or high school football coach had some links to the salmon industry and got him the job. I knew the responsibilities carried by each job in the Alaska canneries, the demographics of who held them, how they lived, even what they ate. I could tell you that "white girls" probably would be clueless about what they were getting into; they usually just wanted to make some quick summer money and probably had tight connections with a company owner or supervisor, or maybe their best friend's father was a bookkeeper for one of the companies, or maybe they had a cousin who worked in one of the companies' Seattle headquarters.

The Filipinos, on the other hand, had layers and layers of ties to the canneries that went back two, sometimes three, generations. People's grandfathers were still regulars at certain canneries, while their uncles were foremen at others. They went to the canneries where their older brothers had gone before them, or the younger guys would try to get their whole *barkada* (clique) up to the same cannery. They'd compete to see who could "score a white girl" by the end of the season. In short, "going to Alaska" was a center-piece of Seattle's Filipino community. The canneries couldn't function without them, yet Filipinos were getting the short end of the stick. Meanwhile, the corrupt union officers had been colluding with the industry for years and did nothing to address the blatant inequality. Silme, his brother Nemesio, Gene, and others took the initiative, went outside the union, and filed a Title VII class-action lawsuit charging racial discrimination against the New England Fish Company in 1972. Then they filed a second suit against Ward's Cove Packing Company in 1973, and that's how our paths crossed and my life changed.

I remember how, at first, Silme used to scare me. He'd barge into the LELO office, filling up all the space with his presence. He'd have on his long black coat, his "big shoes" that shook the floor when he walked; he had long hair, thick and wild. I guess you'd say he had "big hair." Luckily, he didn't wear a "big hat" too, like some of the other Filipino guys. They used to really scare me because they looked like pimps! Anyway, Silme would blow in, cause a lot of commotion, and then say, "I got to go," and be gone.

Gene wasn't as scary to me, mainly because we had more in common. The first day I met him I remember he was wearing his varsity letterman jacket. We were both into sports, so we could shoot the breeze without having to always have heavy political interactions. I also hooked up more with Terri Mast, Silme's spouse; the fact that she was a woman really helped.

I guess I was on the KDP's periphery for a while. KDP members would sell me *Ang Katipunan* on a regular basis, and then they'd talk to me about different articles to make sure I really understood the issues. I enjoyed it. I remember attending the Filipino Far West Convention in Seattle and learning a lot. I helped do fund-raisers for the Rank and File Committee of Local 37 of the International Longshoremen's and Warehousemen's Union (ILWU; the Alaska Cannery Workers Union) during the springs and summers of 1977 and 1978.

In those days, LELO attracted all kinds of political people as staff members, volunteers, and interns. When I look back on it, this was a strange period. In the early 1970s, there were lot of competing revolutionary parties and groups, all trying to out-organize each other. I think I was on everyone's periphery—it seemed like everybody wanted to recruit me, pulling me into all kinds of private meetings and talks. It was sort of hilarious. But the KDP had a special attraction for me. Its members were very serious about their work. I could see this from their role in the lawsuits and their day-to-day organizing activities. Also, these guys didn't feel isolated to me; they had roots in the community, an incredible network of connections. Their political work and their lives seem more connected than in some of the other left groups. Gene constantly sprinkled KDP terminology during our lawsuit work until it also became part of LELO's working language. I can also remember when Terri got pregnant with Ligaya and decided to start a family while being up to her neck in union work. I was impressed and freaked out at the same time. We were both close in age, and having kids was the very last thing on my mind.

I think my first entry into closer, more direct involvement with Local 37 was when the Rank and File Committee successfully recalled the secretary-treasurer, Ponce Torres. I remember Gene asking me to be an impartial observer, to watch the vote counting. I wasn't shocked at the request, but I was hesitant. I said, "I'm not even a union member!" Gene responded, "It's okay, you're a white girl, no one will question it. Besides, you're going to be with us anyway." So I agreed and spent a hot afternoon counting ballots at the union hall.

Today, the Alaska Cannery Workers Union is so dramatically different. I've seen young white women participating in union activities comfortably. They have no idea how difficult it was in the early years of the reform effort. Being a white girl back then was a double-edged sword. It was true that being white and a woman gave us a bit of an advantage to maneuver, to say and do things that the Filipino guys couldn't. For example, I remember Terri and I used to sell *Ang Katipunan* openly in union meetings and during the dispatch. On the other hand, a lot of times it was really uncomfortable. To begin with, mainly Filipinos got dispatched out of the hiring hall because the white crews would be bused in, skirted through dispatch as a group, and then put back on the buses. I imagine it was sort of like being in the South during Jim Crow. Partially because of this, dispatch could sometimes be a nightmare. You'd have to walk through a narrow hallway to get to the dispatch hall. There were only a handful of women, two or three of us white. Meanwhile, the walls were lined with Filipino men of every description, from sixteen to eighty years old, many of them leering at you, especially the gangster types, half of them muttering stuff in Ilocano or some other Philippine dialect as you passed by. It was like walking a gauntlet.

I don't remember exactly when I was finally recruited to do direct Local 37 organizing work, but by then it seemed natural. I'd been a KDP associate member (a semi-active member) for what seemed like a long time already.

I do recall the meeting in which I was asked to make a commitment, quit my job, and work in Alaska. The meeting was with Gene and Terri. By then I was working as a painter at Seattle University, making some decent money. We met at a coffeehouse across the street from the university, owned by a friend of Gene's from high school. Gene was showing off that day. He liked to flirt, and there he was with two women. As I said, though, it was all anti-climactic. I'd been working in the Local 37 collective with these guys since the fall of 1979, so I already knew what the meeting was about. I showed up, let them talk, and then agreed to the assignment.

We discussed the plans to get me dispatched to the cannery in Egegik. I was instructed to "get dressed up" and meet Silme at the union hiring hall. So I put on a real dress, heels, nylons, and makeup—the whole thing! I felt ridiculous, but I showed up. Silme ushered me into Rudy the dispatcher's office, saying, "This is Emily, she wants to go to Alaska." Rudy looked me up and down, but he was respectful of Silme so nothing got out of hand. The whole thing was strange nonetheless. We sat and chatted for forty-five minutes. I'm sure no one had ever been "interviewed" like that just to go up to some fish house in Alaska. Whatever, I got through it. What followed was pretty hellish. I had to show up and wait through every single dispatch. I had to spend weeks at the union hall! Finally, I got dispatched up to Egegik.

Egegik itself, however, was the real initiation from hell. It was a cannery that had been closed for ten years and had deteriorated a lot, even by the low industry standards. It had only reopened a couple of years earlier, and Terri and Lynn Domingo (one of Silme's sisters) had gone up the year before and begun organizing. Still, it was incredibly hard.

Instead of working in the egg house with the other white women, I was in the fish house, on the patching line, with twelve other women, mainly Fili-pinas. A slow day was twelve hours long, 7:00 a.m. to 7:00 p.m. We frequently worked until nine at night. For a week or so when the season peaked, we'd work round the clock, twenty to twenty-four hours. Organizing under such harsh conditions was difficult. The issues got pretty basic. For example, there were not enough gloves, or the food at the 9:00 p.m. "mug up" was pitiful, and so on. In fact, by the end of the season we were eating leftover hot dogs and peanut butter sandwiches. People could hardly find time or energy to do much more than complain to each other, much less try to hold a meeting. I was officially part of the grievance committee and was supposed to help out the steward, who was a *manong*, a nice old guy, but a friend of the foreman and not very effective. So I wound up doing most of the negotiating with management over our grievances.

My main assignment for the Rank and File Committee that season was to gather support for the reform slate in the upcoming union elections. In particular, I was supposed to organize the white women. Much of the organizing work was just about building ties, finding out who was signed up with the union and who wasn't, what different people's attitudes were about the union, and the like. Of course, when you live with your coworkers, a lot of issues aren't directly tied to the job. So I became something like a dorm mom. I was all of twenty-five then and already viewed as an old woman; most of the others were eighteen or nineteen years old.

The women's bunkhouse was a mess! To begin with, it was like a barracks, with bunk beds stacked in tiny cubicles. There was a lock on the front door, but the back door was always kept ajar, so it was easy to "keep in touch with the boys." I spent a good part of my time counseling women how not to turn their boredom into unwanted pregnancy. I distributed a lot of birth control. Also, some very strange and scary things happened. For example, my bunkmate was a white hooker from Seattle who ran around with the Tulisan (Bandits) gang. One night she went out into the tundra with some of the gangster boys; she came back with a bullet in her foot and some wild story that she had accidentally shot herself in the course of their "activities" out there. One reason we had targeted Egegik was because it was a gangster stronghold, but this kind of incident was a little too close for comfort!

Fortunately for me, a couple of women who had been recruited into the Rank and File Committee the year before were back again at Egegik. Terri and Lynn had worked with these women the year prior. They were open to helping me pass out the *Alaskero News* (our reform newsletter; *Alaskero* was the nickname for Alaska cannery workers), and a few workers even liked *Ang Katipunan*. So I wasn't all by myself in this effort. But no matter how you cut it, the work was hard, rough, and slowgoing.

Alaska, especially where a lot of the canneries were located, was still very much frontier territory. Maintaining communication with the Rank and File Committee back in Seattle was difficult. In those days, not only were we without cell phones and e-mail, but we didn't even have access to regular telephones—talk about being isolated. Once a week I'd get a letter from Gene; it would be filled with instructions, questions, and warnings. Have you distributed the *Alaskero News*? Have you signed people up in the union? Have you done this yet? Have you done that? Get close to the white women. Do not get close to the Filipino men. On and on like that! Gene was really hard on us.

I knew that Silme would travel to Diamond E (in Egegik) that summer, but I didn't know when exactly. Finally, toward the end of the season, I remember walking along the boardwalk and hearing behind me, "Ugh, pssst!" Then I heard it again and turned around. There they were, a hundred yards behind me, both Gene and Silme! I was ecstatic. It was wonderful to see their friendly faces in the middle of that wasteland.

A key part of the Local 37 reform slate's program and platform was to put some muscle behind contract enforcement. So the purpose of Gene and Silme's visit was to sign up members and address any grievances that the on-site committee had been unable to resolve. At the union meetings, you could already see the impact of the Rank and File Committee's work: the number of folks attending; the fact that they were not all Filipinos but included many, if not all, of the white workers; the fact that people felt safe enough to speak up about their grievances with the union as well as with the company. Signing up with the union was, for all practical purposes, an issue for the white workers because most had bypassed the union dispatch in getting up to Alaska. So at union meetings, we had to take the resistance head on, responding to comments like "Why do I have to join the union?" and "My uncle got me this job, I'm not joining no Filipino union." Silme was great at handling these types of situations. In fact, one of the best pictures we have of him was taken while he led a union meeting that year, during the reform campaign.

In all, that was my initiation to Alaska. Egegik was the first of several canneries I would be sent to over the years. Although the organizing work became more familiar to me, it never got easier. And when I got back to Seattle after that first season in the canneries, my union work was far from over because we were still in the middle of campaigning for the upcoming union elections.

Two years earlier, the Rank and File Committee had sponsored its first slate of candidates against the entrenched old guard. It put Silme up for dispatcher and Gene for secretary-treasurer. We lost the bid that time, but we did manage to get rank-and-file folks onto the executive board. And since then, the Rank and File Committee had succeeded in getting Secretary-Treasurer Ponce Torres recalled. Soon after, Torres's replacement, Abella, died in office. Silme was then appointed to the position on an interim basis, with the support of not only the executive board but also Tony Baruso.

So now we were running to keep Silme in as secretary-treasurer and to elect Gene as dispatcher. We had not run anyone for president against Baruso. Tactically, the Rank and File Committee felt we didn't have enough experience yet to actually run the union. Also, we didn't think we could beat Baruso yet. Even though the Rank and File Committee was gaining strength among the stewards and membership, Baruso was still entrenched, with a lot of loyal supporters among foremen and cannery bosses, not to mention the thugs.

Since Egegik had one of the shortest seasons, we were back in Seattle by July 20 and had a lot of time left to campaign. We tried to find out exactly when the different canneries were flying workers back from Alaska. Usually, a supporter had to call us from Anchorage with the flight number right before getting on the plane. Then we'd gather up our *Alaskero News* (we actually called it propaganda back then), put on our Rank and File Committee T-shirts, and head out to the airport, usually in the middle of the night or at dawn. When the workers got off the plane, there we'd be to greet them and find out how their season went. People loved it! We encouraged supporters to go to the union hall, get their union book stamped—*and vote* (there were no mailed ballots). Often, we needed to help them with transportation and a place to stay for a day or two, especially those from California or western Washington.

The Rank and File Committee office, which we shared with the Alaska Cannery Workers Association (ACWA), was where we'd hang out, talk about how the season went, figure out ways to encourage supporters to vote, and just *chismis* (gossip). And it all paid off. In 1980, the Rank and File Committee swept the election. Both Gene and Silme were elected, and the reform forces had a majority on the executive board!

The counting of ballots was exciting and scary. I think Baruso knew we were going to win, so he didn't even show up at the hall. But Rudy, the dispatcher, was there, along with his boys, the Tulisan gangsters. We had David Della on the Election Committee to make sure nothing "mysterious" happened during the voting. Even this was not enough protection, so we asked Bob Gibbs, one of the union's lawyers, to be there as an observer during the final count. The atmosphere was tense, and since the union hall was large we had to keep our eye on every single movement anyone made.

When the results were finally read aloud, we were so excited. I turned to see the look on Rudy's face. He was pissed but managed to say, "Congratulations, you guys worked hard." The Tulisan boys left the hall without incident. Then we could relax and enjoy our victory; the Rank and File Committee went off and had a great party that night.

A short time later, we held an inauguration ceremony for the new officers. It was at the downtown Seattle Hilton. I remember we had to argue with Gene about wearing a suit. He said he didn't want to look like an ice-cream cone. Still, we made him get a suit, although he did look silly because his pants were too long. But it was a good time for all of us. The union reform movement had grown steadily stronger through endless hours of difficult organizing and years of persistence. Our victories were all won fair and square. We now had Baruso surrounded and felt confident, which only served to make the shock and anger deeper when Silme and Gene were gunned down in the union hall nine months after the election.

My life would become tied up with the Alaska Cannery Workers Union and the KDP in a way I'd never imagined. For the next seven years, we were all thrown into a whirl of constant political work to clean up and strengthen the union and keep the gains we had made, while grieving the loss of our friends and comrades, Gene and Silme.

A DAY I'LL LIVE WITH FOR
THE REST OF MY LIFE

DAVID DELLA

'LL see you at 4:20 this afternoon," said Silme over the telephone, adding with his usual sarcasm, "Don't vacillate!" I hung up the phone and continued my work sorting banknotes for delivery around the International Division of Seafirst Bank. This was my full-time job that paid for my living expenses and supported my political work that I did in the evenings and on weekends. Silme, Gene, and I were to meet later to discuss the planning for this year's Philippine National Day celebration (or PND, as we called it in the KDP).[1] We were going to meet in the Local 37 union offices downtown and then go to nearby Chinatown to grab a bite at the Four Seas restaurant; then Gene and I would head home to our collective living arrangement, which doubled as the Seattle KDP headquarters. The HQ was a pretty decent ranch-style house on Nineteenth and College Streets on Beacon Hill, better known

---

See "A Little Red Book" for contributor biography.

1   The KDP helped initiate and organize broad Filipino community fiestas throughout the United States on June 12 each year. The date commemorated the Katipunan's 1898 revolutionary struggle against Spain and the later US colonization of the Philippines. The intent of Philippine National Day celebrations was to change the cultural habits of many US Filipino communities, especially on the West Coast, where Filipino "independence" was celebrated on the same day as the US independence, July 4, usually with beauty-queen contests and expensive formal dinner dances. PNDs were more informal, family-oriented affairs, usually held during the daytime and in a park with food, entertainment, and of course, political speeches and exhibits.

as "the Asian ghetto." The house had enough space for chapter meetings and file cabinets and desks, as well as living quarters for three people. It was great not having to travel to chapter meetings; we could just wake up and saunter into the meeting on time.

I worked right up to 4:25 p.m. before I realized that I was going to be late for the meeting and have to listen to Silme ribbing me all night for being late and "vacillating" on taking up the tasks needed to coordinate the PND this year. I worked downtown, less than a mile from the union hall; I could've walked, but I had my car that day. I was driving south on Second Avenue when I saw fire trucks suddenly pull up to the front of the union hall on the Main Street side and an ambulance leave with its siren blaring and lights flashing. Oh my god, was the hall was on fire?

As I drove past the intersection of Second and Main, I could see to my left that Silme's Monte Carlo was parked in its usual space. I cautiously proceeded around the corner and parked just beyond the union hall. I got out and walked toward the building. A fire truck and a police cruiser were parked outside, and I saw a firefighter in full gear walking out of the door. I ran up and asked if there was a fire. He said there was no fire, but a shooting had occurred, and one man was dead inside and another had just been taken to Harborview Hospital. He showed me the small pool of blood on the sidewalk in front of the door, as if to prove that there had in fact been a shooting.

I asked about Silme, and he said he didn't know who Silme was but there was still a dead man inside the union offices. I told him I was on the executive board of the union and that I wanted to go inside. The firefighter asked if I could help identify the dead man. Hesitantly, I said I would try and asked again about Silme; again he told me he didn't know who Silme was. The firefighter went in and brought out a policeman to escort me in and identify whoever was dead. As I walked behind the police officer, I was shaking. Inside, I saw another union member, Mac Callueng. He told me it was Gene who was dead on the floor. I walked into the office area and saw the most hideous sight I've ever seen. Gene was lying on the floor with blood spattered up from his torso over his face. His eyes were still open, with an empty, dead look. Oh, God! I thought I was going to throw up. I turned and bolted out of hall, wanting to get outside, hoping none of this was really happening.

My adrenaline took over. I asked the police officer, who had followed me out, where Silme was. He interrupted, asking if I could positively identify the dead man. I said, "Yes, he is my friend and roommate." I told the cop I'd been supposed to come here and meet with Gene and Silme. He told me that the other man was also pretty badly shot and was being taken to Harborview.

I asked for a ride to the hospital. He said I could get one as soon as they finished up a few things.

I ran across the street to Swannie's, the sports bar, and got to a telephone to call someone. I had to tell someone that something awful had just happened. I was numb, I couldn't cry, scream—nothing. I called Leni's house (Leni Marin had been transferred from the KDP's New York chapter leadership). Leni answered the phone, and I just gushed out the words that there had been a shooting at the union hall, that Gene was dead, that Silme was at the hospital. Leni started crying loudly while simultaneously trying to tell her partner, Mila de Guzman, what had happened. Before long, I heard them both crying. I was still too numb to cry. Leni told me to go to the hospital to check on Silme and that she would call Bruce Occena and others in San Francisco.

I hung up and went back across the street to the union hall. By this time, the coroner's vehicle had arrived and they were preparing to take Gene's body away. I helped with wrapping Gene's body, and then I asked again if I could get a lift to the hospital. The police had a cruiser take me up to Harborview. In the police car, the officers said they thought this was a gangland slaying done by a group called the Tulisan (Bandits), a gang tied to gambling in Chinatown and well known to the police. I heard the words, but nothing was registering. I was numb, scared, my heart was beating out of my chest. I thought to myself, "Man, I know more about the Tulisan gang than you guys ever will," but I said nothing. Nothing mattered at that moment except getting to the hospital to see if Silme was still alive.

A MEMORY OF STRONG WOMEN

LILLIAN GALEDO

Lillian Galedo was recruited into the KDP in 1978 in the San Francisco Bay Area. She was assigned to the organization's National Commission on Immigrant Rights, focusing initially on discrimination against Filipino professionals but quickly expanding in scope to immigration reform. Lillian built coalitions to fight against repressive immigration bills, starting in the early 1980s with what became the Simpson-Mazzoli Act. She is a founding and active member of the National Network for Immigrant and Refugee Rights, the Dignity Campaign for Real Immigration Reform, and Alameda County United in Defense of Immigrant Rights. Lillian has also been involved for over sixteen years in the campaign to win equal status and benefits for Filipino World War II veterans. She recently retired from her position as executive director of Filipino Advocates for Justice (formerly Filipinos for Affirmative Action), where she has worked since 1980, focusing on the needs of the growing Filipino community in the San Francisco Bay Area.

J UNE 1, 1981. Shocking and incredible news is traveling through the KDP grapevine. I can't believe it. This couldn't really have happened. Gene and Silme have been shot! I can't seem to get any hard facts, but they might be dead! They're so young, for Christ's sake. They've barely figured out what they want to do with their lives. Oh, poor Cindy. And what about Terri and her two kids? The parents must be devastated too. How do you handle your kids dying before you do? Especially in the hands of some assassins!

Somebody give me a straight answer. Isn't there something I should be doing? But what? I must be patient. We can't simply fall apart. I know a "summation" will be forthcoming. Wait for the meeting at the national KDP headquarters. Word has it that Geline Avila and Bruce Occena will be flying to Seattle. We'll get all the details soon when we're all together. That'll be good. I need to be with everyone else.

I'll always remember that picture on the front page of *Ang Katipunan*: Terri Mast, Cindy Domingo, Elaine Ko, Leni Marin. I know how much each of them loved Gene and Silme. How could they have found the strength, the courage, to get up at the memorial, in front of everyone, to sing "The Internationale" through their tight throats and tears, so soon after the murders?[1] How could they be so strong?

One thing the KDP had, for sure, were strong women. You couldn't help but admire them. You couldn't help but want to be like them. While I was looking for words to cope with my feelings, trying to handle just myself, I felt like women leaders of the KDP were in motion, getting on top of the situation, addressing the public, helping the rest of us channel our fears into action. Wasn't there something more I could be doing?

On top of everything else, the Far West Convention was supposed to be held in Seattle that year during the Labor Day weekend, just two and a half months later.[2] How in the world were they going to pull that off?

---

1   "The Internationale," the unofficial anthem of the socialist and workers' movement, has been translated into almost every language on earth, including Tagalog. It was commonly sung at KDP functions, usually first in Tagalog and then repeated in English. One week after the murders of Silme Domingo and Gene Viernes, a large memorial service was held at the ILWU Local 37 union hall, where they had been gunned down. To close the memorial, several women in the KDP led everyone in singing "The Internationale," which was introduced as "Silme's favorite song." The atmosphere was quite tense, because some of the people suspected of involvement in the murders were present. The strength of the memorial service gave a clear signal to the murderers that the KDP would not be cowed and would turn grief into action. Much of this was captured in a photo of the women who led the singing. The photo, which is included in this book, was carried on the front pages of *Ang Katipunan* and a number of other left-wing newspapers throughout the country.

2   The Far West Convention (FWC) was an educational event held annually from 1971 until 1982 to update the Filipino community on burning issues in the United States and the Philippines. A local community coalition would plan and host the event, which would draw participants from all over the West

Cathi Tactaquin, from the KDP National Executive Board, came by my office. She was somber, not much kidding around. She explained that she would be leaving for Seattle in a week or so to take over organizing the Far West Convention. She would have only two months to do it. "Our comrades in Seattle need the help desperately," she said. The murder trial would begin soon and community support had to be organized, not to mention dealing with emotional fallout from the murders. It was impossible for the Seattle chapter to do the convention by themselves.

"Would you help? Would you leave your job for two months to go to Seattle?" she asked. I didn't say anything at first. Could I just abandon my job on the spot like that? But maybe this would be my chance to do something. She took my silence as hesitation. She became more intense and said, trying not to get too heavy about it, "Well Lillian, I think it's time you saw yourself as playing more of a leadership role."

Holy shit! How did she know that I had been waiting for someone to ask? I really wanted to do something more. I was about to cry. I felt badly that she even had to ask me, that she had to exert a little extra effort in making the request. Why couldn't I have been as strong as all the other women around me who seemed to take leadership, want leadership, step forward without asking, sometimes even competing for leadership? What the hell was wrong with me? I sat silent for a moment then heard myself saying out loud, "Okay, I could be ready to leave in a couple of weeks."

Coast—three hundred to five hundred people. FWCs were held in Seattle, Stockton, Sacramento, San Diego, Los Angeles, San Francisco, and Berkeley.

THE TEST OF FIRE

HOW DO I SIZE A BULLETPROOF VEST?

KRIS MELROE

Kris Melroe began working with the Seattle KDP chapter in 1975, when she moved to the city at the request of the American Indian Movement (AIM) to organize around Leonard Peltier's case and the Native American struggle at Pine Ridge, North Dakota. This led to working with the KDP on fishing rights and an alternative July 4 centennial citywide event. Kris helped draw the parallels between Marcos and the Pine Ridge tribal chair, Dick Wilson, and was important in organizing Native support for the anti-Marcos movement. As a result of her ties with the KDP, Kris was one of the first activists to be a core member of the Committee for Justice for Domingo and Viernes (CJDV), doing fund-raising, newsletter coordinating, and community outreach. She continued her CJDV work as a member of the Line of March (LOM) and was with the committee when it won the 1989 court victory. Kris returned to school in the late 1980s and earned a master's degree in education. In her semi-retirement, she is training and coaching elementary-school teachers at three Hawaiian homestead schools on Oahu.

I HAD waited a long time for June to come—it was my first day of vacation in over two years. I had been codirector of the Lesbian Resource Center in Seattle, which meant long hours and hard political battles, but now I was finally planning to enjoy a relaxing summer before looking for a new job.

All that evaporated the instant that Gene Viernes and Silme Domingo were killed. The first day of my vacation turned into an eight-year political commitment that taught me a great deal about myself and the human spirit.

On the actual evening of June 1, I had a scheduled meeting with Silme and movement lawyer Jim Douglas at the union hall of Local 37 of the International Longshoremen's and Warehousemen's Union (ILWU; the Alaska Cannery Workers Union). The three of us were leading a study circle on Marxism-Leninism. I had been anxious all day because I was planning to deliver my first criticism to Silme regarding sexism. Around 6:00 p.m., John Foz called to say that the meeting had been canceled, that something had come up. At first he wouldn't say, but then he told me Gene and Silme had been shot. *Stunned* doesn't begin to explain my feelings. The whole thing sounded too crazy, and I waited for someone to call and say it was all a big mistake. This couldn't be true . . . but it was.

The next few days were a mixture of sadness, disbelief, and anger. Apparently, the world went on—people in Seattle still went to work, the buses ran—but I sat on the cold marble floor outside the hospital's family room. I remember snatches of things: going in to see Silme after one of the operations . . . seeing Terri Mast and Silme's mom crying . . . listening to Christopher Hershey write a song that we would all sing over and over again for years to come. Eventually, the hospital saga ended. They couldn't save Silme, and he died.

Just hours after Silme died, someone (I don't exactly remember who) asked me to purchase three bulletproof vests. I was told that my friends were going back to the union offices tomorrow! I couldn't believe it. I couldn't believe it. I was scared that I would lose even more friends. I had been through rough times doing solidarity work with Indians on Pine Ridge, and I didn't want to be there again. Revolutionary politics were so much easier to discuss in the abstract on a Sunday morning . . . and so hard to be a part of when the real world of class struggle crashed in all around you.

Since I had never bought a bulletproof vest, I didn't have a clue as to where to go. One of the police detectives gave me a lead about a store that sold police gear. The store was between First Avenue and the waterfront, in a sleazy part of town, down from the federal building. The basement store had rows of guns, uniforms, and boots, and there was a redneck-type man behind the counter. He eyed me suspiciously, and I was more worried that he would arrest me rather than help me. After I explained who had given me the address and why I was there, he turned out to actually be helpful. He asked me sizes, and since I had no idea how to size the vests, I found myself describing how tall and wide my comrades were (of course avoiding the term *comrades*). As Terri Mast, Silme's widow, later discovered, bulletproof vests were not sized for full-breasted women. The salesman informed me about the types, costs, and warrantees, listing which kinds of bullets a vest would protect against and which it wouldn't. We exchanged this factual data as if I were purchasing a new washing machine. With that information in hand, all that was left was to hunt down the money.

The next task was to figure out who would give me large sums of money first thing in the morning when banks opened. Remember, this was before the days of ATMs on every street corner. Needless to say, the list I came up with was rather short. That night I went to visit an engineer who was active in the movement and a rich woman lawyer whose house I'd cleaned every week a few years before. They gave the money, but it was hard. Asking for money was something I did but never grew to enjoy, no matter how many years I did it.

The next morning, back I went downtown, cash in hand, and purchased the three vests. I remember I felt pleased with my accomplishment as I drove to the union office. When I entered, the sight of the blood and the police markings on the floor outlining just where Gene and Silme had been shot brought me back to reality. Terri and David Della were not there, but John Foz was waiting behind the counter. I handed him the vests and tried to transmit the information the man at the store had given me, but I couldn't finish. I remember I just hugged him, told him to stay safe, and left crying.

That was my first fund-raising endeavor for the Committee for Justice for Domingo and Viernes (CJDV). That's where the fund-raising activities started: very hard, very real, and very urgent. The first six months after the murders were a blur of activity; there were funerals, memorials, community meetings, and rallies. At all these events we passed the donation basket. After a few months, I remember having discussions about needing to approach fund-raising for the long haul. To me, *long haul* meant maybe a couple of years. Ha! Eight years and a hundred thousand dollars later, I'd gain a whole new appreciation for the long haul.

Because I had some experience raising money for the Lesbian Resource Center and American Indian Movement, I was as good a candidate as any to head up fund-raising for the Committee for Justice. Fortunately, an old friend of mine from Minneapolis had "moved on up," so to speak, and was an assistant director at the Ms. Foundation. Before the murders, I'd arranged a meeting with her, Silme, and others to talk about the union movement. After the murders, she became very supportive and helpful to our fund-raising efforts, opening a lot of doors.

At the end of the first year, I was sent to the East Coast to raise money. My first step was to get the Youth Project in Washington, DC, to take on the Committee for Justice as a project under their nonprofit umbrella. With this in place, I dashed off to New York City to meet with some potential donors.

But I didn't raise a dime! I think they thought I was making up the whole story. However, a progressive foundation—Funding Exchange—did give us a good chunk of money. I'll never forget: the key person I dealt with was in political exile from South Africa. He was as abrupt as he was insightful. When he handed me the check, he held onto it for a minute and looked me right in the eye, saying something to the effect that he hoped we wouldn't be so politically naive as to let any more of our people get killed. That was a very hard moment. And over the years there would be other hard moments. For example, a year or so later, on another trip to New York, I met with Joyce Horman, whose husband had died at the hands of the Chilean dictator, Pinochet, in 1973. I remember the night was dark and rainy. I took the subway to some plush section of Manhattan. Her apartment was like a movie set, with a sunken living room. As we talked she offered many valuable insights and contacts. The conversation was very moving because death and tragedy were still so close under the surface for both of us.

Back in Seattle, I spent a lot of my time creating long lists of potential donors and trying to get money from them. Raising money this way was tricky. On some level, it made me feel like a prostitute or a beggar, but I knew that my comrades were counting on the money, so I found the stamina to do it anyway. It's like going on stage. I had a special set of fund-raising outfits (a sweet-looking flowered summer dress and a smart-looking navy blue skirt suit for winter, both quite different from my usual "lesbian wear" of overalls and plaid shirts). Along with this went a sort of staged act, which I played to the hilt, since I was a closeted and frustrated Broadway actress anyway. Rich people could be funny; the trick was to figure out why they gave their money away and try to play that card while educating them in the process. Race played into this scenario in a strange way too: some donors felt more comfortable speaking to a white person (me), while others preferred to see and talk to a person of color. Secrecy was also the name of the game; most rich folks didn't want their names to get out, afraid they might get besieged with all kinds of requests. If the names leaked, your sources dried up, period. Often, when I'd bring money back, comrades would ask with gossip in their eyes, "Who did you get this from?" I became very good at being evasive.

This wasn't the only way we raised money for the Committee for Justice. Quiet as it was kept, we actually raised large sums through direct appeals at outreach and educational events. Ordinary working folks were incredibly generous. After many events, I'd sometimes have thousands of dollars. Then I'd have to figure out how to safeguard it until it could be counted, recorded, and brought to the bank. I'd usually wrap it up like a roast and stick it in my freezer for a couple of days!

But overall, fund-raising was a lonely task. Not many folks wanted to do it, although everyone agreed it needed to be done. Thank God that, for me, it wasn't the only thing I got to do for the Committee for Justice. I also worked on the newsletter and did outreach to the gay and lesbian community.

We printed our first newsletter a week or so after the murders, to let people know what was happening. There were times it could have come out daily. Everyone in the city seemed hungry for news. The newsletter was a creative and exciting process: we sought to disseminate accurate information and analysis; we used the newsletter to expand our base of support in the community; and we had to keep the high priests of politics from writing articles that no one could understand. Help came from all quarters. A number of printers and typesetters in Seattle volunteered and worked extra hours when last-minute rewrites had to be done.

The newsletters around the early trials were the most exciting. I remember as we waited for the jury verdict on Tulisan gang chieftain Tony Dictado's trial, we had two different front pages written and camera-ready, depending on which way the decision went. We spent all night preparing the pages so we would have something to hand out at the community meetings after the trial that night. Back then, there were no fancy computer programs to make this easy; things had to be typeset and proofed, and mistakes had to be corrected and pasted in line by line, sometimes even word by word. But unlike the fund-raising, creating the newsletter seemed much more tangible to me and made me feel like I was making a difference.

Getting the newsletter mailed out, however, was a whole other headache. First-class mail was too expensive for us. So I approached the Lesbian Resource Center board for permission to use the group's newly acquired bulk-mail permit. They agreed, and that's how we did the early mailings for the Committee for Justice. Of course, there's a nice backstory that goes along with this. After the Lesbian Resource Center got its 501(c)(3) nonprofit status, it spent two years in a bitter fight with the postmaster to get a bulk-mailing permit. Apparently, some top administrators at the post office were outraged that a group of lesbians would even be allowed to become a non-profit organization, much less send out "obscene materials" as bulk mail. But the postmaster finally had to give in and register the center's bulk-mail permit. How fitting that one of the first uses of the permit was to send out newsletters from the Committee for Justice for Domingo and Viernes!

WE HAD ALREADY LOST TOO MUCH
TO TURN BACK

TERRI MAST

Terri Mast joined the Seattle KDP chapter in 1976, heavily influenced by a 1973 visit to the Philippines, where she witnessed the people's poverty and the undemocratic nature of the Marcos regime. As a cannery worker, Terri was assigned to the KDP's team at Local 37 of the International Longshoremen's and Warehousemen's Union (ILWU; the Alaska Cannery Workers Union) and worked on the Alaska Cannery Workers Association's Title VII discrimination lawsuits against canneries. She was a rank-and-file reform officer and executive board member of Local 37 at the time of the murders of her partner, Silme Domingo, and Gene Viernes. In 1982, Terri became president of Local 37 and has now worked over thirty years as a labor leader in Seattle. She is currently secretary-treasurer of the Inlandboatmen's Union (IBU), the marine division of the ILWU (ILWU Local 37 is now known as IBU Region 37), and she serves on the Advisory Committee of the University of Washington's Harry Bridges Center for Labor Studies. She is also an executive board member of the International Transport Workers Federation. Terri was the wife of Silme Domingo and together they had two children, Kalayaan and Ligaya.

S ILME and Gene had been dead maybe two months the day David Della and I sat down to draft the petition calling for the recall of Tony Baruso as president of the International Longshoremen's and Warehousemen's Union (ILWU). Once we got started, we couldn't stop listing stuff. We had an endless list of reasons and incidents why he had to go. Everything was there, from his not filing grievances, to not servicing our contracts, to failing to attend union meetings, to his habit of taking half-day lunches. I think we might have even charged him with taking bribes at dispatch! At that point it seemed we had everything to gain and nothing to lose. We then edited the petition to make sure that every member of the union could read and understand it, that every member could find something in it that matched their own experience and would give them a reason to sign it. Fortunately, it was still the height of canning season, so we could catch most of the members as they came back from Alaska.

Of course, it's not like we had just discovered Baruso was a bad guy. Our whole rank-and-file reform effort for the past five years had been about breaking Baruso's hold on the union and fighting everything he stood for. Besides weakening the union, Baruso played a reactionary role in the community as an outspoken champion of the Marcos regime. The move to recall him was about bringing into the open the challenge we had been planning for a long time. After the murders, things were more urgent, more black and white. From the day Silme and Gene were shot, we all knew in our guts that Baruso was involved somehow. So our decision to go back into the union was all about getting him out. Of course, the real question was when and how. It was all about tactics, which are never easy because they can't be worked out neatly beforehand; it's more about remaining flexible and alert. It's so hard to capture those times. The events moved so fast and are so interwoven, both in my memory and in real life.

Right after the murders, we went back into the union. But things were very, very tense. Baruso hadn't yet been publicly implicated in the murders, so he was still around, going through the motions of running the union. But he was edgy and nervous around us. And I think that on some level, he couldn't believe it himself that we'd go back into the union and get up in his face so soon after the shootings. The Tulisan gangsters, on the other hand, were more arrogant (at least on the surface) and were still swaggering around Chinatown—even though the police had arrested the gunmen due to Silme's dying declaration and had picked up some of them for questioning. But in Chinatown, the police had a terrible track record in solving these kinds of crimes because of the code of silence among the gangster elements. Ordinary folks who had to deal with the Tulisan on a day-to-day basis also feared retaliation. There was no reason to believe that Gene's and Silme's murders would be any different unless we stepped in to assist the police and the prosecutor.

I had been appointed by Local 37's executive board to accompany Baruso and the union's lawyer, Mike Withey, to Alaska to service the Bristol Bay contracts. Needless to say, Mike and I were freaked out; Bristol Bay was a

Tulisan stronghold, and one of the suspects in the murders was at a cannery there. Mike and I both wore bulletproof vests and were jittery as hell.

During the trip, I talked to a foremen who had been a supporter of the rank-and-file reform movement years earlier, but now we weren't sure where his loyalties lay. I said, "Hey, weren't we supposed to have an election for the ILWU international officers?"

"Oh, that one, we did it during the dispatch. Don't you remember?"

"No, I can't say that I do," I replied. I thought that maybe I'd zoned out and missed this one, since so much had happened. So when I got back to Seattle, I started asking around. Did we have an election? Did you vote for the international officers? Sure enough, no one had. I called the international in San Francisco just to check. They said, "Oh, yeah, Local 37? We got your ballots right here." I told them that no election had been held, so they'd better consider initiating an investigation into possible fraud. Was this the opening we'd been waiting for? It still wasn't clear.

Then, shortly after we returned from Bristol Bay, we had our first real indication that all was not well in the Baruso camp. The falling out among thieves had begun. The police got an anonymous tip that led them to a dumpster in West Seattle—they found a gun. Ballistics determined that it was the murder weapon that killed Silme and Gene. The real news was that it was Baruso's gun, registered to him and everything. The police arrested Baruso. We all rushed down to witness his arraignment. He was shaken. You could see it in his face. And we were emboldened to push him even harder. (Afterward, I remember how we all rolled with laughter at the sight of Baruso handcuffed in his cute little orange jumpsuit; those few moments of emotional release were so important during that tense period.) Baruso must have seen in our eyes that we were convinced he was involved in the murders. He called the union's lawyer from his jail cell, shouting that he was being framed and that the Rank and File Committee better not touch anything in his office or get any "bright ideas" while he was away.

These were the events that led to our drafting the petition calling for Baruso's recall. We knew we had to move quickly and decisively, in spite of our own fears and uncertainties. Here's where our union's history also weighed in on our side. In the formative years before the anticommunist McCarthy era, Local 37 had been built up by progressives—by folks like Chris Mensalvas, Ernesto Mangaoang, Carlos Bulosan—and was part of the ILWU. As a result, our union by-laws were extremely democratic. I think we only needed one hundred signatures on a petition to ask for a special election. And in this case, we actually gathered several hundred. Then we submitted the petition to the union's board where, by this time, the Rank and File Committee held a majority of seats. This was near the end of August, and the special election was set for October. Mail ballots were sent out to everyone on the active membership list. And a special elections committee was set up, and it included two of our Rank and File Committee members, Emily and Peter, who were not on the union's board.

As for Baruso, he was really pissed. But fortunately for us, he had his hands full with other headaches at the time (the police were questioning him about involvement in the murders, the ILWU international was investigating him regarding possible election fraud, etc.), so he wasn't able to direct his full venom at our recall effort. Also, he knew that the tables were turning, and we did too. It was really inspiring.

Once we'd found the courage within ourselves to stand up and fight back, hundreds of union members quietly stood up behind us; this was really the force that changed the union. People who had supported the reform effort years earlier came back; those who previously had been noncommittal began to show support. Many activities and special meetings took place around the union hall that summer and fall right after the murders, and it was not uncommon to have over a hundred members at each meeting! If the numbers began to decrease, we only needed to make a few phone calls and get word out that we still needed people's participation and support, and they were back again. The backbone of this support was the core of Filipino union members, both young and old, people who shared the same community and often the same family networks with Baruso and the Tulisan boys; but they were making it clear that they drew the line at murder. Without that support, we never would have won, no matter how determined we were or how hard we worked.

I remember the afternoon and early evening that we counted the recall ballots. The union hall was filled with anticipation and underlying tension. Baruso didn't show up. The Tulisan boys were spotted a couple of times, circling the union hall with their cars; but by now they no longer felt free to come in and out of the hall as they pleased. When the election committee announced the results—that Baruso was to be removed from the union's presidency—we felt satisfaction for sure, but I wouldn't call it jubilation. Things were much too tense for that, and there was still too much left to do. The board appointed Nemesio Domingo Sr. (Silme's father) to move up from vice president to fill Baruso's position. I was appointed vice president. Regular union elections were scheduled for a few months after the recall. That's when I ran for the position of president and won.

I've often been asked what it felt like living through that period. Honestly, I was emotionally numb through most of it. If any memory sticks out for me, it's the one of experiencing sheer terror on all levels. I felt ambivalent about everything we set out to do. On one level, I didn't want to do any of it—it was too scary. At the same time, we'd already lost too much to turn back. Besides, what signal would that give for all the folks who had believed in us?

On the deepest personal level, the murders of Silme and Gene terrorized me because I knew all the players involved. It wasn't like I was some sheltered housewife struck by this tragedy. I had been working in Alaska years before we even started the rank-and-file movement. I had worked in the canneries with a lot of the Tulisan gangsters. In fact, the season I was shop steward at Egegik, both gang leader Tony Dictado and Jimmy Ramil were there with me. Ramil got into a fight, broke a beer bottle, and mercilessly sliced up someone's face. I can still remember looking at him and not seeing the slightest trace of remorse. I told him, "There's no way I can help you. The company's going to send you home." (Of course, as soon as Ramil got back to Seattle, Baruso dispatched him to another Alaska cannery. And at that second cannery, Ramil actually did kill someone.) When the season was over, I said to Silme, "Watch that guy, he's cold-blooded."

About a month before Silme was shot, Ramil was in Alaska at Dutch Harbor, where we had an organizing drive under way. By this time, Silme and Gene were doing almost all the day-to-day paperwork to keep the union functioning. One day, I went into the office to help catch up some of Silme's work. I was at Silme's desk, and Baruso was in his own office and didn't know I was there. Suddenly, I looked up and who's standing in front of me but Jimmy Ramil! I felt a shiver go down my spine.

He said, "You remember me?"

I said, "Yeah, I sure do."

Baruso came out of his office and looked startled to see me. Ramil made some comment to Baruso in Ilocano; they laughed and then went into Baruso's office and closed the door behind them. I can remember thinking to myself, "What are those two up to? How come Ramil has such easy access to the union's business office?" (The office had a service counter and members rarely came to the other side of it, because one had to pass through a locked door to enter the office.)

I was at the hospital the day Silme was shot. The detective must have seen the blood drain out of my face when he told me that the name *Ramil* was part of Silme's dying utterance. To this day, it gives me the creeps to even think that I might have been right there, in the next room, the day the contract on Silme and Gene was sealed.

In the months after the murders, a lot of the terror we experienced was intentionally inflicted to scare us off. Although it didn't work, I personally stayed scared most of the time. The Tulisan gangsters would circle the union hall in their cars or park outside and watch us. We'd get strange phone calls at home at all times of the day and night. Warnings and rumors about what was going to happen to us would circulate in the community. For me, the worst was when I thought my two girls might be harmed in some way. Often, my daughters would stay at my mother's house. When I'd go to pick them up, there would be one of the Tulisan cars waiting somewhere along the way so I couldn't miss seeing it. It's the kind of terror I never want to live through again. I would ride home with my kids, convinced that my car was rigged to blow up at any second.

Of course, it wasn't just about terror. I've come to understand how it's possible to be afraid and act courageously at the same time, mostly because we were so damn mad at what they'd done to us. And as I mentioned earlier, the support of the union membership became very tangible and real. There were moments, in the middle of all the fear and pain, when we could see how different the union could be, even if Silme and Gene wouldn't be there to share the vision with us.

I remember my first open challenge to Baruso. It was the first special union meeting called after the murders. The hall was packed, with a hundred members or more, and a representative from the international union was also there. Our meetings were usually extremely polite (partly because of the Filipino influence on the union), except for Baruso, who acted like an ass on a regular basis, shouting at people, cutting them off, and so on. On this occasion, Baruso was ranting on about something, trying to show off in front of the international. Next thing I know, he's referring to the work of Silme and Gene, claiming responsibility for it and describing how he intends to continue it. I thought, "He must be nuts talking like this to us!" I looked around, and eyes were on me from all points of the room, looks that were questioning whether we'd let him get away with this, looks nudging me to do something, asking for leadership. I knew we had nothing more to lose, but I felt paralyzed. I wasn't sure what to do and I hated to speak in front of large groups of people.

Then I remember someone interrupting Baruso to try to ask a question, and Baruso shouted at the person to sit down and shut up. All of a sudden I was on my feet, saying "Excuse me, Tony, excuse me . . ." as I proceeded down a side aisle toward the front of the room. It was an out-of-body experience for me, like a film that gets thrown into slow motion. I could see the expressions on people's faces, the looks in their eyes as they followed me to the front of the room. The silence was deafening. I could hear my own voice as though someone else was speaking.

"You're not going to stand up here and tell people to shut up anymore. We're tired of that bullshit and we're not putting up with it. This is our union and everyone has the right to speak and be heard. And another thing, I'm not going to let you stand up here and claim credit for Silme's and Gene's years of hard work." I said some other stuff too, but by that time I was just so angry it didn't matter. I may have even raised the possibility that he had some connection to the murders . . . I don't remember exactly, but I sure was on a roll!

When I finished, there was a silent and hesitant pause—then the room exploded in thunderous clapping. I don't remember what happened next, but some things were different from then on.

When I think back on the way we pursued the struggle for justice surrounding the murders of Silme and Gene, one word comes to mind: *relentless*. From day one, we knew Baruso was at the center of the conspiracy, and we refused to rest until we saw him properly charged, convicted, and shut permanently behind penitentiary doors. But that took almost ten years! Recalling him as the union president wasn't the end of it. He deserved to be recalled simply because he did nothing to build or strengthen the union; in no way did it settle the debt he owed for the murders. Once he was ousted from the union, we were able to uncover that he had embezzled about $5,300 (that's all we could prove). The US Department of Labor conducted an official investigation that culminated in a federal trial in which Baruso was sentenced to five years in prison (about a year for every thousand dollars—not bad). Of course, he was locked up at one of those fancy low-security prison ranches; but it still knocked him out of commission for a while.

By the time Baruso eventually got released, Marcos had been overthrown. We pressed the King County prosecutor to reopen the criminal case. And this time we were successful in getting Baruso charged and convicted of conspiracy in the murders of Silme and Gene. By the time Baruso finally made his journey to Walla Walla state prison, he was a broken man. I'm sure that the day he set the murder conspiracy in motion, he never dreamed he'd ever get caught or would have to pay. But we pursued him relentlessly and squeezed him tighter and tighter into a corner from which he couldn't escape. The broader issue for us was never about revenge against one individual; it was about how determined we would be in defending ourselves and our movement against outright fascist attacks. Baruso's fate became the symbol for that whole struggle. And in the end, the message came across loud and clear—especially in the Filipino community.

After we got hold of the union, we still had a lot of work to do. It took us a few years to get rid of the organized gambling at the canneries and the gangster elements that ran those operations. Dillingham Cannery was the last holdout. Finally we told the company, "You guys have got to help us put a stop to this," and they did. The gambling was tied to the foreman, so they cut him off and made him get all his work crew from the union hiring hall. Without any of his own soldiers, he couldn't keep the gambling going.

Today we have a good union, with a solid democratic foundation. A lot of our members are young people and students; yet somehow they know about our history and what we've been through. Much of it is passed on by word of mouth, not just about the murders, but about the whole reform effort. Still, it's an uphill battle all the way and probably always will be. Largely because work in the canneries is seasonal and tends to be transitory for most of the young workers, we don't have much leverage or strike power. The union is not as strong as I'd like it to be, but we try our best to defend the interests of our members, and the industry takes us seriously.

So many years have passed, yet people in the labor movement still encourage us to share our story and the lessons from our difficult struggle to clean up Local 37. Often, these are folks engaged in similar reform efforts in their own unions. Most of the time I don't know exactly what to say, where to start, what to include, what to leave out. Sometimes the story gets romanticized, and it makes me uncomfortable.

It's nice to have an opportunity to tell a part of this story in my own words. In the beginning of our reform effort, we shared a vision, we had a plan, and we were organized—and a lot of that is about the KDP. After the murders, and the struggle that followed, it was bigger than the KDP. We never set out to become heroes or heroines. I certainly never did! I was just trying to raise my family, take some labor studies courses, and do some union work. Events overtook me, events I never would have asked for. Bottom line, I think we were pretty ordinary people faced with an extraordinary challenge; and we managed to do some courageous things. But we were scared most of the time and uncertain lots of the time. And too often, the fear gets dropped out of the story. But when we tell it, we can't leave that out.

A NIGHT IN CAMELOT

MICHAEL WITHEY

Michael Withey was a member of the Line of March (LOM) and a movement lawyer in 1981 at the time of Silme Domingo's and Gene Viernes's murders. Mike dropped out of corporate law practice for two and a half years to become lead counsel in the case Estates of Domingo and Viernes v. Ferdinand Marcos. *Mike has served as a public interest and human rights attorney for forty-four years, specializing in international human rights, constitutional law, and personal injury practice. He retired in 2014 and is currently writing a book,* Summary Execution: The Political Assassinations of Silme Domingo and Gene Viernes. *Mike served as president of the Public Justice Foundation and in 2014 was honored with the American Bar Association's Pursuit of Justice Award.*

MANILA, *September 1986.* I couldn't breathe. I gasped for air. My lungs burned hot. The night was humid and smoky. I felt like the exhaust of a thousand jitneys was being mainlined straight into my lungs. I was going to pass out! It was midnight at Manila International Airport. The baggage-claim area was spinning around and around, my knees were buckling, my head felt light. I started to slump down. "Are you all right?" Rene Ciria Cruz asked.

Coming to, I tried to mumble, "Sure, just jet lag." But no sound came out of my mouth, just a faint gasp. I was dying of carbon monoxide poisoning. The heat and fumes were unbearable. My shirt was soaked.

"You look terrible, do you want some water?" Rene asked.

"Sure, thanks," I said, taking the cup of water he offered and pouring it over my head. I looked into his face. He was calm, not even sweating.

"Cindy's at the Camelot Hotel," he said. "She'll meet us there. You can get some sleep."

I picked up my luggage and headed to Rene's car, dragging one foot after the other. It seemed like miles; it was probably one hundred yards. Throwing my suitcase in the backseat, I sat in the front and rolled the window up to avoid a blast of exhaust from the bus on our right.

"It won't take long. You look terrible," Rene said again. I wanted to pass out. But instead I spent the next forty-five minutes until we arrived at the hotel rolling my window up and down—first to get fresh air and then to avoid the next exhaust blast from passing buses.

Our trip to Manila was an attempt to take advantage of the tremendous opening brought about by the recent overthrow of the Marcos regime. We wanted to discover smoking-gun proof of Marcos's involvement in the murders of Silme Domingo and Gene Viernes. Our lawsuit, filed in 1982, had survived the dictatorship's motion to dismiss by the slenderest of threads. Up until now, we had failed to uncover solid evidence of the Marcos regime's extensive surveillance of its opponents. We were seeking documents and possibly witnesses that could verify that Gene had been surveilled by Marcos intelligence during his trip to the Philippines, shortly before his murder.

The Camelot Hotel looked like an Arthurian castle, complete with towers and long, dark halls and rooms with very little light. It was dim throughout, almost sinister. I fumbled for my room keys, entered my room, flopped onto the narrow bed, and passed out. That night, and most of the next day, I had nightmares about running up and down the dark corridors, escaping Marcos agents, exchanging gunfire with pro-Marcos coup plotters, tossing this way and that, waking, sleeping, but rarely reaching consciousness.

The phone rang. It was across the room. I thought I jumped up and bounded over to it, but in fact I couldn't move. My legs felt like tree trunks, my arms dead branches. It rang ten times. I didn't move. It stopped ringing. I slept and dreamt of Marcos agents and pro-Marcos putschists some more. The phone rang again, what seemed like a few minutes later. This time I managed to pick it up. It was Cindy Domingo.

"You hungry?" she asked. "You've slept all day."

"I have no idea. I can't wake up. I can't move. Where are you?" I replied.

"At dinner. We planned on starting tonight."

"Okay, I'll get up and come right down," I said apologetically.

"You better not try going down, you're on the first floor," she laughed.

"Okay, okay. I'll come over."

Rene and Cindy were sitting at the table, drinking coffee, deep in some intense conversation when I walked up. They looked at me and started laughing. "Jet lag?" they asked. "You slept all day." (I thought about George H. W. Bush's speculating that he must've had jet lag when he'd complimented Marcos a few years earlier for his "love and adherence to democracy"!)

"No," I responded. "I dodged bullets and Marcos agents all night long." They looked at me quizzically as I explained my nightmares.

Rene cut in, "OK, here's the plan. Tonight I need to use your room, Mike, while you and Cindy . . ."

"What for?" I questioned.

"A meeting. You and Cindy will go to see Senator Diokno, and . . ."

"A meeting with who?" I asked.

"With the chairman of the National Democratic Front," he replied nonchalantly. "Now, as you know, Diokno heads the Human Rights Commission . . ."

"Wait, wait a minute. You want to have a meeting with the chairman of the National Democratic Front in my room?" I asked incredulously.

"Yes, it's more secure there; less likely to be bugged."

"No, they just run armed Marcos agents in and out of the hotel. I tell you my room got real busy last night."

"You were dreaming. The political situation is very different now that Cory [Corazon Aquino] is in power. Marcos loyalists are holed up at the Manila Hotel, not here. We need your room, Mike," Rene explained, more informing me than persuading me.

"Okay, I'm just warning you guys, there are agents in this hotel." They both looked at each other, then at me, dismissing my comments and waiting for me to get a hold of myself so we could get down to work.

After a pause, Cindy went on to explain that Senator Diokno would see us at his house because he was ill, and therefore we couldn't stay long. She explained that tomorrow morning we would visit lawyer Rene Saguisag at the Presidential Palace and the day after that we might have an appointment with General Fidel Ramos, which Boni Gillego (a former military intelligence officer who was an anti-Marcos ally in the United States) was attempting to arrange. Ramos was serving as President Aquino's chief of staff of the Philippine armed forces. He had joined the "People Power" uprising that had overthrown the dictator.

We knew we needed to see if the Philippine military had any documents we could use in our civil suit, any evidence that Gene had been tailed in his meetings with the Kilusang Mayo Uno (KMU, or May First Movement) or other resistance groups. Our problem, of course, was that General Ramos was at best a very late convert to Philippine democracy Aquino-style. Under Marcos, Ramos had been second in command of the armed forces after General Fabian Ver. Was it conceivable that he didn't know of the thousands of extrajudicial killings and human rights violations that Marcos had visited upon the Philippine Left? Unlikely. Was it possible that Ramos didn't know about the Domingo and Viernes murders? Unlikely. Yet here we were, going into his heavily guarded headquarters to ask him point-blank for proof that Marcos had been behind the murders of Silme and Gene. Would we get his cooperation? Again, unlikely. But we were used to pursuing slim leads.

So when the fateful day came, Cindy, Boni, former senator Raul Manglapus (head of the US-based Movement for a Free Philippines, or MFP), and I all set off for Fort Bonifacio to meet General Ramos, full of hope and trepidation. That very same day, by coincidence, the morning newspapers were filled with articles about the antics of a Philadelphia lawyer who had filed suit against Marcos and the Philippine government, seeking compensation and punitive damages for ten thousand victims of Marcos's terror. This lawyer had asked a court in Manila to order the Philippine military to turn over the location of "safe houses" used by Marcos intelligence to interrogate and torture human rights victims.

As we left, choking exhaust filled the air of metro Manila and shrouded the stately and well-groomed grounds of Fort Bonifacio. Our discussions ceased. Rumors of a coup d'état were in the air. Ramos's headquarters was a heavily armed camp, surrounded by crack paratroopers armed with M16 assault rifles, on the lookout for military mutineers.

My thoughts went back to Gene and his trip here five years earlier. It was such a different world. I tried to imagine how he must have felt meeting with Felixberto Olalia, head of the KMU, the largest anti-Marcos trade union, with students from the University of the Philippines, with fighters from the New People's Army. In my wildest imagination, I never thought we would be in a position to meet with leading members of the Philippine government to try to enlist their support in this lawsuit. In my mind, General Ramos was still very much an enemy, part of Marcos's and General Ver's repressive apparatus. Yet here we were, on the doorstep of Ramos's headquarters about to ask him to help us.

Our escort from the car to the building was all business; an extensive search was conducted of our persons and our belongings. My pocket Dictaphone didn't pass the inspection and was "salvaged," never to be seen by me again. Boni's face tightened as he informed the adjutant of our identity and the purpose of our visit. Raul, who was close to Cory but no friend of the Philippine military, conversed quietly with one of the secretaries, a townmate whose father had fled the Philippines after martial law was declared. As time went by, Cindy and I speculated that maybe Ramos would be too busy with the potential coup to meet with us.

"Oh well, we tried!" We started to prepare to leave. Then a door opened and a colonel asked us to step inside.

The room was large, ornately decorated and cool, a welcome relief from the noonday sun. General Ramos was seated at his desk, piles of paper and files in front of him. He did not rise. His eyes were dead cold, his jaw tight, clenching a short, fat cigar. The colonel asked us to sit down around a small rectangular table perpendicular to Ramos's large desk. No food, no drinks, no small talk. Ramos was silent.

The silence was filled with tension. Finally, Raul spoke first, in English: "Thank you, General Ramos, for taking time from your busy schedule and your important duties in defending the People's Power revolution against our domestic enemies." Ramos looked sternly at Raul, unmoved by the polite formalities. Raul cleared his throat and continued, "With me is Bonifacio Gillego, a former intelligence officer of the armed forces of the Philippines; Cindy Domingo, whose family comes from Cebu and sister of Silme Domingo, who was killed in Seattle; and her lawyer, Mike Withey of Seattle. We have come to ask you to direct your subordinates to conduct a search for documents of the military that might help Cindy and Mike present their case in a US court. We only ask . . ."

Ramos interrupted. "What you ask for no military would ever agree to," he said, taking his cigar from his mouth. His back was stiff and his eyes were steely.

"I'm sorry, general?" Raul responded with some confusion—although we'd all heard every single word Ramos had said.

Ramos shot back quickly, "We cannot give you what you ask for; it would severely compromise our security. It's unthinkable." It seemed that after just two minutes with Ramos, the main goal of our whole trip had gone up in his cigar smoke. My heart sank. I looked at Cindy, who also looked perplexed.

Suddenly, but hesitantly, she began to speak. "You see, General Ramos, my brother, Silme Domingo and our friend, Gene Viernes, were murdered in 1981 in Seattle. We have reason to believe that Ferdinand Marcos had known about . . ."

Ramos, still glaring at Raul, interrupted Cindy. "I'm sorry about your brother, but we will never turn over to the American courts, or even to the Philippine courts, the location of our safe houses. Some of them are still being used and we need them. You might as well go home."

Safe houses? I thought to myself, what's he talking about? We aren't asking for the location of any safe houses. He must have us confused with that other lawsuit in Philadelphia.

Cindy was speaking up again, "No, general, we would never ask you for the location of safe houses. The security of the Aquino government is very important to us as well. You may have us confused with the case recently filed in Philadelphia. That's a different case altogether."

Looking straight at me for the first time, Ramos said, his face softening, "I thought you were the lawyer asking for the locations of our safe houses." To all of us, "What is it that you want?"

As I began to explain our case and our request, the tension oozed right out of the room. At the end of my presentation, Ramos stood up and signaled the colonel. Suddenly, the coffee, soft drinks, and *merienda* (snacks) appeared. Smiling broadly, Ramos came out from behind his desk, joined us at the table, and asked us for a list of documents we wanted and which agencies should search for them. He gave orders to his adjutant to cooperate fully with our requests. As he walked us to the door a half hour later, he reached to shake all our hands, promising to do whatever he could.

I knew the chances of ever getting the documentation we wanted from the military were slim and that Ramos's abrupt change in demeanor was probably more an expression of his relief that we were not there to press him for the safe house locations. Nevertheless, for us it was a mission accomplished! The documents we eventually received were used in the trial of our civil suit to establish that the organizations Gene had met with during his trip in April 1981 were, in fact, heavily spied on by Marcos intelligence and that it was highly likely that Gene himself was caught on surveillance cameras or reported by informants. Although we did not locate a smoking gun, the use of documents from the Philippine government's own files led the civil jurors to believe that our case was authentic. These documents also came in handy when cross-examining Marcos at his depositions while he was in exile in Hawaii, because he had a hard time denying statements made in them.

The last day of our trip we decided to relax in the restaurant of the Camelot Hotel. We ate a gigantic Filipino meal, which was excellent, and started to chat with the other hotel guests, mostly men, who said they were attending a convention. Before long our thoughts turned to music. As one after another of the hotel guests stood to sing songs, I was encouraged to play the piano. I launched into a medley of Beatles songs. In unison, the restaurant guests stood around the piano and sang "Yesterday," "She Was Just Seventeen," and "With a Little Help from My Friends." On into the night we played and sang with the other guests. The nightmares from my first day in the Philippines had become a distant memory.

The following morning, the day of our departure, broke cool and fresh. I had an hour to kill, so I went across the street to the hotel pool. Looking up into the hillsides, I reflected on the beauty of the Philippines. The heat wave had broken and the green vegetation surrounding the pool was a welcome respite from the previous days' heat and smog. As I lay on the lounge chair, a small boy asked me if I wanted to buy a paper. Why not, I thought. Handing him some change, I lay back, unfolded the paper, and read the front page's top headline: "Marcos loyalists convene confab at Camelot Hotel, seek return to power." Marcos henchmen in the hotel had not been an imaginary nightmare after all.

LONG ROAD TO JUSTICE

CINDY DOMINGO

THERE are still times when in the midst of a joyous event or an important meeting, I find myself silently thinking that my brother Silme should be there. I want to see him strut into the room, bringing with him the life of the party, joking and giving everyone a high five as he passes every person who knows him. With his shaggy, stylish black hair, his red leather coat, velveteen pants, and platform shoes that distinguished him from other activists, he wouldn't be out of place amid today's quirky fashion styles. Even the burgundy Chevy Monte Carlo that Silme drove, which became his trademark, would be seen as a classic today. For a moment when I think of him, I am stuck in time. It seems impossible that Silme has been dead for over thirty years.

At the time of Silme's and Gene's murders in 1981, I was assigned to the national headquarters of the KDP in Oakland, in the National Education Department, designing and guiding internal studies for the organization. However, much of my political work was the development and guidance of study circles for the Marxist-Leninist Education Project (MLEP), a new project launched by the Line of March (LOM), a communist formation. As part of my work, I was assigned to assist the MLEP in Seattle, thus requiring tracking down Silme for discussions.

In early May I joined many of the Seattle KDP people, including Silme and Gene, in Hawaii to attend the International Longshoremen's and Warehousemen's Union (ILWU) international conference. Gene was flying in directly from the Philippines, bringing with him a letter from Felixberto Olalia, president of the Kilusang Mayo Uno (KMU, or May First Movement),

---

See "Fighting US Imperialism with a Master's Degree" for contributor biography.

inviting the ILWU to send a labor delegation to the Philippines to investigate the working conditions of Filipino workers under the regime of Ferdinand and Imelda Marcos. ILWU Local 37 (the Alaska Cannery Workers Union), which Silme and Gene represented, sponsored Resolution R-34 to send the investigating team. It was one of two controversial resolutions at the convention. The other concerned the power that pensioners, led by legendary ILWU president emeritus Harry Bridges, would continue to have in the ILWU.

I had never attended a labor convention, and even though my main reason for being in Hawaii was to vacation, I sensed the historical importance of this event and attended some of the sessions. For months, Local 37 had been preparing for this resolution. The proposal was carefully worded so as not to completely arouse the full opposition of the ILWU's pro-Marcos members—the Local 37 KDP members understood the dangerous implications of the resolution.

While Gene's first visit to the Philippines fulfilled an important personal purpose—to visit his father's family—the trip was also part of a historical strategy that had been handed down from Carlos Bulosan and Chris Mensalvas Sr., officers of Local 37 decades before. When Silme and Gene first started doing research on Local 37, they came across its 1957 yearbook, edited by Bulosan. It contained a section supporting the Huk guerrilla movement in the Philippines. Further research and discussions with the *manongs* (older Filipino men) who had been part of Local 37's first reform movement in the 1940s and 1950s revealed that their labor perspective had been internationalist. Local 37 was a union of immigrants, and part of reforming its politics was incorporating support for the struggle of workers in the Philippines for democracy and improved conditions. Well taught by the *manongs*, Silme and Gene always brought their anti-Marcos politics into the union whenever possible. Now the two had been elected officers of Local 37, and Silme and Gene knew they could use their positions to benefit the anti-Marcos movement. Thus, Gene's trip was also carefully planned to lay the groundwork for reestablishing ties between Local 37 and the progressive labor movement in the Philippines, this time through the KMU.

It seemed that the Local 37 reform movement people at the convention, headed by Silme and Gene, spent the entire four days lobbying for the resolution. Heavy resistance was coming from within the powerful Local 142 from Hawaii, the largest local affiliated with ILWU. Marcos supporters led by one of Marcos's godson's, Bart Alcarez, were trying to gather opposition to the resolution, stating that it was an attempt to condemn martial law and thus the Marcos government. Tony Baruso, president of Local 37 and longtime supporter of the Marcoses, also wanted to oppose the resolution. However, in a sly move at the debate, he rose in support of the investigating team, hoping to guarantee himself a seat in the delegation. Baruso had already received word that Local 142 president Carl Damaso had received consensus from his union that they would vote in overwhelming support of the resolution. It passed, but somehow the feeling of victory eluded Silme and Gene.

A few hours later that night, Gene dragged me over to the tables where the convention photographer was selling pictures for a dollar apiece. Gene said he would give me a dollar to buy the picture of him at the podium speaking in support of the Philippine resolution and presenting Olalia's letter to the convention delegates. Knowing that Gene thought of himself as a ladies' man, I told him to buy it himself if he liked it so much. But this time, Gene wasn't joking; he said he was afraid that if I didn't buy it, Marcos agents would. Thinking he was still joking, I took his money and bought the picture and kept it for myself. Little did I know that this picture would be shown hundreds of times in the years after the murders and would become a treasured memento for Gene's KDP comrades.

Two weeks later, Silme and Gene came to Oakland for a meeting with the national KDP leadership team to discuss their work in Local 37 and the upcoming ILWU investigating team. Geline Avila, in charge of the Philippine support work, also wanted to get a briefing on Gene's visit to the Philippines and his discussions with labor leaders in the KMU.

Silme's serious side seemed to be overshadowing his usual jolly character. I thought perhaps he was under criticism again for refusing to take his leadership responsibilities more seriously in the Seattle KDP chapter. I already knew that Silme was refusing to do the MLEP work in addition to his Local 37 work. Gene, on the other hand, was always fairly serious. However, the two seemed to cheer up as they drank beer, enjoying the salmon meal Silme usually prepared for my household collective whenever he came to visit. As Silme drank more, I could tell he was bothered by matters I knew little about. I didn't really understand why Silme talked about carrying a gun in his briefcase, or why he was afraid to be out drinking in the International District by himself at night. But Silme's other trademark was that he never really let people know what was going on with him emotionally, and the same could be said about Gene.

Two weeks later, on June 1, 1981, Silme and Gene were shot in broad daylight at four o'clock in the afternoon as they worked in Local 37's offices, a high-traffic area at that time of the day in Seattle's Pioneer Square. Gene died immediately, trying to dodge two bullets, one that went through his heart.

Silme was shot five times in the stomach but made his way out of the union hall, called for help, and gave the first paramedic on the scene the names of their two assassins.

Precisely at the same time, I was thinking of returning Gene's 3:30 p.m. call regarding the tennis shoes he had left in Oakland just two weeks earlier. But I figured they had already closed the Local 37 office for the day, and the call could wait until the next day. At 6:00 p.m., Dale Borgeson from the KDP National Executive Board and cofounder of the Seattle chapter, came to the downstairs duplex where we all lived and asked if he could talk privately with me. Dale, who had been sent to Seattle in 1973 to form the KDP chapter and was a good family friend, told me with great difficulty and tears in his eyes that Gene was dead and Silme was in critical condition. There was very little information to share other than that Dale would accompany me home to Seattle in a few hours.

I packed my carry-on suitcase in disbelief. I folded a black dress for the funeral and gathered my KDP work, believing I would be back in Oakland the following week for a scheduled meeting on the MLEP. I called Vangie, my older sister in Phoenix, repeating the few details that I'd been told. I thought it was misinformation, and soon I would be in Seattle seeing Silme and Gene both alive and well.

Upon arriving in Seattle, comrades took Dale and me directly to Harborview Hospital to await news of Silme's condition. More than a hundred people passed through the waiting rooms, the majority of whom our family didn't know, bringing us food, asking if there was anything they could do, comforting us and giving support to the others that were also there. Conspicuously missing was Baruso. He finally came to the hospital after my mother called him, questioning why the president of the union was not interested enough to see Silme or inquire about his condition. All Baruso asked was, "What do you know? Who did it?" After Baruso was told, he said nothing. What could he say? After all, he was close to one of the murderers, Jimmy Ramil. His silence spoke of his complicity in the crime.

Twenty-five hours later, at 5:00 a.m., after several operations, dozens of pints of blood, and attempts on Silme's part to name another accomplice in the murders, he died in the trauma unit at Harborview. Our family was allowed to see him one more time to say good-bye, but the doctors warned us that the trauma Silme had gone through had left his body almost unrecognizable. I felt guilty that I had sent Vangie and my father home earlier, as they would've wanted to be there. I guess the gravity of the situation hadn't really sunk in at the time. In fact, it wasn't until a week after the funerals and memorials had ended that I realized I would never see my brother again. The week following the murders was nonstop activity. On top of funeral arrangements, our comrades were trying to pull us into political discussions to figure out why Silme and Gene had been murdered and how to use the funerals and memorials to build support for efforts to bring their killers to justice. There was no time for grieving. There were too many interviews, too many details, too many speeches to write. All that mattered was finding the truth behind the murders.

All the KDP and Local 37 activists were thrust into leadership positions after June 1. Most of us were in our middle to late twenties, and although we had experience in community organizing, we were unprepared to run a union or spearhead a campaign that would challenge both the US and Philippine governments. But there was no opportunity to flinch, to say no, and it was the unified approach of the Local 37 members, KDP, and Line of March that gave each one of us the strength to accept our new responsibilities as leaders of a movement. Lynn, my younger sister, bravely volunteered to take Silme's position as secretary-treasurer of Local 37 when no one else stepped forward; John Foz, Angel Doniego, and David Della formed the Local 37 dispatch team to fill Gene's shoes, fearing that it was too dangerous for just one person; and David and Terri Mast would lead the Local 37 Executive Board. The comrades in the union knew the challenges would be difficult. Baruso was still president, and other members of the gang that killed Silme and Gene were still coming to get dispatched and attending union meetings, mainly to intimidate the officers with their presence.

The Committee for Justice for Domingo and Viernes (CJDV) was formed by Elaine Ko, my eldest brother, Nemesio Domingo Jr., and me one week after the murders, with other members of Local 37 and individuals from the Filipino community participating. Our mission was to form a legal team to assist the prosecutor's office in finding witnesses and information to help prosecute those who had been arrested for the murders. We also needed to educate people in Seattle about the political nature of the assassinations, to build broad support for Local 37's implementation of a fair dispatch system, and to totally rid the union of corruption.

I was just twenty-seven years old at the time and I had to become one of the spokespersons for the CJDV—first, at the local level; and then in 1982, when the civil lawsuits were filed, I became the national coordinator. Elaine Ko used all her organizing and journalism skills to build the CJDV and put out newsletter after newsletter. Only a juggler like Elaine, could have led the committee, organize her wedding, have a baby, and go through two murder trials in the year after the murders. At its height, the CJDV had eight outreach committees composed of one hundred people doing education in every community imaginable. Through two murder trials and three life-without-parole convictions of the suspects, the committee operated efficiently and effectively. The commitment of those at the center of the CJDV and Local 37 was unquestionable.

The pace of the first year and a half after the murders was grueling. There was very little time for a personal life, whether for family, socializing, or even going to movies. Life was filled with meetings every night—collective preparations for the weekly community meetings, meetings with the prosecutor's office, speaking engagements to educate various organizations throughout the city, tracking down clues and witnesses. It was no wonder that in the first year of the work, stress had me chain-smoking and barely eating, to the point of weighing just over a hundred pounds. Clumps of my hair started falling out.

Working a regular job was out of the question, but so was receiving a regular paycheck from the CJDV. I even had to pay for my own health coverage out of my three-thousand-dollar annual salary. But we all sacrificed. Mike Withey gave up partnership in his law firm to become the full-time lawyer for the CJDV. Members of the KDP were transferred temporarily or permanently to Seattle, some with just a few weeks' notice, to bolster the work in the KDP, CJDV, and the union. Therese Rodriguez and Lourdes Marzan of the New York KDP chapter leadership were asked to move to Washington, DC, so Therese could become national coordinator of the East Coast CJDV office. No one turned an assignment down, for everyone knew there was too much at stake.

In September 1982, the civil lawsuits were filed, and the CJDV work went national. Slowly, more evidence was uncovered through the murder trials of the hit men. Moreover, the findings of a private investigator with ties to government intelligence confirmed what we already knew—that the orders for the murders came from the Philippines and that the US government was fully complicit in the surveillance and harassment of the US-based anti-Marcos movement. We filed our federal civil suit to coincide with the Marcoses' first state visit to the United States at the invitation of then-president Ronald Reagan. As activists, we knew that timing was everything, and since the national press would cover the Marcos visit, our civil suit had a good chance of getting picked up. But Seattle was a backwater town then, without its no. 1 in the nation status for its traffic problems or its no. 1 ranking as the most livable city. The media were not interested in what seemed an implausible international murder case. While the press and legal circles laughed behind our backs, we knew the US and Marcos governments continued to watch us closely.

However, just as we had been so naive about the seriousness of Silme's and Gene's work at the time of their deaths, we were caught by surprise when the federal judge assigned to our civil suit, Judge Donald Voorhees, dismissed almost all the defendants, including the Marcoses and the US governments agencies. We were left with the Philippine government, Baruso, and the hit men as defendants. By the end of December 1982, there was little hope that we would be able to continue our work. The Marcoses had won this round. Even in Washington, DC, our lobbying efforts for assistance in uncovering US complicity in the murders were met with little support. Therese tried to coach me to be the grief-stricken sister and not to come on too heavy with the anti-Marcos politics. "Leave that to Odette and me," Therese said. "You must try to appeal to their humanity."

But I left Washington, DC, unable to feel any humanity, when one congressional aide told me that we should come back when something more serious happened. I asked myself, "What could be more serious than the murders of two US citizens by a foreign dictatorship on US soil?" Our requests for a public congressional hearing on the use of Philippine and US agents to infiltrate, spy on, and harass members of our movement fell on deaf ears. Only Democratic congressmen Ron Dellums (California), Mike Lowry (Washington), and John Conyers (Michigan) lent their support from the beginning, but their demands for US government accountability were silenced.

By the second anniversary of Silme's and Gene's deaths in June 1983, the reality that our civil suit would be on appeal for a long time had hit home. At the annual memorial, we stated again that we would not rest until we received full justice, but the emotional and physical strain of the prior two years was beginning to wear people down. For myself, the inability to grieve for Silme and Gene was compounded by another KDP comrade's sudden death due to illness. Cynthia Maglaya, often seen as the mother figure in KDP and everyone's confidante, died just weeks before the second memorial in the same trauma unit where Silme had died. In an effort to save my sanity, I tried to go for counseling, but unfortunately, after a hilarious session in which I listened to my counselor go on and on about the trauma she was experiencing after she'd cut her hair short, I decided I was okay.

Within a few weeks, the assassination of Benigno Aquino Jr. on August 21 swept most of us back into an upsurge of work. The whole world witnessed on television the boldness of the Marcos regime as the film footage of the Aquino assassination was shown repeatedly. Whatever doubt people had about the true nature of the regime was quickly erased in those ninety seconds of tape. No soldier would have been so bold as to murder Aquino without orders from Malacañang Palace, especially just as Aquino was exiting the plane and in front of the international media.

In a tragic sense, we knew that the Aquino assassination would help our cause, and in the end we were right. For the next few years, the international attention on the Philippines gave us the platform to bring attention to Silme's and Gene's assassinations. In every demonstration and literature piece calling for an end to US support for the Marcos regime, Silme's and Gene's names were mentioned. Every June at our annual memorials, we reminded people that we would not rest until justice was served in Silme's and Gene's deaths, even though there was little movement in our civil suit and Baruso still walked the streets of Seattle a free man.

Finally, in 1986, when the Marcoses were overthrown, Mike Withey and I traveled to the Philippines in the hope that the Corazon Aquino administration would help us. After all, I thought, even though Cory Aquino was president of the Philippines, she could understand the need for justice, especially since her husband had also been so brutally murdered. Call it naïveté again, but that help never materialized. Perhaps it was because Cory had other things to worry about, including warding off several coup attempts. Perhaps she was unwilling to implicate her own military and the US government in the deaths of thousands of opponents of the Marcos dictatorship, including Silme and Gene. After all, in the end, Cory never received justice in her own husband's murder.

In 1989 we succeeded in bringing our civil suit to trial. When we said that we would not rest until we brought the Marcoses to court, we didn't realize it would take us eight and a half years of work. I remember clearly the final day of the trial in 1989, as December 14 was also my thirty-sixth birthday. As Mike prepared to give his closing statement, I looked around the packed courtroom of over a hundred people. Standing room only. After so many years, people remembered Silme and Gene, and even though everyone had gone their own separate ways over the years, they had all come back to fulfill the promises they'd made back in 1981. Mike Kozu, who in 1981 had slept on my mother's living-room floor to ensure our family's safety, came back to Seattle to help us. Marlene Pedregosa worked her magic and pulled together an organizing team to mobilize for the trial, since the KDP, Coalition Against the Marcos Dictatorship, and Line of March no longer existed. For a moment, the movement that we had known before existed again, and for the first time I felt that I had fulfilled my promise to Silme and Gene that I would not rest until justice was served. It was such an emotional moment, and my eyes filled with tears. I didn't need the verdict to tell me what I already knew. We had won because Silme and Gene were present in the faces of people who were in the courtroom. To me that was what justice was—building a movement that would not forget.

I stayed with the CJDV until the very end—the spring of 1991. By then we had won the civil suit, seen Tony Baruso finally tried and imprisoned for life without parole (in 1990), and collected damages from the Marcoses' estate. The judge and jury awarded the families a total of $23.3 million, but hunting down the Marcos family money turned out to be a difficult task. We eventually settled for a much smaller amount, and the Domingo Viernes Justice Fund was formed, a portion of the money going to continuing some of the political work that Silme and Gene had begun. Movie and book deals came and went, and some became quite controversial within our leadership collective.

People always used to ask me how I stuck it out for so long, because others in the CJDV came and went, moving on to other things in their lives, whether having children or becoming involved in other issues and political arenas. But for some like myself, we knew there was no option—we had to see this to the end.

As I remember my old CJDV speeches (many of which are still in my files in my mother's cramped garage), I really believed that we would get justice for Silme and Gene no matter how long it took. In fact, when I look at some of my work now, I'm still trying to get justice for Silme and Gene by ensuring that people do not forget their legacy. Recently, my son's physical education teacher asked him if he was related to the guy who was murdered years ago because my son's middle name is Silme Domingo. My son said yes. I know through such incidents that Silme and Gene are remembered. My only wish now is that Mike Withey would come to me today and tell me that a piece of damning evidence has surfaced, revealing the US complicity in the murders. Without any hesitation, I know that Mike and I would be ready to organize again to write the final chapter of this work.

DEFEATING THE MARCOSES IN A COURT OF LAW

JIM DOUGLAS

Although lawyer Jim Douglas was not a member of the KDP, he was practically one, like fellow lawyer Mike Withey with whom he worked on the Committee for Justice for Domingo and Viernes (CJDV) legal team. Jim had known Gene and Silme through political activities before their murders in 1981. Having gone through the twists and turns of the Estates of Domingo and Viernes v. Ferdinand Marcos *wrongful death civil lawsuit, being in the courtroom when US District Court judge Barbara Rothstein announced the jury's verdict against the Marcos estate, he says, remains one of the most memorable moments in his career as a lawyer.*

DECEMBER 15, 1989. The legal team had received a phone call from the judge's clerk that the jury had reached a verdict. It was only six hours after they got the case. We tried to be calm as we charged uphill to the federal courthouse. An out-of-town reporter who had followed the trial yelled to us from across the street, "It must be bad news for them to come back so soon, don't you think?" He was just like everyone else who, for more than eight years, doubted our theory about the murders of Gene Viernes and Silme Domingo. Our allegations in the civil case were only for movie scripts, they thought; things like that don't happen in real life.

Lawyers, the families of Gene and Silme, and activists in the Committee for Justice for Domingo and Viernes (CJDV) gathered at an hour's notice in Judge Barbara Rothstein's courtroom. I was totally unprepared for the intense emotions that charged the next few minutes. Thousands of hours of political and legal work for dozens—hundreds—of people had come down to this moment. I remember that Jeff Robinson, a criminal lawyer who brought to our team his experience with conspiracy law, and I seemed on the verge of fainting from hyperventilation. I was too dazed to notice much else.

The judge calmly read the jury's verdict: Were Ferdinand or Imelda Marcos members of the conspiracy we had alleged? *Yes*, for both! Were the murders of Gene and Silme an overt act of that conspiracy? *Yes* . . . And the judge went on to slowly and deliberately read the nine separate damage figures, totaling $15 million awarded by the jury! We had triumphed in a way unimaginable when we first filed the case back in September 1982. We had taken on one of history's most powerful dictators in a case most observers thought to be a product of our overly active, collective imaginations. How far we had come, and against what odds! We had won. We didn't know whether to laugh or cry, so most of us did both. By coincidence, one of the Committee for Justice's regular community meetings was planned for that evening. But the agenda had suddenly changed to a celebration.

Within a few days of Gene's and Silme's murders in June 1981, a group of us met to form a legal team. We knew it would be uphill all the way—US courts were not known for holding pro-US dictators liable for murder. But we were determined to give it our best shot.

Mike Withey, who quit his law practice to devote himself full-time to the case, was the best at generating creative ideas and thinking big. John Caughlan was our elder statesman, a seasoned veteran who brought decades of experience in political-legal struggles from which we could draw lessons. Liz Schott worked tirelessly outside her nine-to-five job at Legal Services and brought experience with procedural problems, as well as a healthy dose of skepticism about the legal theories and strategies we hatched up. Jeff Robinson, who joined us six months before we went to trial, was our conspiracy expert. Me? I was the details guy who tried to keep us all working on the same page, which at times was much easier said than done.

For the next eight and a half years we had a million meetings. That may be a bit of an exaggeration, but it felt like a million. Certainly we spent thousands and thousands of hours working on the case (that's not an exaggeration). We could always find some minute legal point to argue about. Terri Mast and Cindy Domingo frequently participated and sometimes must have wondered whether we were starting to lose our marbles. But as the months and years went by, we actually did a lot of innovative legal work.

Most of us on the legal team had known Gene and Silme personally, and that was probably motivation enough for our initial involvement. However, by the time we filed the case, we were collectively convinced—based on our analysis of the facts we had uncovered—that both comrades had in fact been killed as a result of the Marcos regime's conspiracy to suppress opposition in the United States. We felt we had the facts to support our theory. But, unfortunately, we had a hard time convincing anyone else in mainstream legal circles. Sheer determination pushed us on nonetheless.

In the first months after the murders, we hired an investigator, a real cloak-and-dagger type. (We hired him with proceeds that Terri had donated from a life-insurance policy Silme had fortuitously purchased for union officers only a few weeks before he was murdered.) Our private eye had worked on the case that tried to fix responsibility for the death of nuclear whistleblower Karen Silkwood, but he still spooked us really badly. We weren't used to people entering a room and scanning the place for electronic surveillance before every meeting. We had to communicate with him using public phones and code words. To add to the drama, our mail was being intercepted at the time—opened and resealed in a way intended to be obvious to us. Meanwhile, our investigator was being followed by some burly, Filipino-looking guys, one of whom he was able to photograph. It was all pretty unnerving.

Our cloak-and-dagger man still had contacts in military intelligence circles from his years in the Marines. After several months, he gave us a report, which confirmed our worst suspicions. He informed us that US government intelligence knew that the Marcos dictatorship was monitoring opposition in the United States and there had been communications between US and Philippine intelligence regarding Gene's trip to the Philippines in the months before his murder. Supposedly, US agents conveyed incorrect information to Philippine agents that Gene was carrying almost $300,000 with him, intended for the opposition, the New People's Army (NPA) in particular. In addition, our investigator's source said that Tony Baruso, president of Local 37 of the International Longshoremen's and Warehousemen's Union (ILWU; the Alaska Cannery Workers Union), had made three phone calls to the US State Department within twenty-four hours of the murders. Although we were never able to uncover US government documents to verify all this, the information formed the cornerstone of our theory that the conspiracy resulting in the deaths of Gene and Silme was far larger than gambling operations at the canneries.

In the first few months after the murders, we also did some of our own investigating. Mike somehow got a copy of a secret Senate committee report about Marcos agents' activities in the United States. We also got our hands on a Defense Intelligence Agency report that introduced to the US intelligence community five Philippine military attachés assigned to the Philippine embassy in Washington, DC. Their role was explicitly "to monitor and possibly operate against anti-Marcos dissidents in the United States."

While we were convinced, early on, that the conspiracy reached as far as the Presidential Palace in the Philippines and the US State Department, the immediate fight against fascist terror required that we concentrate on punishing the hit men, the little guys. If we failed to defend ourselves on that basic level, any future organizing work would be impossible.

Within the first few months of the murders, the hit men, Jimmy Ramil and Pompeyo "Ben" Guloy Jr., were brought to trial and convicted based on Silme's dying declaration and the prosecution's theory that the murders were motivated by a dispute over Local 37 dispatching for cannery work. The prosecutor, Joanne Maida, argued that the men were Tulisan gang members who, because of union reforms, stood to lose their gambling operations in the Alaska fish canneries.

Even at that first trial, it was evident that larger, more powerful forces were involved. A certain LeVane Forsythe surfaced as a last-minute surprise witness for the defense, saying he had been on the murder scene. He attempted to contradict key evidence, most importantly claiming that he had spoken with Silme right after Silme had been shot and stumbled out of the union office. According to Forsythe, Silme told him he didn't recognize any of the gunmen. Forsythe's story was preposterous, but what tripped him up was a critical detail—he testified that Silme spoke with a foreign accent. Silme, however, was born and raised in the United States and spoke with no accent. (Forsythe also admitted on the stand that, coincidentally, he would be a surprise witness in the Howard Hughes trial involving the "Mormon Will.") Fortunately, the jury disregarded Forsythe's testimony.

As unlikely as Forsythe's story seemed, we came to believe that he had indeed been at the murder scene, acting as a US government agent. We believed he had been instructed to try to get an acquittal for Ramil and Guloy and derail our efforts early on. We learned that Forsythe had a long history as an FBI operative. He told us years later, in a deposition for the civil suit, that his role was often initiated by a call from a control agent, who would instruct him to go to a location at a specific time and keep his eyes and ears open. He then would write a report about what he observed. He said he had dictated a tape of what he observed on the day of Gene's and Silme's murders, but he "lost it."

The early period immediately after the murders was a very active time for everyone involved in the justice efforts. Hundreds of people participated in community meetings and observed the criminal trials. Hundreds more organized and participated in teach-ins that drew parallels with similar cases, such as the Silkwood murder and Chile's murder of former diplomat Orlando Letelier and his aide Ronni Moffitt in Washington, DC.

The first stage of our legal struggle took about a year. It concluded with the trial in April 1982 of Tulisan gang leader Tony Dictado. While he claimed to be innocent, he kept testifying that he was unable to say what he knew because he feared for his family's safety in the Philippines. While this added to the intrigue that there was something bigger and more sinister going on, it didn't help Dictado. He was found guilty and became the third gang member sentenced to life imprisonment without possibility of parole.

Even after two successful criminal trials, the chief prosecutor steadfastly refused to prosecute former Local 37 president Tony Baruso. This was more because of politics than disbelief by the prosecutor's office about Baruso's involvement in the conspiracy. Baruso had already been discovered to be the owner of the murder weapon, which was mysteriously found in a parks department trash bin. Unbelievably, Baruso told the police he had never seen the gun—he had bought it in a paper bag, which he never bothered to open to see the gun before it was supposedly stolen.

Another startling event involved Boy Pilay, the third gunman. Pilay disappeared soon after the murders, but not before telling a witness that Baruso was supposed to pay each gang member five thousand dollars for the hit. Pilay was clearly the weak link in covering for Baruso. Yet the police seemed to drag their feet in tracking him down. The Committee for Justice did all the footwork for them. We told them that a rumor in Chinatown had it that Pilay was back East with his family. Then we found the address in Maryland and even confirmed that he was there. But still the police botched it. When Pilay resurfaced in Seattle, we surveilled his movements ourselves and literally led the police to him. Once he was in custody, we attempted to pressure the prosecutor's office to indict Pilay and Baruso together. Instead, the prosecutor released Pilay—and he was killed, execution-style, within a few days.

There was no other way to interpret this incompetence than to assume that the FBI must have been exerting even greater pressure on the Seattle's prosecutor's office than we were—in order to stop the prosecutor from pursuing the criminal case any further, thereby protecting Baruso. We realized we were at a dead end, but politically we could not afford to break our alliance with the prosecutor's office. Instead, we turned our attention to what became known as the civil suit. We filed in civil court in September 1982 after all the hit men had been successfully imprisoned or, in the case of Boy Pilay, otherwise accounted for.

It was thrilling to finally get the civil case started. A Jesuit priest and member of the Silkwood legal team, Bill Davis, was working with us. He managed to successfully serve Ferdinand Marcos with our legal papers while Marcos was at a press conference in connection with his state visit to the United States. Bill also chased Alexander Haig down a slippery footpath in front of Haig's home to serve him papers. But despite these moments of high drama, it was clear from the beginning that we would have an uphill battle all the way.

First, we didn't have a warm reception from Donald Voorhees, the judge assigned to our case. He dismissed Ferdinand and Imelda Marcos from the case out of hand, based on the US State Department's "suggestion of immunity" owing to their being "heads of state." Without our even realizing it, we got lucky when the State Department, for whatever reason, failed to get an additional final order, which would have forced us to appeal the decision at that time, an appeal we would have surely lost. But because no final order dismissing the Marcoses was ever entered, years later we were able to reinstate them back into the lawsuit—after they had been forced to flee from Manila in 1986.

Our original complaint also alleged that US agents knew the Marcos regime posed a threat to its critics in the United States yet did nothing to halt operations against anti-Marcos forces and, in fact, even shared intelligence with the dictatorship. But we were never able to get hard evidence to substantiate these claims. Our discovery requests led nowhere, and the US government successfully resisted our separate cases under the Freedom of Information Act. So within months of filing the case, Judge Voorhees ruled that our allegations were insufficient and let all defendants from the US government out of the case as well.

The only early ruling that benefited our cause involved the government of the Philippines, which was named as a defendant under a federal law making a foreign government liable for its agents' actions that lead to injuries in the United States. Although the judge initially dismissed the Philippine government, he gave us the right to redraft the complaint; then he recognized our amended allegations as adequate and kept the government in the case. However, he put the entire case on hold while the Philippines appealed the decision. (We were unable to get a favorable decision from the US Ninth Circuit Court of Appeals until several years after we filed.) So, while we were not completely dead in the water, we obviously were getting nowhere fast.

While Marcos was in power, the Philippine government was represented by the prestigious Washington, DC, firm Covington and Burling, where some of my Ivy League classmates had chosen to ply their trade after law school. The firm treated our case as a ridiculous annoyance, but somehow we kept at it, trying to gather information as best we could. Mostly we were hoping for a break of some kind.

And, of course, we finally got the biggest break we could have ever dreamed of—the "People Power" revolution in 1986 that led to the overthrow of the Marcos dictatorship. This historic event changed the fortune of the Filipino people, but it also changed our fortunes as well. Overnight, the long struggle of the anti-Marcos movement in the United States was vindicated, showing that all along it had represented the broad democratic interests and sentiments of the Filipino people. Suddenly, our case did not seem as much of a long shot.

Although the new government of Corazon Aquino was legally responsible for the actions of its predecessor, the change was astounding. We started to get cooperation from a new law firm representing the Philippine government, to the point that the new lawyers went to the Philippines themselves to make sure that a proper search was made for documents relevant to our claim. A second fortuitous change was that Judge Barbara Rothstein took over the case because of the failing health of the first judge. The new judge, no doubt in part because of the political changes in the Philippines, proved to be much more receptive to our case. Finally, we were on a more optimistic trajectory—maybe we'd get somewhere after all.

Ferdinand Marcos made a lot of mistakes, and surely one of them was bringing certain documents with him when he fled the Philippines for Hawaii. They were seized by the US Customs Service and we were able to subpoena them. Although we didn't find the smoking gun we were hoping for, we discovered a piece of paper that was pretty close. It was a statement of expenses from a certain Mabuhay Corporation. It showed how the Marcos regime had illegally spent almost one million dollars in the United States between 1979 and 1981 on various activities, including political campaigns (sometimes contributing to both sides in one election) and the attempted purchase of a popular Bay Area radio station, KJAZ. But most interesting was the intriguing item called "special security projects."

As it turned out, Marcos's man in San Francisco was a physician, Leonilo Malabed, who managed the Mabuhay Corporation. A lifelong friend of Marcos, the good doctor drove a white Rolls-Royce convertible and bought and sold expensive real estate. But amid all the large transactions on the statement of expenses, one small entry under "special security projects" jumped off the page: fifteen thousand dollars spent on May 17, 1981, two weeks before Gene and Silme were killed. This electrified us because that date was the very same weekend Baruso had made a quick trip to San Francisco. Years earlier, we had subpoenaed Baruso's travel records. We could place him in San Francisco on that weekend and knew it had some significance, but we had nothing solid to tie it to; it was a piece of the puzzle we had set aside hoping to find other pieces to connect to it. Now we had something. This was also the same weekend of a pro-Marcos gathering in nearby San Jose. Last, but not least, the amount exactly matched the story, attributed to Boy Pilay, that the three gunmen had been promised five thousand dollars apiece.

This circumstantial evidence was the closest we got to catching Baruso red-handed. Naturally, he tried to squirm out of it. Back in his first deposition in 1982, Baruso had denied taking such a trip. Then, when we showed him the records, he remembered going but couldn't remember the reason. Finally, in another deposition several years later, he all of a sudden remembered that the trip was for "fraternal lodge business," and he could even remember the names of all the "lodge brothers" he met with. The only (convenient) hitch was that every single one of them had died in the interim. Not surprisingly, Baruso insisted under oath that he didn't know and had never laid eyes on Dr. Malabed. When we inquired about ten thousand dollars deposited into his bank account shortly after the murders, again he couldn't remember but said lamely that maybe he had been "lucky at bingo" or that the money may have been race-track winnings.

After the People Power revolution, the tables quickly turned on Marcos. Not only were we able to examine his seized papers, but shortly after his arrival in Hawaii, we were able to take his deposition under oath. By simply being allowed to question him, we had accomplished something inconceivable only a few months earlier.

We were the first lawyers to get to question the man who still insisted on being referred to as "the duly elected president of the Philippines." It was a hot, humid day. We questioned him on the lanai. He was very uncomfortable. Perhaps it was the weather, or perhaps his failing kidneys, but he repeatedly and abruptly excused himself to change clothes. (But his wife, Imelda, kept the same shoes on all day. She was livid at our intrusion, but the most she could do was play "Send in the Clowns" on the piano as we returned from lunch.)

As usual, we were persistent. Because of Marcos's failing health, the deposition was done in short stints. Nonetheless, we questioned him for a total of fourteen hours. Predictably, he gave self-serving accounts of the freedoms allowed by his regime. However, he also was careful to hide behind the right not to incriminate himself when asked whether his intelligence funds paid for the murders of Gene and Silme.

By the time our civil trial began in November 1989, Marcos was dead. His son, Bongbong, or Ferdinand Jr., was substituted as the party to represent the Marcos estate. We had already settled with the new government of the Philippines, and its lawyers would not be participating in the trial. We also decided to dismiss other defendants, such as the gang members, in order to focus on the Marcoses, Malabed, and Baruso. This put the triumvirate at a decided disadvantage, because their lawyers had had very minimal involvement with pretrial preparation, in stark contrast to us. For years, while Marcos was still in power, they had sat back complacently and relied on the Philippine government's high-powered legal counsel, not to mention the unspoken sympathy of the US State Department. But now they had to work and work hard, and they weren't ready.

November 1989. As we waited for prospective jurors to be selected on the first day of the trial, Mike Withey and I recalled how, for years, our main goal had simply been to get the case to trial. Now here we were allowing ourselves to think we could win it. Our plan was that Mike and Jeff Robinson would question the witnesses; I was still keeping track of the details; Rebecca Cate and Gary Iwamoto had also joined our legal team, doing legal research and helping organize the massive amounts of paper.

The three-week trial would be the distilled version of all we had learned since 1981. We didn't set out to prove that Marcos had personally ordered the murders or that Malabed had knowingly paid for them. Instead, we would show that they had created and run the overarching conspiracy—in both the Philippines and the United States—which intimidated, harassed, and sometimes murdered its opposition. We would try to convince the judge and jury by "clear and convincing evidence" that the murders of Gene and Silme were the result of that conspiracy, paid for partially out of Malabed's Mabuhay fund.

Terri, Cindy, Gene's sister Barbara, other activists, Local 37 members, and family members took the stand, once again, to describe the kind of people Gene and Silme were, their participation in the struggle against Marcos, and their efforts to reform the union. Witnesses testified about Gene's trip to meet with the labor opposition in the Philippines shortly before the murders and explained why they concluded that he had come under intense Marcos surveillance. They testified as to how Gene, returning from the Philippines, met up with Silme and others at the ILWU convention in Honolulu, and how together they led a floor fight to pass a resolution critical of the Marcos regime that would send an ILWU investigating team to the Philippines to look at labor conditions.

Prominent leaders of the anti-Marcos opposition also testified, including then–foreign minister Raul Manglapus by videotape. They told of the threats against them and of the people who had disappeared or been murdered for their anti-dictatorship activities. The jurors were particularly stunned by the videotape of the last flight to Manila by returning exiled leader Benigno Aquino Jr., in 1983, including his being taken off the plane by uniformed men, followed by the gunfire that rang out, killing him right on the tarmac.

Ex-CIA agent and critic Ralph McGehee vividly described the range of intelligence techniques used by US-client governments against their democratic opposition. Princeton international law professor Richard Falk told of the Marcos regime's human rights violations and its particularly strong reaction to the threat of instability caused by the worsening economic situation and resulting labor unrest. The final witness was former intelligence chief and then–Philippine congressman Bonifacio Gillego, who had been trained by the CIA as a young man and later became an outspoken critic of Marcos. He convincingly testified that Marcos operatives would certainly have had Gene under surveillance, given his activities in the anti-Marcos opposition, his trip to the Philippines, and his role in passing the resolution at the ILWU convention.

There were also a few lighter moments in an otherwise intense trial. We put the Marcoses on the stand via the videotaped depositions we had done with them. As Imelda droned on and on about the interrelationship between beauty, independence, and honor, the jury grew restless and started to fidget. After half an hour of the tape, Judge Rothstein interrupted with a sharp command, "Would counsel approach the bench." As the lawyers rushed up to sidebar, the judge whispered to Mike Withey, "How much more of this woman do we have to listen to?"

Mike stammered, "Well, uh, it should be done in about another hour or so."

The judge's eyes turned into saucers. "Can't you cut it back?"

"Well, it's hard to edit the tape now," Withey said apologetically.

"Well, you've got to do something," she said.

"Okay," Mike offered, "let's play another five minutes so it doesn't look like you cut us off, and then we'll put the tape in as an exhibit."

"Agreed," Judge Rothstein said.

A few minutes later, Withey pulled the plug on the video machine, and Imelda was unceremoniously pushed off center stage in midsentence.

We also put Baruso on the stand, and Jeff Robinson completely disemboweled him. Baruso repeated invoked the Fifth Amendment. His lawyer kept motioning to him conspicuously when to plead self-incrimination. "I decline to answer that question on advice of counsel, based on the Fifth Amendment," Baruso would stammer.

Still, Jeff bore down. "Mr. Baruso, Ade Domingo, mother of slain union leader Silme Domingo, testified that you once told the Filipino community that you had personally met President Marcos and that he was a close friend of yours."

"I never said that," Baruso countered.

Jeff turned to the overflow crowd in the courtroom and motioned for Ade to stand up. "Ade Domingo, are you present?" Jeff thundered.

"Yes, I'm here," she said, standing hesitantly.

Jeff swiveled to stare at Baruso. "You recognize Ade Domingo, do you not?"

"Yes, that's her," Baruso said.

"Are you telling this jury that Ade Domingo lied under oath in this courtroom?" Jeff asked defiantly.

Baruso shifted in his seat, avoiding Jeff's and Ade's stares. "Yes, that woman lied," he said.

Jeff jumped to his feet. "So, Ade Domingo's a liar, is that what you're saying?"

Baruso finished, "Yes, she's a liar."

Jeff sat back triumphantly. Here was Baruso, repeatedly taking the Fifth while accusing the mother of Silme of lying under oath—it was a high point of the trial. "That's all, your Honor," Jeff said.

After three weeks of our witnesses, the defendants' case was over in an afternoon. Baruso presented no defense at all. Malabed elected to have his case decided by the judge, not the jury. He also chose to not even show up in the courtroom. His testimony was offered from the tapes of five previous depositions, where he had spent most of the time invoking the Fifth Amendment. Through his lawyer, Malabed presented a dozen receipts the day before the trial began, but these seemed only to weaken his case. Some of the receipts were on Marcos's presidential stationery and some on the good doctor's prescription pads. They showed that Malabed had passed large sums of cash—up to $66,000 at a time. He admitted that a lot of the money was in cash, passed in plain brown envelopes. The receipts used different code words; for example, "payment for 33 of your reinvigorating vitamin tablets." Clearly these guys never thought they would get caught—they were so confident they could afford to be cute. The receipt for the critical May 17 expenditure documented the sale of fifteen thousand copies of *Bataan News*, a pro-Marcos tabloid that Malabed published and that sold on the newsstand for just fifty cents apiece. Malabed's only witnesses were two men, involved in the same black-bag operation, whom he sent to testify about the receipts. But he hadn't prepared their stories well enough, and they contradicted each other on a number of critical details regarding the suspicious fifteen-thousand-dollar transaction.

As for the Marcoses' defense, their lawyer Richard Hibey made no rebuttal to the damaging testimony we had presented. As the trial was rapidly drawing to a conclusion, Hibey did object to having the jury hear Malabed's two witnesses. "Your Honor," Hibey began, "these are witnesses called by Dr. Malabed in his defense. They do not pertain to the case against my clients."

Judge Rothstein, a bit perplexed, called for another sidebar.

"Well," Withey volunteered, "I suppose the court could hear the witnesses with the jury out of the room."

The judge looked at Hibey. "Well, Mr. Hibey, you are going to call Intelligence Agent James Nach by deposition, is that correct?"

"Yes, your Honor," Hibey offered.

"Well then, why doesn't the jury listen to you read Mr. Nach's deposition while I take the testimony of Dr. Malabed's witnesses upstairs," she said.

"But," Hibey objected, "that may look like nobody cares about my witness."

Rothstein said, "Well, I'll explain to the jury that I have already read the deposition of Mr. Nach and will consider it."

And with that, the courtroom cleared. The jury, the judge, the Marcoses' lawyers, and I were the only people left in the room. The judge, the rest of our legal team, Malabed's attorney, and all of the audience went upstairs to hear Malabed's witnesses. It was obvious to the jury that whatever deposition Marcos's lawyer was going to read, it had little significance whatsoever. How far the mighty had fallen.

When the judge and everyone else returned, and the court was called back into session, Mr. Hibey rose and stunned us all. "Your Honor, the defense rests."

The look of incredulity on several jurors' faces was obvious. Linda Barber, the jury foreperson, leaned forward, her eyes wide open and mouth agape. The entire defense of a multilayered conspiracy ended with Hibey offering but one witness, who testified by deposition to an almost-empty courtroom. It was a fitting ending to a defense that really had no defense.

Mike's closing argument brought people to tears, including some jurors. He urged people to see through the cover-up that Baruso had devised when he paid the Tulisan gang members, who had their own motives due to union reforms to do the dirty work for the Marcos regime. Mike finished by asking the jury for a verdict that, in the words from the Old Testament as adapted by Martin Luther King, would allow "justice to flow down like a mighty stream," and the jury heard him.

A month later, Judge Rothstein issued her formal written decision bolstering the jury's verdict and awarding damages at $8.3 million in addition to the previous jury award of $15 million. We had convinced not only a jury but also the presiding judge of the federal court for the western district of Washington. Judge Rothstein noted the "overwhelming, and essentially unrebutted evidence" establishing Marcos's illegal intelligence operations in the United States, which "committed numerous acts of harassment, intimidation, and violence" against the opposition. She found that Gene and Silme had "posed a substantial threat to the Marcos regime" because "they were rising young leaders with ties to powerful labor organizations in the U.S. and they were active and effective members of the anti-Marcos opposition." Regarding Dr. Malabed, the judge said that his testimony "vacillated between a total lack of memory and outright fabrication," and his two witnesses' testimony "the court found singularly unbelievable." Last but not least, Judge Rothstein held that there was "overwhelming evidence regarding [Baruso's] involvement in the murders" and that "he offered almost nothing to contradict this evidence." She said, "As to questions Baruso did answer, his testimony was evasive and wholly unbelievable."

We hadn't quite won everything. One big loose end was tied up, however, when the prosecutor's office, spurred on by the success of our civil suit, finally decided to bring criminal charges against Tony Baruso for conspiring to murder Gene and Silme. The trial was swift and the justice was final; by this time Baruso was a broken man. The final chapter ended when the penitentiary gates slammed behind Baruso—life imprisonment without possibility of parole. The only party to the conspiracy to get off was the US State Department and the intelligence community. Surprise!

On a more personal note, the other disappointment was that no one ever made the movie. A scriptwriter took the time to write it all down, but HBO wouldn't buy it. I guess it was too political or didn't have enough sex or car chases in it. That's too bad, because we did have the brave heroines (Terri and Cindy), tense courtroom scenes, and international intrigue. Cindy and Terri had wanted to play themselves in the movie, but only if someone handsome played Mike's role. Everyone was agreed that Pee-wee Herman would be perfectly cast to play me, but just my luck, the movie would have been released just when Pee-wee's compromising peep-show escapades broke out into the open.

PART FOUR

LOOKING BACK

TODAY, former KDP activists have diverse careers, and many are still engaged in various political causes. For some, not all their past experiences were positive, although when former members get together in reunions big and small, it is the camaraderie of the past that prevails and colors the occasion. There is always an underlying poignancy during these invariably joyous gatherings that comes from the commonly shared realization that some of the truths they all embraced in the past have become uncertainties today. All former KDP activists—and some of their children too—however, acknowledge that their years with the organization are an indelible part of their lives.

REVOLUTIONARY BABY

REBECCA APOSTOL

*Rebecca Apostol is the daughter of KDP activists Bo and Sorcy
Apostol. She is proud to write her father's story as a tribute to his KDP
activism and its impact on her own life. Rebecca was born and raised
in Sacramento, where she began as a community and political
organizer. She has focused her professional life on building strong,
progressive, and politically active communities of color. This has led
her to work with and build programs for esteemed organizations like
the AFL-CIO, Asian and Pacific Islander American Vote (APIAVote),
and Mobilize the Immigrant Vote.*

WAS a revolutionary baby. Born a short eight months after the 1986 fall of
the Marcos regime in the Philippines, I always felt that I was the culmina-
tion of my parents' love, dedication, and hard work for their country and
the beginning of their full investment in the family they sought to build in
America.

Like many red diaper babies (as KDP activists' children are affectionately
called), I grew up learning of my parents' activism and the movement through
community storytelling. Each new recitation revealed new details. Since my
parents' love story is intertwined with their activism, my favorite tellings
came from their fellow KDP activists with whom they remained close friends;
these versions usually gave away juicy information that my parents had forgotten or chosen not to reveal.

I remember being about eleven and running up to my mother, laughing,
"You tried to set Dad up with who?!" Auntie Nonie (Briones) had just told
me about my mom's initial efforts to divert my father's advances. When my

parents and their friends would all join together at the table, stories would naturally come out about demonstrations, discussion groups, strategy sessions, writing and publishing *Ang Katipunan*—it was like dinner theater! The characters, the varied settings (as far as New York and Hawaii), the triumphs, the tears, and the learning of lessons all fully captured my attention. I was never asked to leave the table. I was in awe of their real life experiences and admired their dedication to the greater movement and most of all, to humanity.

My father's story is one not often heard even within KDP, as many of the men who traveled with my dad chose not to become activists and returned to the Philippines from their exploitative 4-H trainee program. Up-and-coming young people from the Philippines' rural areas were promised training in modern agriculture but found themselves being used as cheap, if not free, labor on private US farms, often in unbearable conditions. My father was among those who, with the help of the KDP, exposed the program and caused its suspension. I recall first hearing references to his story while going through the produce section of the supermarket, as Dad referred to particular fruits and vegetables, how he had worked on farms where they grew on the West Coast (central and northern California, Oregon, Washington), and how easy or difficult it was to grow them.

When I was seven, we bought a house that had a small garden in the back, and I learned what an incredible gift my father had—not just a green thumb, a green hand. Everything he touched grew, and grew beautifully. As we tended to and picked strawberries on the weekend, he shared how things that grow well are loved and cared for by those who grow them, like the rice he used to plant with his dad back home. He said it was very much unlike the farming system here in the United States, where the workers weren't given credit as the growers but were treated poorly and used as migrant labor. Worse, he explained, was that the owners—who rarely, if ever, touched the soil or their fields—were given the titles of grower and farmer. It was misleading that those who did the work never received the credit they deserved.

This may seem like heavy conversation for weekend gardening with your daughter, but I cherished every moment of it. My dad worked two full-time jobs during the week, and we got to spend time together as a family on the weekends. And when we weren't out being a family of community organizers, my parents made sure to pass on their dedication to social justice and equality through their personal experiences and stories.

We talked about how the *manongs* (older Filipino men) of the 1920s and 1930s went through trials similar to my dad's and much worse, due to racism and the racist laws that supported unfair and at times less than human treatment. We spoke of Philip Vera Cruz, the Filipinos of the Agricultural Workers Organizing Committee and the Delano Grape Strike, and how Filipino and Mexican farmworkers had organized together during the labor movement. And finally, I learned of my father's own gross mistreatment when he'd come to the United States in 1977, having been promised higher education only to be used as cheap labor, forced to work long hours in the sweltering heat and freezing cold, for as many days a week as the host farmers made him.

My father worked hard every day of his life and continues to do so, to provide for himself and his family. We certainly did not have a privileged upbringing, but he made sure that we all had health care and food on the table. He sacrificed his own health, working eighteen to twenty hours a day for nearly thirty years, barely catching up on sleep over the weekend. He taught me an old-school work ethic with a new-school attitude. Work was always going to be hard, because anything worth taking pride in takes great effort. As a janitor, he learned that work also wouldn't always be fulfilling; so for his children, he taught us to follow our passion in life and become experts so we can make a living from it.

In my short twenty-seven years, and through the passing of my Auntie Nonie Briones and some of my parents' other KDP activist friends over the years, I have learned that our legacies lie in our stories—the ones we tell and, eventually, the ones that are told about us. For my unassuming father, I honor his legacy by retelling his story as he told it to me while I was growing up.

Through one of his most difficult trials as an undocumented student, thousands of miles away from home at the young age of seventeen, being demeaned as cheap labor in a profession he loved, my father found love, his voice, and activism, and he built a family. Oh, and did I mention that after the KDP and the community exposed the exploitative 4-H international program, it was suspended?

This is my father's extraordinary immigrant legacy.

SCOOBY DOO: GROWING UP WITH THE KDP

SILAHIS M. TAVERNA

Silahis M. Taverna (fondly called Sinag by her family and close friends) was born in Washington, DC. Growing up in the nation's capital, she attended many protest marches and pickets, including actions protesting the Marcos dictatorship. As a young adult with an independent, free-spirited streak and spiritual character, she expressed herself in her art and her determination to make this world better than when she found it. After graduating from college, she moved to Hawaii, where she found her voice and connected with local environmental organizations on the North Shore of Oahu and in Maui. She advocated for the protection of the islands' cultural heritage, ecosystems, and endangered species. And she fought against unfettered development. Sinag unfortunately passed away in 1986 at age twenty-eight, but her spirit and ideals live on in the continuing advocacy and community work of the Save Honolua Coalition (SHC), of which she was a board member when she died.

"N ASAAN si Mommy?" I remember demanding of my dad, always inquiring about my mom's whereabouts.

"Your mom is at a meeting," he would always reply.

Meeting, such a strange word, yet already part of my two-year-old vocabulary. I learned that word almost at the same time as I did *inom* (drink) or *matulog* (sleep).

I would often accompany my parents to these strange gatherings. They (the grownups) would assign me tasks to keep my restlessness under some degree of control. At the tender age of four, I mastered the art of envelope stuffing. I would make a game of my task, turning those important leaflets and flyers into paper airplanes.

Despite all the chaos I caused at meetings, I actively participated in the events my parents helped organize. I attended everything my parents did. I picketed in front of the White House, cheered on my Tito Jon Melegrito as he led many of our rallies, helped at fund-raisers, and even sang for President Corazon Aquino when she visited the United States after the fall of Marcos. To me, these things were part of everyday life.

Having a child's outlook on my parent's causes, I figured that they were always right: I sensed the seriousness of the battles fought but never fully grasped their entirety. To me, everything resembled the plot of my Saturday-morning cartoon, *Scooby Doo*. There was only one conflict—the good guy versus the bad guy. If you were the good guy (which I thought I was), you could do anything you wanted; and the bad guy (for example, Marcos and Ronald Reagan) could do nothing to hurt you. So, acting on instinct, I drew "No Marcos" and "No Reagan" signs, taped them on our doors, and picketed by myself on our front lawn.

I grew up always voicing my opinions and later continued to act on them. Most parts of radical politics were second nature to me. So you can imagine my surprise when I entered Meeker Junior High in Kent, Washington (a suburb of Seattle). People in Kent lived in a suburban bubble. Most of my classmates were like, "Duh . . . huh? Politics?" They seemed so different from me. The biggest concern many of my friends had was what to wear on Friday night. Most of them hadn't even thought about the kind of things I had already done. I remember often thinking, "Thank God I'm not that ignorant!"

A while later, another realization hit me as I was talking to my boyfriend, Jay, on the phone one night. We were humorously comparing our childhoods and some of the different obstacles we faced growing up. His world was based on the streets of Beacon Hill, where you were always "kickin' it thuggish style." Gangs, fights, drugs, guns, and dying "homies" were part of everyday life. It was almost funny when I told him that I had practically dedicated my life to the principles of nonviolence, equality, and civil rights. Although our battles were different—Jay fought for survival and respect, whereas I fought for peace and justice—I learned that everybody has a struggle, and there are many shades of gray between the black and white I saw so innocently as a child.

Growing up with the KDP has taught me many lessons I use in life. I have seen the world from many different perspectives. I know about my parents' struggles that opened doors for my generation. By teaching me their beliefs and causes, my parents have given me the best gift possible: at fifteen, I had knowledge and an understanding most of my friends did not. I thank my parents for these experiences and gifts.

ONE FEBRUARY NIGHT IN SAN FRANCISCO

FELY VILLASIN

Fely Villasin, born on December 24, 1941, arrived in Toronto in 1974. Her then-husband, Ruben Cusipag, a journalist, was arrested by the Philippine military when Marcos installed himself as dictator in September 1972. After his release, they left for Canada. Fely was a brilliant student who skipped grades in high school and graduated with a degree in foreign service from the University of the Philippines when she was just fifteen. She earned a French government scholarship to the Sorbonne, where she studied for four years with Algerian and Vietnamese students at the height of the Algerian War and the French counterinsurgency in Vietnam. Fely learned about cultural awakening and anticolonialism, and when martial law was declared in the Philippines, she knew that resistance was the only option. Upon arriving in Toronto, she led the organizing of a KDP counterpart as a leading member of the International Association of Filipino Patriots, which received all the training and theoretical education available to KDP members. Fely quickly became known as an energetic presence in the Toronto Filipino community, leading the anti-dictatorship work and helping found the Kababayan Community Centre, Kapisanan Philippine Centre, and Carlos Bulosan Theatre. Fely was also well known in the Canadian women's movement; she was a member of the executive committee of the National Action Committee on the Status of Women (Canada) in the 1990s. In 1981, Fely was transferred to the San Francisco Bay Area to help coordinate the nationwide activities of the Coalition Against the Marcos Dictatorship (CAMD) in the United States and Canada. Returning to Toronto after Marcos's ouster, she became the coordinator of Intercede in 1987, which champions the rights of domestic workers, caregivers, and new immigrants. She ceaselessly campaigned for landed status and workplace protections for domestic workers. She also traveled frequently to the Philippines,

*building ties with the women's movement and the democratic Left
there. Fely, a leader of Toronto's Filipino community, women's rights
activist, playwright, and theater director, died on December 27, 2006,
after a three-year battle with cancer. Fely had one daughter, Nadine,
who continues her mother's love for cultural work.*

YELLOW confetti is raining on us. I strain my neck looking up as my face catches pieces of paper torn from the Yellow Pages of telephone directories. The news has reached us. It traveled like thunder through the massive crowd of demonstrators. The dictator Marcos has just fled Malaca-ñang Palace.

For almost a week before this night, we have been demonstrating in front of the consulate, the crowd growing larger each day. On the first day, a thunderstorm sent many of our friends scampering for cover, thinning our picket line. I panicked at the thought that our action would prematurely end. We were left to sustain the protest, continuing our circle. We doggedly held up wilting placards and shrinking banners against the pouring rain, shouting louder, "Marcos dictatorship has to go!" Then, one by one, some sheepishly, those who sought cover, came back to the picket line. No rain was going to keep anyone away from this vigil until Marcos was gone for good.

Tonight, our victorious demonstrators are wildly cheering and scattering confetti from the fifth-floor windows, as down below we shriek and whoop and dance madly and hug and cry. The occupation of the Philippine consulate on Sutter Street in San Francisco has just been accomplished. Protesters broke through the tight security shield and stormed into the consulate quarters.

I feel a strange calm as I stand still amid the frenzy, just watching the tiny pieces of paper catch reflections from the neon lights as they fall softly to the ground below. It is a moment of pure, unadulterated calm, frozen in time and in my memory. As yellow confetti pelts my face, I see eleven years of my life flash through my mind. I stand in the middle of the huge crowd that is delirious with the news of the end of the Marcos dictatorship—and I feel a rush of mixed emotions.

There was the loneliness of the early years of organizing the Filipino community in Toronto, Canada; the feeling of isolation while handing out information leaflets to Sunday churchgoers. There were insults and threats hurled at our demonstrations. There was the intimidation from police and security agents. There was the sheer insecurity of our lives. For all the years that I led the Coalition Against the Marcos Dictatorship (CAMD) chapter in Toronto, I was working as a secretary in a benefits consulting firm in the city's equivalent of Wall Street. It was an ordinary day for me to do a nine-to-five job and then spend nights and weekends in meetings, organizing demonstrations or campaigns as part of supporting the resistance against the Marcos dictatorship.

I remember the copious little notes left for me by my daughter, Nadine, who grew up missing her goodnight kisses, reminding her absent mom to tuck her in. And the end of a marriage that inevitably came yet still surprised and saddened me. I had led a double life and worked triple days, combining paid work on Bay Street and unpaid work caring for a family and organizing a community.

Like many other activists, I parceled out my annual two-week holiday to attend regional and national meetings of the CAMD and the KDP. The annual CAMD conference was always a high point of my existence during those years of intense work in one of the twelve chapters of the organization. This yearly assembly promised an exciting reunion of friends brought together by a common cause. From cities spread across the United States and Canada, we gathered in one place—at times up to three hundred of us—to validate our experiences and clarify the direction of our individual efforts and actions, as one movement in the fight against fascist rule in the Philippines. The gradual piling up of our luggage and backpacks at the back door of the conference site as we arrived, one by one from the airport, paralleled the mounting anticipation we felt as we geared up for the next three to four days of sharing and planning.

This process of collectivizing our experiences and evaluating the effectiveness of our coordinated campaigns strengthened our resolve and reinvigorated us. It gave us a coherent view of what it was we were accomplishing, giving some sense to what seemed to be small and insignificant tasks: the endless meetings, phone trees, leafleting, funny skits, Christmas caroling, letters to the editor, petitioning. It helped ease the frustrations and anxieties we lived with every day. We energized one another, valued our existence as an organization, and validated our individual contribution. At the CAMD conference every year, I came away convinced it was all worth it.

But how I resisted doing things I thought I couldn't do but ended up doing anyway for some higher goal. Like writing for the *Taliba* or talking to the media. And how I even surprised myself with my own conviction by packing up and moving to the San Francisco Bay Area to be one of the national coordinators of the CAMD. It was a painful effort to set aside my personal distaste for certain members of the elite opposition and persist in working with them as part of strengthening the political resistance front abroad.

Through it all, I struggled day in and day out with my insecurity in taking up the leadership roles that I felt pressured to play.

This night in San Francisco, these memories flash through my head. Marcos has just fled the wrath of Filipinos beating at the gates of the Presidential Palace. Yellow confetti rains mercifully on Sutter Street. And I have just seen the end of one part of my turbulent adult life as an activist.

I HAVE NOT STOPPED DREAMING

ESTELLA HABAL

ALTHOUGH my experience in the KDP, in particular during the last few difficult years, may seem harsh, I would never trade it for anything. For me, as a Filipino American of the 1960s generation, the KDP provided the most concentrated, transformative experience politically, socially, and ideologically. The greatest feeling was the sense of empowerment, optimism, and destiny. KDP members worked tirelessly to accomplish concrete tasks that yielded tangible results, while at the same time holding a broad vision that encompassed not only our Filipino struggles but also the whole world.

The KDP changed my perspective and my life. On the one hand, I was always attracted to seeking out my roots as a Filipino, because so much of my history was kept secret from me and other Filipino youth. But sentimentally looking to the Filipino past was not enough. My identity had to also be forged in the direction of the future. And the future I found was full of promise and optimism, revolution and Marxism. The risks were great and some of the sacrifices were heavy, but I was convinced I was dedicating my present life for a better future, not just for me, but for humankind. In some ways, my faith in the revolution was somewhat idealistic and utopian, but I have not stopped dreaming.

When people learn the bits of my history that I relate in this collection, they may wonder how a teenage mother, then a single mother with three children on welfare, and later a mother of four could have done so much under such extreme circumstances. Certainly, my personal background as a child of a poor immigrant family gave me the work ethic to try to succeed. But I believe that many of us did extraordinary things because the revolutionary

See "Running Away to Life" for contributor biography.

times we lived in called for that. Our generation of youth knew no boundaries or limits. Youth all over the world were turning the tables, demanding to be heard, wanting to change the world with a sense of urgent necessity. The rallying cry of the French students in 1968 captures our youthful optimism and audacity: "Be realistic. Demand the impossible!"

Activists and revolutionaries seemed to be at the forefront of everything in those days. If you were a woman like myself, we did it all and then some. We had our children, divorced the men we didn't love, organized childcare for our kids, all the while fighting hard to win battles we passionately believed in. My individual energy and power were doubled, quadrupled by the social movement of the times and an organization like the KDP.

Of course, there were intense social and personal costs. I was reminded of the heartaches of being an activist and mother when I read an article awhile ago about a woman leader who was being honored for her activism during a world conference, and how she shared her pain of being estranged from her children. My heart still aches when I think of how my own children must have suffered during my activist days due to the splintered attention I paid to them. Although they all survived to become compassionate and productive human beings, I still wonder if they could have accomplished more had I been able to pay more attention to their schooling.

Perhaps, the greatest affirmation of my activist life comes from my own children. During the tenth anniversary commemoration of the International Hotel eviction in August 1987, my oldest son, Anthony, said, "Mom, I finally understand why you fought so hard. You did real good. I'm proud of you. I am glad you did this." His comments helped heal some of the guilt I carried around for years.

The revolutionary movement opened my eyes to the vastness of human potential, both collective and individual. The movement gave me invaluable social and organizing skills, as well as an analytical proficiency, which I probably would not have learned anywhere else. It's no small wonder that today I find myself back in school, working hard to finish my PhD and become a college professor. I keep dreaming, I keep struggling.

DEEP HORIZON

GIL MANGAOANG

AGENTLE breeze blew on that balmy tropical night. The sand beneath gently massaged the soles of my feet. I couldn't believe that I had done what I had always dreamed of doing—living in Hawaii. The crunch of my feet on the sandy beach combined with the rhythmic splashing of the surf. Even though it was evening, the sky was bright. The moon was full, casting enough light for me to see the foam left by the receding tide. Each time the surf came ashore, it laid down an exquisite one-of-a-kind filigree pattern.

I was lost in thought about what had happened in the last forty-eight hours. But my thoughts were interrupted by the vision of beauty that suddenly stepped into view. Walking toward me was a strikingly gorgeous young man. My pulse quickened as my heart began beating faster. As he approached, I became more aware that this young man was no more than sixteen or seventeen years old.

My thoughts went back to the day before and the subdued revelry at my KDP farewell picnic party. Following my work with the northern California Regional Executive Board, I became a National Council member and was eventually elected to the National Executive Board. The last National Council session had assessed that our work in Hawaii needed bolstering.

"Here it was—the opportunity for me to get away from it all, and of all places in Hawaii!" spoke the voice in my head. Leaning forward in my chair, I said spontaneously, "I would like to be considered for that assignment, but would have to give it more thought." I shocked myself and sat back to contemplate what I just said. "Where did that come from? Are you out of your mind?" the voice said.

See "Hitting the High Notes" for contributor biography.

I knew it would be a life-changing experience; I just didn't know what to expect. What I did know was that I was restless and uncomfortable with how my life was proceeding. So much was in tumultuous motion that I felt smothered. I needed some sorting through so I could breathe again. There were so many issues I was struggling to understand and manage in some cohesive fashion.

I was having difficulty sorting out my political commitment. My belief that I would see revolutionary change with the creation of a socialist society would not come true. The Soviet Union was no more. Disillusionment had begun to erode my resolve to continue. I wanted out, but to whom do you go for approval?

My hero had failed, and I was politically floundering. I was disheartened by the fact that Bruce Occena, whom I'd considered my mentor and a source of inspiration throughout my political involvement, had succumbed to drug addiction and was in a downward spiral. I was devastated. I felt abandoned.

Just a day ago I had been in Tilden Park at a potluck farewell party held in my honor and organized by the KDP national staff. It wasn't a joyous experience for me. In fact, it was uncomfortable, and I felt awkward. I felt somehow betrayed by the movement—I had devoted a good portion of my early adult years to working for revolutionary change. I so much wanted the revolution to happen. But it was not to be.

How I chose to handle myself at the picnic reflected my deep resentment. All the friends I had worked with so closely over the years were present and seated around various tables. I chose to ignore them for the most part. It was awkward and tense because there must have been at least fifty of the best people I would ever meet and in whom I still had complete trust. Instead, I chose to sit at the table with my immediate family rather than interact with anyone from the KDP. I had to get away and start all over again.

On the beach, as the young man stepped closer, I could see his bright smile caused by the full moon's luminosity.

"Hi," I said as he walked by.

He paused and turned, "Hi." I stood there for a few seconds just to enjoy the freshness and beauty of his masculinity. His voice was deep for such a young face. "Nice night. I just got here an hour ago and had to get down to Waikiki. Wow, dude!"

"Nice! Is this your first time in Hawaii?"

"Yeah, I'm here with my mom. I got a USC scholarship. She was so pleased that she brought me here for a week's vacation."

"You're a lucky guy. This is my third time here and I don't plan to leave anytime soon—in fact I moved here."

"Wow dude, I wish I could do that!"

"You never know what will happen in life, you're still young."

Instantly, my thoughts flashed back to Juan and all that had happened in our shared life. We had been together since 1977. We had met by way of my boyfriend at the time, Michael Jerry Krause.

Michael and I had just gotten together in March 1976. We were cultivating a loving, supportive relationship that was based on an anti-imperialist political foundation. He was in the June 28th Union, a gay left group in San Francisco. It was named after the date the New York City police had raided the Stonewall Inn in 1969, leading to an all-out brawl between the police and the primarily black and Latino transgender patrons, who fought back. Michael was the chair of the group's leadership body. He was eager to understand how the KDP developed its structure and ideological orientation. His intent was to apply what he learned through our exchanges to the work of his group.

The 1976 Gay Pride March in San Francisco was the first gay public event I participated in. Michael and I held a Bay Area Gay Liberation (BAGL) banner at the front of the parade. BAGL was a radical gay organization with membership open to all. At the end of the march, Michael had to return the banner to his friend who lived on Polk Street. And that was where I met Juan Joseph Lombard for the first time.

But that night would be the last time I was ever with Michael. The next evening, while riding down the Dolores Street hill, he ran a yellow light at Nineteenth Street and was fatally struck by a car. The irony was that Michael had just graduated from nursing school and was set to start work at Saint Mary's Hospital. The driver of the car that killed him was the chief of trauma surgery at San Francisco General Hospital.

"Are you okay?" came that deep voice. It brought me back to the beach. "You seem a little spaced-out. Whatever you're on, I want a hit!"

"I was spacing out. So what are you doing now?"

"Just walking the beach before I saw you."

"Mind if I join you on your walk?" I wanted to give him the option to refuse my company should he choose.

"I don't mind. Lots of guys I passed on the beach were leering at me and making comments."

"I'm sure."

"I think they were queers! Maybe if I'm with you they won't stare so much." I rolled my eyes.

It was such a thrill to walk along the Waikiki surf on a full-moon night with this young man by my side. The water felt cool on my toes, making squishing sounds as I walked. I heard his feet making the same sound in syncopation to my footsteps.

Juan is a wonderful, caring, and thoughtful man. During our initial years together, we enjoyed traveling when we could. But for the most part we were so thoroughly engaged in our political work that we had little time together. In the mid-1970s there were still very few openly gay men of color. And there were even fewer with any sense of political or social consciousness focused on revolutionary change. Juan was an independent thinker, but we both shared the same anti-imperialist perspective.

We were very domestic. Usually I cooked and cleaned while Juan made the real money. Most of the time I worked part-time at different nonprofit social service agencies. With the flexibility afforded me in those jobs, I was able to do nearly full-time KDP activities most weeks. Like any relationship, ours was contentious at times; yet we were caring in our own special way toward each other.

But I still couldn't shake out that empty feeling. There was a call inside me to be free. I just wasn't sure if I wanted to spend the rest of my life with Juan. I knew I had to physically remove myself from his presence, and a geographic move to Hawaii would suit me fine. I had to get away.

"Well, you're easy to look at." The young man stiffened at my comment, so I knew he was uncomfortable with what I'd just said. Oops! "I meant it in a complimentary way. With your looks, you probably have lots of girlfriends back home."

Slyly, he said, "Yeah, one. Two. They don't know about the other. My best buddy always tells me that the one I decide not to go for, he'll take her."

We walked along the beach until Queen's Surf Beach. "Want to sit on the rocks for a while?" I carefully asked.

With a smile in his voice he quickly said, "Sure."

It was so peaceful sitting there, our toes teased by the surf. The moon reflected off the glimmering ocean, making the sea look like rippling waves of black satin rolling up and onto the beach. The surf crawled up to our toes and stopped. Only the sound of the gentle waves could be heard. There was no need for talk.

I was in Hawaii, and that was all that mattered. I had no plan of what I wanted to do. I just wanted to start all over again. In Hawaii I felt that there would be no constraints as to how I would conduct my gay social life. There would be no prying eyes to judge me. While in the KDP national and the northern California regional bodies, I never had the opportunity to explore my gay identity to its fullest. The scope of political responsibilities left scant personal time. Also, I felt the constraint of not disclosing that I was gay within the Filipino community, for fear of damaging the KDP's political work. Now that was no longer an issue for me. I had chosen to no longer be constrained by being in the KDP.

In Hawaii I could assume a different identity, which enabled me to enjoy and explore the gay life that I felt I'd been deprived of in prior years. I could pick up where I'd stopped before becoming politically active.

"I have to go, my mom is waiting to take me out for dinner."

"And it's time for me to get something in my stomach too."

We rose and looked at each other. It was an awkward moment. Neither of us knew what to do or say next.

"Well, enjoy your vacation."

He looked me in the eyes and said in his husky voice, "Thanks," and then turned around and walked back up the beach in the direction he came from.

Before he got too far I called out to him, "Hey, I don't even know your name."

He stopped and looked back, "Jason."

"Gil." I decided to go ahead and say it. "And I'm gay."

A look of shock fell over his face momentarily, and then he smiled, "Cool."

"Have a good life!" I waved. Then he turned and I watched till his profile melted into the deep horizon. Breathe.

NO REGRETS

EDWIN BATONGBACAL

*Edwin Batongbacal became a student activist while studying at De La
Salle University, Manila, in the late 1970s. Upon graduating in 1979,
Edwin worked for about a year in the underground support branch of
the eastern central Luzon regional organization of the New People's
Army and National Democratic Front. In 1980, Edwin immigrated to
the United States with his parents, and he joined the KDP National
Secretariat shortly after his arrival. Edwin was assigned to a KDP
housing collective and was deployed to the International Association
of Filipino Patriots, which was formed to do organizing, propaganda,
and international support work outside the Filipino community.
Edwin subsequently worked in KDP chapters in San Francisco and Los
Angeles. Like other activists, Edwin eventually went back to school,
where he studied to become a social worker. He now works for San
Francisco County, and he continues to be active in supporting
pro-democracy efforts in the Philippines.*

WHY was I ever drawn into the movement? Answering this question is important because I now look back at how my life diverged from those of my schoolmates and friends. Their current lives of material success and power might have also been mine if I had walked the path they did, especially since I, like them, was privileged with the best education money could buy in the Philippines. I seek some explanation, some reason that will satisfy and assure me that what I did during all my years in the movement was worthwhile and that my life today is all the better for it.

No regrets is where I want to be.

I wrote to my friend in the Philippines, Maita Gomez, around 1990, that it's no use wringing our hands in despair and regretting that we spent such a good part of our lives sacrificing for a movement that didn't get to where it wanted to go. (Maita was a famous former model and beauty queen who joined the revolutionary underground in the Philippines; she passed away in 2012.) Maita was the person who recruited me into the National Democratic Front some forty years ago. In recent years, we both found ourselves at a crossroads, struggling to make sense of the death of our movement and lamenting the wasted lives and delayed dreams that would never blossom to their fullest.

I wrote her that it's no use regretting what we had done, because if we really looked at it, took into account who we were and the times we were living in, we could not but have done what we did. But this type of deterministic theory quiets my soul only temporarily, because an inevitable tragedy is tragedy nonetheless. To be truly at peace, I must instead reconnect with the fire that burned in my heart a lifetime ago. To have no regrets, I must regain that firm belief in the cause that I embraced so wholeheartedly, even as I continue to live the new life I have today, and even as I remain aware of the paradigms that history seems to have disproved.

I guess I miss believing. The collapse of existing socialism and the derailment of the Philippine revolutionary movement have taken its toll on my capacity to believe. My hope is to find peace in discovering what remains true of my old leftist convictions, determining which truths I can believe in as firmly today as I did back then. I sense that what remains true is to be found, not merely in polemics about debatable truths in political philosophy, economy, and strategy, but also in the subjective and personal realms of what truly constitutes a life worth living.

AFTERWORD

RENE CIRIA CRUZ

WHEN the remaining members of the KDP held a national meeting in Berkeley and voted to disband in 1986, most were well into mature adulthood and had begun to pursue postponed careers or schooling, build families, and otherwise tend to their private lives. Some who had worked with the Line of March (LOM), which also disbanded, tried to continue political work by joining efforts to regroup US leftists in an informal network. Meanwhile, the US Committee core that led the KDP's Philippine support work persisted for a year or so, seeking out new political relationships with socialist formations and dissident elements in the Communist Party of the Philippines (CPP) that were critical of the party's hardening sectarian and dogmatic orientation. This core continued publishing *Katipunan* until 1991, but by 1992 this group had also ceased all political activity.

Former KDP activists have generally kept in touch with one another through a national e-mail group as well as social media, maintaining a comradeship forged over more than a decade. There have been periodic reunions, which were nostalgic, sometimes bittersweet, but always happy occasions. A few former members have returned to the Philippines. Individually, many have gone on to serve as activists in their own fields, leading advocacy groups for immigrants and women in the Filipino communities in the United States and Canada, working in labor unions, and gaining important responsibilities in civil society and even in government, both in the United States and the Philippines. A few have continued forging ties with progressive elements in the Philippines to support the building of a united democratic left alternative to the CPP. Wherever they are today, most of these Filipino progressives continue to value and rely on the political, analytical, and organizational skills they acquired during their intense years of activism with the Union of Democratic Filipinos. As the personal narratives in this collection show, it is an experience they will treasure for a lifetime.

APPENDIX I: ABBREVIATIONS

ACWA	Alaska Cannery Workers Association
AMLA	Anti–Martial Law Alliance (local chapter of AMLC)
AMLC	Anti–Martial Law Coalition (later became the CAMD)
CAMD	Coalition Against the Marcos Dictatorship
CAMD-PSN	Coalition Against the Marcos Dictatorship–Philippine Solidarity Network (merger of the two groups)
CJDV	Committee for Justice for Domingo and Viernes
CPP	Communist Party of the Philippines (founded 1968 by Jose Maria Sison)
CTF	Congress (Education) Task Force of the CAMD
FFP	Friends of the Filipino People
ILWU	International Longshoremen's and Warehousemen's Union
KDP	Katipunan ng mga Demokratikong Pilipino (Union of Democratic Filipinos)
KM	Kabataang Makabayan (Nationalist Youth)
LELO	Legacy of Equality, Leadership and Organizing (founded as Northwest Labor and Employment Law Office)
LOM	Line of March
MFP	Movement for a Free Philippines
NAFL-FNG	National Alliance for Fair Licensure for Foreign Nurse Graduates
NCRCLP	National Committee for the Restoration of Civil Liberties in the Philippines
NDF	National Democratic Front
NPA	New People's Army
PKP	Partido Komunista ng Pilipinas (Communist Party of the Philippines) (founded 1930)
PND	Philippine National Day (June 12)
PSN	Philippine Solidarity Network
SDK	Samahang Demokratiko ng Kabataan (Democratic Association of Youth)

APPENDIX II: *ANG AKTIBISTA*,
"ORIENTATION TO PHILIPPINE SUPPORT
WORK IN THE CURRENT PERIOD"

This following article from the April 16, 1984, issue of *Ang Aktibista*, the internal theoretical bulletin of the KDP, is included as an appendix to show the organization's side in the final schism that broke the KDP's bonds with the Communist Party of the Philippines (CPP) and the National Democratic Front (NDF).

This article was a response to fast-moving developments in the Philippines after the assassination of anti-Marcos leader Senator Benigno Aquino Jr. upon his arrival in Manila on August 21, 1983. The assassination triggered a largely spontaneous protest movement of thousands of citizens, in which both the organized Left and liberal forces intervened to provide direction. For Filipino leftists, the unprecedented flow of open, popular opposition to the dictatorship raised the question, what is to be done?

The KDP's response, formulated by its national leadership, analyzed the new political situation and provided an orientation for its activists that, two years later, would lead the KDP to support the bourgeois opposition candidacy of Aquino's widow, Corazon Aquino, against Ferdinand Marcos during the 1986 snap presidential election. That election would lead to the dictator's downfall. The KDP's position contradicted that of the CPP and the NDF; these two groups called for a boycott of what they considered a rivalry within the ruling-class enemy. In addition to revealing differences over Maoism and the "international line," as well as the program for organizing Filipinos in the United States, the KDP analysis and policy expressed in this excerpt finalized the break between the KDP and the leadership of the revolutionary movement in the Philippines.

ANG AKTIBISTA

Theoretical Bulletin of the KDP National Headquarters

APRIL 16, 1984

"Orientation to Philippine Support Work in the Current Period"

INTRODUCTION

The period following the Aquino assassination has required significant changes in our policies and methods of work in the Philippine support arena. Our activists have had some difficulty implementing these policies and methods thoroughly, both because these are new and we have not had the benefit of systematic study. This *Ang Aktibista* is the basis for a mass study of our concrete assessment of the period and of our orientation, policies and methods. It presents the political and theoretical basis for the major refinements we have made especially in the area of forging popular front of opposition to the Marcos dictatorship. At our summer theoretical school, we will study the universals of united front practice and their application to all our areas of work.

The level of abstraction of this *Ang Aktibista* (AA) is relatively high. We are assuming that comrades have followed in sufficient detail the political events in the Philippines through *Ang Katipunan* and *Taliba*, and the materials and updates that the NDC [National Democratic Commission of the KDP National Secretariat] has struggled hard to collect. (We will not attempt to reproduce those details here.) If not, comrades should rectify their practice immediately. We go to all lengths just to monitor the situation and scrounge up hard-to-get materials from the Philippine movement so that our activists can keep up with fast changing political data. To neglect the responsibility of updating ourselves is to diminish our political and propaganda capacities.

Not only is the level of abstraction of this AA relatively high, it has not undergone a thorough enough editing due to the pressure to get it out. As a result, the sentence structures, (especially of the first half) tend to be complex, dense, and even downright awkward. Leading comrades, then, have the responsibility of preparing thoroughly for the main discussions to lead membership in plowing through the material. Leading comrades already had a few hours of discussion here at the National Headquarters when everyone gathered for the CAMD conference. But if in the preparations those comrades encounter difficulty themselves, they should raise their questions to either Kas _R_ or _G_. Please do not fail to do this in the interest of a lively and elucidating study process. The next stage of our orientation will be the careful summation of our practice in the following years on the basis of the line presented here and the extraction of lessons that will improve our practice as well deepen and refine the line itself.

THE NEW POLITICAL SITUATION IN THE PHILIPPINES

The existence of the Marcos fascist regime is itself a reflection of the global political crisis that has faced U.S. imperialism for the last two decades. Along with its attempt to reestablish nuclear blackmail over the Soviet Union and the socialist camp, it has stepped up counter revolutionary activities against national liberation movements. This has included imposition of dictatorial regimes in the neo-colonies and the reestablishment of its capacity for open military intervention should these client regimes fail to stem the advance of the revolutionary movements.

As in other victimized countries, the imposition of fascist rule in the Philippines meant a qualitative change in the people's political existence. The destruction of nominal bourgeois altered the terms of their political struggle. While the imposition of fascist rule marked a stage in the short term, the vicious attack set back the people's movement and pushed it on the defensive all-sidedly. For reformists and national democratic revolutionaries alike, all avenues for peaceful and open political struggles were closed off.

The 10 years that followed was an ebb in the people's movement. Fascist terror spread a blanket of fear and intimidation nationwide. Disenfranchised bourgeois democrats, accustomed only to legal parliamentary struggles, were paralyzed. National democrats went underground and took up the painstaking task of building up the people's army on a nationwide scale while preserving their forces in the face of brutal fascist attacks. Although severely hunted down, the revolutionaries immediately undertook political agitation through illegal and semi legal means. Only after two years or so were the bourgeois democrats able to regain their bearings and initiate legal forms of antifascist agitation.

Meanwhile the objective conditions faced by the people continued to deteriorate, setting the basis for continued discontent. The regime's economic policy of heightened subservience to foreign finance capital wreaked havoc on the people's livelihood and living standards. By the end of the decade, the country was irretrievably trapped in a $22 billion debt to foreign lending institutions. Benefitting most from this influx of borrowed capital were the

Marcos cronies. On top of the steady pauperization, the people also chafed at the severe restriction of their rights. Arbitrary one man decrees, savage abuses and repression by the military and the paramilitary were accomplished by Marcos' KBL [Kilusang Bagong Lipunan, or New Society Movement] party power monopoly. The country was kept in the dark by the controlled media, which specialized in the trumpeting the first lady's ostentatious display of wealth and in feeding the president's vanity.

Throughout the last decade, the broad democratic resistance managed to establish a visible anti-fascist pole that fed the spontaneous discontent already arising from the oppressive economic and political conditions. The existence of this pole—from the revolutionary resistance to the bourgeois opposition—was an important factor in the quantitative weakening of the regime during the last 10 years. The activity of the subjective forces became part of the objective conditions that bit by bit, and year by year, eroded the regime's political strength. But during this ebb the political struggles tended to be more scattered and sporadic. The subjective forces, particularly the revolutionary left, had to exert great effort to draw out the connections between issues and maximize the political and mobilizing impact of each particular struggle. Disheartened or intimidated, the masses were relatively difficult to mobilize.

Aquino's martyrdom, and the outrageous manner in which he was killed, set off a complex set of factors already building during the ebb (the combination of oppressive conditions and the efforts of the subjective forces) and let loose the current flow. With the Aquino assassination, the "connections" suddenly became "clear." The people's anger became concentrated. Overnight the fear of fascist reprisal was set aside, and the mass response broke the back of the fascist intimidation. From a period of relative calm, emerged a period of conspicuous change with the masses being drawn into a struggle on a wide scale, on various levels, fronts and organizational forms. The obsolescence of fascist rule, previously exposed only in an uneven matter surfaced in an all-sided way. This has placed a tremendous strain on the regime and its institutions whose purpose had been to obscure the nature of Marcos' autocratic rule. The politicization of the people is now growing by leaps and bounds; the class struggle is intensifying day to day and the fascist institutions are experiencing a severe crisis.

No doubt the U.S.-Marcos regime still has the upper hand militarily. Despite its rapid expansion nationwide, the NPA [New People's Army] is still not in a position to lock the AFP [Armed Forces of the Philippines] in a stalemate. Politically, however, Marcos has been placed on the defensive overnight. His popularity is at an all-time low. With his isolation from all sectors of Philippine society on a qualitative level, even the U.S. is in danger of being exposed on a wide scale as the instigator behind the fascist imposition.

Literally all sectors of Philippine society are represented in the open protest and defiance of the fascist regime. Workers, students, peasants, the religious and the urban poor—areas of traditional left influence—are being mobilized in almost daily demonstrations and marches. What is most significant, however, is the spontaneous activation of the so-called "middle-class"—sectors that had remained relatively passive and oblivious to anti-fascist and revolutionary agitation in the past, i.e., white collar workers, professionals, small businessmen, artists and liberal intellectuals. Among them, various democratic organizations have emerged (ATOM, ROAR, etc.). In addition, opposition literature and newspapers have sprung up. To make matters worse for the regime, even its potential allies among the business elite have broken ranks. These are compradors who have been victimized by presidential favoritism or who fear that Marcos' mishandling of his power is making the country ripe for revolution. In other words, the regime no longer has any friends beyond its own narrow clique and its imperialist sponsors.

The broadness and militance of the spontaneous movement have shaken the regime and exacerbated the factional tensions within the ruling camp. Some of Marcos' KBL party followers have begun to worry about their political futures and are looking for ways to position themselves safely should the need to jump ship arrive. There have been minor defections to the opposition circles. Within the military, some disgruntled officers have begun feeding damaging information to the panel investigating the Aquino assassination, and to the legal opposition. This political crisis also comes at a time when the U.S.-Marcos regime has to resolve a delicate succession question. Ill and getting on in years, Marcos clearly cannot serve imperialism forever. Even though no single individual within his camp can replace his capacity to lord over the ruling machinery and to mediate factional disputes, imperialism already has to set in place a succession process that would not result in destabilizing factional struggles. The pressure of the protest movement is what imperialism needs the least at this point. Now, the need for a speedier transition is arising. At the same time, the danger of internecine struggles within the ruling camps—as factions jockey for positions—increases in proportion to the strain imposed by the political unrest.

To make matters worse, Marcos' political crisis coincides with a severe turn in the economy towards deeper crisis. Hard on the heels of the assassination, which itself had a serious negative impact on tourism and the rate of investment, came a major devaluation of the peso—a measure dictated by the regime's international lenders. Thus, the people's economic condition including those of the middle classes have become even more deplorable. This, while the regime's dependence on foreign capital, its corruption and the greed of its crony system are being exposed in a concentrated way by the protest movement. Definitely, the economic crisis will only serve to fuel the political conflagration.

U.S. imperialism, of course, is extremely worried about the deterioration of its ally's capacity to hold itself up politically. Its most immediate concern is how best to diffuse the political unrest that is destabilizing the regime. Because Marcos is already extremely on the defensive over the Aquino murder, open and violent repression is a politically unacceptable tactic in the immediate period. Imperialism has to devise a political maneuver—"democratization"—that can put the opposition off-balance, isolate the left and co-opt the bourgeois wing. At the same time, such a political maneuver can be used as a rationale to impose violent repression against those who "impede democratization" if the maneuver fails to neutralize the unrest.

This is also a moment when imperialism is forced to think and quickly decide on its long-term options, on the variants of forms for its class rule in the Philippines. The first assessment it has to make is whether, as in the words of the former U.S. ambassador William Sullivan, "Marcos' days are numbered." It has to assess whether the current crisis is only temporary setback for the regime or whether it is irreversible. Both sides of the U.S. bourgeoisie realize it is irreversible. And, even if the protest is diffused, Marcos' health problems and old age require the decisive settling of the succession question sooner than later. Just this matter alone introduces strains between Marcos and the U.S. as the former tries to get the best out of the deal; for example the Imelda-as-successor issue. The political unrest exacerbates matters and, if sustained, will accelerate the ripening of the secondary master vs. puppet contradiction.

To sum up, imperialist class rule has entered a period of increased instability. The massive protest movement that emerged in response to the Aquino assassination together with a profound economic crisis, a ripening succession question, and the rise of conflicts within the U.S.-Marcos alliance make for a potentially devastating combination. How this period can be turned into a setback of historical proportions for the U.S.-Marcos regime depends on the astuteness and decisiveness of the revolutionary national democratic forces.

The Challenge to Revolutionaries

A. The Character of the Movement

For the left, the new political situation presents a complex and exciting challenge. As the conscious element, the communists must establish a decisive orientation towards this phenomenon and determine how this spontaneous upsurge can be linked to the overall revolutionary agenda. How can this mass movement be sustained, and how can its political direction be established? First, we must assess as objectively as possible the character of the mass protest movement, its strengths and limitations.

The most impressive feature of the current protest is the number of people it has mobilized. The number of participants easily dwarfs any previous political mobilizations—including the 1970 first quarter storm. Another positive characteristic is the active participation of the "middle-class" sectors, such as white collar workers, entrepreneurs, and professionals, who had not been "politically involved." These features show the extent of the dictatorship's isolation and the generalized anger at the present dispensation. Also, they reflect a spontaneous but objective coalescence of classes and political forces never before ranged against the reactionary ruling system.

However, it is a largely spontaneous movement with the unorganized easily outnumbering the organized, conscious forces of the various political trends—from bourgeois democrats, social democrats, to communists—interacting with it. Without the intervention of a politically conscious core, this spontaneous movement will peter out, despite favorable objective conditions for its sustenance.

In addition, the spontaneous movement is mainly anti-fascist and reformist in character. It is centered in the rejection of the Marcos regime and its peaceful replacement by a bourgeois democratic government. This is reflected in the popular demand for the resignation of Marcos and his minions and the varied calls for a caretaker government and genuinely democratic elections. This is understandable. Fascism may have placed itself in contradiction with the broadest number of people, but it is still a form of indirect imperialist rule. Hence, while the fascist regime stands exposed U.S. imperialism is not yet as exposed. Also, the majority of those who now actively oppose fascist rule gravitate towards reformist solutions. Peaceful reform is a more attractive direction, given that it requires less sacrifice; and for as long as this alternative appears viable it will command a popular following—not only among the middle classes, but even among the basic masses not yet under the influence of the revolutionary forces.

The reformist, bourgeois-democratic impulse of the spontaneous move-ment is the basis for the reinvigoration and prominence of bourgeois reform-ist leaders and their organizations, even aside from the fact that these bourgeois forces can operate openly. The bourgeois reformists may have rela-tively small and loosely organized bases, but their influence is larger than their actual organized strength. Both the bourgeois reformist political lead-ers (and the middle classes that they have immediate influence on) play a significant role in the politics of the nation. Articulate, and heir to the retarded bourgeois democratic traditions of the nation, they still command respect even among the most oppressed classes and sectors of the masses, especially if they maintain a stance of opposition to fascist rule. (Aquino was an excel-lent example of this.) As such, they have an inordinate amount of influence on the political temper of the people.

The class character of the bourgeois reformist forces and their fear of a Communist-led revolution make them a potential reserve of imperialism. In fact, imperialism looks at them as horses-in-reserve, as a source of puppets should the present one prove no longer capable of serving imperialism's inter-est. However, we should note the gradations among the bourgeois reform-ists. This camp has three identifiable wings based on their outlook towards imperialism, the left, and revolution.

The right wing consists of the most pro-imperialist and anti-Communist of the forces. They pose themselves to the imperialist as the viable alterna-tive to both Marcos and the left, and actively campaign for the imperialist sponsorship. This wing has absolutely no interest in seeing the people take the initiative in instituting social change, and would prefer to "critically col-laborate" with the Marcos camp than ally with the revolutionary left.

The left wing is composed of bourgeois reformist who are more critical of imperialism's role and who lean towards political independence. They pur-sue a more consistent opposition to the regime and constitute the resistance pole, as opposed to the collaborationist or reconciliation pole, within the reformist camp. While they have a strategic fear of the left, they are open to a cooperating with it and to armed revolution as a last resort.

This reformist camp has a large middle—political leaders, rank and file members, and lieutenants—who swing to whichever wing is strongest at a particular moment. It would be safe to say that the majority of the unorga-nized elements in the current protest movement also constitute this camp's middle. Prior to the Aquino assassination, the bourgeois reformists were in their darkest period. Marcos' ruthlessness and Ronald Reagan's rise deprived them of whatever opening President Carter had provided. Collaboration was rising to dominance within their camp as the polarization between the regime and the left emerged more visibly. Very few struck to principled resistance and went into clandestine alliance with the left. The Aquino assassination, however, produced a larger and more militant middle, politically and morally undercut the trend towards collaborationism and strengthened the hand of the left or resistance wing. With the regime on the defensive politically, more room has emerged for open, reformist political activity.

B. Communist Intervention

For the Communists, who are also a force (in fact, the most organized force) within the new protest movement, the point of knowing the political character, impulses and forces within this movement is to answer the question: "How can this spontaneous anti-fascist and reformist movement be turned into a reserve of the revolution"?

From a distance, we observe that the left is actively grappling with this very question. The prevailing orientation of the CPP and the NDF, at this time, takes note of the importance of interacting with the protest movement—including entering into alliances, utilizing electoral openings—within the framework of the strategy of people's war. However, according to "Plaridel Papers," a publication that reportedly involves some "incapacitated" Communist and NDF forces: "Within such a framework, the participation of the revolutionary forces in the current protest movement seems to be aimed *only* at intensifying the atmosphere of the protest to heighten the political isolation of Marcos. . . . The revolutionary forces, of course, are steadily 'harvesting' recruits from the spontaneous movement." (Emphasis ours.)

Plaridel notes the "politically destabilizing combination" of the protest movement, the succession problem, the emergence of the master-puppet contradiction, and the economic crisis—and raises the question: "*Should* (revolutionaries) *set more ambitious goals for the protest movement?*" (Emphasis ours.) It went on to state, "If we consider the basic character of the actual movement rather than the explicit goals formulated by the legal organization, we can accept the view that the same protest movement that is now following a reformist line can develop into a conscious component of a *revolutionary uprising.* In the eyes of many observers, including Marcos, it is in fact, already contributing to the making of a revolutionary *situation.*" (Emphasis ours.)

This is an extremely significant assertion, a not-so-implicit criticism of the (as of this writing) prevailing approach of the NDF and the CPP to the current situation. Rather than simply look at the current situation as presenting improved new conditions for increased revolutionary propaganda work and organizational expansion, *Plaridel* calls for the conscious effort to transform it into a *revolutionary situation*. A revolutionary situation is an extremely crucial historical moment of the class struggle. It is a nationwide crisis affecting both the exploiters and the exploited, when the masses no longer want to live in the old way and the ruling class can no longer carry on in the old way. Meaning, when the majority of the basic masses (workers and peasants) "fully realizes that revolution is necessary and that they should be prepared to die for it" and when the ruling classes "are going through a governmental crisis, which draws even the most backward masses into politics (symptomatic of any genuine revolution is a rapid, tenfold and even a hundredfold increase in the size of the working and oppressed masses—hitherto apathetic—who are capable of waging political struggle), weakens the government and *makes it possible for the revolutionaries to overthrow it.*" (Lenin, *Left-Wing Communism, an Infantile Disorder*; emphasis ours.)

Indeed, if the protest can be sustained, expanded, and directed correctly, it can exacerbate the economic crisis, the succession problem and the secondary contraction (master and puppet) and push the regime into a revolutionary crisis. At that point, the left's ability to seize power depends on the strength of its own base and the extent of its allies domestically and internationally. It is already admitted that the NDF's independent base, including its armed strength, is not yet sufficient for a direct seizure of power by the left. However, in our opinion, its entry into the corridors of the state power, despite this limitation is *not* completely out of the question.

It is within the *realm of possibility* that in a revolutionary crisis, this particular regime can be overthrown and replaced by a government that includes the left, even if the latter's strength remains only at the current level. It becomes principally a question of allies. It depends on how the left, despite its insufficient base, can forge, prepare and motivate its allies. It depends on how its allies are prepared to move, and how far they are willing to go. It depends on how broad and vibrant such alliances are to the point that they can create splits within enemy institutions, even within the reactionary army. We may hasten to add that it also depends on the strength of a international front that can politically, diplomatically and materially flank the popular seizure, i.e., the left's links to the socialist camp and its ties with the progressive or independent governments, and peoples. (The impact of this external factor on the capacity of the internal forces to seize and consolidate historic gains should not be underestimated, given the strategic importance of the Philippines to the most powerful imperialist country in the world.)

It is within the realm of possibility that a coalition of anti-fascist forces can force the Marcos camp to step down; reconstitute the Philippine army by winning over its democratic elements, cutting off its ties with the U.S. and integrating into its command and ranks units of the people's army and other armed groups; and proceed to reestablish institutions of democratic rule. Even if the left is not the dominant force within such a coalition government, it can utilize its new position to widen and strengthen its revolutionary base and influence. And assuming a favorable international balance of forces—if imperialism is preoccupied by serious revolutionary challenges elsewhere—the left, through peaceful democratic contests [elections], can even proceed to construct a more all-sided national democratic or transition regime that will lead towards socialism. Such a post-Marcos coalition stage, however, would be highly unstable and precarious, and the left must always be prepared for an orderly retreat in the event of an overwhelming imperialist counterattack.

It is more likely that such a coalition victory would be short-lived. But even the bourgeois democratic respite prior to a full imperialist counterattack would be of great advantage for the left politically and organizationally. Such a respite, if skillfully utilized, can enable the revolutionary forces to strike deep political roots nationally at a rapid pace, freely construct lasting international alliances and even prepare to minimize the damage that the eventual counterattack will inflict. Even now, the partial [political] relaxation is already a relative boon for the left, giving its revolutionary efforts more room for maneuver.

It is most likely, however, that if a revolutionary situation matures, imperialism will clamp down before any of the left's and its allies' attempts can succeed. Even so, the left still stands to gain from the situation, assuming that is has prepared the popular forces for an orderly retreat. First of all, the political struggles leading to the crisis will be a source of tremendous lessons and valuable experience both in the "art of politics" and the "art of insurrection." Secondly, depending on the left's political skills, the masses in their millions can be trained in the political struggle and, as a result of their experience, the anti-imperialist revolutionary alternative can gain hegemonic influence over all resistance efforts, greatly enhancing the people's war and accelerating its pace. Thirdly, even if the imperialist clamp down, the revolutionary situation would deepen the crisis of imperialist rule. It would at least prove fatal to the Marcos regime. Imperialist rule would be so unstable because short of a direct occupation of the country, it would have to rely on a succession of unwieldy puppets to maintain order.

But a simplistic approach to the current situation will fail to bring out any of these above-mentioned possibilities. Simply intensifying the atmosphere of protest and recruiting new adherents to the revolutionary program will not lead to a qualitative maturation of the current protest movement or of the regime's political crisis. Bringing out the maximum historic potential of the present protest movement is a question of political line, of mapping out a complex set of political tactics capable of cohering the spontaneous movement and of setting its political direction. The implementation of these tactics will be more demanding and will require more of the cadre than any directive to mainly increase and intensify revolutionary propaganda and organizing. It will require of the Communist the mastery of the "art of politics." Lenin said this art "consists in correctly gauging the conditions and the moment when the vanguard of the proletariat can successfully assume power, when it is able—during and after the seizure of power—to win adequate support from sufficiently broad strata of the masses, and when it is able thereafter to maintain, consolidate, and extend its rule by educating, training and attracting ever broader masses of the working people."

C. Zigzag and Compromise

The Communists would be the first to agree that currently the revolutionary forces are not in a position to assume power through a "direct path." Meaning, the basic worker-peasant alliance is not yet in a position to directly wrest political power from the enemy. The present political juncture (the regime's crisis) must therefore be considered a period that presents a detour or zigzag in the direct path to revolutionary power. But Communists must recognize it as such, otherwise the direct path could be fetishized, and the opportunity offered by the zigzag may be lost.

> As it happens, revolutionary periods are mainly periods in history when the clash of contending social forces, in a comparatively short space of time, decides the question of the country's choice of a direct or a zigzag path of development for a comparatively very long period of time. The need for reckoning with the zigzag path does not in the least do away with the fact that Marxists should be able to explain to the masses during the decisive moments of their history that the direct path is preferable. (Lenin, "Against the Boycott")

In other words, the need to reckon with a zigzag path of history does not automatically negate the validity or the desirability of the direct path. In the same article, Lenin explained: "Marxism's attitude towards the zigzag path of history is essentially the same as its attitude towards compromise. Every zigzag turn in history is a compromise, between the old, which is no longer strong enough to negate the new, and the new, which is not yet strong enough to overthrow the old. Marxism does not altogether reject compromises. Marxism considers it necessary to make use of them, but that does not in the least prevent Marxism, as a living and operating historical force, from fighting energetically compromises. Not to understand this seeming contradiction is not to know the rudiments of Marxism."

It is important to grasp this lesson in order to banish any fears that "setting more ambitious goals" for the present protest movement might deviate from the general line of the Philippine revolution. Relative to the socialist revolution, the two-stage strategy or the necessity for a national democratic stage is itself a recognition of a zigzag path of historical development. In the attainment of the first stage, the direct path is the seizure of power by the worker-peasant alliance through a protracted people's war. This strategy is the decisive factor that gives the communists the historic initiative and the leverage over other political forces and trends contending for power. Recognizing in the current crisis a zigzag course, and refocusing the communists' efforts towards seizing the political possibilities offered by this historical moment in no way requires the abandonment of the direct path. It would constitute a right error of grave proportions were the communists to abandon their strategic orientation and squander their leverage. But what is required is the integration of the essence of the direct path into new forms of struggle, forms that will of necessity be shaped by compromise. Zigzag in relation to direct path is tactic in relation to strategy.

How, then, must communists proceed to "seize the hour" in the present crisis? The experience of the world communist movement has yielded valuable lessons. Consider the following observation from Georgi Dimitrov ("Report before the 7th World Congress of the Communist International, Aug. 2, 1935"; emphasis in the original):

> It is a common mistake of a "leftist" character to imagine that as soon as a political (or revolutionary) crisis arises, it is enough for the communist leaders to put forth the slogan of revolutionary insurrection, and the broad masses will follow them. No, even in such a crisis the masses are by no means always ready to do so. We saw this in the case of *Spain*. To help the *millions* to master as rapidly as possible, through their own experience, what they have to do, where to find a radical solution, and what Party is worthy of their confidence—these among others are the purpose for which transitional slogans and special forms of *transition* or *approach*, to the proletarian revolution are necessary. Otherwise, the great mass of the people, who are under the influence of petty

bourgeois democratic illusions and traditions, may waver even when there is a revolutionary situation . . . may stray, without finding the road to revolution—and then come under the axe of the fascist executioners.

In the current crisis, it is *not enough* to raise the call for national democratic revolution, to raise the slogan "Dismantle the U.S.-Marcos Dictatorship," or to accelerate individual recruitment into the revolutionary ranks, or even to intensify calls to oppose the regime, or to deepen the crisis. These are not erroneous calls, but they are not enough to sustain the present protest movement, or to politically train the masses in their millions, or to win them over to the necessity of revolutionary struggle. Even from the point of view of "rendering the bourgeois reformists incapacitated as a third force" as some CPP cadre put it, simply intensifying revolutionary propaganda and agitation will not effectively turn a significant portion of the bourgeois opposition into a reserve of the revolution (as opposed to a reserve of imperialism).

The Communists need a transition approach. Dimitrov pointed out that Lenin attached exceptionally great importance to forms of transition "Because (Lenin) had in mind the *fundamental law of all great revolutions*, the law that for the masses, propaganda and agitation alone cannot take the place of *their own political experience*, when it is a question of attracting really broad masses of the working people to the side of the revolutionary vanguard." The left needs to popularize a tactical political program that can cohere the spontaneous movement, and unite the revolutionaries and the organized bourgeois reformists as this movements' core. This tactical (compromise) program should include among others, a commonly-agreed-upon alternative to the present regime, and the principal means of fighting for this alternative. The forces at this movement's core should necessarily organize a common center and formulate a general plan for the immediate political struggle.

From the communists' point of view, all of this is compromise—an exercise in flexibility. For in uniting the current protest movement, which is both spontaneous and reformist, this tactical program will have to be principally anti-fascist in character; a program for the restoration of democracy; for the setting up of a bourgeois democratic government which will not principally be under the workers-peasant class leadership (as we maximally want) but under the *shared* (equally weighted) leadership of the revolutionaries and the anti-fascist bourgeoisie. Given the reformist character of the movement— and the left's own assessment that an armed overthrow is not possible in the immediate period—the anti-fascist program will be pursued through peaceful but militant means. The only condition that must be placed on this broad anti-fascist unity is that all forces must direct their fire at the fascist regime and its supporters and not at one another; that all forces must direct their fire at the fascist regime and its supporters and not at one another; that all forces subordinate their strategic differences and be accountable to the established programmatic unity of the front.

The left has to have a clear standpoint on this transition, on this compromise approach. This is not a communist trick "in lieu" of our inability to seize power by ourselves. Our interest in an anti-fascist compromise is not fake. It is precisely because we cannot yet take the direct responsibility for putting an end to the source of the people's oppression that for the communists, the bridling of the fascist beast and the strengthening of *all* democratic forces (even if these be principally bourgeois democratic forces) in order to preserve the people's democratic gains, is *not* a small matter.

It would be extremely irresponsible for any communist to ignore the danger faced by democratic forces, even by bourgeois democratic forces, or to fail to range before the fascist enemy all the possible forces that can oppose it just because such an effort will not yield an immediate and unqualified left victory. In addition, Lenin called upon revolutionaries to study all questions of all democratic struggles, "to expound and emphasize general democratic tasks before the whole people, without for a moment concealing our socialist convictions" (*What Is to Be Done?*). This responsibility arises from the fact that "Only the proletariat can be a consistent fighter for democracy" while the bourgeoisie "will impart an inconsistent and self-seeking nature" to the democratic struggles ("Two Tactics").

The anti-fascist compromise will be positive for everyone, except the fascist regime and the imperialists. Even if it will *objectively strengthen the hand of the reformists and the bourgeois democrats*, it will not necessarily weaken the hand of the revolutionaries. Should the transition approach succeed, and a compromise democratic government replace the present regime, *even for a brief period*, it will not necessarily be a diversion from our revolutionary program—for as long as we do not for a moment conceal our revolutionary intentions. "Political changes of a truly democratic nature, and especially political revolutions, can under no circumstances whatsoever either obscure or weaken the slogan of a socialist revolution. On the contrary, they always bring it closer, extend its basis and draw new sections of the petty bourgeoisie and the semi-proletarian masses into the socialist struggle" (Lenin, *Collected Works*, Vol. 21 p. 339). And should a democratic transition regime successfully assume power, it becomes a substage in the political struggle for a truly national democratic regime.

A clear orientation that the transition approach serves the interest of the democratic whole and that it is neither a trick nor a sell-out on the communists' part, will enable the left to take the valid democratic interests of its allies seriously. With nothing to lose in this compromise, except if it surrenders its strategic outlook, the left can be broadminded, above-board and flexible. Such an orientation will establish the communists' political and moral superiority over other political forces whose anti-fascist stand may be flawed by their "self-seeking" strategic and class perspective.

D. The Concrete Struggle

The call for a broad anti-fascist front and its program must be concrete and detailed. Various opposition forces in the Philippines, in fact, have instinctively attempted to hammer out such a call, e.g., KOMPIL, COMPACT, JAJA, etc. However similar most of the calls and programs are, no unified front or an umbrella encompassing the majority of the opposition has gelled. The perhaps unspoken reason for this is that everyone wants to know what the CPP-NDF has to say. The left has become such a central force in Philippine politics that its policies and actions carry a considerable, if not decisive, weight.

For its part, the left has apparently focused on the formation of the Nationalist Alliance for Justice, Freedom and Democracy. As an "anti-fascist, anti-imperialist" formation, the NAJFD has drawn the left-led groups and forces broadly sympathetic to the national democratic movement. As a legal expression of NDF politics, the NAJFD is an important formation. In the midst of a reformist movement, an open left pole makes up for the limitations that clandestinity imposes on the revolutionary forces. However, *if* the NAJFD is meant to be the unifying formation that will cohere the spontaneous movement, it has serious limitations. Politically, it does not extend enough accommodations to forces who have not yet arrived at a relatively developed anti-imperialist critique. Parts of its program of action are the repudiation of foreign loans that never benefitted the Filipino people; the nationalization of all basic industries; and the dismantling of the U.S. bases. While the spontaneous movement is prepared to oppose U.S. support for the Marcos regime, the imposition of more sophisticated anti-imperialist demands as a condition for broad unity will be counterproductive. The NAJFD program does not compromise enough.

"The term compromise in politics implies the surrender of certain demands, the renunciation of part of one's demands, by agreement with another party. . . . The usual idea the man in the street has about Bolsheviks, an idea encouraged by the press, which slanders them, is that the Bolsheviks will never agree to a compromise with anybody. . . . The idea is flattering to us . . . for it proves that even our enemies are compelled to admit our loyalty to the fundamental principles of socialism and revolution. Nevertheless, we must say that this idea is wrong." (Lenin, *On Compromises*).

There is, however, another motion from the left, which bears watching. We have obtained a badly reproduced copy of an outline proposal for a Congress for the Restoration of Democracy (CORD) formulated by a certain "Bayani C. Aquino." We do not know CORD's relationship to the *Plaridel Papers*, but if they are from the same quarters, we would not be surprised. They have essentially similar political thrusts.

CORD calls for a united anti-fascist movement that would force the resignation of Marcos, his cabinet, all his appointees in all services of the Armed Forces "to give way to a democratic transition government headed by a committee of retired justices . . . and other outstanding individuals acceptable to all political parties and people's organizations. The transitional government will nullify Marcos' constitution, restore democracy, release all political prisoners and declare general amnesty. It must call for general elections from the presidency down either under the 1935 constitution or rules adopted by said transition government." To facilitate the resignation of Marcos and his top officials and the assumption of office by a transition government, a national reconciliation council may be formed . . . etc.

A powerful, peaceful, but militant mass movement led jointly by all organized opposition groups must utilize demonstrations, marches, general strikes and various forms of civil disobedience to press for the resignations and to pave the way for the democratic transition government. Such powerful and militant mass actions must be sustained; all concessions offered by the U.S. or Marcos short of resignation and the assumption of a transition government must be rejected, boycotted, exposed and discredited.

The CORD proposal can be the left's approach to the "zigzag." Its points are broad and acceptable to all democratic forces. Given the existing capabilities of all opposition forces, its goals, the means it prescribes are practical. The call for a transition government can provide the present spontaneous movement a centerpiece, a unified vision of an alternative it can fight for, thereby providing it a direction and giving it sustenance. CORD also has the potential of cohering the organized left and bourgeois democratic forces as the core of the mass anti-fascist movement.

A sustained, politically focused protest movement can put tremendous pressures on the regime and its institutions. It can potentially cause regime officials to desert; it can create splits in the military; it can force imperialism to undertake risky political maneuvers thereby opening itself to exposure; it can exacerbate the master-puppet contradiction. This non-violent mass movement's call for a democratic transition government is so reasonable it places the people on clearly higher political ground vis-à-vis Marcos and imperialism. Their refusal to accede to this reasonable democratic alternative will heighten their exposure and isolation: that they are the obstacle to democracy, peace and national reconciliation.

Should the movement succeed and consolidate its historic gain, it would be a tremendous setback for imperialism and a victory for the revolutionary forces. Should it succeed only briefly and be counterattacked by imperialism, the U.S. will stand exposed before all Filipinos and before all the world. Should the U.S. maneuver by ousting Marcos, and replacing him with another puppet, it would only succeed in deepening the crisis of its rule. Should Marcos crack down it will be at a high political cost. His isolation will get even worse so that the U.S. might have to replace him anyway. In other words, the movement's reasonable demand for a democratic transition government can place the U.S.-Marcos regime in a no-win situation. It will be damned if it accedes, damned if it doesn't.

The CORD proposal has a secondary but important feature. It proposes a discussion among all opposition forces on the need to banish any illusions as to how the regime will respond. That while the movement will pursue its goals through non-violence, it must also prepare for self-defense and for the protection of its ranks and leaders. It calls on the movement to extend democratic influence into the ranks of the armed forces; to organize counter-surveillance on military and police agents "so as to distinguish the diehard fascist elements from the good and the honest elements" and so as to cause the arrest or disarming of bad elements; to secretly gather arms; etc. Presumably, the left will contribute much in setting up provisions for an orderly retreat, offering sanctuaries, routes to new posts in the countryside or abroad; or, *as the front's unity matures*, in setting up provisions for *armed insurrection* or an offensive. While the call for self-defense is not the principal feature of the transition approach, it is an essential feature that checks any idealistic notions about the real dynamics of struggle. It also mass lines the armed struggle to the reformist movement, not as a programmatic assertion by the left, but as a need to prepare for all eventualities.

A CORD-style approach to the present crisis facilitates a number of things for the communists. Firstly, a broad but detailed compromise program systematizes the work with allies. The program—its aims and methods—sets a clear standard of political accountability for the entire front. It makes easier the determination of who is and who is not in the front, or who has broken from it, or is about to break from it. This is how a carefully formulated program of reforms can be directed also against the opportunists. Secondly, the CORD approach rescues the movement from spontaneity and enables the communists to "train the masses in their millions in the political struggle" and through "their own political experience." The tit-for-tat with the enemy's maneuvers, the enemy's refusal to budge and its attempts to respond with violence can teach the masses "in their millions" the obsolescence of reforms and the need for a revolutionary solution. Ironically, a carefully formulated reformist transition approach can, in the end, prove to be a better recruiter of revolutionaries that the most tireless cadre who, without a transition program, tries to recruit people in their tens or hundreds. Finally, depending on the communist's skill in leading the transition, the Communist Party can emerge as the most reliable, practical and trustworthy leader of the entire resistance. The dynamics of the transition approach facilitates the differentiation and radicalization not only of the masses but also of the bourgeois democratic forces. If the communists respect the compromise, defend the front's unity, work well with the other forces, and stand fast against the regime, a point will be reached in the front where, according to Dimitrov, considerable proportions of the non-communists—including bourgeois democrats—will "demand ruthless measures against the fascists and other reactionaries, fight together with the communists against fascism and openly oppose the reactionary section of their own party which is hostile to communism." In other words, a considerable proportion of the bourgeois reformists can become the reserve of the revolution, not the imperialists. Perhaps, an example that comes to mind is how significant Salvadoran bourgeois democratic forces (their version of the Tañadas, the Macapagals and the Dioknos) have become welded within the FDR component of the FMLN-FDR.

Struggle within the Front/Independent Work

The left must, however, avoid any illusions about the smoothness of the transition approach. While the left "must fight most resolutely to overcome and exterminate the last remnants of self-satisfied sectarianism within its ranks," Dimitrov warns that the tactics of the united front "are not a reconciliation with social Democratic (bourgeois reformist) ideology and practice."

Apart from the enemy's maneuvers, dangers lurk from within the front itself. The front represents the mediation of strategic class interest and is therefore inherently unstable. There will be a need to struggle against the vacillations, tendencies towards collaborationism and inconsistencies of the non-proletarian forces. The left has to be vigilant against divisive practices.

It must also bear in mind that the danger of opportunism to the right will increase in proportion as the front broadens. There will be attempts to reduce the role of the Party and to sacrifice the interest of the left especially when instances of negotiations with the enemy arise. Communists must learn when the need for criticism and struggle arises; when to criticize with restraint and when to move for the expulsion of any force from the front.

The principle of independence also has to be established within the front. Left propaganda will be crucial in summing up for the millions of front adherents the key junctures, advances and setbacks of the common struggle against the fascist regime. In particular, the exposure of the role of imperialism falls on the shoulders of the CPP-NDF. As the anti-fascist struggle intensifies so must revolutionary education, agitation, and organization-building. The left cannot allow the independent voice of any party to be muzzled, so long as independent actions do not contravene the unity of the front and are relatively subordinate to the demands of the common work and plans. Revolutionary propaganda carried out within the context of a broad and united popular movement packs a more effective wallop, as it is revolutionary propaganda rooted in the experience of millions in the political struggle.

Implications to Philippine Support Work in North America

A. The Broader Fronts

The current political crisis in the Philippine impacts mainly the Filipino community, as opposed to the broader anti-intervention, anti-imperialist movements in the U.S. (and Canada). This is largely due to the fact that the Philippine conflict has not yet ripened to the level of a decisive confrontation between imperialism and the revolutionary forces (or of a military stalemate at least). Objectively, there is no imminent necessity or possibility for a more direct and active U.S. military role that will polarize U.S. society (and the international scene) over the issue of imperialist intervention in the Philippines.

Understandably, the broader anti-intervention and the anti-imperialist movements are focused on the struggle in Central America, and there is no need on our part to insist that these movements bring the Philippine issue to the top of their agenda at this time. However, if the Philippine left takes the current tactical juncture by the horns, the political situation could change within a year or two, requiring the broader movements to begin placing greater attention on the Philippine struggle. There is therefore a need to consistently update key sectors of the broader movement on the current political dynamic and where these could lead to. We need to give more attention to how "Philippine Solidarity Network (PSN)-type" work gets conducted, for while it will not yet be the principal character of the support work, our positioning in the broader fronts needs to be more consciously approached even now.

While Marcos' governmental crisis has not become the U.S. bourgeoisie's round-the-clock preoccupation, it has nevertheless intensified the debate over how best to preserve the U.S. position in the Philippines. Both sides of this debate recognize the need for a transition from an ally that has become a political liability, to a more stable puppet regime. Both sides also agree that the transition should not be messy, to prevent the left from taking advantage of "contradictions within the enemy camp." The Reagan administration, however, holds that while it is willing to give up Marcos, the new regime must retain the fascist core of the Marcos camp and include only the most pro-imperialist and anti-communist elements of the bourgeois opposition.

But the U.S. liberal bourgeois wing believes such a regime would not be able to appease the Filipino masses, would not have enough popular consensus to rule and, therefore, would be inherently unstable. Its prescription is to "loosen up" by giving a more significant role in the new regime to bourgeois reformists that are more bourgeois democratic than fascist and would definitely be pro-imperialist and anti-communist (Benigno Aquino Jr.'s vision of a post-Marcos regime). The U.S. bourgeois liberals believe it is not yet "too late" for this type of transition. Meaning, that unlike in El Salvador, the revolutionary left has not yet co-opted or won over a considerable portion of the bourgeois democratic opposition into a solid resistance coalition. They believe the bourgeois reformists can still be split from the left and turned into a reserve of imperialism.

There are favorable opportunities for exacerbating this debate by bringing to Congress, the media, influential liberal circles, human rights and academic groups that have closely interacted with the Philippine issue, the exposure of the fake democratic maneuvers of Reagan and Marcos and the continuing abuses of the fascist regime. With a compromise program in the Philippines—a "reasonable demand" for a democratic transition government on the part of the people—the movement has a "realistic" alternative that U.S. liberals cannot reject outright. The conditions for extending the popular front more broadly and isolating the Reagan transition plan are favorable. However, while exploiting these responsibilities, we must check the anti-communism that can intensify if liberals both in the broader front and the Filipino opposition movement attempt to popularize the argument "democratize now or else the left will take over."

B. The Opposition Front in the Filipino Community

The flow of opposition following the Aquino assassination has changed the political atmosphere and balance of forces within the Filipino community [in North America]. The Philippine consulates and the reactionaries grouped around them are on the defensive. Except for the most unabashedly reactionary elements, there is a trend of "neutralism" within the organized sectors of the community as leaders and organizations keep a safe political distance from the regime's positions. Some have gone beyond neutrality and have taken open anti-Marcos postures. In the community as a whole, there is an upsurge of democratic, anti-fascist sentiments and a flow of opposition activity. No doubt the propaganda work done by all the organized opposition forces over the years has facilitated the entry of hundreds of new forces into the active ranks of the movement.

The conditions for extending and broadening the anti-fascist popular front in the community are therefore, excellent. But in order to gain from these favorable conditions, the left here must also have a clear and precise orientation towards the new protest movement among Filipinos.

First of all, let us not deceive ourselves as to the character of this movement. It is of course not revolutionary. It is a reformist movement dominated by bourgeois democratic politics. In fact, the majority of those in the community who have stepped forward into political activity have gravitated to formations led by exiled bourgeois reformist leaders. And due to the shortcomings and limitations of this bourgeois reformist leadership, the new movement still remains largely spontaneous.

We can cite a number of factors that help strengthen the movement's political characteristics: the bourgeois reformist leaders are more "prestigious"; most Filipino immigrants are of petit-bourgeois origins; their different set of political and material conditions here tend to buffer their views from the real dynamics of the struggle in the Philippines; etc. But the main thing is bourgeois democracy is not yet regarded as obsolete by most Filipinos, and their experience living in the most advanced bourgeois democratic society in the world certainly bolsters that outlook. Comrades should therefore not conclude that only the petit-bourgeois elements in the community gravitate to M_____ or H_____. Even among working class Filipinos, bourgeois democracy is not yet obsolete and we should not be surprised to discover that the majority of the people in the bourgeois reformists' base are your regular wage slaves.

No amount of anti-imperialist and revolutionary propaganda in the past several years could have basically altered the reformist impulses of this new movement. As in the Philippines, people can only be won over to revolution as a result of their own political experience, including, but not solely, their experience with revolutionary propaganda. But what are ten years of anti-imperialist and revolutionary propaganda has achieve is no small matter. Within this new movement, anti-imperialist views and positions supportive of the national democratic revolution are not considered illegitimate. The CAMD and the KDP are seen in legitimate political forces, even though many people maintain their differences with us. Even though many people, especially the newly activated elements have a lot of anti-communist fears and prejudices, their general tendency is to negotiate their apprehensions with us rather than to avoid us altogether. Only a handful of backward elements attempt to reduce the left into an outcast.

Maximally, our propaganda work has neutralized the more blatantly backward positions of the right. Ten years ago, for example, M_____ and [his organization] were only willing to "criticize" U.S. military aid to Marcos and not the economic aid. Now, they are even opposed to the U.S. bases. Ten years ago, any mention of the NPA in joint events tended to invite controversy. Although our propaganda work was not solely responsible for the changes in the right's positions, the *Ang Katipunan*, the *Taliba*, the CAMD forums, leaflets, etc. have insured the amplification of a sophisticated political perspective that others could not ignore. These forms of propaganda improved the community's receptiveness to "radical" ideas and perspectives. Among key middle forces in M_____'s organization, for example, the CAMD is now sought after for political updates and "framework sharing." As we had predicted, our systematic propaganda work during the ebb has helped reduce the political primitiveness of the current flow, even though this flow remains principally reformist and non-revolutionary in character.

What should our attitude be towards this new movement and its limitations? How should we take the fact that it is reformist and that most people who join it gravitate to bourgeois reformist formations? If a new M___ or N____ chapter forms in our local areas, is that a bad thing or a good thing? It is no exaggeration to say that most of our activists had a hard time making up their minds. The initial impulse was to be critical of the underdevelopment of the political forces and the incompetence of the reformist groups and to feel threatened by their growth. Much of this reaction comes from a good place, from our grasp of our revolutionary politics and intentions, and our concern that the community's political response to the Philippine situation not be influence by backward perspectives. However, the purpose of analyzing this moment's character and the historical factors that shape it is to arrive at an objective appraisal that would enable us to gain our bearings.

We must grasp that on the whole the new movement—despite its spontaneous shortcomings and the self-seeking or incompetent behavior of quite a few of its bourgeois reformist leaders—is a positive thing. Even the growth in membership of the reformists is, on the whole, a good thing.

The new movement, despite its limitations, contributes profoundly to the popularization and strengthening of anti-fascist sentiments among Filipinos. And to the extent that reformist formations provide an organizational form for large numbers of people who are stepping forward into political activity for the first time, their growth should not be viewed by our activists with dismay. The flourishing of anti-fascist sentiments in the Filipino community keeps the pro-Marcos reactionaries on the defensive; extends the isolation of the Marcos regime; and contributes to the difficulties of U.S. imperialism in the Philippines. A broad democratic movement injects a valuable progressive current in community politics overall. And for the left's purposes, a broad and vibrant anti-fascist movement among Filipino provides extremely fertile ground for anti-imperialist and national democratic propaganda.

It should be clear to us then that the left shares a common interest with other political forces in seeing to it that the anti-fascist sentiments in the Filipino community are strengthened and extended to new sectors. We therefore also share the common responsibilities of sustaining the new protest movement and setting its political direction. The KDP has to exercise leadership in struggling with all the organized forces to take up these responsibilities. In the context of performing the task and those that we share in common with all other forces, the left must extend and deepen the influence of the anti-imperialist national democratic line.

C. Building the Popular Front

Reinforcing and expanding the climate of opposition requires sustained propaganda work on a community-wide scale against the Marcos regime, its representatives and its allies. Anti-fascist propaganda has to reach as many of the unorganized as possible and as consistently as possible. At the same time, recent experience has shown that the consulates' traditional hold on the organized sectors can be shaken depending on the strength of the anti-fascist climate. In the final analysis only a few diehard reactionaries are willing to stand up for the fascists when the going gets rough. These community organizations have to be targeted for propaganda. They can be encouraged to realign with the opposition or be "neutral." More realistically many of their individual members can be drawn into the organized networks of the opposition. The point is, anti-fascist propaganda has to permeate all sectors of the community—the organized and the unorganized. It is clearly a task that cannot be shouldered by the left alone. The requirements of community-wide propaganda work done at the pace of the flow should dissolve any remnant sectarian notions on our part that it is more desirable for us to "go it alone," or that we have absolutely no use for the "incompetently led" reformists groups that have suddenly abounded.

Key to the maintenance of a sharp community-wide polarization over the issue of fascist rule, is how the left can get the other opposition groups to consciously share the responsibility of sustaining the new protest movement based on a commonly agreed upon direction. In other words, the key is the cohering of an organized common front, a popular front of opposition among the various political forces who otherwise cannot come together due to fundamental and strategic ideological and political differences. Right now, the movement's efforts are dispersed and the lack of a common direction weakens its consistency. In addition, such a state of spontaneity is advantageous to bourgeois opportunist leaders whose narrow agendas and self-promotion antics cannot be collectively checked.

The principal thrust of our work in the Filipino community, therefore, is the setting into operation of an actual, substantial and self-conscious popular front of opposition. Take note that we place a premium on the operative, working character of this front. It will therefore take a lot of complex struggles to build. But building the front is first of all, a political question. The pooling of efforts, the coordination of joint activities is best set in motion if all political forces can reach a set of political unities appropriate to the broadness of the movement and to the objective tasks before the entire opposition. As in the Philippines, the left here also has to be prepared to compromise and exercise flexibility. We will place no condition on the formation of this front other than the condition that all political forces train their guns at the common enemy and not at anyone within the front; that all forces subordinate their strategic differences in the interest of the common task. We will only object to any attacks against the left here and in the Philippines, or any attacks or anyone else, or any acts that violate or undermine the unity of the front. Other than this, we will remain extremely open to any proposal or initiative directed against the common enemy.

The most obvious concession we are willing to give is that we are not going to impose a revolutionary or a "national-democratic" unity on this broad front. Instead, all forces can realistically reach unity on an uncompromising opposition to the Marcos fascist regime (or to the "Marcos dictatorship" as some of the reformist forces prefer to call it). We are not going to demand a unity based on a thorough critique of U.S. imperialism. However, no one in this movement can conceivably be *for* the continuation of U.S. support to Marcos. Therefore, opposition to U.S. aid is a necessary point of unity.

In the past, joint efforts usually ran into the "problematic" question "what is your alternative." Usually any joint panel in a forum, for example, would break down on this with forces having no choices but to go "to each its own." In other words, while forces from time to time could reach workable unity on what they were opposed to, the absence of a *common* alternative or of a *positive* elaboration of political unity served to undermine any unity effort. Here is where the development of a compromise opposition program in the Philippines would be of tremendous impact here. The opposition here would have the possibility of uniting not only in opposition to Marcos and U.S. aid, but also in support of a popular demand for a democratic transition government, and in support of non-violent but militant mass efforts to institute that government. For the first time, the broad opposition would be able to place before the community a common solution (while still holding onto their strategic alternatives), thereby giving the protest movement a common direction and a clearer vision. We will proceed with the assumption that the CORD proposal is the appropriate transition approach and we will actively struggle for it the as the common alternative of the popular front.

What are the conditions like for struggling with the reformist wing of the opposition to cohere this front with the left?

The bourgeois-led opposition, or the reformists, have undergone significant changes especially since the Aquino assassination. Prior to the assassination, the bourgeois oppositionists here reflected the despair felt by their counterparts in the Philippines over their waning viability as a "Third Force." Organizational weaknesses and demoralization prevented them from pursuing any significant political activity. The Marcos state visit caught them unprepared and it became obvious that the CAMD was better positioned to center the nationwide protests. After the assassination, however, new life was breathed into this wing with hundreds of new people joining the reformists ranks. Aside from the M___, new groups were formed largely with overlapping memberships: N_____, J_____, etc. A new dynamic, however, has emerged in the flow. A__, leeching on to the Aquino family, proceeded to turn N_____ into a base of his own after drawing members from the M's organization. This opportunism and A's sectarian practices have angered M and many leading figures in the [his organization].

As things stand, A__ and his top leadership now constitute the right wing of the reformist camp. Their limelighting has attracted the most anti-communist and pro-imperialist elements in the camp. While A__ himself is not an out and out pro-imperialist, his personal opportunism encourages backward and sectarian behavior. Because of his opportunism A's organization, of all reformist forces, has taken a consistently vacillating position on the May 14 [elections to Marcos-controlled parliament] boycott movement. While M___ remains an anti-communist and pro-imperialist force, his contradictions with A__ has neutralized his most rigid postures towards the left. Meanwhile, a small but potentially influential left wing has become visible within M's organization (left wing in relation to the right wing of the reformist camp, but center in relation to the overall reformist camp-left camp polarity.) Individuals like G_, B_ and BB_ are social democratic types who are also the workhorses or the more serious forces within the M's group. They are non-collaborationists in relationship to the regime, more critical of the U.S. role, are outraged at A__'s opportunism, and are extremely open to working with the left. They exert a still underdeveloped influence among some of the rank-and-file that intersects [the various reformist groups] who are beginning to be critical of the incompetence and the egotism of some of their leaders.

Through the initiative of the national leadership, we have actually set in motion the forging of ties with center forces. A number of informal discussions have been conducted that resulted in low-key cooperative work. So far, the trends are positive. The serious and principled approach of the left has been tested a few times in the concrete, and is making itself felt. Already word about "the CAMD-M__ unity front" is getting around the immediate circles of the left-wing reformists. To show comrades the extent to which we are willing to be flexible, we have been asked and have agreed to help the center forces (through advice and resources) in developing the M into a more competent organization. Relative to general task in the community and to the goal of checking the backward tendencies of the right, this is a positive concession.

Whatever steps we have taken are but the beginning of a complex process of struggle. As Dimitrov repeatedly warned, any "doctrinaire narrowness" or satisfaction with "simplified methods of solving the most complex problems . . . on the basis of stereotype schemes" will easily lead us to sectarianism. We cannot, therefore, look for a blueprint on how to deal with every dynamic that would confront us in building this front. Our day-to-day tactics of unity and struggle will have to be defined by the concretes of the situation; we have to train "on-the-job." However, we can map out a general approach. But first of all, activists have to grasp the interest of the whole, which is, the sustenance of an opposition to U.S. support and on the struggle for a democratic transition government. This is *not* a "propaganda or public relations line" that hides a "real line" which calls for the destabilization of everyone else but the left.

Assuming a correct stand, we will proceed with building the front from "above and below." There is no question as to which comes first; it has to be done simultaneously. The CAMD has already designated campaigns that are specifically for joint work. We will initiate this joint work on a local level, working closely with the center forces. At the same time, we will formally propose to the national leadership of the various organizations these campaign as national undertakings. We will be open to taking up other forms of joint work that may be initiated by other forces. These campaigns are only building blocks to ensure that the front already becomes operative even on a limited scale. In the course of joint work, we must begin to popularize the concept of a common front that has a common direction. Without delay, we will initiate discussions on a national level on the need for the formalization of the front. The reasons for approaching front building from above and below are simple. Regardless of the backwardness of many of the reformists' leaders, they are still the only forces that have the mandate to formulate their groups' decisions and policies. While it may be "easier" for us to work with the rank-and-file, there is no avoiding the sometimes distasteful negotiations with higher officials. Otherwise, the front and its unities will never be formalized. Meanwhile, working from below is also crucial as the only possible way internal pressure can be applied on the official decision-makers. Working from below also assures us direct political contact with the rank-and-file.

While we place a premium on the actual life of the front, the formal aspects of it (actual organizational structure, points of unity or program, plan) cannot be disregarded. These are the aspects that spell out the rules of accountability, which make clear the political and organizational standards on which to base the struggle and criticisms within the front. Without these, it will be extremely difficult to check the more backward tendencies of the bourgeois forces or to determine who is within the front or who has already broken from it. In fact, this is the very reason why opportunists will tend to hesitate in officially constituting the front. A formally constituted front systematizes our alliance work. Thus, while will not settle for just the formal trappings, neither will we settle for just an "objective" front.

D. Struggle within the Front

Our readiness to work with opportunists and backward elements within the broad opposition movement does not mean we are willing to reconcile with opportunism and backwardness. The left must be vigilant and be ready to criticize and struggle against divisiveness, sectarianism, anti-communism, and vacillations and collaborationism in the face of the enemy's attacks or offers of seductive concessions. But criticism must be concrete and based on the front's common standard and unities. We must also be willing to accept valid criticisms [which] must be concrete and based on the front's common standards and unities. We must also be willing to accept valid criticisms or to make self-criticisms.

We have to learn how to unfold struggles with precision, and how to bring them to a close; when to struggle with restraint and when to be relentless. Each instance of struggle will have its own concrete conditions; thus while we must be vigilant, we must avoid mechanical or knee-jerk responses. Spontaneity will not serve us any in the struggles. Furthermore, we are not struggling for joint and close-quarters work with other forces just so we can "expose and isolate the right" every chance we get and in every meeting we happen to be in.

Our approach to the exposure and isolation of the most backward forces must be a protracted one. This does not mean postponing struggles even when they are called for. We must always consider the center forces who will be able to see through the opportunists and the pretenders only through their own political experience. The center forces will have to be brought through these struggles each step of the way. We must consciously imbue them with a respect for the front's unities and with an appreciation for the front's valuable function. The center forces also have to be trained to be militant against the enemy's propaganda and political maneuvers and to accurately sum up the movement's collective experiences. Only through such conscious work can a considerable proportion of the center forces reach a point where, to paraphrase Dimitrov, they not only demand ruthless measures against the Marcos dictatorship, but they also "openly oppose the reactionary section of their own party which is hostile to communism." Needless to say, in the course of working in this popular front, our activists must do meticulous social investigation on the configuration of forces within the reformist groupings. We must especially identify center forces "above and below" (not all reformist leaders are opportunist and reactionary and not all rank-and-filers are necessarily honest and progressive) and seek ways to work closely with them.

Comrades should be sobered up by the evident complexity of building the popular front. This work is extremely challenging. The varying levels of detail and the endless possibilities of knotty political situation and dynamics are overwhelming. Furthermore, some of the opportunist elements are highly skilled and trained in bourgeois politics. Definitely, this work requires activists to function at a very high level of consciousness at all times. No wonder Dimitrov noted in his own time that "there are still quite a few . . .

doctrinaire elements, who at all times and places sense nothing but danger in the policy of the united front. . . . For such comrades, the whole united front is one unrelieved peril." There is simply no getting around the task of turning the spontaneous movement into an organized detachment of the broad anti-fascist front in the Philippines. There are no simplified methods of solving the most complex problems of the people's movement. The "self-satisfied "go-it-alone" approach is too amateurish in light of the objective political demands, to be considered a serious alternative method of work.

Comrades will notice that the orientation laid out in this AA departs from our previous attitude towards forces in the reformist camp. To be accurate, that attitude had been shaped a lot by objective conditions that dictated certain policies. At the same time, there were indeed weaknesses towards "leftism" in our united front practices.

Early in its history, the KDP already broke from the gross infantilism of the U.S. Maoist trend. In Philippine support work, our initial impulse was in fact correct: to build a broad anti-fascist front that includes reformists and bourgeois opportunists. (This was a far cry from the practice of U.S. Maoist groups who always impose the highest level of unity on every front—including unity against "Soviet revisionism.") The vision of a broad anti-fascist front was the basis for the National Committee for the Restoration of Civil Liberties in the Philippines (NCRCLP) prior to the KDP's formation and for the struggle to build the AMLC [Anti–Martial Law Coalition] right after the KDP's founding. M_____ was the key right force that had to be dealt with. Initial discussions were taken up with him, in one of which we even offered him the chairmanship of the front. After the AMLC founding, we pressed the M___ to be part of a common front, but to no avail.

Despite our correct impulse, the conditions were unfavorable for such a front. To begin with, the movement as whole was relatively narrow—it was us and the M's right circle. In the years following, we tried looking for middle forces who had enough clout within the M's organization, and we could not find anyone of significance. (A__ even volunteered to be the "key middle force!") Still smarting from their loss of influence during the First Quarter Storm in the Philippines, M___ *et al.* chose to stress their anti-communism, necessitating militant responses on our part. The right also downplayed the U.S. role—most especially during the Carter years when they wanted to keep their channels to the White House open, which led to frequent political clashes with us.

In general, our response to their backward tendencies was correct. In fact, our policy of struggling with the right even while seeking unity with them was a product of line struggle within the KDP. An influential line of "all unity and no struggle," of "unite with the right to win over the middle" had been championed by RR and DB and tended to gag the left. A bitter struggle defeated that line and established the line "Unite the left, win over the middle, and isolate the right." This was an important demarcation. The victorious line was one of unity and struggle within the front and a line that allowed the independence of the left to propagate its strategic perspectives. It was also correct to educate our ranks on the bankruptcy of reformism and on the class character and strategic interests of the bourgeois opposition, as compared to the naiveté, and political abdication promoted by the defeated line.

However, our distaste for the consistent opportunism and anti-communism of the right reinforced remnant leftism in our practice. Instead of the need to strengthen the movement through cooperation, the need to expose and isolate the right became the operating object of front-building. This led to mechanical practices of "isolating the right" such as contending with them at every instance or drawing them to joint activities so we can discredit their reformist programs. We lost sight of the protracted character of the right's isolation because of our subjectivism. To be sure, M___ et al. were no angels either, and there was still the need to challenge their sectarian and anti-communist practices when these occasions arose. Finally, we gave up on forging a front with the right and kept our distance unless the need for joint work came up. This was our policy right up to the Marcos visit and the Aquino assassination (whereupon, our orientation started to change). In hindsight, the years of "cooling off" was probably a good thing. However, in keeping our distance, a self-satisfied go-it-alone orientation also became operative in our ranks.

All in all, the damage done by incorrect "left" tendencies on our part is not quantitative. While we obviously need more time to bring out the fruit of our new orientation, the work of repairing our ties with center forces and even with right forces already look very promising. In consolidating our orientation, the summation of experience and the extraction of lessons will be key. In consolidating its theoretical underpinning, we will rely mostly on the summation of the Bolshevik experience during the Russian revolution. The Leninist summation is by far the richest, the most complex yet precise body of work that deals with the political art of front building.

E. Independent Anti-imperialist Work

Our approach to the popular front is extremely broadminded, yet by no means does it call for a reconciliation with the ideology of reformism. While compromise is one component of turning the spontaneous reformist movement into a reserve of the revolutionary movement, the *independent political work of the left is the other component.*

The popular front we are building is inherently unstable, given the co-existence of contending strategic class interests within it. It is completely necessary, therefore, to extend to as many center forces to those who are honestly concerned about the fate of the alliance the anti-imperialist and revolutionary influence of the National Democratic united front. This work contributes to the immediate though temporary stability of the front. In the long run, this work done well will make sure that a considerable portion of the center forces will move with the National Democratic forces once the popular front breaks apart for reasons historically valid.

It cannot be expected that reformist elements who are under the influence of bourgeois ideology, which had been instilled in them for decades, will break with reformism of their own accord. It is the business of the left to free them from the hold of reformist ideology. The work of explaining the principles of the National Democratic revolution, the critique of imperialism as a system, and the flaws of reformism must be carried on in a patient and comradely fashion. The work must also be adapted to the level or degree of development of the center forces. For some leading and politically sophisticated center forces, it may be the principles of scientific socialism that need to be explained.

The "national democratic education" of the center forces has to be done creatively and not mechanically. Dimitrov said, "Our criticism of Social Democracy must become more concrete and systematic, and must be based on the experience of the Social Democratic masses themselves. It must be borne in mind that primarily by utilizing their experience in the joint struggle . . . will it be possible and necessary to facilitate and speed up the revolutionary development of the Social Democratic worker" ("Concluding Speech before 7th Congress, Comintern 1935"). In other words, apart from direct propaganda on its strategic program, the left must lead in the careful summation of the front's experience in the Philippines and here, be these about key political junctures or the political behavior of certain forces and tendencies within the front. A word of caution: The essence of winning over center forces is their *realignment to the left's perspective and lines,* not their mechanical recruitment into the CAMD.

The left must also stand for the principle of independence of all parties within the popular front. The best way for us to squander our leverage is to do everything through the popular front; to forget that the anti-imperialist united front is more strategic and to thereby abandon independent propaganda work and base-building.

CAMD's perspectives, amplified through its propaganda work, exert a broad impact on the politics of the movement as a whole. It sets up a broad, unspoken of standard, which other political views have to reckon with. The consistent perspective of the *Taliba*, for example, objectively raises the standards for assessing the political trends in the Philippines. Other political forces also recognize the *Taliba* as the voice of the "left" in the opposition and take seriously its contents, regardless of their disagreements.

Instead of waning, CAMD's anti-imperialist propaganda must intensify, and become even more conscious and timely as the popular front takes more recognizable shape. As the front systematizes the movement's work and creates closer interaction among various groups and their bases, the ground for expanding the political influence of the CAMD and for expanding the anti-imperialist united front becomes even more favorable. And for the other political forces in the popular front, it is the consistency of the left's presence and base, along with the caliber of its activists, who serve as its clout. The CAMD has designated certain campaigns that are meant for its independent presence and base-building (NPA support work etc.). These are to be implemented faithfully and not to be needlessly sacrificed to popular front work.

APPENDIX III: KDP ACTIVISM TIMELINE

Compiled by Helen Toribio

1970 Search to Involve Pilipino Americans (SIPA) conference in Los Angeles
Ating Tao guerrilla theater founded in San Francisco
Youth conference in San Francisco
  - 150 delegates from San Diego, Los Angeles, Stockton, San Jose, Seattle
  - San Diego and Seattle delegates move for resolution on Philippine situation, denouncing "the vicious oppression and exploitation perpetrated by the fascist Marcos puppet regime in the doggish service of the American imperialists."
  - Plans discussed for communication network and information center in the Philippines

1971 San Joaquin Valley students from University of the Pacific and San Jose Delta College join the Asian contingent of antiwar protest in San Francisco
Kayumanggi student association established at California State University, Sacramento
Coconut drama by Ating Tao staged at San Francisco State University, City College of San Francisco, and California State University, Hayward (now Cal State East Bay)
June: Kalayaan collective publishes a newspaper called *Kalayaan*
July 23–25: Second SIPA conference, "Are You Curious (Brown)?"
September 3: Young Filipino People's Far West Convention in Seattle

1972 Kalayaan collective establishes Kilusan publications to provide progressive materials about the Philippines

Support Committee for a Democratic Philippines in New York City
organizes cultural group called Sining Bayan (People's Art)

February–March: Kalayaan collective calls for development of a
"progressive organization" to come out of the Pilipino People's
Samahan "Panahon na" conference in San Diego to bring together
all locally based progressive and revolutionary organizations into
one group

- Local collectives to be included: Kilusan ng Masang Pilipino (New
York; newsletter *Ang Masa)*, *Panahon Na* newsletter (San Diego),
Kabataang Katipunan organization, *Bagong Silangan* newspaper of
San Jose student coalition, *Kaibigan* newsletter (Seattle)
- Principles of organization: (1) clear statement of progressive
principles and goals, (2) activist in nature, (3) based on collectivity
and struggle
- Areas of collectivity: "We should learn to relax and have fun
together; we should learn to work and discuss things seriously
together; we should learn to study together."

March: Andres Bonifacio chapter of Ad Hoc Committee of San Diego
State University initiates statewide student conference

March 3–5: Pilipino People's Samahan "Panahon Na" conference, San
Diego State University

June: Kalayaan collective reports on Filipino workers' victory at Blue
Shield of California and on Youth Guidance Centers

July 24–26: "Serve the People" conference, Los Angeles

August 9–12: Filipino People's Far West Convention in Stockton,
with multiple sponsorships from student and community
organizations

- Theme: "Lakas ng Pagkakaisa/Power through Unity"
- Name changed to Pilipino People's Far West Convention

September 21: Martial law declared in the Philippines

September 23: National Committee for the Restoration of Civil Liberties
in the Philippines (NCRCLP) established to (1) oppose martial law,
(2) demand restoration of civil liberties, (3) release political prisons,
(4) oppose US support of Marcos

December: Samahan youth conference at San Diego State University

1973 KDP proposal to develop a "united front"; that is, a coalition of anti-
dictatorship forces

May 20: *Isuda ti imuna* cultural program by Pilipino American Alliance
(PAA) in Berkeley

July 27–28: Katipunan ng mga Demokratikong Pilipino (KDP, or Union of Democratic Filipinos) Founding Congress, Santa Cruz, California

- Program: (1) support for national democracy in the Philippines, (2) support for socialism in the United States
- Identity as a "revolutionary mass organization"
- "The KDP will concentrate its political work among the Pilipino community in the United States. It will seek to develop close ties with the broadest numbers of the Pilipino people here by encouraging its activists to be in the midst of the people and their struggles; to address themselves to the people's concrete needs and problems and to serve the people whole-heartedly and always fight militantly for their long-range interests."
- "The KDP plans to develop chapters wherever there are Pilipino communities and become a significant progressive and revolutionary force among Pilipino people. Although the KDP will remain principally a Pilipino organization, revolutionaries of non-Pilipino origin whose political work among Pilipino people or around support for the Philippine revolution, will also be welcomed within its ranks."

August 24–26: Third Far West Convention, in San Jose

October 1–15: First issue of *Ang Katipunan*, twice-monthly newspaper. Reports on the Third Far West Convention and its resolution passed against martial law; also on the September 22 founding in Washington, DC, of Movement for a Free Philippines (MFP).

October 20: Friends of the Filipino People (FFP) founded in Philadelphia

November 24: First issue of *Ang Aktibista*, theoretical and internal bulletin of KDP. Establishes democratic centralism as KDP's organizational structure for "the unity of both the democratic participation in decision-making and in the election of leadership, as well as for centralized guidance and decision-making for the entire organization."

December 17: *Ang Aktibista* issue, "The Role of Propaganda in the Struggle"

- Encourages national (*Ang Katipunan*) and local propaganda "to politicize the masses" through a "propaganda war between . . . revolutionary activists and the imperialists"
- Stresses the importance of a "mass line" (adaption of a party position, used in doing work in the community)

- Stresses "the importance of study": study of history, imperialism, revolutions, and revolutionary theory

1974 March 8: *Ang Aktibista* issue on the first KDP National Council report
- Distinction between *cadre* and *revolutionary mass organization*: *cadre*—"most experienced and tested revolutionaries with basic grasp of Marxist-Leninist theory"; *revolutionary mass organization*—"strives to bring many new people into the movement who see . . . the necessity for a fundamental and revolutionary change without necessarily being Marxist-Leninists, i.e., anti-imperialist activists recruited by education through 'lower-level organizations'"
- Policy: No dual membership in the KDP and a cadre pre-party communist organization
- National Secretariat established distinct from Bay Area chapters; activists cannot be members in both
- Call for transfers to Hawaii and Seattle
- Ideological: Struggle against individualism (putting individual interest above the whole) and liberalism (lack of militancy)

May: United States–Republic of the Philippines agreement for 4-H exchange program

August 15: *Ang Aktibista* issue, "Unite the Left, Win Over the Middle, and Isolate the Right"

September: KDP Seattle chapter founded

November 6: *Ang Aktibista* issue, "Revolutionary Line on Parliamentary Struggle" about petitioning US Congress
- Assessment and rectification in East Bay KDP chapter: chapter problems include "[being] mechanical in giving political and organizational guidance . . . lack of democracy . . . [being] bureaucratic . . . [and that the] center of leadership became weak and isolated"

December 28–29: First national anti–martial law conference in Chicago
- KDP is "assigned to centralize all information from the resistance movement in the Philippines and organize a historical archive for the anti–martial law movement in the U.S."
- New campaign proposed by KDP regarding political refugees: "those dislocated, evicted, or forced to abandon their lands by military intrusion, infrastructure projects, Imelda's beautification drives and landgrabbing by Marcos' officials," affecting especially national minorities (e.g., on Mindanao)

1975 Chicago KDP chapter splits away "to focus on Philippine support work"

February: *Ang Aktibista* issue on KDP National Council report

- Article to deepen the differences between proletarian versus bourgeois ideology in approaching KDP work
- Article about the "socialist field": Far West Conventions, organizing local communities
- Reports from National Secretariat, including all its commissions and departments
- Publication of re-edited pamphlet *People's War*, used for education on national democracy

May: *Ang Aktibista* issue, "Grasp Firmly the General Trend of History, Study Carefully the Day-to-Day Developments"

- Article on liberation of Vietnam
- Article titled "General Trend: People Want Revolution"
- Political analysis of Southeast Asia and international situation in aftermath of Vietnam's victory

June 22: Pro-Marcos "Magdalo II June 22 Movement" conference in Pittsburgh, California, condemns the Movement for a Free Philippines and KDP for urging suspension of US aid to the Philippines and rejects "the claims that KDP is the spokesman" of the Filipino people in the United States because of its espousal of an ideology "alien and destructive to Filipino traditions"

June 29: New York City immigrant rights conference "Filipino Immigration Problems: Roots and Solutions" addresses the issues of foreign medical graduates and undocumented Filipinos. Jointly sponsored by KDP, New York Philippine Jaycees, Philippine Medical Association of America (PMAA), Philippine Nurses Association (PNA), Philippine Executive Council, and Philippine Forum of New York.

July–August: Sectoral conferences in northern California in preparation for the Far West Convention at University of California, Berkeley

- July 20: Education conference in Oakland
- August 2: Housing and elderly conference at Project Manong, Oakland, cosponsored by International Hotel
- August 2: Health conference in Sacramento cosponsored by Mga Kapatid and the Delta Organizing Committee
- August 9: Labor conference in San Francisco cosponsored by Sandigan, the Filipino Newcomers Service Center

August 29–31: Far West Convention at University of California, Berkeley. Establishes Filipino Education Task Force to address racist portrayals of Filipinos and the treatment of Philippine-US relations in textbooks such as *Let Freedom Ring* (published by Silver Burdett) and *The American Adventure* (published by Allyn and Bacon).

Fall: KDP members attend Goddard-Cambridge School in Social Change

September 10: Apprehension for deportation of three Filipino maids protesting slave conditions at Philippine consulate; maids receive support from International Drop-in Center (IDIC) and the KDP Seattle chapter and are criticized by the pro-consulate Filipino Community Council

October 26: KDP develops Emergency Defense Committee for Foreign Medical Graduates (EDC-FMG) to aid foreign doctors, nurses, dieticians, nonmedical workers facing immediate deportation. Cosponsored by Philippine Medical Association of America (PMAA), Physicians National Housestaff Association (PNHA), Asian-American Legal Defense Committee (AALDC), and Immigration Committee of the National Lawyers Guild.

November 1–2: Anti–Martial Law Coalition (AMLC) founded in Chicago

1976 Chicago KDP split is resolved after the National Executive Board sends Geline Avila to reunite chapter

KDP develops International Support Commission

Premiere of *Philippines: Bangon! (Arise!)* album of nineteen revolutionary songs, from the 1896 revolution (led by Andres Bonifacio, founder of the Katipunan) to the 1970s Philippine national democratic movement; produced over a three-year period

Pandayan founded, the KDP's US publishing arm and distributor of Philippine materials

- *Philippines: Bangon! (Arise!)* distributed by Paredon Records
- *Makibaka* (Dare to struggle) calendar
- KDP collection of essays *Four Years of Martial Law* published
- *What's Happening in the Philippines* pamphlet published by *Far East Report*

April: Dameron Hospital in Stockton fires Dr. Antonio Saqueton for admitting and treating an eighty-year-old Filipino who could not afford to pay; KDP chapter takes up the issue

July 2: *Ang Aktibista* issue, "Expand and Consolidate Our Ranks to Meet the Need of the Mass Movement"

- Advocates building propaganda-organizing teams (POTs) as base of organization
- Proposes affiliate memberships

- Summarizes New People's Army (NPA) anniversary and medical aid campaign

September 16: Court decision in *Regents of the University of California v. Bakke* affirms "reverse discrimination"

Winter: The group MAKIBAKA (Malayang Kilusan ng Bagong Kababaihan, or Free Movement of New Women) produces 1977 "people's calendar" of Philippine, Filipino American, US, and world histories

1977   *Human Rights and Martial Law in the Philippines* pamphlet published by Friends of the Filipino People and Anti–Martial Law Coalition

International Solidarity Commission becomes the International Association of Filipino Patriots (IAFP)

Jose Maria Sison, chair of the new Communist Party of the Philippines (CPP), is arrested in the Philippines; KDP and IAFP publish a jointly signed statement protesting his arrest

March 1: Start of Filipina Narciso and Leonora Perez trial in Detroit for the murders of thirty-five patients at the veterans' hospital in Ann Arbor, Michigan.

April 13: California State Board of Education approves racist textbooks in spite of Filipino Education Task Force protests

April 23–24: Western States Conference at University of California, Berkeley, about the *Regents of the University of California v. Bakke* decision, where the National Committee to Overturn the Bakke Decision (NCOBD) was founded. This was an important campaign for the KDP.

April 30–May 1: National conference in New York City on foreign nurse graduates organized by National Alliance for Fair Licensure for Foreign Nurse Graduates (NAFL-FNG), an organization headed by KDP leader Aimee Laurel

June: *Ang Katipunan* publishes exposés on conditions of 4-H trainees, top agricultural students recruited in the Philippines and used as slave labor on US farms

June 17: Narciso and Perez found guilty of conspiracy to poison patients at Michigan veterans' hospital

August 4: International Hotel tenants evicted after a long campaign to resist ouster from their homes

November 25: Benigno "Ninoy" Aquino Jr.; Bernabe Buscayno, also known as Commander Dante, founder of the New People's Army; and Victor Corpus, member of the Central Committee of the Philippine Communist Party and former Philippine military officer,

are sentenced to death in the Philippines by firing squad. Anti–
Martial Law Coalition activists occupy Philippine consulates in
Seattle, Chicago, San Francisco, and New York City in protest.
Winter: 1978 "people's calendar" published by KDP, titled *Tala-arawang
bayan*; commemorates progressive struggles of Filipinos and Filipino
Americans and features reproductions of paintings by Filipino artists

1978　US Congress proposes the Criminal Code Reform Act (S. 1437), which
supersedes 1977's Criminal Justice Reform Bill (S. 1) and has negative
implications for 4-H trainees and H-1 visa nurses, who protest their
treatment
Anti–Martial Law Coalition publishes *Democracy in Form, Dictatorship
in Substance*
February 1: Victory for Narciso and Perez when US Attorney General
declines to refile criminal charges for poisoning and murder, the
judge having ordered a retrial after ruling that there had been
prosecutorial misconduct
June 13: Proposition 13 passes in California, linking property tax raises
to an inflation rate of no more than 2 percent of the 1975 assessed
property value. This limitation caused severe economic crisis in the
state budget, resulting in drastic cuts in human services and
education funding.

1979　Publication of *Conditions of the Filipino People under Martial Law*
pamphlet by Friends of the Filipino People and Anti–Martial Law
Coalition investigation team goes to the Philippines
US publication of Jose Maria Sison's book *Philippine Society and Revolution*
and his pamphlet *Specific Characteristics of Our People's War*
International Association of Filipino Patriots publishes *500 Mile Island:
The Philippine Nuclear Reactor Deal* pamphlet
Ang Katipunan establishes West Coast editions; describes additional
mission as "Not only report the news, we help make it"
March: Split develops within Friends of the Filipino People
May: *Philippine News*, a US-based Philippine publication, publishes
red-baiting articles about split within FFP
June 8: Formation of defense committee for Dr. Bienvenido Alona, a US
Navy physician of Filipino descent framed for the malpractice of
white doctors
August 31–September 2: Far West Convention in Sacramento;
establishes National Task Force for the Defense of Immigrant Rights

1980 February: San Francisco KDP chapter organizes community meeting to
          address youth violence in aftermath of the slaying of a Filipino youth
          by rival Latino youth
       April 21: Marcos visits Hawaii
       May 8: Benigno "Ninoy" Aquino Jr., former Philippine senator and
          outspoken anti-Marcos leader, arrives in United States for heart
          surgery. Aquino does not return to the Philippines until August 21,
          1983, whereupon he is immediately assassinated.
       June 18: Attempted arson at KDP headquarters in Chicago, home of
          Mayee Asidao
       September 21: KDP member Jerry Espejo assaulted and threatened at
          gunpoint at Filipino American Community of Los Angeles (FACLA)
       October 31: Founding of Philippine Solidarity Network (PSN) in
          Berkeley, made up of former Friends of the Filipino People members
       November 22–23: First conference of the National Task Force for the
          Defense of Immigrant Rights, in San Francisco; renaming and
          formalization of the group as National Filipino Immigrant Rights
          Organization (NFIRO)

1981 Rene Ciria Cruz becomes editor of *Ang Katipunan*
       Geline Avila becomes national coordinator of the Anti–Martial Law
          Coalition
       Anti–Martial Law Coalition becomes the Coalition Against the Marcos
          Dictatorship (CAMD) in response to "lifting" of martial law in the
          Philippines
       April 27–May 1: International Longshoremen's and Warehousemen's
          Union (ILWU) international convention in Honolulu, where Gene
          Viernes of Seattle-based Alaska Cannery Workers Union (Local 37)
          presents a resolution to send an ILWU investigating team to look at
          labor conditions in the Philippines and at Marcos's repressive labor
          practices
       June 1: ILWU Local 37 union leaders Silme Domingo and Gene Viernes
          are murdered in Seattle
       June 16: Marcos holds Philippine election for president; boycott called
          by opposition
       June 21: Committee for Justice for Domingo and Viernes established in
          Seattle
       September 4–6: Far West Convention held in Seattle
       November 27: US-Philippine extradition treaty proposed, includes Rene
          Ciria Cruz on its list of those to be extradited

1982 September: Marcos state visit to Washington, DC; Coalition Against the
      Marcos Dictatorship organizes nationwide protests that follow
      Marcos's itinerary

1983 Freedom of Information Act documents received in the case of Silme
      Domingo and Gene Viernes reveal detailed surveillance by FBI and
      US Naval Intelligence of KDP, particularly of its leaders
      March 11–13: Coalition Against the Marcos Dictatorship and the
      Philippine Solidarity Network merge at the annual CAMD
      conference in Berkeley; CAMD-PSN becomes explicitly
      anti-imperialist
      May 23: Death of Cynthia Maglaya, founding member of KDP
      August 21: Benigno "Ninoy" Aquino Jr. assassinated at Manila
      International Airport as he leaves the plane, igniting spontaneous
      mass ferment against Marcos dictatorship
      September: *Ang Katipunan* supplement published for KDP's tenth
      anniversary summarizes the group's decade of political work and
      publicly announces the KDP as a "socialist organization"

1984 Filipinos join the Rainbow Coalition and form Filipinos for Jackson, in
      support of Jesse Jackson's candidacy as Democratic nominee for US
      president
      April 16: *Ang Aktibista* issue, "Orientation to Philippine Support Work
      in the Current Period." Analyzes mass protests following the Aquino
      assassination, predicts a fatal crisis for Marcos dictatorship, in
      preparation for which the paper prescribes building a broad
      "popular front" against the dictatorship.
      May: Philippine national elections; boycott called by opposition

1985 *Line of March Journal*, no. 18, article "The Filipino Nationality in the
      U.S.: An Overview" by Bruce Occena, former chair of KDP National
      Executive Board

1986 February 7: Snap election ordered by Marcos in October 1985 takes
      place; Marcos declared winner by the Marcos-controlled Batasang
      Pambasa (Philippine Parliament); KDP and the Coalition Against
      the Marcos Dictatorship support Corazon Aquino for president
      February 22–25: "People Power" uprising overthrows Marcos amid
      charges of massive election fraud; Marcoses flee to Hawaii on US
      helicopter; CAMD-PSN and other anti-Marcos organizations

celebrate in front of Philippine consulates across the United States;
Corazon Aquino becomes the first female president of the
Philippines

CAMD-PSN becomes Campaign to Advance the Movement for
Democracy and Independence (CAMDI)

July: KDP formally disbands

1987 January: Line of March (LOM) formally establishes the Filipino
Commission in the United States, part of its national organizational
structure and an informal left network of Filipino activists to
continue the work of developing a political analysis and line guiding
the establishment of true democracy in the Philippines

June: *Ang Katipunan* publishes its final issue as an organ of KDP

September–October: *Katipunan* published, an independent left
publication produced by Katipunan Publications

1989 December 15: US District Court judge Barbara Rothstein in Seattle
issues decision in the Domingo-Viernes civil suit, ordering Tony
Baruso and Leonilo Malabed to pay $8.3 million in damages; the
estates of Ferdinand and Imelda Marcos, $6.7 million. In
January 1990, Judge Rothstein adds $8.3 million to the award.

1991 October: *Katipunan* (formerly *Ang Katipunan*) ceases publication

SUGGESTED READING

Alegado, Dean T. "Carl Damaso: A Champion of Hawaii's Working People." In *Filipino American History: Identity and Community in Hawaii*, ed. John Okamura, Social Process in Hawaii, no. 37, 26–35. Honolulu: University of Hawai'i Press, 1996.

Bulosan, Carlos. *America Is in the Heart: A Personal History.* Seattle: University of Washington Press, 1973.

Churchill, Thomas. *Triumph Over Marcos: A Story Based on the Lives of Gene Viernes and Silme Domingo, Filipino American Cannery Union Organizers, Their Assassination, and the Trial That Followed.* Seattle: Open Hand, 1995.

Espiritu, Yen. *Filipino American Lives.* Philadelphia: Temple University Press, 1995.

Karnow, Stanley. *In Our Image: America's Empire in the Philippines.* New York: Ballantine Books, 1989.

Letters in Exile: An Introductory Reader on the History of the Filipinos in America; A Project of Resource Development and Publications, UCLA Asian American Studies Center. Los Angeles: The Center, 1976.

"The Salinas Lettuce Strike of 1934." In *Roots and Routes: Cultivating Filipino American History on the Central Coast*, an online exhibit for sharing knowledge about Filipino American history on California's Central Coast, created in collaboration with South County Historical Society, Cal Poly San Luis Obispo Ethnic Studies Department, and Central Coast Filipino American communities. https://sites.google.com/site/centralcoastroutesandroots/strikes/the-salinas-lettuce-strike-of-1934-1.

Scharlin, Craig, and Lilia Villanueva. *Philip Vera Cruz: A Personal History of Filipino Immigrants and the Farmworkers Movement.* Seattle: University of Washington Press, 2000.

Schirmer, Daniel B. *Republic or Empire: American Resistance to the War in the Philippines.* Cambridge, MA: Schenkman Publishing, 1972.

Takaki, Ronald. *A Different Mirror: A History of Multicultural America.* Rev. ed. New York: Back Bay Books, 2008. First published 1993.

Avila, Geline, 68, 143, 165, 170, 194, 209, 233; children of, 68; and Marcos 1982 state visit, 135, 138; and recruiting Odette Polintan, 140, 141; sent to Chicago, 16
Ayson, Felix, 163

Bacho, Norris, 81, 85
Bacho, Reme, 89, 91
Bantayog ng mga Bayani (Monument to the Heroes), 195
Barber, Linda, 251
Barros, Lori, 24
Baruso, Tony: and Alaska Cannery Workers Association, 88; and assassinations of Domingo and Viernes, 187, 194–95, 217–18, 222, 234, 235, 238, 242, 244, 246–47; corruption of, 84, 87, 187, 220 (see also Tulisan); president of ILWU Local 37, xxiii, 202–3, 216, 232–33; rank-and-file opposition to, 194, 202–4, 216, 217–19, 221–22; support of Marcos, 194, 232–33; trial and conviction, 187, 194–95, 222, 237, 239, 250–52
Batongbacal, Edwin, 136, 272–73
Bello, Walden, 135, 140, 141, 142
Benavidez, Richie, 24
Black Power, xii
Bonifacio, Andres, xvii, 316
Borgeson, Dale, 61, 68–70, 81–91, 136, 190, 193–95, 234; establishing Seattle KDP chapter, 68
Borromeo, Abel, 91
Bridges, Harry, 232
Briones, Nonie, 115, 255, 257
Bulosan, Carlos, xvii, 5–6, 70, 149, 151, 218, 232
Buscayno, Bernabe, 12

Cabildo, Sabino, 88, 91
Callueng, Mac, 206
Camacho, Josie, 105

Carlos, Sixto, 24
Catague, Emma, 89, 91
Cate, Rebecca, 248
Caughlan, John, 241
Cayetano, Ben, 93
Chavez, Cesar, 83. See also United Farm Workers
Chin, Donnie, 91
Choy, Catherine Ceniza, xv
Chung, So, 163
Churchill, Thomas, xxii
Ciria Cruz, Rene, xxi, 3, 16, 24, 26, 89, 127, 136, 224–26, 319; protesting Marcos's 1979 Hawaii visit, 93; on US-Philippine extradition treaty list, 142, 144
Claraval, Vicki, 87, 89, 91
Clark, Ramsey, 140, 147
Coalition Against the Marcos Dictatorship (CAMD), 12, 130, 135–36, 136n1, 139–47, 164, 238, 261, 263–64, 319, 320
Committee for Human Rights in the Philippines (CHRP), 93, 104
Committee for Justice for Domingo and Viernes (CJDV), 74, 117, 139, 141, 187, 194, 211, 213, 235, 240, 241
Communist Party of the Philippines (CPP), xiv, 7, 10–11, 13, 17, 27n5, 33, 42, 59n1, 167, 172, 174, 274, 278; KDP schism with, 278–310. See also Partido Komunista ng Pilipinas (PKP)
Communist Party of the United States (CPUSA), xiv, 5–6, 42
Congress (Education) Task Force (CTF), 12–13, 126, 140–42, 145
Constantino, Renato, 70
Conyers, Congressman John, 237
Coquio, Gigi, 95, 108
Cordova, Dorothy, 81–83, 88
Cordova, Fred, 81–83, 88
Corpus, Victor, 12
Corsilles, Diony, 87, 89, 91
Covington and Burling law firm, 245–46

Furukawa, Rick, 88
Furutani, Warren, 85–86

Galedo, Lillian, 208–10, 210
Garcia, Marcial, 36–37
Garcia, Romy, xix, xviii, 34–43
Gatus, James, 24–25
Geaga, Wicks, 137, 138
Gibbs, Bob, 203
Gillego, Bonefacio, 228, 249
Glenn, Kasamang, 151
Gomez, Maita, 273
Guerrero, Amado, 59
Guerrero, Kalayaan, 99
Guloy, Pompeyo "Ben," Jr., 194, 243.
    See also Tulisan
Guzman, Emil de, 155, 158
Guzman, Mila de, 207

Habal, Estella, xviii–xix, xxi, 52–58,
    99–103, 265–66
Haig, Alexander, 245
Hatten, Barry, 151
Hearst, Patty "Tania," 47, 52–53
Hearst, Randolph, 53
Hermoso, Mang Mario, xviii, 6, 41–43
Hernandez, Nena, 16
Hershey, Christopher, 212
Hibey, Richard, 251
H-1 visa nurses, 129, 131–34, 318
Hongisto, Richard, 162
Horman, Joyce, 214
Hughes, Howard, 243
Hukbalahap (Huks), 25n1, 232

Immigration and Naturalization Service
    (INS), 13, 73, 131–33
International Association of Filipino
    Patriots, 261, 272, 317, 318
International Hotel (San Francisco),
    55–56, 266, 315; eviction from, 103,
    317; and Kalayaan collective, 99;
    movement to save, xv, xxi–xxii, 14,

32n2, 52, 100, 102–3, 155–63; Tenants
    Association, 28, 159
International Longshoremen's and
    Warehousemen's Union (ILWU), 14,
    83, 84, 196, 216, 242; resolution
    critical of Marcos, xv, 194, 232–33.
    See also Local 37 of the ILWU
Isuda ti imuna (Those who came first),
    63, 149, 150n2, 312
Iwamoto, Gary, 248

Jackson, George, 46, 55
Jackson, Reverend Jesse, xvi

Kabataang Makabayan (Nationalist
    Youth), xii, 10, 24, 57
Kalayaan (newspaper), 8, 9, 33n, 44, 48,
    50, 51, 57, 311
Kalayaan collective, 44, 52, 53, 81, 110,
    157, 311, 312; formation, 8, 47n2;
    politics of, 8–9, 99; as precursor to
    KDP, 31, 47; and United Filipino
    Association, 32n2
Katipunan, xvii, 8, 316
Katipunan ng mga Demokratikong
    Pilipino. See KDP (Union of
    Democratic Filipinos)
KDP (Union of Democratic Filipinos),
    93, 103, 133, 278; activism timeline,
    311–21; activists' life histories, 21–78;
    activists look back on their
    experiences, 253–75; anti-
    discrimination campaigns, 13–14;
    conditions for emergence of, 5–8;
    consolidation, 9–12; day-to-day
    political operations, 79–185; decline
    and dissolution, 16–19; "dual-line"
    program, xiv, xix, 9, 13, 16–17, 86,
    175; founding congress of, 9, 85, 313;
    opposition to Marcos dictatorship,
    12–13; overview, 4–5; reaction from
    the Right, 14–16; structure, 9–10, 21
KDP National Congress, 9, 10, 84, 85

KDP National Council, 9, 10, 16, 100, 267; reports of, 314, 315

KDP National Education Department, 90, 100, 103, 117, 231

KDP National Executive Board, 9–10, 68, 91, 93, 118, 120, 133, 316

KDP National Finance Commission, 9

KDP National Propaganda Commission, 9, 138

KDP National Secretariat, 9, 52, 93, 110, 113, 314, 315

KDP Regional Executive Boards, 9; Bay Area, 28, 52; East Coast and New York, 23, 126, 127, 128; northern California, 100, 105, 110, 113, 267

Keeler, Christine, 48

Kennedy, Robert, xii

Kennedy, Senator Ted, 143

Kerry, Senator John, 143

Kilusang Mayo Uno (KMU), 165–66, 168, 226, 227, 231, 232, 233

King, Martin Luther, Jr., xii

King, Thelma, 111

Knowles, Catherine, 163

Ko, Elaine, 91, 194, 209, 235

Kozu, Mike, 91, 238

Krause, Michael Jerry, 269

Lantos, Congressman Tom, 147

Laranang, Julia, 80, 81

Laurel, Aimee, 24, 26, 73, 132, 317

Lawson, Vincent, 89

Lazam, Frank, 159

Lazam, Jeanette Gandionco, xix, xxii–xxii, 28–32, 93, 155–63

Legacy of Equality, Leadership and Organizing (LELO), xxix, 34. See also Northwest Labor and Employment Law Office (LELO)

Legaspi, Joaquin, 156, 157, 163

Letelier, Orlando, 244

Linda, Ka, xxi, 172–85

Line of March (LOM), 17, 18, 52, 68, 104, 211, 224, 235, 238, 274; formation of, 11; many KDP leaders join, xvi; and Marxist-Leninist Education Project (MLEP), 72n1, 231, 235

"line" struggle, 165, 175–77. See also KDP (Union of Democratic Filipinos): "dual-line" program of

Ling, Fook, 163

Liu, Wing, 163

Local 37 of the ILWU, 152, 199, 223; assassination of Domingo and Viernes in offices of, 187, 209; corrupt leadership of, 84, 87, 152; efforts to reform, 14, 59, 194, 196, 202, 216–18, 232–35. See also International Longshoremen's and Warehousemen's Union (ILWU)

Lopez, Flora, 80

Lowry, Congressman Mike, 237

Maglaya, Cynthia, 9–10, 70, 81–82, 86; cofounder of KDP, xix; death of, 237, 320; personality and background of, 57–58

Maglaya, Letty, 111

Mahaguna, Supasit, 155, 158

Maida, Joanne, 243

Malabed, Leonilo, 246, 248, 250, 251

Malayang Pagkakaisa ng Kabataang Pilipino. See MPKP (Free Association of Filipino Youth)

Maleng, Norm, 195

Mangaoang, Ernesto, xvii, 6, 87, 110, 218

Mangaoang, Gil, 110–16, 267–71

Manglapus, Raul, 8, 12, 93, 227, 228, 249

Mao Tse-tung, 27, 46, 49n5, 99–100, 167, 173

Marasigan, Bullet, 156

Marasigan, Pete, 157

Marcelo, Nonoy, 25

Marcos, Bongbong, 248

Marcos, Ferdinand: and civil suit for assassinations of Domingo and Viernes, 145–46, 188, 226, 228, 236–39, 247–48, 321; compared to world dictators, 47; and corruption and repression, xiii, 40, 194, 229, 246; death of, 248; declaration of martial law, 8, 30, 82, 92, 173; installs self as dictator, 261; and 1979 Hawaii visit, 93–94, 96–97, 98; and 1982 state visit, 136, 144–45, 236; and 1986 snap election, 18, 147, 278, 320; overthrow of, 23, 195, 222, 262, 264 (*see also* "People Power" revolution); US support for, xii, 47, 142, 144

Marcos, Imelda, 237, 239, 241, 245, 249

Marin, Leni, 26, 207, 209

martial law in the Philippines, 28–32, 70, 81, 130

Marx, Karl, 10

Marxist-Leninist Education Project (MLEP), 231, 232, 234

Marzan, Lourdes, 126–28, 141, 236

Mast, David, 235

Mast, Terri: in aftermath of Domingo and Viernes assassinations, xxiii, 209, 212, 216–23, 252; children of, 191, 199, 208; and civil suit against Marcos, 241, 242, 248; as ILWU Local 37 activist and leader, 88, 201, 235; as KDP activist and leader, 88, 198, 199, 200

McGehee, Ralph, 249

MEChA (Movimiento Estudiantil Chicano de Aztlán), 55, 88

Melegrito, Jon, 123–25

Melroe, Kris, 211–15

Mensalvas, Chris, Jr., 190

Mensalvas, Chris, Sr., 6, 87, 151, 151n3, 218, 232

Mizuki, Andy, 91

Moffitt, Ronni, 244

Montemayor, Jeremias, 172

Moscone, Mayor George Richard, 158, 160

Movement for a Free Philippines, xiii, 8, 12

MPKP (Free Association of Filipino Youth), 27n5

murders of Domingo and Viernes, xv, 15, 77, 141, 171, 187, 194, 204, 205–7, 208, 233–34, 319. *See also* Domingo, Silme; Viernes, Gene

Murkowski, Senator Frank, 61n2

Nach, James, 251

Narciso, Filipina, xv, 13, 76, 101, 129, 133, 317, 318. *See also* Narciso-Perez defense campaign

Narciso-Perez defense campaign, 23, 105, 114–15, 129, 133–34, 318

National Alliance for Fair Licensure for Foreign Nurse Graduates (NAFL-FNG), 12, 13, 23, 71, 73, 132

National Association of Filipinos, 7, 173

National Committee for the Restoration of Civil Liberties in the Philippines (NCRCLP), 70, 80, 81, 130

National Democratic Front (NDF), xiv, 16, 140, 170, 174, 226, 272, 273, 278

Navarro, Gene, 87

Navarro, Nelson, 26

Nemenzo, Princess, 147

New England Fish Company, 198

New People's Army (NPA), xxi, 27n5, 75, 169, 227, 242, 281, 317; established, xii, 164; KDP support for, xiv; participation in, 75, 174, 175–76, 178, 272; reception among Filipino American activists, 7

Ningas Cogon, 11

Northwest Labor and Employment Law Office (LELO), 196–97, 198. *See also* Legacy of Equality, Leadership and Organizing (LELO)

Silva, John, 149

Simpson, Esther Hipol, 129–34

Sining Bayan (People's Art), xxi, 9, 14, 63, 148, 150, 150n2, 153, 154, 311; and KDP's cultural work, xix

Sino Na Gang, 35, 36, 37

Sison, Jose Maria, xii, xviii, 59n1, 317, 318

Stark, Pete, 146

Students for a Democratic Society (SDS), xii, 55

Support Committee for a Democratic Philippines (SCDP), 3, 7, 173, 312

Suson, Alonzo Glenn, 91, 189–92

Suson, Mario, 88, 91

Suson, Mario Parama, 189

Symbionese Liberation Army (SLA), 53

T., Ding, 123–25

Tacazon, Moy, 95

Tactaquin, Cathi, 105, 210

Taliba (AMLC newsletter), 12, 263, 279, 300, 310; distribution, xxiii, 41, 41n4, 43, 89, 123, 124

Tampao, Wahat, xxii, 158, 160, 161, 162, 163

Tangalan, Sylvestre, 87, 89

Taruc, Luis, 24–25, 83, 91

Taverna, Silahis M., 258–60

Ti mangyuna (Those who led the way), 63, 150n2, 153

Toribio, Helen, 3, 311

Torre, Father Ed de la, 172, 173–74

Torres, Ponce, 199, 202

Triumph over Marcos, xxii

Tulisan, 201, 215, 219, 244, 251; hit men in Domingo and Viernes assassinations, 194–95, 207; intimidation by, 203, 217–18, 219, 220–21, 243

Ubalde, Reverend Tony, 156

United Farm Workers, 48, 148, 149–50, 196

US-Philippine extradition treaty, 15, 135, 142–44, 319

Valdez, Pablo, 6

Valparaiso, Russell, 85–86

Van Bronkhorst, Emily, xix, 88, 196–204

Veloria, Velma, xxviin32, 74–78

Ver, General Fabian, 227

Vera Cruz, Philip, 49, 83, 90, 257

Viernes, Gene, 90, 189–91, 193–94, 195, 196, 198–99; aftermath of assassination of, xx, xxii–xxiii, 165, 211–13, 216–52; assassination of, xv, 15, 77, 141, 171, 187, 194, 204, 205–7, 208, 233–34, 319; and discrimination lawsuits, 198; as ILWU Local 37 activist and leader, xv, 88, 91, 187, 200, 201–3; and ILWU resolution to oppose Marcos, xv, 231–33, 249, 319; as KDP activist and leader, xix, 60–61, 68, 87, 90, 118–19, 190; memorial service for, 209n1; trials and civil suit for assassination of, xxi, xxii, 15, 117, 145–46, 187–88, 194, 215, 222, 224–30, 236–52, 321; as young activist, 84

Villasin, Fely, xx, 261–64

Villones, Maxie, 136

Vinluan, Ermena, xvii, xxi, 148–54

Voorhees, Judge Donald, 237, 245

Ward's Cove Packing Company, 61n2, 84, 90, 190, 198

Wilson, Dick, 211

Withey, Michael, xxi, 194, 217–18, 224–30, 238, 239, 240, 241–43, 249

Wong, Janelle, xi

Woo, Ruth, 78

Woo, Shari, 91

World Bank, 123–25

Yonn, Walter, 104–9

Zapata, Emiliano, 55

Zaragoza, Tessie, 137

Zogby, James, 144